Transition from Illegal Regimes under International Law

Yaël Ronen analyses the international legal ramifications of illegal regimes, namely illegal annexations of territory or illegal claims of statehood, with reference to the stage of transition from an illegal regime to a lawful one. Six case studies (Namibia, Zimbabwe, the Baltic states, the South African Bantustans, East Timor and northern Cyprus) are used to explore the tension between the invalidity of the illegal regimes' acts and their effectiveness, with respect to the international relations of such territories, their domestic legal systems, the status of settlers, and land transfers. Relying heavily on primary and previously unconsidered sources, Dr Ronen focuses on the international legal constraints on the post-transition regime's policy, particularly in the context of international human rights law.

YAËL RONEN is Senior Lecturer at Sha'arei Mishpat Law College, Israel, and a former diplomat in the Israeli Foreign Service. Her areas of expertise are statehood and territorial status, international human rights law, humanitarian law and international criminal law. She is also editor of the *Israel Law Review*.

Transition from Illegal Regimes under International Law

Yaël Ronen

CAMBRIDGE
UNIVERSITY PRESS

CAMBRIDGE UNIVERSITY PRESS
Cambridge, New York, Melbourne, Madrid, Cape Town,
Singapore, São Paulo, Delhi, Tokyo, Mexico City

Cambridge University Press
The Edinburgh Building, Cambridge CB2 8RU, UK

Published in the United States of America by Cambridge University Press, New York

www.cambridge.org
Information on this title: www.cambridge.org/9780521197779

First published 2011

Printed in the United Kingdom at the University Press, Cambridge

A catalogue record for this publication is available from the British Library

Library of Congress Cataloguing in Publication data
Ronen, Yaël, 1968–
Transition from illegal regimes under international law / Yaël Ronen.
p. cm. – (Cambridge studies in international and comparative law ; 78)
Includes bibliographical references and index.
ISBN 978-0-521-19777-9 (hardback)
1. State succession. 2. De facto doctrine. 3. Legitimacy of governments.
4. Regime change. I. Title. II. Series.
KZ4024.R66 2011
341.26 – dc22 2011001413

ISBN 978-0-521-19777-9 Hardback

Contents

Abbreviations

ACHR	American Convention on Human Rights
ANC	African National Congress
Annan Plan	Draft Comprehensive Settlement of the Cyprus Problem
CAT	Convention against Torture and Other Cruel, Inhuman or Degrading Treatment or Punishment
CEDAW	Convention on the Elimination of All Forms of Discrimination against Women
CERD	International Convention on the Elimination of All Forms of Racial Discrimination
CMATS	Certain Maritime Arrangements in the Timor Sea
Codesa	Convention for a Democratic South Africa
CRC	Convention on the Rights of the Child
CSCE	Commission on Security and Cooperation in Europe
ECHR	European Convention for the Protection of Human Rights and Fundamental Freedoms
ECJ	European Court of Justice
ECtHR	European Court of Human Rights
FAO	Food and Agriculture Organization
Fretilin	Frente Revolucionária de Timor Leste Independente
HCNM	High Commissioner on National Minorities of the CSCE
HRC	Human Rights Committee
ICCPR	International Covenant on Civil and Political Rights
ICESCR	International Covenant on Social, Economic and Cultural Rights
ICJ	International Court of Justice
ILC	International Law Commission
ILO	International Labour Organization
IPC	Immovable Property Commission

ITU	International Telecommunications Union
IUA	International Unitization Agreement
JDA	Joint Development Agreement
MPNF	Multi-party Negotiation Forum
OAU	Organization of African Unity
PACE	Parliamentary Assembly of the Council of Europe
PCIJ	Permanent Court of International Justice
PF	Patriotic Front
SPSC	Special Panel for Serious Crimes
SWAPO	South West African People's Organization
TBVC	Transkei, Bophuthatswana, Venda, Ciskei
TFSC	Turkish Federated State of Cyprus
TGT	Timor Gap Treaty
TRNC	Turkish Republic of Northern Cyprus
TST	Timor Sea Treaty
UCR	United Cyprus Republic
UDHR	Universal Declaration of Human Rights
UDI	Unilateral Declaration of Independence
UDT	União Democrática de Timor
UNCLOS	United Nations Convention on the Law of the Sea
UNCN	United Nations Council for Namibia
UNGA	United Nations General Assembly
UNIN	United Nations Institute for Namibia
UNMIK	United Nations Mission in Kosovo
UNSC	United Nations Security Council
UNTAET	United Nations Transitional Administration in East Timor
VCLT	Vienna Convention on the Law of Treaties
VCSPAD	Vienna Convention on Succession of States in Respect of State Property, Archives and Debts
VCST	Vienna Convention on Succession of States in Respect of Treaties
ZANU	Zimbabwe African National Union
ZAPU	Zimbabwe African People's Union

Acknowledgements

This monograph is the expanded version of the PhD thesis I defended at Cambridge University in August 2005. I had the privilege of being supervised by Professor James Crawford SC, Whewell Professor of International Law, chair of the Law Faculty and then director of the Lauterpacht Centre of International Law. Under his guidance I learned to enjoy steering through the many shades of grey in international law even while seeking an essential truth. I am grateful to him for his patient advice and unwavering confidence in my ability. I am also grateful to the examiners of my PhD thesis, Professor John Dugard, professor of international law at the University of Leiden, and Sir Daniel Bethlehem QC, then director of the Lauterpacht Centre of International Law and presently legal adviser to the United Kingdom Foreign and Commonwealth Office. Thanks are also due to the anonymous reviewers of this monograph's proposal.

Much of the material presented in this work was collected in visits to South Africa, Namibia and Cyprus. I am grateful to the many sponsors of these visits, including the Smuts Memorial Fund; the UAC of Nigeria Travel Fund; the Royal Historical Society; the Gilbert Murray Trust; and New Hall (now Murray Edwards College), Cambridge. Research on Chapter 6 was made possible under generous support of the Minerva Center for Human Rights at the Hebrew University in Jerusalem.

Chapter 6 draws on my article 'The Status of Settlers Implanted under an Illegal Regime under International Law', (2009) 80 *British Yearbook of International Law* 194–263.

In obtaining original documents, many of them unavailable publicly, I have relied on the help of legal officers in several foreign ministries and international organizations, as well as archivists and librarians. Many other people have taken the time to meet or correspond with me. I am indebted to all those who have helped me understand the legal, political, historical, social and economic contexts in which the events described took place, and who have opened new worlds for me. In particular, I would like to thank, in Namibia: Dr Sackey Akweenda, then-Prime Minister Theo-Ben Gurirab, Mr Werner Hillebrecht, Dr Justine Hunter, Minister Joel Kaapanda, Adv. Peter Koep, Mr Andrew Matjila, Dr Arnold Mtopa, Judge Bryan O'Linn, Mr Reuben Philander and Adv. Hartmut Ruppel; in South Africa: Mr Gerrit Grove, Mr Verne Harris, Mr Sello Hatang and the SAHA team, Dr Jonathan Klaaren, Mr Roelf Meyer, Dr Michèle Olivier, Mr Zam Titus, Mr Dire Tladi and members of the Unisa Law Department, Prof. François Venter and Prof. Marinus Wiechers; in Timor-Leste: Mr Louis Gentile and Mr Warren Wright; in the TRNC: Adv. Achilleas L. Demetriades, Ms Ayla Gürel, Mr Zaim Necatigil, Dr Kudret Özersay; Dr Costas Paraskeva; and elsewhere: Prof. Roger Clark, Prof. Martti Koskenniemi, Ms Marja Lehto, Ms Suzannah Linton, the late Adv. Willem van Manen, Mr Dan Nicholson, Mr Mart Paberit, Ms Claire Palley, Dr Vello Pettai, Mr Arnold Pronto, Mr Tony Rogers, Ms Tiina Runthal, Dr Ilan Saban, Mr Salman Salman, Mr Rytis Satkauskas, Mr Claude Schenker, Mr Bradford Smith, Prof. Stefan Talmon, Prof. Gillian Triggs, Sir Michael Wood, Mr Warren Wright and Dr Ineta Ziemele.

Numerous colleagues have kindly read drafts of various sections of this manuscript. I am grateful to Dr Frank Madsen, Dr Cedric Ryngaert, Dr Robbie Sabel, Prof. Yuval Shany, Ms Irys Weinrib and numerous anonymous reviewers. Mr Ohad Abrahami's painstakingly detailed work on the bibliographical sources was invaluable in bringing the manuscript to print.

Last but not least, I am grateful for the diligent work and help of the editors and staff at Cambridge University Press, especially Finola O'Sullivan, Nienke van Schaverbeke, Richard Woodham, Dan Dunlavey and John Gaunt.

Foreword

Dr Ronen's book deals with an important modern topic – how to move from an unlawful regime on the outer in international society to a secure, recognized society – normally a state member of the United Nations and of other international organizations. How to transition?

This is, of course, not just an issue of conflict management (though it is that), and the study is not just a detailed description of particular instances of transition (though it is that). For the focus of study raises the old question of the relationship between two broad elements underpinning international law, legality and effectiveness, as expressed in a discrete category of situations: transition from illegal territorial regimes under international law. Dr Ronen examines how the tension between the two elements informs the policy of post-transition regimes, in particular the extent to which they attempt to reverse the factual situation created by the preceding regime, and the extent to which they succeed, in light of the legal and political constraints in which they operate. These include the need to take account of the interests of third parties, as well as of international human rights law. On the basis of doctrinal analysis and a thorough review of practice, her study seeks to contribute towards a response to the more general question: how, and to what extent, the transition from an unlawful regime is substantively different from the 'ordinary case' of succession of states; and, further, whether the obligation of non-recognition is an effective tool of international legal enforcement.

Specifically she examines six instances of transition following lengthy periods of non-recognition of illegal regimes: the Baltic States, Rhodesia (Zimbabwe), Namibia, the Bantustans, Timor-Leste and the Turkish Republic of Northern Cyprus. In Chapters 1–3 she lays the background, recounting the legal history of the process of transition in the various cases, and examining the evolving doctrine of non-recognition, which has served as the basis for identifying the legal situation facing the post-transition regime in each territory considered. Then, in Chapters 4–6, she addresses the issues thematically: treaty relations, domestic law in general, the status of settlers, and land rights.

Both on the inter-state and on the domestic level, reversion by the post-transition regime to the *status quo ante* has proven difficult and has rarely led to a reversal of acts already carried out by the illegal regime. Political and legal considerations have combined to induce post-transition regimes to maintain existing practices. Thus the illegality of a previous regime does not automatically lead to the invalidity of all its acts and their consequences. Non-recognition, both as a legal obligation and as a policy choice, is subject to major exceptions for the protection of individuals and third parties. As the book shows, international human rights law has been influential here; indeed, its effect may be that non-recognition will become a tool applicable almost exclusively in inter-state relations. To that extent, emergence from an illegal regime is not very different from emergence from a legal regime which has adopted a clean-slate policy. The power of non-recognition as a means of enforcing international law is limited. If it fails politically to induce an illegal regime to revert to legality, it also does not preserve the legal freedom of action of the post-transition regime. When all is said and done, non-recognition has proved to be a weaker tool of international law enforcement than many of us had hoped. But the fact is that – given the comparative poverty of the toolbox – it is one of the few things available.

This is a steely-eyed work of realism – one written by a young scholar who cares as much about truth-telling as she does about the integrity of international law. It is a further contribution to the profession – building on her collaboration with the late Shabtai Rosenne in his magisterial fourth edition on the International Court of Justice. It underlines Dr Ronen's potential as a significant Israeli scholar of the next generation.

James Crawford
Lauterpacht Centre for International Law
University of Cambridge

Table of treaties

Multilateral treaties and similar international instruments

Bilateral treaties

Table of case law

Table of UN documents

Security Council resolutions

General Assembly resolutions

International Law Commission documents

Miscellaneous documents of the UN and specialized agencies

Table of domestic legislation and similar acts

Estonia

English translations of Estonian legislation are available on the website of the ELLC (under the Estonian Ministry of Justice) www.legaltext.ee/endefault.htm

Latvia

English translations of Latvian legislation are available on the website of the TTC (established by the Latvian Government) www.ttc.lv/advantagecms/LV/tulkojumi/meklet_dokumentus.html

Lithuania

English translations of Lithuanian legislation are available on the website of the Seimas (Lithuanian parliament) http://www3.lrs.lt/n/eng/DPaieska.html

Namibia

Zimbabwe (Southern Rhodesia/Rhodesia/Zimbabwe/UK)

Zimbabwean legislation is available on the parliament's website: www.parlzim.gov.zw/

South Africa/TBVC

TRNC/Republic of Cyprus

Timor-Leste (Indonesia/UNTAET/Timor-Leste)

Unofficial English translations of Indonesian legislation are available at www.eastimorlawjournal.org/Indonesian_Laws_regarding_East_Timor/Index.html; UNTAET legislative material and official Portuguese versions of Timor-Leste legislation and their unofficial translations to English are available on the website of the United Nations Integrated Mission in Timor-Leste (UNMIT) at www.unmit.org/legal/index-e.htm

USSR

Soviet legislative material in English is available in J. L. Black (ed.), *USSR Documents Annual* (1989)–(1991), Gulf Breeze, Florida, c.1993

Table of documents of intergovernmental organizations

1 Introduction

This book concerns the relationship between two broad elements underpinning international law: legality and effectiveness. The element of legality is embodied in the maxim *ex injuria jus non oritur*, according to which a violation of international law cannot produce legally valid outcomes. In some situations, however, effective practice does generate normative consequences, particularly through international human rights law. This phenomenon is embodied in the maxim *ex factis jus oritur*. This book studies the balance between the two elements as it is expressed in a discrete category of situations: the transition from a territorial regime that is illegal under international law to a legal territorial regime.

The term 'territorial regime' denotes an entity in which a functioning governing apparatus exercises control over a population in a territory, and makes a claim of sovereignty over that territory.[1] Territorial status is a matter not only of fact but also of law. A territorial regime is considered in this book 'illegal' when its creation involves the violation of a peremptory norm of international law, principally the prohibition on the use of force or the obligation to respect the right of peoples to self-determination. This is not to say that territorial claims do not at times involve other violations of international law, but those are less likely to result in an objective illegality of the regime. For example, the establishment of the German Democratic Republic (GDR) was regarded by the Western Allies

[1] Accordingly, the term 'illegal regime' does not refer to the governing body alone, as in expressions such as 'the Taliban regime', 'the Rabuka regime', 'the Habré regime' or 'the Khmer Rouge regime', which denote the identity of the individuals in power and not the international status of Afghanistan, Iraq, Fiji, Chad or Cambodia respectively. Regarding claims to territorial status other than sovereignty, see below.

(France, the UK and the US) as a violation of the Potsdam Declaration of 1 August 1945.[2] But this violation operated only among the parties to the declarations. There was nothing illegal about the emergence of the GDR as far as states other than the four occupying powers (the Western Allies and the USSR) were concerned.[3] In contrast, the illegality of a territorial regime which comes to exist in violation of a peremptory norm has effect *erga omnes*,[4] thereby creating an objective status. This objective character of the territorial regime also permits an analysis of the consequences of illegality as a matter of general international law rather than as the result of specific undertakings by individual states.[5]

The link between the peremptory character of certain basic rules and the criteria for the legality of a territorial regime, noted by Crawford in his treatise on the role of law in the creation of states,[6] has evolved through both doctrine and practice. Norms regulating territorial status include first and foremost the prohibition on the use of force, which provides the well-established principle that territory cannot validly be acquired by an unlawful use of force.[7] The prohibition on the use of force is generally

[2] Protocol of the Proceedings of the Berlin Conference, Declaration of 1 August 1945, 'Section II: The Principles to Govern the Treatment of Germany in the Initial Control Period', in United States Department of State, *Foreign Relations of the United States: Diplomatic Papers: The Conference of Berlin (the Potsdam Conference), 1945* (Washington, DC: US Government Printing Office, 1960), Volume II, 1478, 1481–1483.

[3] The refusal of states other than the Western Allies to recognize the GDR was a political stance, not a legal one. It was not universal, and ultimately it did not prevent the recognition of the GDR, even before the treaties of 1972 (involving the Federal Republic of Germany, the GDR and the four powers) regulated the situation. Thomas D. Grant, 'Hallstein Revisited: Unilateral Enforcement of Regimes of Nonrecognition since the Two Germanies' (2000) 36 *Stanford Journal of International Law* 221, 226.

[4] On the *erga omnes* character of peremptory norms, see Maurizio Ragazzi, *The Concept of International Obligations* Erga Omnes (Oxford: Clarendon Press, 1997); André de Hoogh, *Obligations* Erga Omnes *and International Crimes: A Theoretical Inquiry into the Implementation and Enforcement of the International Responsibility of States* (The Hague: Kluwer Law International, 1996), particularly 53–56; Lauri Hannikainen, *Peremptory Norms (Jus Cogens) in International Law: Historical Development, Criteria, Present Status* (Helsinki: Finnish Lawyers' Publishing Company, 1988).

[5] John Dugard, *Recognition and the United Nations* (Cambridge: Grotius, 1987); Alexander Orakhelashvili, *Peremptory Norms in International Law* (Oxford University Press, 2006).

[6] Crawford, *The Creation of States in International Law* (Oxford: Clarendon Press, 1979), 84.

[7] Report of the Committee on General Welfare, Recommendation of the International American Conference adopted 18 April 1890, 2 International American Conference. Reports of Committees and Discussions Thereon (Revised under the Direction of the Executive Committee by Order of the Conference Adopted 7 March 1890) 954, 1148 (second declaratory paragraph). Tripartite Conference in Moscow, Anglo-Soviet-American Communiqué, 1 November 1943 (1944) 38 *American Journal of International Law*

accepted as a peremptory norm that operates *erga omnes*.[8] While originally the test of legality was applied to territorial acquisitions by existing states, practice indicates that the *creation* of states, previously perceived as a matter of fact only, is also regulated by the prohibition on the use of force.[9] Through the years, the prohibition on unilateral territorial acquisition has expanded further, to cover territorial situations resulting from any use of force, even lawful use.[10] However, the consequences of territorial change following lawful use of force are presumably less far-reaching than those that follow unlawful use of force, which is a violation of a peremptory norm.

Another parameter for testing the legality of a territorial regime is the obligation to respect peoples' right to self-determination.[11] The right to self-determination is generally accepted as a peremptory norm which operates *erga omnes*,[12] although its precise content and limitations are controversial. The obligation to respect the right to self-determination is, in some instances, the corollary of the prohibition on the use of force: the breach of the right to self-determination is an illegal use of force when looked upon from the perspective of the victimized people rather

supplement 3, 7; Ian Brownlie, *International Law and the Use of Force by States* (Oxford: Clarendon Press, 1963), 410–423; Robert Y. Jennings, *The Acquisition of Territory in International Law* (Manchester: Manchester University Press, 1963), Chapter 5; Charles de Visscher, *Theory and Reality in International law* (revised edn, translated by P. E. Corbet, Princeton, NJ: Princeton University Press, 1968), 323–324; Robert Langer, *Seizure of Territory: The Stimson Doctrine and Related Principles in Legal Theory and Diplomatic Practice* (Princeton, NJ: Princeton University Press, 1947); see also Sharon D. Korman, *The Right of Conquest: The Acquisition of Territory by Force in International Law and Practice* (Oxford: Clarendon Press, 1996), particularly 234–248. For an account of the development of the prohibition on the use of force, see Brownlie, *Use of Force*, particularly Chapter 5.

8 *Military and Paramilitary Activities in and against Nicaragua (Nicaragua* v. *US) (Merits)* [1986] ICJ Rep 14, 100–101, [190]; ILC, *Draft Articles on State Responsibility*, Article 40 Commentary, paragraph 4.

9 Crawford, *The Creation of States*, 131–148; Antonio Cassese, *Self-Determination of Peoples: A Legal Reappraisal* (Cambridge: Cambridge University Press, 1995), 188–189.

10 Declaration on Principles of International Law Concerning Friendly Relations and Co-operation among States in accordance with the Charter of the United Nations, annexed to UNGA Resolution 2625(XXV).

11 J. E. S. Fawcett, 'Security Council Resolutions on Rhodesia' (1965–1966) 41 *British Yearbook of International Law* 103, 112; Crawford, *The Creation of States*, 107–131; David Raič, *Statehood and the Law of Self-Determination* (The Hague: Kluwer Law International, 2002), Chapter 4, particularly 128–140.

12 ICJ, *East Timor Case*, [29]; ICJ, *Wall Advisory Opinion*, [155]–[156]; ILC, *Draft Articles on State Responsibility*, Article 40 Commentary, paragraph 5.

than from that of the victimized state.[13] The right to self-determination can also be violated irrespective of any use of force, for example when a territorial regime is established in order to deprive the population of its right to internal self-determination.

Another norm recognized as peremptory is the prohibition on racial discrimination.[14] While not inherently related to territorial status, it may be implicated when a territorial regime is established for the sole purpose of maintaining a racially discriminatory political entity. When racial discrimination is institutionalized, for example through apartheid, it can amount to a violation of the right to self-determination.

Territorial regimes may take many forms: entities purporting to be states, established states purporting to hold sovereign title over territory outside their boundaries (annexation), occupation, international administration and more. All of these regimes can be tested against legal yardsticks.[15] This book is limited to the first two categories – purported states and purported annexations – which concern claims of full sovereignty. Limiting the discussion to claims of sovereignty permits a focus on the effect of illegality in isolation from other factors which limit the international functioning of a territorial regime, such as the inherently limited international personality of non-state actors. For example, it would be irrelevant to examine the effect of illegality on the capacity of an illegal occupant or an illegal international administration to grant its nationality to residents of the occupied territory, since even a legal occupant may not grant such nationality, while an international administration has no nationality to grant.

The consequence of a violation of a peremptory norm is a legal nullity which operates *erga omnes*. To maintain this nullity, states are prohibited from recognizing the legality of a situation created in violation of a

13 Cassese, *Self-Determination of Peoples*, 55, 90–99.

14 ICJ, *Barcelona Traction Case*, [33]–[34]; Dugard, *Recognition and the United Nations*, 156–158.

15 On the legal parameters for occupation see Yaël Ronen, 'Illegal Occupation and Its Consequences' (2008) 41 *Israel Law Review* 201; Orna Ben-Naftali, Aeyal Gross and Keren Michaeli, 'Illegal Occupation: The Framing of the Occupied Palestinian Territory' (2005) 23 *Berkeley International Law Journal* 551; Benjamin Matthew Clarke, 'Occupation, Resistance and the Law: Was Armed Resistance to the Occupation of Iraq Justified under International Law?', PhD thesis, University of Melbourne, 2009, unpublished, Appendices 2 and 3 (on file with the author); on the legality of international administration see Enrico Milano, *Unlawful Territorial Situations in International Law* (Leiden: Martinus Nijhoff, 2006), 237–251.

peremptory norm,[16] irrespective of the effectiveness or apparent success of those responsible for the conduct in question.[17] By non-recognition, states deny the competence of the governing apparatus to act on behalf of the territory and its people, and thus prevent the acts of the illegal regime from producing valid consequences.[18] This, in turn, is intended to prevent the regime in question from reaping the fruits of its violation of law, and to induce it to restore legal order.[19] Non-recognition is thus an expression of the maxim *ex injuria jus non oritur* (illegal acts cannot create law). This nullity operates not only towards third states, but also towards the illegal regime itself (at least if it is a state and therefore bound by general international law), as well as towards the ousted, legal regime, recognized as sovereign over the territory (where such a regime exists).[20] Needless to say, the illegal regime is unlikely to accept the illegality of its actions and their consequent nullity, although it is not unprecedented that arguments concerning the regime's status arise before its own authorities.[21] The peremptory character of the violated norm also means that the illegality is not curable by consent of states.[22]

[16] ILC, *Draft Articles on State Responsibility*, Article 41; Sir Hersch Lauterpacht, *Recognition in International Law* (Cambridge: Cambridge University Press, 1947), 413; Robert Y. Jennings, 'Nullity and Effectiveness in International Law', in *Cambridge Essays in International Law (Essays in Honour of Lord McNair)* (London: Stevens, 1965), 66.

[17] Vera Gowlland-Debbas, *Collective Responses to Illegal Acts in International Law: United Nations Action in the Question of Southern Rhodesia* (Dordrecht: Martinus Nijhoff, 1990), 276–277; Raič, *Statehood and the Law of Self-Determination*, 109.

[18] For simplicity, when describing the non-recognized regimes (as states or annexations), their institutions (governments, courts) and acts (laws, treaties, administrative acts), the qualifying terms 'purported', 'so-called', 'aspirant' etc. will be used only where they are necessary to avoid ambiguity. Nonetheless, these qualifications should be assumed wherever appropriate.

[19] Lauterpacht, *Recognition in International Law*, 340–341.

[20] Orakhelashvili, *Peremptory Norms*, 401; ILC, *Draft Articles on State Responsibility*, Article 45 Commentary, paragraph 4.

[21] Namibia, *Binga* v. *Administrator-General, South West Africa and Others*; Rhodesia, *Madzimbamuto and Baron* v. *Lardner-Burke (GD)*; Rhodesia, *Madzimbamuto and Baron* v. *Lardner-Burke (AD)*. In *Demopoulos and Others* v. *Turkey*, [107], the ECtHR acknowledged that 'it can hardly be expected, for evident practical reasons, that the [illegal regime] authorities themselves proceed to pronounce the legal and administrative system . . . to be null and void in order to satisfy the points of principle'. The case of the Turkish Republic of Northen Cyprus (TRNC) is unique in that despite the Greek-Cypriot claim that the TRNC is illegal, despite Turkey's claim that it is not responsible for the TRNC, and despite the TRNC's claim to be independent, all three parties appear, in one form or another, before the ECtHR and accept its authority to adjudicate the disputes.

[22] Christian Tomuschat, 'International Crimes by States: An Endangered Species?', in Karel Wellens (ed.), *International Law: Theory and Practice: Essays in Honour of Eric Suy* (The Hague: Martinus Nijhoff, 1998), 259.

Moreover, to waive this illegality or acquiesce in it would in itself be a violation of an international obligation,[23] even if the waiving or acquiescing state is the one directly injured by the original violation.

The obligation of non-recognition was pronounced by the ICJ in the *Namibia Advisory Opinion*, although the court did not expressly tie it to the violation of a peremptory norm. Formally, the obligation of non-recognition was triggered by the obligation of states under Article 25 of the UN Charter to comply with the decisions of the Security Council. The Security Council resolution in question, Resolution 276(1970), confirmed the revocation of the South African mandate over Namibia by the UN General Assembly, following the violation of peremptory norms, as discussed in Chapter 2. It declared that the continued presence of South Africa in Namibia was illegal and consequently that South Africa's acts on behalf of or concerning Namibia were invalid.[24] In other words, substantively the obligation or non-recognition arose from the violation of a peremptory norm which affected Namibia's status. The obligation under UN Charter Article 25 can itself be analogized to a peremptory norm, given the normative superiority under UN Charter Article 103 of Security Council resolutions over other international obligations of states. Admittedly, this normative superiority is institutional rather than substantive.

The link between peremptory norms and the obligation of non-recognition is clearly stipulated in the ILC *Draft Articles on State Responsibility*, which, interestingly, regard the *Namibia Advisory Opinion* as an authority on the application of the doctrine despite the fact that the *Advisory Opinion* relies only indirectly on the peremptory character of the norms.[25] The ICJ itself subsequently twice linked the obligation of non-recognition to peremptory norms. In the *Case Concerning East Timor*, Judge Skubiszewski suggested that the obligation of non-recognition of forcible acquisition of territory might in the future develop into a peremptory

[23] E.g. Swedish recognition of the Soviet annexation of the Baltic states in 1940 – William J. H. Hough III, 'The Annexation of the Baltic States and Its Effect on the Development of Law Prohibiting Forcible Seizure of Territory' (1985) 6 *New York Law School Journal of International & Comparative Law* 303; and the Australian recognition of the Indonesian annexation of East Timor in 1979 – *Australian Practice in International Law* (1978–1980) 8; *Australian Yearbook of International Law* 253, 279; ICJ, *East Timor Case (Portugal* v. *Australia)*, Counter-memorial of the Government of Australia (1 June 1992), [175]–[176]; ICJ, *East Timor Case (Portugal* v. *Australia)*, Rejoinder of the Government of Australia (1 July 1993), [44]–[54].

[24] ICJ, *Namibia Advisory Opinion*, [112]–[115]; UNSC Resolution 276 (30 January 1970) paragraph 2.

[25] ILC, *Draft Articles on State Responsibility*, Article 41 Commentary, paragraph 8.

norm as a corollary of the prohibition on the use of force.[26] If this process does occur, recognition of a territorial claim despite the existence of an obligation of non-recognition will itself constitute a violation of a peremptory norm. In the *Wall Advisory Opinion*, the majority opinion again mentioned the peremptory character of certain norms in the context of the obligation of non-recognition. However, it did so chiefly as an indication of the norms' *erga omnes* character, which is where the court lay the basis for the obligation of non-recognition.[27] The linkage between non-recognition and obligations *erga omnes* was criticized by two of the judges, who instead alluded to the peremptory character of the norms as the direct trigger for the obligation of non-recognition. Judge Higgins in a separate opinion referred to the commentary of the ILC *Draft Articles on Responsibility of States for Internationally Wrongful Acts*, which deal with obligations regarding peremptory norms.[28] Judge Kooijmans, also in a separate opinion, took issue with the notion that a violation of an obligation *erga omnes* by one state can lead to an obligation for another. He noted, however, the overlap between *erga omnes* obligations and peremptory norms at least where claims to sovereignty over territory are concerned.[29] This opinion, in particular, relies on and reinforces the link made in the ILC *Draft Articles on State Responsibility* between the obligation of non-recognition and the violation of peremptory norms, in the context of territorial claims.

The obligation of non-recognition should be distinguished from a policy of non-recognition that is adopted on political grounds or on domestic legal grounds,[30] even if such a policy is in some cases universal. It is not always easy to determine whether a refusal of recognition is politically or legally grounded, particularly since governments that refuse to lend legitimacy to territorial claims often attempt to strengthen their position by couching it in international legal terms. In addition, claims of illegality are sometimes grounded in domestic law. For example, secessionist entities which come to exist in violation of the law of the state from

26 ICJ, *East Timor Case*, dissenting opinion of Judge Skubiszewski, [125].

27 ICJ, *Wall Advisory Opinion*, [155]–[159].

28 ICJ, *Wall Advisory Opinion*, separate opinion of Judge Higgins, [37]–[38], referring to ILC, *Draft Articles on State Responsibility*, Chapter 3 Commentary paragraph 2.

29 ICJ, *Wall Advisory Opinion*, Separate Opinion of Judge Kooijmans, [40]–[43].

30 The grounds for non-recognition are distinct from the motive for the adoption of a non-recognition policy. Whether the motives of a state in a specific situation are political or legal is immaterial. What is important is whether it can base its policy in international law.

which they emerge or without its consent are often referred to in common political parlance as 'illegal'.[31] But neither non-recognition based on a political stance nor domestic illegality create the objective legal status that a violation of a peremptory norm creates.[32]

The negatively formulated objective of the obligation of non-recognition, namely to prevent the consolidation of the illegal regime, assumes that non-recognition is a temporary measure. Practice, however, reveals the weakness of non-recognition in restoring legal order. Illegal regimes have at times existed for lengthy periods of time. This book examines six cases, where the illegal regimes have lasted for periods ranging from fifteen to fifty years. During the period of existence of the illegal regime, a disparity exists between law and practice. Within the territory under the illegal regime's control, the effectiveness of the illegal regime's conduct remains by and large unhindered; outside the territory, the invalidity of the regime's status, and its acts, may reign unchallenged by the need to meet factual changes on the ground, other than in exceptional cases. When the illegal regime comes to an end, the new regime (the post-transition regime) is confronted with the need to resolve the large-scale conflict between law and fact. Its policy may be informed, inter alia, by the lack of legitimacy of the previous regime, by that regime's effectiveness or by some balancing mechanism between the two.

Non-recognition is a means to an end. Once that end is achieved, i.e. the illegal regime ceases to exist, the *raison d'être* of the obligation disappears. As a matter of law, the post-transition regime should not be bound by the obligation of non-recognition, and thus it should not be prevented from giving retroactive effect to the acts of the illegal regime that non-recognition failed to prevent. Equally, however, the post-transition regime should not be held bound by the effectiveness of the illegal regime, and thus should not be obligated to give effect to acts that non-recognition

[31] This is the case of practically all secessions, since the law of the parent state usually prohibits secession. E.g. on the American Constitution see *Texas* v. *White* (1868); the attempted secession of Katanga was in violation of the Loi Fondamentale of the Congo: Dugard, *Recognition and the United Nations*, 88. The absence of a prohibition does not mean that the parent state would peacefully accept secession, of course. James Crawford, 'State Practice and International Law in Relation to Succession' (1998) 69 *British Yearbook of International Law* 85, 85.

[32] E.g. Henry Cattan, *Palestine and International Law* (London: Longman, 1973); Nathan Feinberg, *The Arab–Israel Conflict in International Law* (Jerusalem: Hebrew University, 1970), particularly 71–79.

has failed to prevent. In principle, the post-transition regime should be able to decide whether and to what extent to revert to the situation that prevailed prior to the emergence of the illegal regime.

If the post-transition regime opts to adapt law to facts by giving blanket effect to the acts of the illegal regime, it may avoid most practical and normative problems, although where the acts of the illegal regime were illegal for reasons other than the regime's status, the post-transition regime would still have to address that illegality. If, on the other hand, the post-transition regime opts to return to the legal *status quo ante*, its ability to do so may be constrained by the normative consequences of factual changes that have taken place. International law at times gives effect to such changes through the protection of third parties' reliance and through international human rights law.

The focus of this book is on the manner in which the tension between the illegality of the regime and its effectiveness informs the law and policy of post-transition regimes. To what extent can the post-transition regime reverse the factual situation to put it back in line with the law? To what extent do post-transition regimes attempt to do so? How do the interests of third parties play into the equation? Does international human rights law affect the post-transition regime's freedom of action? On the basis of doctrinal analysis and practice review, this book seeks to contribute a response to a more general question: whether, overall, transition from an illegal regime is substantively different from an ordinary transition from a legal regime, and, by implication, whether the obligation of non-recognition is an effective tool of international legal enforcement.

This book examines six instances of transition following lengthy periods of non-recognition of illegal regimes. These instances are, in chronological order: (1) the purported annexation of the Baltic states by the USSR (1940–1991); (2) the purported statehood of Rhodesia under the Ian Smith regime (1965–1980); (3) South Africa's administration in Namibia (1966–1990); (4) the purported statehood of the South African homeland states Transkei, Bophuthatswana, Venda and Ciskei (collectively referred to as the TBVC) (1976–1994); (5) the purported annexation of Timor-Leste by Indonesia (1976–1999);[33] and (6) the purported statehood of the Turkish Republic

[33] For convenience, the names Namibia and Timor-Leste are used also with respect to the periods prior to independence, during which the territories were referred to as South West Africa and East Timor (or Timor Timur) respectively.

of Northern Cyprus (TRNC) (since 1983), which persists at the time of writing.[34]

The main criterion for choosing these cases was that an obligation of non-recognition in response to a violation of international law was (or is) generally considered to exist in their respect, and that a policy of non-recognition was instituted in practice. With regard to Rhodesia, Namibia, the TBVC and the TRNC, the illegality of the regimes and the obligation of non-recognition were prominently declared in international fora, and a policy of non-recognition was instituted and implemented. The situation is different with regard to the Soviet annexation of the Baltic states and the Indonesian annexation of Timor-Leste. In both cases, the illegality of the annexation was never formally declared, nor was a policy of non-recognition instituted on a collective basis. Indonesia's intervention in Timor-Leste was a matter of concern in the UN until 1982, although apart from deploring the violation of Portuguese Timor's territorial integrity,[35] the UN has never referred directly to the illegality of the annexation. For obvious reasons, the Soviet annexation of the Baltic states was also never even put to debate in the UN. These cases are nonetheless pertinent in view of the convergence of three factors. First, the obligation of non-recognition is triggered directly by the violation of the peremptory norm; it does not depend on any formal declaration. Difficulties of analysis can arise when that obligation is not fully complied with, but with respect to both the Baltic states and Timor-Leste, this difficulty is mitigated by the second factor, namely the practice of non-recognition on the part of many states, which can be seen as confirmation that they considered the annexations illegal.[36] Third, and most importantly for present purposes, the post-transition regimes in both cases acted on the premise that their territories had previously been subject to an illegal regime.

This work does not provide an exhaustive catalogue of territorial regimes that were, or are still, denied recognition because of their illegality. Conspicuously absent from its coverage are Manchukuo, the Japanese puppet state established in China's Manchuria in 1932; Iraq's purported annexation of Kuwait in 1990; Israel's claims of sovereignty over Jerusalem since 1967 and over the Golan Heights since 1981;[37] and Western Sahara's status under Moroccan control since 1975.

[34] For the reasons for including the TRNC in this work despite the fact that no transition has yet occurred, see Chapter 2 below.

[35] UNGA Resolution 3485(XXX) (12 December 1975).

[36] See Chapter 2 below.

[37] Adam Roberts, 'Prolonged Military Occupation: The Israeli-Occupied Territories since 1967' (1990) 84 *American Journal of International Law* 44, 67; Stephen M. Schwebel, 'What

Manchukuo, while in many respects the precursor of the other cases, offers little in the way of evaluating the law governing transitional arrangements. This is for legal reasons, as the notion of peremptory norms and the obligation of non-recognition were in their infancy at the time; and for historical reasons, as the reversion to Chinese rule did not signal a return to legality but was accompanied by civil war and revolution which disposed of all earlier arrangements in a summary fashion. The Iraqi annexation of Kuwait lasted only seven months,[38] a relatively short period, during which few significant problems have arisen, particularly since armed conflict prevailed throughout.[39]

Israel's claims of sovereignty over East Jerusalem and the Golan have been labelled 'illegal' occupation and declared 'null and void' and to constitute 'a flagrant violation of international law' by the UN Security Council[40] and the General Assembly.[41] Despite its apparent centrality to the issue at hand, this case has been excluded for a number of reasons. First, Israel acquired its control over these territories by action in self-defence, i.e. through lawful use of force. Such use of force cannot, by itself, give sovereign title to territory,[42] but in the absence of a violation of a peremptory norm, it also does not give rise to the kind of obligation of non-recognition that is examined here. A practical reason for the exclusion of the annexations by Israel from the study is that this book focuses

Weight to Conquest?' (1970) 64 *American Journal of International Law* 344; Elihu Lauterpacht, *Jerusalem and the Holy Places* (London: Anglo-Israel Association, 1968), 51–53.

38 UNSC Resolution 662 (9 August 1990).

39 But see *Kuwait Airways Corporation (Consolidated Appeals)*, [113]–[118].

40 E.g. UNSC Resolution 497 (17 December 1981).

41 E.g. UNGA Resolution 32/20 (25 November 1977); UNGA Resolution 33/113 (18 December 1978); UNGA Resolution 41/63 (3 December 1986), [3]. Roberts, 'Prolonged Military Occupation', 67; Korman, *The Right of Conquest*, 250.

42 According to the Golan Height Law, 5742-1981, Israeli 'law, administration and adjudication' apply in the area. The effect of this legislation is tantamount to a claim of sovereignty, but formally Israel has avoided claiming to have annexed the Golan Heights. In HCJ 210/67 *David Levi* v. *Chief of Staff and Others* PD 21(2) 166, Justice Zilberg of the Supreme Court sitting as the High Court of Justice mentioned the Golan Heights as 'occupied territory abroad'. However, this was prior to the enactment of the Golan Height Law – Leon Sheleff, 'The Application of Israeli Law to the Golan Heights Is Not Annexation' (1994) 20 *Brooklyn Journal of International Law* 333; and Asher Maoz, 'The Application of Israeli Law to the Golan Heights Is Annexation' (1994) 20 *Brooklyn Journal of International Law* 355. On Jerusalem, see Lauterpacht, *Jerusalem and the Holy Places*, 51–53; but also James Crawford, 'The Right of Self-Determination in International Law: Its Development and Future', in Philip Alston (ed.), *People's Rights* (Oxford: Oxford University Press, 2001), 35.

on transition from illegal regimes rather than on the illegal regimes themselves. The overwhelming bulk of legal debate on the conflict in the Middle East concerns the means of bringing the current situation to an end,[43] while there is almost no discussion of the practical consequences of such an eventuality.[44] The same lack of substantive discussion of the transition stage characterizes Western Sahara. With respect to these conflicts, a different normative framework for discussion may also be appropriate, namely the law of occupation. This book does not engage with the law of occupation in depth, because this body of law has featured only marginally in the lead-up to, or process of, transition. When mentioned by relevant actors, the law of occupation was used principally as a rhetorical tool, rather than as a legal one.

Also excluded from this study are situations where the illegal regime ultimately achieved international endorsement. This category includes instances such as the Indonesian annexation of West Papua, the Indian annexation of Goa and Bangladesh's acquisition of independence from Pakistan. In all of these cases, the endorsement of the new regime by the international community left the question of illegality unattended. Since this book offers a qualitative analysis rather than a quantitative one, the non-exhaustive list of cases examined does not detract from the validity of its findings, which indicate trends and directions in law and practice.[45]

[43] The following offer examples of different approaches: Moshe Hirsch, Deborah Hausen-Couriel and Ruth Lapidoth, *Whither Jerusalem? Proposals and Petitions Concerning the Future of Jerusalem* (The Hague: Martinus Nijhoff, 1995); John Quigley, 'The Role of Law in a Palestinian–Israeli Accommodation' (1999) 31 *Case Western Reserve Journal of International Law* 351; Gershon Baskin and Robin Twite (eds.), *The Future of Jerusalem* (Jerusalem: IPCRI, 1993); 'The Future of Jerusalem: A Symposium' (1995–1996) 45(3) *Catholic University law Review*.

[44] Exceptions are Eyal Benvenisti and Eyal Zamir, 'Private Claims to Property Rights in the Future Israeli–Palestinian Settlement' (1995) 89 *American Journal of International Law* 295; Eyal Benvenisti and Eyal Zamir, *The Legal Status of Lands Acquired by Israelis before 1948 in the West Bank, Gaza Strip and East Jerusalem* (Jerusalem: The Jerusalem Institute for Israel Studies, 1993) (in Hebrew). For an international legal perspective of the current situation (concluding that little can be done to reverse it), see Ardi Imseis, 'Facts on the Ground: An Examination of Israeli Municipal Policy in East Jerusalem' (2000) 15 *American University International Law Review* 1039.

[45] With respect to Kosovo, it is argued that its independent existence violates Serbia's right to self-determination. With respect to South Ossetia and Abhkazia, it is argued that they have been established through use of force by the Russian Federation against Georgia. Even assuming that the assertions of independence by these entities are based on violations of international law, they are at present too far from reversion to legality to be considered in this book.

Most of the cases examined in this book have featured some degree of UN involvement. Nevertheless, UN action has not been taken as an independent criterion for inclusion (or exclusion) of cases, mainly because the book focuses on the consequences of non-recognition on transition under customary international law, rather than on specific obligations under UN law, undertaken ad hoc with respect to specific disputes (such as the enforcement measures adopted against Rhodesia or South Africa, or the establishment of UNTAET in Timor-Leste). In addition, UN action often concerns the period of the illegal regime's existence and its non-recognition, while this work focuses on the period of transition to a lawful regime. Nevertheless, UN action plays an important historical and political role in substantiating the categorization of certain territorial regimes as illegal, and its practice has led to policies of non-recognition which might not have been so uniformly adopted had they been left to individual states' discretion. Since the criteria for inclusion in this work include the actual practice of non-recognition by third parties, it is helpful to rely on UN action to establish the existence of this practice.[46]

The first part of this book sets the factual and normative background for the current study. Within it, Chapter 2 provides an overview of the case studies and the basis for their inclusion in this study. It describes the political context in which each of the illegal regimes emerged, the international legal reaction to it and the process through which the territory reverted to a lawful regime. This chapter also discusses the illegality underlying the creation of each of the regimes. Since the emphasis in this chapter is on the legal standards for evaluating the illegality of the regimes, the case studies are discussed by chronological order of the emergence of these regimes. Chapter 3 examines the evolving doctrine of non-recognition. Its point of departure is the *Namibia Advisory Opinion* of 1971, which is still universally recognized as the most authoritative text on this matter; but this chapter also examines earlier and subsequent jurisprudence and scholarship. This serves as the basis for identifying the legal situation facing the post-transition regime in each legal area considered in the following, thematic chapters.

The book then moves on to examine the law and practice relating to post-transition regulation of specific areas of substantive law, on both the

46 Although such reliance is not free from conceptual difficulties, e.g., the illegality of the TRNC as asserted in Security Council resolutions is questionable as a basis for an obligation of non-recognition, as discussed in Chapter 2.

international and the domestic levels. There follow several thematic chapters. Chapter 4 concerns treaty relations, where the freedom of action of the post-transition regime is legally constrained by the reciprocal character of rights and obligations. Chapter 5 concerns the adoption of domestic law as a general question. Chapters 6 and 7 continue to examine two specific issues regulated by domestic law. Chapter 6 concerns the status of settlers brought in by the illegal regime to the territory, where the freedom of the post-transition regime to pursue its national interest is legally constrained primarily by its international human rights obligations towards the settlers. Chapter 7 concerns changes made by the illegal regime to land rights in the disputed territory. The post-transition regime's choice is legally constrained in this context principally by its human rights obligations towards both dispossessed owners and current occupants. The case studies are examined in an order that corresponds mainly to the date of transition from the illegal regime.

Each thematic chapter begins with a doctrinal analysis of the legal situation facing the post-transition regime. This analysis addresses the consequences of the obligation of non-recognition that had prevailed during the existence of the illegal regime. This is followed by consideration of the constraints which the various bodies of international law place upon the post-transition regime's freedom of action with respect to maintaining the invalidity of acts and reverting to the *status quo ante*, or, alternatively, preserving the existing situation. The theoretical background is followed by a study of practice. Following a review of the illegal regimes' conduct in the specific area of law, this study examines whether the post-transition regimes attempted to revert to the *status quo ante* by upholding the invalidity of the illegal regime's acts, and the extent to which their attempts were successful.

Finally, Chapter 8 identifies certain commonalities and differences in the responses of post-transition regimes to the acts of illegal regimes. These are indicative of the perceived role of non-recognition; they also constitute the actual legacy of the obligation of non-recognition once the illegal regime comes to an end.

Although the purpose of this book is first and foremost to assess the law and policy of non-recognition as they emerge from the process of transition to a legal regime, a significant part of the text is devoted to describing the legal history and policy of both the illegal regimes and the post-transition regimes. With less than a handful of exceptions – the policy of the Baltic states with respect to nationality, Indonesian land policy and the Annan Plan for the reunification of Cyprus – these stories have until today remained untold by legal scholars and are rarely known to them. It is hoped that this book will contribute to bridging the gap between history and law, and help incorporate a wealth of international practice into the study of international law.

2 The case studies

2.1 The Baltic states

2.1.1 The annexation of the Baltic states by the USSR

Caught between the USSR and Germany ever since their emergence as independent states following the First World War, Estonia, Latvia and Lithuania (the Baltic states) had to handle their relations with their two neighbours with great care. With the advent of Nazi Germany, this became increasingly difficult. The three states signed individual non-aggression pacts with the USSR,[1] but evaded proposals for guarantees of closer protection, which would have entailed the stationing of Soviet troops on their territories.

On 23 August 1939 the Soviet and German foreign ministers signed the Treaty of Nonaggression between Germany and the USSR (the Molotov-Ribbentrop Pact), to which a secret Supplementary Protocol provided,

> On the occasion of the signature of the Nonaggression Pact between the German Reich and the Union of Socialist Soviet Republics the undersigned plenipotentiaries of each of the two parties discussed in strictly confidential conversations the question of the boundary of their respective spheres of influence in Eastern Europe. These conversations led to the following conclusions:
>
> 1. In the event of a territorial and political rearrangement in the areas belonging to the Baltic states (Finland, Estonia, Latvia, Lithuania), the northern boundary of Lithuania shall represent the boundary of the spheres of influence of Germany and the USSR . . .[2]

[1] 1932 Treaties of Non-aggression between Estonia and the USSR and between Latvia and the USSR; 1926 Treaty of Non-aggression between Lithuania and the USSR.

[2] 1939 Secret Supplementary Protocol.

On 28 September 1939, the Supplementary Protocol was amended to provide for the transfer of Lithuania to the Soviet 'sphere of influence'.

As Germany invaded Poland, the USSR began its gradual takeover of the Baltic states. It demanded of each of the three states that it sign a 'mutual assistance' pact with the USSR and acquiesce in the establishment of Soviet military bases on its territory. It threatened to carry out a military invasion in the face of refusal. The three states all capitulated and signed the pacts, which allowed Soviet forces to enter their territories. Each of the pacts nonetheless provided that:

> [t]he implementation of this Agreement shall in no way interfere with the sovereign rights of the Contracting Parties to the Agreement, especially with their constitutional, economic and social system, military measures, and in general, with the rule of non-interference with domestic affairs.[3]

During 1939 and 1940, the Soviet government made several claims that its own security was at risk because of actions by the Baltic states, and staged certain events to justify its allegations.[4] In June 1940 this campaign reached its peak, when the Soviet government issued ultimatums to all three Baltic states, requiring full occupation and reconstruction of their governments under Soviet supervision. Again, the three states surrendered to the demand.[5] The puppet governments established under Soviet military guard arranged for elections, following which the elected assemblies in each state petitioned the Supreme Soviet (the legislature) of the USSR for admission to the Union. In August 1940 the Supreme Soviet passed legislation admitting the Baltic states into the USSR as Soviet republics.[6] The organs of governance established after the annexation were dependent on the support of the Soviet armed forces, which maintained a visible presence in all three states until the 1990s.[7]

3 1939 Pacts of Mutual Assistance between Estonia, Latvia and Lithuania and the USSR.

4 Susan E. Himmer, 'The Achievement of Independence in the Baltic States and Its Justifications' (1992) 6 *Emory International Law Review* 253, 266.

5 Anatol Lieven, *The Baltic Revolution: Estonia, Latvia, Lithuania and the Path to Independence* (New Haven: Yale University Press, 1993), 79–80.

6 On 3, 5 and 6 August 1940; Boris Meissner, 'The Occupation of the Baltic States from a Present-Day Perspective', in Jundzis Tālavs (ed.), *The Baltic States at Historical Crossroads* (Riga: Academy of Sciences of Latvia, 1998), 480.

7 In the late Brezhnev era, there were over 100,000 troops stationed in Estonia. Toivo U. Raun, 'Post-Soviet Estonia 1991–1993' (1994) 25 *Journal of Baltic Studies* 73, 75. Latvia was the headquarters of the Soviet Army's north-west military unit.

2.1.2 The international reaction to the annexation of the Baltic states

International reaction to the annexation was limited. Europe was in the throes of war, with many states themselves being occupied by Germany. The hope that the USSR would be an ally in defeating the Germans deterred opposition to its actions.[8] The response was not, then or later, uniform.[9]

Some states, including the US, the Holy See and Ireland, firmly refused to recognize the legal validity of the annexation. The US issued a statement on the 'Baltic Republics' on 23 July 1940, which stated:[10]

> The people of the United States are opposed to predatory activities no matter whether they are carried out by the use of force or by the threat of force. They are likewise opposed to any form of intervention on the part of one state, however powerful, in the domestic concerns of any other sovereign state, however weak... The United States will continue to stand by these principles...

However, in the Potsdam Conference held at the end of the Second World War, the US and the UK agreed in principle to the Soviet proposal concerning the ultimate transfer of Königsberg and adjacent areas to the USSR.[11] Such a transfer could not be accomplished without giving effect to the incorporation of Lithuania into the USSR.[12]

Several European and Latin American states, as well as Canada, recognized the de facto absorption of the Baltic states into the USSR, but refused to recognize it de jure.[13] New Zealand recognized the Soviet

[8] Romain Yakemtchouk, 'Les Républiques Baltes en droit international, échec d'une annexion opérée en violation du droit des gens' (1991) 37 *Annuaire Français de droit international* 259, 267.

[9] William J. H. Hough III, 'The Annexation of the Baltic States and Its Effect on the Development of Law Prohibiting Forcible Seizure of Territory' (1985) 6 *New York Law School Journal of International & Comparative Law* 303, 427.

[10] Statement by Acting Secretary of State Sumner Welles, 23 July 1940, III Bulletin DoS No. 57 48 (27 July 1940), quoted in Marjorie M. Whiteman, *Digest of International Law* (Department of State, Washington, 1965), Volume V, 942.

[11] Protocol of the Proceedings of the Berlin Conference, Declaration of 1 August 1945, 'Section VI: City of Koenigsberg and the Adjacent Area', in United States Department of State, *Foreign Relations of the United States: Diplomatic Papers: The Conference of Berlin (the Potsdam Conference), 1945*, Volume II (US Government Printing Office, Washington, DC, 1960) 1478, 1489.

[12] Robert A. Vitas, 'The Recognition of Lithuania – The Completion of the Legal Circle' (1993) 24 *Journal of Baltic Studies* 247, 254.

[13] Hough, 'The Annexation of the Baltic States', 430–442. For the UK see *A/S Tallinna Laevauhisus* v. *Tallinna Shipping Co*; Hansard HC Volume 433 Column 5 (10 February 1947), cited in *In the Estate of Feivel Pikelny* (1955); Hansard HC Volume 776 Column 583 (22 January 1969); Hansard HC Volume 172 Column 172 (8 May 1990). For Canada see

annexation de jure.[14] Australia initially granted the incorporation of the Baltic states de facto recognition,[15] but in July 1974 this was converted into de jure recognition.[16] In December 1975, following a change of government, Australia withdrew de jure recognition and reverted to de facto recognition only,[17] indicating that it 'does not accept the legality of the Soviet annexation'.[18] The Australian diplomatic staff in Moscow would no longer visit the Baltic states, and the Latvian honorary consul resumed his function.

The matter is complicated further by ambiguous positions, some of which were clarified only after the Baltic states re-established independence. Some states maintained silence and their practice was inconclusive.[19] Some later claimed that their silence reflected a policy of non-recognition.[20] For example, in 1991 the Dutch minister for foreign affairs explained that when the Netherlands established diplomatic relations with the USSR in 1942, it did not recognize the annexation; it made no reservation to that effect, because the Baltic states were under German occupation at the time.[21] This statement does not adequately explain the Dutch practice. The German occupation did not purport to extinguish prior sovereignty,[22] and thus did not eliminate the question of principle of whether or not the USSR was sovereign in the Baltic states. Indeed, the

Estonian States Cargo and Passenger Line v. *S S Elise and Messrs Laane and Balster* (1949). On the practical significance (or lack thereof) of the distinction between de jure and de facto recognition with regard to the annexation, see below. In general on the distinction, see Stefan Talmon, *Recognition of Governments in International Law: With Particular Reference to Governments in Exile* (Oxford: Clarendon, 1998), Chapter 2.

14 Lauri Mälksoo, *Illegal Annexation and State Continuity: The Case of the Incorporation of the Baltic States by the USSR* (Leiden: Martinus Nijhoff, 2003), 121.

15 (1967) *Australian Yearbook of International Law* 241.

16 Parliamentary debates, House of Representatives, 15 October 1974, 229, 27 November 1974, 4216, reprinted in (1974–1975) 6 *Australian Yearbook of International Law* 229–230.

17 (1978–1980) 8 *Australian Yearbook of International Law* 278.

18 Statement on behalf of the minister of foreign affairs, 7 April 1976 (1976–1977) 7 *Australian Yearbook of International Law* 432.

19 Hough, 'The Annexation of the Baltic States', 437, 440–443; Pierre Michel Eisemann and Martti Koskenniemi (eds.), *State Succession: Codification Tested against the Facts* (Dordrecht: Martinus Nijhoff, 2000), 52; Mälksoo, *Illegal Annexation and State Continuity*, 122.

20 Rytis Satkauskas, 'The Practice of France with Respect to the Baltic States' (2001) 1 *Baltic Yearbook of International Law* 111, 113.

21 Eisemann and Koskenniemi, *State Succession*, 282.

22 Raphael Lemkin, *Axis Rule in Occupied Europe: Laws of Occupation, Analysis of Government, Proposals for Redress* (Washington, DC: Carnegie Endowment for International Peace, 1944), 117.

Dutch position had earlier been taken as an implicit recognition of the annexation.[23]

When the Federal Republic of Germany (FRG) established relations with the USSR in 1955, it formulated a reservation concerning the recognition of the territorial possessions of both parties. This, according to the FRG, reflected non-recognition of the annexation of the Baltic states.[24] Later, the 1970 Treaty between the FRG and the USSR provided that the two countries 'share the realization that peace can only be maintained in Europe if nobody disturbs the present frontiers. They undertake to respect without restriction the territorial integrity of all states in Europe within their present frontiers'.[25] This phrase caused consternation in the Baltic diaspora, despite the FRG's declaration that it had never recognized the incorporation of the Baltic states and that the Treaty did not constitute a change of policy. The same issue arose with regard to the 1975 Helsinki Final Act, where thirty-five states held that they would 'refrain from any demand for, or act of, seizure and usurpation of part or all of the territory of any participating State'.[26] Participating states denied that this phrase constituted a change to the refusal to recognize the annexation of the Baltic states.[27] Such denials thwarted any claim of implicit or inferred recognition, but did little to clarify the meaning of the text as understood by the relevant states. If the Helsinki Final Act did not reflect a change of policy on their part, this was partly because of disagreement over what the Final Act actually meant.[28]

Although the validity of the annexation of the Baltic states was never generally recognized, the three states were also not treated as still independent or existing in any real sense. The UK, for example, did not recognize the annexation but considered that the Baltic states had ceased to exist.[29] The international community had largely resigned itself to

[23] Eisemann and Koskenniemi, *State Succession*, 50; Mälksoo, *Illegal Annexation and State Continuity*, 50.

[24] Statement of the minister of state of the Federal Republic of Germany, 16 October 1990, cited in Eisemann and Koskenniemi, *State Succession*, 211. This statement contradicted Nazi Germany's position following the Molotov-Ribbentrop Pact. For an explanation that Germany had never granted de jure recognition to the annexation, see Hough, 'The Annexation of the Baltic States', 425.

[25] 1970 Treaty between the Federal Republic of Germany and the Union of Soviet Socialist Republics, Article 3.

[26] 1975 Helsinki Final Act, Section 1(a) III.

[27] Yakemtchouk, 'Les Républiques Baltes', 275.

[28] The criticism that the Helsinki Act constitutes recognition of the annexation is somewhat vindicated by the fact that the Act on the Re-establishment of the State of Lithuania refers to the 1975 Helsinki Final Act as determining Lithuania's borders; see Chapter 4 below.

[29] Hansard HC Volume 195 Column 363 (22 July 1991); Switzerland held a similar position. Eisemann and Koskenniemi, *State Succession*, 342–343.

the annexation of the Baltic states in all but name.[30] This resulted in a variety of stances, not all of which were wholly coherent or consistent. For example, after the Second World War, Baltic refugees in the US were 'repatriated' to the USSR.[31] The US continued to recognize and accredit the Baltic diplomatic and consular missions in its territory, but did not maintain normal diplomatic relations with them. It also remained unclear to what authority these missions were responsible and whose interest they represented.[32] Through the years, the recognition of these missions became more symbolic than legally meaningful.[33] The nationalities of the Baltic states remained recognized in principle but without full juridical weight. Even countries that continued to recognize the existence of the Baltic states would not admit persons carrying only Baltic passports into their territories, because such passports did not guarantee the ability of their holders to return to their countries of origin.[34]

To conclude, in 1989, when the three Baltic states began mobilizing public support for independence, the majority of the international community regarded the annexation of the Baltic states by the USSR as legally invalid, although the exact status of the Baltic states remained unresolved.

2.1.3 The illegality of the annexation of the Baltic states

Two main grounds are invoked for the illegality of the Soviet annexation of the Baltic states. One is that it was the consequence of an illegal threat to use force and an act of aggression. The other is that it violated the right of the Baltic peoples to self-determination.

30 Yakemtchouk, 'Les Républiques Baltes', 268; Mälksoo, *Illegal Annexation and State Continuity*, 122. E.g. Hansard HC Volume 776 (5th series) Column 583 (22 January 1969); Hansard HC Volume 172 Column 172 (8 May 1990) and Oral Answers to Questions Hansard HC Volume 172 Column 179 (8 May 1990). This resignation was the grounds for Australia's de jure recognition of the annexation, as noted by the Australian prime minister in October 1974, (1978) 6 *Australian Yearbook of International Law* 230.

31 Vitas, 'Recognition of Lithuania', 254.

32 Thomas D. Grant, 'United States Practice Relating to the Baltic States, 1940–2000' (2001) 1 *Baltic Yearbook of International Law* 23, 48. Talmon, *Recognition of Governments*, 194; Mälksoo, 'Estonian Government in Exile'.

33 For the ambiguity of such situations compare Yakemtchouk, 'Les Républiques Baltes', 273; Eisemann and Koskenniemi, *State Succession*, 50.

34 Satkauskas, 'The Practice of France with Respect to the Baltic States', 114–115. Other states recognized these persons as refugees, and issued them travel documents. Daniel C. Turack, 'Selected Aspects of International and Municipal Law Concerning Passports' (1970–1971) 12 *William and Mary Law Review* 805, 826.

There had been various bilateral and other treaties of limited participation, in force between the USSR and the Baltic states, that renounced the use of force;[35] the annexation was in contravention of these treaties. However, in 1940 the use of force and specifically the threat to use force were not clearly prohibited under customary law (so as to justify an obligation of non-recognition). The International Military Tribunal in Nuremberg considered threats of use of force, carried out in 1938, to be acts of aggression. Its statement to this effect, when examining the implications of the German annexation of Austria,[36] was based not on specific conventional undertakings by Germany, but on general international law. As such it could also apply to the use of force by the USSR. In contrast, scholarly opinion from the period does not support this assertion.[37] Only at a later stage was the existence of a customary prohibition on the use of force considered undisputed.[38]

Moreover, strictly speaking, the annexation of the Baltic states was not carried out by use of force, but through a *threat* to use force. Some Russian authorities and legal scholars claim that at the time of the annexation, a mere threat, as opposed to direct use of military force by one state against another, was not prohibited under international legal instruments.[39] In contrast, Brownlie considered that although the Pact of Paris did not expressly prohibit threats, a threat to resort to war for political motives would have constituted 'recourse to war for the solution of international

[35] E.g. the 1928 Pact of Paris; the 1932 Treaties of Non-aggression between Estonia and the USSR and between Latvia and the USSR; the 1926 Treaty of Non-aggression between Lithuania and the USSR; 1929 Protocol between Estonia, Latvia, Poland, Roumania and the USSR for the Immediate Entry into Force of the Treaty of Paris of August 27, 1928, Regarding Renunciation of War as an Instrument of National Policy; the 1933 Convention on the Definition of Aggression (to which the USSR, Estonia and Latvia were parties, and which was later extended to Lithuanian–Soviet relations through the Lithuania–USSR Definition of Aggression Convention, 1933). See further Mälksoo, *Illegal Annexation and State Continuity*, 91–93.

[36] *Judgement of the Nuremberg International Military Tribunal*, 1 October 1946 (1947) 41 *American Journal of International Law* 172, 192–194.

[37] Herbert Wright, 'The Legality of the Annexation of Austria by Germany' (1944) 38 *American Journal of International Law* 621; James W. Garner, 'Non-recognition of Illegal Territorial Annexations and Claims to Sovereignty' (1936) 30 *American Journal of International Law* 679. Brownlie does not mention the Soviet annexation of the Baltic states, while Jennings takes for granted that their annexation was forcible. Robert Y. Jennings, *The Acquisition of Territory in International Law* (Manchester: Manchester University Press, 1963), 81.

[38] ILC, 'Draft Articles on the Law of Treaties – Report by Mr H Lauterpacht, Special Rapporteur' (24 March 1953), UN Doc A/CN.4/63 (24 March 1953), Comment to Draft Article 12, paragraph 3; Jennings, *Acquisition of Territory*, 52–67.

[39] See sources mentioned in Dainius Žalimas, 'Legal Issues on the Continuity of the Republic of Lithuania' (2001) 1 *Baltic Yearbook of International Law* 1, 4–5.

controversies . . . as an instrument of national policy', and would thus have been prohibited by Article 1 of the Pact, if made in circumstances which did not justify the use of force.[40]

With respect to the violation of the right of the Baltic states' peoples to self-determination,[41] reference is often made to the bilateral undertakings in the 1920 peace treaties between the then Russian Socialist Federal Republic and the Baltic states. These note the right of 'all peoples freely to decide their destinies, and even to separate themselves completely from the state of which they form a part'.[42] However, the peace treaties refer to a constitutional right of secession within Russia, which is not identical to the right to self-determination under international law. In 1940 the latter did not yet form a general – and peremptory – norm of international law.[43] Nevertheless, under the law of treaties, when a new peremptory norm of general international law emerges, any existing treaty which is in conflict with that norm becomes void and terminates.[44] With the expansion of the concept of peremptory norms beyond treaty law, the principle of invalidity of acts contrary to a peremptory norm should also expand, extending also to unilateral acts (such as annexation) that are in conflict with a peremptory norm. Accordingly, once the right to self-determination has consolidated as peremptory norm, the annexation became a violation of it;[45] the USSR should have withdrawn from the Baltic states even if its presence had until then been lawful.[46]

40 Brownlie, *Use of Force* (1963), 364; see also Hersch Lauterpacht (ed.), *Oppenheim's International Law*, 6th edn (London: Longmans, 1940), 153, note 6, noting the Pact of Paris's prohibition on threats of war. However, it seems that the prohibition was not yet considered customary law.

41 Boris Meissner, 'The Right to Self-Determination after Helsinki and Its Significance for the Baltic Nations' (1981) 13 *Case Western Reserve Journal of International Law* 375, 381–385; Mälksoo, *Illegal Annexation and State Continuity*, 91.

42 1920 Tartu and Riga Peace Treaties; 1920 Peace Treaty between Lithuania and the Russian Socialist Federal Republic.

43 Cassesse notes that the right did not ripen until the 1960s. Antonio Cassese, *Self-Determination of Peoples: A Legal Reappraisal* (Cambridge: Cambridge University Press, 1995), 262; but see Jean Salmon, 'Pays Baltes' (2001) 24 *Revue belge de droit international* 262, 266.

44 VCLT Article 64.

45 PACE Resolution 189 (1960) notes the 'forcible incorporation into the USSR of the three European states of Estonia, Latvia and Lithuania' and that 'this illegal annexation took place without any genuine reference to the wishes of the people'.

46 Theoretically the same inter-temporal rule is applicable with respect to the prohibition on the use of force, which is also a peremptory norm. However, practice differs with respect to the two norms: the right to self-determination led colonial powers to divest themselves of territories which they acquired validly under the law applicable at the time of acquisition. The prohibition on the use of force has not led to a similar

The Baltic states themselves did not invoke the right to self-determination (or the denial of its exercise since 1940) as a ground for restoration of their independence. Instead they focused exclusively on the unlawful use of force. This emphasized the invalidity *ab initio* of the annexation, and asserted their continuity from the pre-1940 states in distinction from the other Soviet republics that were seeking independence.[47]

2.1.4 The restoration of independence of the Baltic states

Nationalist aspirations did not disappear in the Baltic states during the period of annexation, but they were repressed by the Soviet authorities.[48] In the late 1980s the Soviet government became more tolerant of grass-roots political movements, and popular fronts formed in the three Baltic states, advocating independence from the USSR. One of the issues raised in this context was a demand that the central government of the USSR declare the Molotov-Ribbentrop Pact and the legislative acts of annexation void. On 24 December 1989 the Supreme Soviet declared the Molotov-Ribbentrop Pact invalid from the day of its conclusion.[49] However, the Soviet government maintained that regardless of this invalidity, the annexation of the Baltic states was valid, and that their campaign for independence was a constitutional rather than an international issue.[50]

Between March and May 1990, the legislatures of the three Baltic republics declared the restoration of the pre-1940 states. Lithuania declared independence with immediate effect.[51] Estonia and Latvia proclaimed a period of transition that would end with the formation of constitutional state organs.[52] Estonia further proclaimed Soviet rule unlawful from the moment it had been imposed. The USSR rejected these declarations,[53] and passed a law on the modalities for exiting the

requirement that states withdraw from territory acquired by (lawful) force prior to the existence of the prohibition.

47 Cassese, *Self-Determination of Peoples*, 260–261.

48 Himmer, 'Independence in the Baltic States', 266–267.

49 Congress of People's Deputies Resolution on a Political and Legal Appraisal of the Soviet–German Non-aggression Treaty of 1939 (24 December 1989).

50 Yakemtchouk, 'Les Républiques Baltes', 277.

51 Lithuania, Act on the Re-establishment of the State of Lithuania, 11 March 1990.

52 Estonia, Resolution on the State Status of Estonia, 30 March 1990. Latvia, Declaration of the Supreme Council of the Latvian SSR on the Restoration of Independence of the Republic of Latvia, 4 May 1990.

53 Decree of the President of the USSR on Declaring Invalid the Resolution of the Supreme Soviet of the Estonian SSR 'On the State Status of Estonia' (14 May 1990); Decree of the President of the USSR on the Declaration of the Supreme Soviet of the Latvian SSR 'On Restoring the Independence of the Latvian Republic' (14 May 1990); Decree of the President of the USSR Decree on Additional Measures to Assure the Rights of Soviet

USSR.[54] The law called for a referendum in each republic, in which Soviet military forces would have been able to participate. It also presented various hurdles to independence that would have delayed its realization almost indefinitely. However, the three republics refused to accept this law, on the ground that they were not subject to Soviet legislative jurisdiction. They refused the demand to hold central government-run referenda on their political future, and each conducted its own referendum, in which the overwhelming majority of the population opted for independence.[55]

In January 1991, the conflict with the central government of the USSR escalated, with Soviet troops entering the capitals of the Baltic republics. Despite the tense atmosphere, the political rebellion continued. Following the failed coup in Moscow in August 1991, Estonia and Latvia, which until then had postponed their formal declarations, also declared their complete independence.[56] International recognition did not follow immediately. Although the illegality of the annexation excluded the Baltic states from the sphere of domestic Soviet affairs, and thus recognition would not have constituted intervention in domestic affairs, states were reluctant to enter into a direct conflict with the USSR. Moreover, the Baltic states did not yet exercise full and effective control over their territories.[57] By early September 1991, however, some forty states, including European Community member states, the US, Canada, Norway and Argentina, acknowledged the independence of the three Baltic states. On 6 September 1991, the USSR also acknowledged it. On 17 September 1991 all three Baltic states were admitted to the UN.

An important element in the policy of the Baltic states is their self-perception as continuators of the international personalities of the

Citizens and Protect the Sovereignty of the USSR in the Territory of the Lithuanian SSR (21 March 1990).

54 Law on Procedure for Resolving Questions Connected with the Secession of Union Republics from the USSR (3 April 1990).

55 Yakemtchouk, 'Les Républiques Baltes', 277; Riina Kionka, 'Estonia Says "Yes" to Independence' (1991) 3(11) Report on the USSR (FRE/RL Research Institute, New York) 25; Dzintra Bungs, 'Poll Shows Majority in Latvia Endorses Independence' (1991) 3(11) Report on the USSR (FRE/RL Research Institute New York) 22; Dzintra Bungs, 'Voting Patterns in the Latvian Independence Poll' (1991) 3(12) Report on the USSR (FRE/RL Research Institute New York) 21; Saulius Girnius, 'Lithuania Votes for Independence' (1991) 3(8) Report on the USSR (FRE/RL Research Institute New York) 24.

56 Estonia, Resolution on the National Independence of Estonia (20 August 1991), noted in Mälksoo, *Illegal Annexation and State Continuity*, 47. Latvia, Law on the Statehood of the Republic of Latvia.

57 Rein Müllerson, *International Law, Human Rights and Politics: Developments in Eastern Europe and the CIS* (London: Routledge, 1994), 120.

pre-1940 states.[58] All three states also regard Soviet rule as having been an occupation.[59] This position is accepted by many states, but not universally. Sweden, which recognized the annexation, proceeded on the premise that the Baltic states were newly established.[60] The Russian Federation (as successor to the USSR) maintains that the Baltic states had been annexed lawfully and that, accordingly, their independence was the result of secession.[61] Although this controversy is largely a matter of principle and rhetoric rather than of practice,[62] it permeates various aspects of the legal relations between Russia and each of the Baltic states, particularly the conclusion of boundary treaties.[63] For example, both Estonia and Latvia have concluded boundary treaties with the Russian Federation which allocated to the Russian Federation territory that until 1940 had been under Estonian or Latvian sovereignty. Both have also made declarations referring, respectively, to the 1920 Tartu and Riga peace treaties. These references implied that notwithstanding these new boundary treaties, the two states maintain their pre-1940 territorial claims to the areas in question. The Russian Federation refused to ratify the treaty with Latvia until the mention of the 1920 Riga Peace Treaty was obscured by

58 E.g. Latvia, Declaration of the Supreme Council of the Latvian SSR on the Restoration of Independence; Lithuania, Act on the Re-establishment of the State.

59 E.g. Estonia, Persons Repressed by Occupying Powers Act, Article 1(1), Resolution on Restoring the Continuity in the Right of Ownership, Article 1; Latvia, Declaration on the Restoration of Independence, preambular paragraph 1; Lithuania, Resolution Regarding the Process of Enforcement and Application of the Law of the Republic of Lithuania on the Procedures and Conditions of the Restoration of the Ownership Rights of Existing Real Property, Article 2, Law on Rehabilitation of Persons Repressed for Resistance to the Occupying Regime.

60 Eisemann and Koskenniemi, *State Succession*, 96, 314–315. Nonetheless Sweden acknowledged some link between pre-1940 and post-1991 Estonia – in 1992 it sought to compensate Estonia for gold deposited before 1940 in the Bank of Sweden. Tai-heng Cheng, *State Succession and Commercial Obligations* (Ardsley: Transnational, 2006), 350.

61 Vladimir Socor, 'Kremlin Assails Baltic States', *Eurasia Daily Monitor*, issue 93, 11 May 2005, www.jamestown.org/single/?no_cache=1&tx_ttnews%5Btt_news%5D=3039,3; Peter van Elsuwege, 'State Continuity and Its Consequences: The Case of the Baltic States' (2003) 16 *Leiden Journal of International Law* 177.

62 Igor Torbakov, 'Rift between Moscow and Baltic states: Is It All about History?', *Eurasia Daily Monitor*, issue 49, 10 March 2005, www.jamestown.org/single/?no_cache=1&tx_ttnews%5Btt_news%5D=2767,5. Among the symbolic matters in dispute is the return of the Estonian state symbol and the presidential necklace and badge. Vladimir Socor, 'Moscow Signs Border Agreement with Estonia', *Eurasia Daily Monitor*, issue 99, 19 May 2005, www.jamestown.org/single/?no_cache=1&tx_ttnews%5Btt_news%5D=3042,7.

63 Van Elsuwege, 'State Continuity and Its Consequences'; Wayne C. Thomson, 'Citizenship and Borders: Legacies of Soviet Empire in Estonia' (1998) 29 *Journal of Baltic Studies* 109.

indirect references.[64] It has yet to ratify the treaty with Estonia. Although both Estonia and Latvia maintain that they do not have any concrete territorial demands against the Russian Federation, they both insist on their declarations as symbols of the illegitimacy of the changes made to their territory while the states were under forcible annexation.

2.2 Rhodesia

2.2.1 The unilateral declaration of independence

Until 1965,[65] Southern Rhodesia was a *sui generis* British colony.[66] It enjoyed a large measure of autonomy, including a limited international

64 See Chapter 4 below.

65 On Rhodesia's declaration of independence, the international reaction and the reversion to colony status, see also Douglas G. Anglin, 'Zimbabwe: Retrospect and Prospect' (1979–1980) 35 *International Journal* 663; Simon Beynham (ed.), *Zimbabwe in Transition* (Almqvist & Wiksell International in co-operation with the Africa Institute of South Africa, Stockholm, 1992); Dermott J. Devine, 'Status of Rhodesia in International Law' (1967) *Acta Juridica* 39', Dermott J. Devine, 'The Status of Rhodesia in International Law' (1973) *Acta Juridica*; John Dugard, 'Rhodesia: Does South Africa Recognize It as an Independent State?' (1977) 94 *South African Law Journal* 127; John Dugard, *Recognition and the United Nations* (Cambridge: Grotius, 1987); Pierre Michel Eisemann, *Les sanctions contre la Rhodésie* (Paris: A Pedone, 1972); Peter Godwin and Ian Hancock, *'Rhodesians Never Die': The Impact of War and Political Change on White Rhodesia, c. 1970–1980* (Oxford: Oxford University Press, 1993); Robert C. Good, *UDI: The International Politics of the Rhodesian Rebellion* (London: Faber & Faber, 1973); L. C. Green, 'Rhodesian Independence – Legal or Illegal?' (1968) 6 *Alberta Law Review* 37; Miles Hudson, *Triumph or Tragedy? Rhodesia to Zimbabwe* (London: H. Hamilton, 1981); Desmond William Lardner-Burke, *Rhodesia: The Story of the Crisis* (London: Oldbourne, 1966); Wyndraeth H. Morris-Jones, *From Rhodesia to Zimbabwe: Behind and Beyond Lancaster House* (London: Cass, 1980); David J. Murray, *The Governmental System in Southern Rhodesia* (Oxford: Clarendon Press, 1970); John Parker, *Rhodesia: Little White Island* (London: Pitman, 1972); Alison Quentin-Baxter, *Rhodesia and the Law: A Commentary on the Constitutional and International Law Aspects of the Rhodesian Situation* (Wellington: New Zealand Institute of International Affairs, 1970); Lord Christopher Soames, 'From Rhodesia to Zimbabwe' (1980) 56 *International Affairs* 405; Colin Stoneman, *Zimbabwe: Politics, Economics and Society* (London: Pinter, 1989); Harry R. Strack, *Sanctions: The Case of Rhodesia* (Syracuse, NY: Syracuse University Press, 1978); Elaine Windrich, *The Rhodesian Problem: A Documentary Record, 1923–1973* (London: Routledge, 1975); Henry Wiseman, *From Rhodesia to Zimbabwe: The Politics of Transition* (New York: Pergamon, 1981); John D. Yeadon and Terence O. Ranger (eds.), *Past and Present in Zimbabwe* (Manchester: Manchester University Press in association with Africa Journal of the International African Institute, 1983); Kenneth Young, *Rhodesia and Independence: A Study in British Colonial Policy* (London: Dent, 1969); Ralph Zacklin, *The United Nations and Rhodesia: A Study in International Law* (New York: Praeger, 1974).

66 After the declaration of independence, Southern Rhodesia renamed itself Rhodesia. Following the internal settlement of 1978, its name changed to Rhodesia-Zimbabwe, and upon independence in 1980 it was renamed Zimbabwe, the African name which reflects the realization of Black African self-determination. For convenience, this book

personality. In 1961 it adopted, with the agreement of the British government, a new constitution, which enhanced the colony's autonomy. This constitution also introduced, for the first time, Black representation in the legislative assembly. However, the electoral system was such as to assure White minority rule, in a country where less than 5 per cent of the population was White. The Black nationalist parties, mainly the Zimbabwe African People's Union (ZAPU) and the Zimbabwe African National Union (ZANU), rejected the constitution. The UN General Assembly responded to the adoption of the constitution by designating Rhodesia a non-self-governing territory, and called on the UK to take appropriate measures to transfer power 'to a representative government in keeping with the aspirations of the majority of the people'.[67]

During the early 1960s, the British government and the Southern Rhodesian government negotiated independence for the colony. Opinions differed on the notion of majority rule, with the Southern Rhodesian government objecting to the British government's demand that more Blacks be allowed to participate in the electoral process.[68] The last round of negotiations on the terms of independence was held in October 1965, and did not bear fruit. On 11 November 1965, the Southern Rhodesian government, headed by Ian Smith, issued a unilateral declaration of independence for Rhodesia (UDI).[69] On 3 March 1970, Rhodesia declared itself a republic, breaking, as far as the Smith government was concerned, the final ties with Britain.[70] There is no doubt that Rhodesia satisfied the traditional, factual requirements of statehood, namely an independently functioning apparatus governing a population in a defined territory.[71]

uses the name 'Rhodesia' for the period until 1980, and 'Zimbabwe' for the following period, except where the designation of the territory as the Colony of Southern Rhodesia is pertinent.

67 UNGA Resolution 1747(XVI) (27 June 1962); UNGA Resolution 2012(XX) (12 October 1965).

68 Documents Relating to the Negotiations between the United Kingdom and Southern Rhodesian Governments November 1963–November 1965 (Cmnd 2807 London 1967).

69 'Proclamation by Prime Minister' (1966). This was clearly in excess of the Southern Rhodesian government's powers under the 1961 constitution. Initially Rhodesia purported to remain a monarchy, with the queen as head of state, but in 1970 it proclaimed itself a republic.

70 Richard M. Cummings, 'The Rhodesian Unilateral Declaration of Independence and the Position of the International Community' (1973) 6 *New York University Journal of International Law & Policy* 57, 63.

71 On the functioning of the Smith government, see Jeffrey Herbst, *State Politics in Zimbabwe* (Berkeley: University of California Press, 1990), Chapter 2.

2.2.2 *The international response to UDI*

In anticipation of UDI, the UN General Assembly had called on all states 'not to recognize any government in Southern Rhodesia which is not representative of the majority of the people'.[72] Once UDI was issued, the General Assembly condemned it.[73] Subsequent action was taken mostly by the Security Council. Resolution 216 (11 November 1965) called upon all states 'not to recognize this illegal racist minority régime in Southern Rhodesia'. Resolution 217 (12 November 1965):

> 4. *Condemns* the usurpation of power by a racist settler minority in Southern Rhodesia and regards the declaration of independence by it as having no legal validity . . .
>
> . . .
>
> 6. *Calls upon* all States not to recognize this illegal authority and not to entertain any diplomatic or other relations with it.

In Resolution 277 (18 March 1970), the Security Council:[74]

> 1. *Condemns* the illegal proclamation of republican status of the Territory by the illegal régime in Southern Rhodesia;
>
> 2. *Decides* that Member States shall refrain from recognizing this illegal régime or from rendering any assistance to it;
>
> 3. *Calls upon* Member States to take appropriate measures, at the national level, to ensure that any act performed by officials and institutions of the illegal régime in Southern Rhodesia shall not be accorded any recognition, official or otherwise, including judicial notice, by the competent organs of their State;
>
> . . .

Immediately following UDI, the British Government promulgated the Southern Rhodesia (Constitution) Order of 1965, which declared that 'any instrument made or other act done in purported promulgation of any constitution for Southern Rhodesia except as authorized by Act of Parliament is void and of no effect'.[75] The British Government also rescinded the limited international personality that Rhodesia had enjoyed prior to

[72] UNGA Resolution 2022(XX) (5 November 1965).
[73] UNGA Resolution 2024(XX) (11 November 1965), paragraphs 1, 3.
[74] See also UNSC Resolution 288 (17 November 1970).
[75] Southern Rhodesia (Constitution) Order 1965 Article 2(1).

UDI and assumed direct responsibility for the territory's international relations.[76]

The adherence to the policy of non-recognition was universal. Not one state recognized the statehood of Rhodesia, although some doubts were raised concerning the stance of South Africa. The latter did not recognize Rhodesia as an independent state, but it also did not recognize the UK's complete and exclusive sovereignty over the territory following UDI.[77] The Smith government and South Africa continued to maintain their pre-1965 missions in each other's territory. Finally, South Africa (and Portugal) also had commercial and other dealings with Rhodesia, although those did not amount by themselves to recognition of statehood. South Africa appeared to hold that its relations with Rhodesia were the same as those maintained by it prior to UDI, and therefore did not constitute recognition of independence.[78]

Later resolutions of the Security Council did not expressly refer to non-recognition.[79] This was unnecessary as all states had by then heeded the call for non-recognition.[80] Instead, these resolutions called on states to carry out their obligations under the UN Charter. Since those included compliance with Security Council resolutions, the obligation of non-recognition that had already been stipulated by the Security Council was implicitly reaffirmed. The Security Council also adopted resolutions imposing mandatory economic enforcement measures on Rhodesia under Chapter VII of the UN Charter.[81]

[76] Dermott J. Devine, 'The Status of Rhodesia in International Law' (1974) *Acta Juridica*, 110–111; S. A. de Smith, 'Southern Rhodesia Act 1965' (1966) 29 *Modern Law Review* 801.

[77] Dugard, 'Rhodesia: Does South Africa Recognize It?', 127.

[78] Jericho Nkala, *The United Nations, International Law and the Rhodesian Independence Crisis* (Oxford: Clarendon Press, 1985); Vera Gowlland-Debbas, *Collective Responses to Illegal Acts in International Law: United Nations Action in the Question of Southern Rhodesia* (Dordrecht: Martinus Nijhoff, 1990), 70, 75.

[79] UNSC Resolution 318 (28 July 1972); UNSC Resolution 320 (29 September 1972); UNSC Resolution 388 (6 April 1976); UNSC Resolution 409 (27 May 1977); UNSC Resolution 423 (14 March 1978).

[80] Dugard, *Recognition and the United Nations*, 93.

[81] UNSC Resolution 232 (16 December 1966); UNSC Resolution 253 (29 May 1968); UNSC Resolution 277 (18 March 1970). For a detailed discussion of the enforcement measures imposed on Rhodesia by the UN, see Nkala, *The United Nations, International Law and the Rhodesian Independence Crisis*; Gowlland-Debbas, *Collective Responses to Illegal Acts in International Law*.

The Commonwealth and the Organization of African Unity (OAU) also took action with regard to Rhodesia. These organizations had an important role in ensuring that the Rhodesia problem remained a priority for global action.[82] The OAU Assembly of Heads of State and Government and its Council of Ministers, for example, adopted resolutions in anticipation of UDI and following it, in which they called 'upon all governments and all international Organizations to withhold recognition of a European minority government in the event of a unilateral declaration of independence'.[83] They later renewed the appeal 'to all Member States of the United Nations and all peace loving nations of the world not to recognize the racist minority regime in Rhodesia'.[84]

2.2.3 The illegality of Rhodesia's independence

The inequitable allocation of governmental power in Southern Rhodesia guaranteed the dominance of the White population despite the existence of an overwhelming Black majority. The intention behind UDI was to secure this White domination. In other words, the creation of an independent Rhodesia was carried out in violation of the right to self-determination and in order to perpetuate this violation.[85] This is reflected in UN General Assembly Resolution 2012(XX), which notes:[86]

> the repeated threats of the present authorities in Southern Rhodesia immediately to declare unilaterally the independence of Southern Rhodesia, in order to perpetuate minority rule in southern Rhodesia . . .
>
> the perpetuation of such minority rule would be incompatible with the principle of equal rights and self-determination of people proclaimed in the Charter of the United Nations and in the Declaration on the Granting of independence to colonial Countries and Peoples contained in General Assembly resolution 1514(XV) of 14 December 1960 . . .

[82] Margaret Doxey, 'Strategies in Multilateral Diplomacy: The Commonwealth, Southern Africa, and the NIEO' (1979–1980) 35 *International Journal* 329, 337.

[83] Organization of African Unity (Assembly of Heads of States), 'Second Ordinary Session of the Assembly of Heads of States held in Accra, Ghana from 21 to 26 October 1965' (22 October 1965) AHG/Res 25 (II), paragraph 5.

[84] Organization of African Unity (Council of Ministers), 'Sixth Ordinary Session of the Council of Ministers held in Addis Ababa, Ethiopia, from 28 February to 6 March 1966', CM/Res 75 (VI) paragraph 1.

[85] Gowlland-Debbas, *Collective Responses to Illegal Acts in International Law*, 225–237.

[86] UNGA Resolution 2012(XX) (12 October 1965), preambular paragraph 2, operative paragraph 2.

In Resolution 2022(XX),[87] the General Assembly recalled the 1960 Declaration on the Granting of Independence to Colonial Countries and People, which stipulated the right of peoples to self-determination, and noted 'the manifest intention of the present authorities in Southern Rhodesia to proclaim independence unilaterally, which would continue the denial to the African majority of their fundamental rights to freedom and independence'.[88] Resolutions adopted by the Security Council also reaffirmed the 1960 Declaration, either directly[89] or indirectly.[90]

The existence of a right to self-determination under international law was controversial at the time when Rhodesia declared independence. Devine advocated the conservative view that this right was 'too controversial, unaccepted and vague to be used by the Rhodesians as a shield or by anyone else as a sword against them'.[91] Others considered the right to be established,[92] and although it was conceded that the exact content and criteria for its application had not been fully defined, it was generally accepted that the right had been violated in the creation of Rhodesia.[93] However, it was clearly an innovation that the right to self-determination was of such importance that its violation would have the consequence of precluding an entity from becoming a state.[94]

Another norm violated by the creation of independent Rhodesia was the prohibition on racial discrimination. UN General Assembly Resolution 2022(XX) '[c]*ondemns* the policies of racial discrimination and segregation practices in Southern Rhodesia, which constitute a crime

[87] UNGA Resolution 2022(XX) (5 November 1965), preambular paragraph 5.

[88] UNGA Resolution 1514(XV) (14 December 1960).

[89] E.g. UNSC Resolution 217 (20 November 1965), paragraph 2; UNSC Resolution 253 (29 May 1968); UNSC Resolution 318 (28 July 1972).

[90] E.g. UNSC Resolution 320 (29 September 1972); UNSC Resolution 388 (6 April 1976); UNSC Resolution 409 (27 May 1977); UNSC Resolution 423 (14 March 1978).

[91] Devine, 'Status of Rhodesia' (1973), 77; Devine, 'Status of Rhodesia' (1974), 183–209.

[92] E.g. Julius K. Nyerere, 'Rhodesia in the Context of Southern Africa' (1965–1966) 44 *Foreign Affairs* 373.

[93] Myres S. McDougal and W. Michael Reisman, 'Rhodesia and the United Nations: The Unlawfulness of International Concern' (1968) 62 *American Journal of International Law* 1, 17–19.

[94] J. E. S. Fawcett, 'Security Council Resolutions on Rhodesia' (1965–1966) 41 *British Yearbook of International Law* 103, 112–113; James Crawford, *The Creation of States in International Law*, 2nd edn (Oxford: Clarendon Press, 2006), 129–131.

against humanity'. The Security Council also referred in its resolutions to the 'illegal racist minority regime'[95] and to the 'racist settler minority'.[96]

None of the OAU resolutions directly addressed the grounds for the illegality of Rhodesia. The first resolution noted the statement of the British government that it would regard UDI as 'illegal and amounting to an act of rebellion and treason punishable solely by the imposition of economic sanctions and non-recognition'.[97] Not only did the OAU not take a position of its own, but, to the extent that its call for non-recognition was based on the UK position, it considered non-recognition a sanction against violation of British constitutional law rather than a response to a violation of international law. After UDI, the OAU also noted the situation resulting from 'the illegal seizure of power by the white, racist settler minority in that country', and called for non-recognition on the same grounds.[98] The OAU referred extensively to the duty of the UK to commit itself to independence on the basis of majority government, to guarantee universal adult suffrage and free elections.[99] It did not mention self-determination expressly until 1972, when it upheld the 'inalienable rights of the people of Zimbabwe' and 'the right to self-determination'.[100] Finally, in 1977 the OAU Council of Ministers clearly mentioned the illegality of Rhodesia under international law, but without elaborating the grounds for such illegality: 'Reaffirming the illegal character of the Salisbury regime by virtue of its original nature'.[101]

95 UNSC Resolution 216 (12 November 1965).

96 UNSC Resolution 217 (20 November 1965). The significance of the term 'minority regime', as opposed to 'state', is examined below.

97 Organization of African Unity (Assembly of Heads of States), 'Second Ordinary Session of the Assembly of Heads of States held in Accra, Ghana from 21 to 26 October 1965' (22 October 1965), AHG/Res.25 (II), paragraph 1.

98 Organization of African Unity (Council of Ministers), 'Sixth Ordinary Session of the Council of Ministers held in Addis Ababa, Ethiopia from 28 February to 6 March 1966' (undated), CM/Res 75 (VI), paragraph 1.

99 Organization of African Unity (Assembly of Heads of States), 'Second Ordinary Session of the Assembly of Heads of States held in Accra, Ghana from 21 to 26 October 1965' (22 October 1965), AHG/Res 25 (II), paragraphs 2, 4(c).

100 Organization of African Unity (Council of Ministers), 'Nineteenth Ordinary Session of the Council of Ministers Held in Rabat, Morocco from 5 to 12 June 1972', CM/Res 267(XIX), preambular paragraphs 5, 7.

101 Organization of African Unity (Council of Ministers), 'Twenty-Ninth Ordinary Session of the Council of Ministers Held in Libreville, Gabon from 23 June to 3 July 1977', CM/Res 547(XXIX), preambular paragraph 5.

2.2.4 *The distinction between government and state*

The international and constitutional perspectives for addressing the Rhodesian crisis illustrate the fine – but crucial – distinction between the non-recognition of a *government* and the non-recognition of a *state*.[102] The *legal* obligation of non-recognition only applies with respect to a territorial claim, not to the right of a government to be in power at a specific moment.[103] Non-recognition of governments, to the extent that it is still practised, is a political act with consequences beyond the scope of this study.[104]

According to Dugard, the terms 'regime' and 'authority' used by the UN in resolutions related to Rhodesia were rooted in the persistence of the Security Council in continuing to view Southern Rhodesia's status as that of a British colony rather than an independent entity.[105] Yet, as he notes, Resolution 277(1970) dispels any doubts that the issue was perceived as one of contested statehood. The resolution calls upon UN member states to suspend the *membership* of the illegal regime of Southern Rhodesia in the specialized agencies and other international or regional organizations, in an effort to isolate the purported *state* of Rhodesia and not merely to prevent participation of a government.[106]

The position taken by the Security Council is not self-evident. Since it was the government's policies that were in violation of the right to self-determination, a refusal of recognition should possibly have been restricted to the Smith government rather than to Rhodesia as a territorial entity. After all, had 'Zimbabwe' made a unilateral declaration of independence and established itself as an effectively self-governing entity, it could lawfully have taken its place among sovereign states; only 'Rhodesia' could not.[107] However, the reality was that the purported state of Rhodesia would not have come into existence had it not been for

[102] See *Namibia Advisory Opinion*, separate opinion of Judge Castro, 218, likening the South African administration to a 'usurping government'. Compare in the context of change of government and state succession with Oscar Schachter, 'State Succession: The Once and Future Law', (1993) 33 *Virginia Journal of International Law* 253, 255.

[103] Colin Warbrick, 'The New British Policy on Recognition of Governments' (1981) *30 International & Comparative Law Quarterly* 568, 569.

[104] On recognition of governments see Talmon, *Recognition of Governments*.

[105] Dugard, *Recognition and the United Nations*, 93, 94.

[106] Devine, 'Status of Rhodesia' (1973), 158.

[107] Brad R. Roth, *Governmental Illegitimacy in International Law* (Oxford: Clarendon Press, 1999), 239–240.

the attempt to perpetuate the denial of the right to self-determination. Accordingly, it was the very existence of the state *at the time and under the terms in which it was carried out* that was tainted by illegality,[108] not just its government's policies.[109]

The ambiguity of the situation was apparent in the work of the OAU. On the one hand, there was continuous condemnation of the failure of the British government to bring the Smith regime to an end, a condemnation that assumed British responsibility and therefore implied that at issue was the right to govern the territory rather than its international status. On the other hand, the OAU referred to 'the illegal seizure of independence', calling upon all states 'to continue to refuse recognition to the present Government of Southern Rhodesia and to refuse recognition to any independent regime which the present talks between Britain and the Southern Rhodesian rebels may bring about'.[110]

2.2.5 The reversion of Rhodesia to colonial status

Throughout the 1970s abortive attempts were made to resolve the Rhodesia problem through negotiated settlements and UN-imposed sanctions.[111] In some instances negotiations were held between the British government and the Smith government; later on, efforts were made to mediate between the White and Black communities of Rhodesia. In the meantime, the fighting within Rhodesia escalated, resulting, by 1978, in some 12,000 victims of guerrilla action.[112] By that time, the Smith government was unilaterally seeking a solution to the conflict that would

108 Nyerere, 'Rhodesia', 373–374.

109 Dore claims that Rhodesia should be regarded as a state with a non-recognized government. However, he ignores the problem of illegality, under international law, of Rhodesia's independence, and considers the non-recognition of Rhodesia merely as a political stance. Isaak A. Dore, 'Recognition of Rhodesia and Traditional International Law: Some Conceptual Problems' (1980) 13 *Vanderbilt Journal of Transnational Law* 37, 37.

110 Organization of African Unity (Council of Ministers), 'Seventh Ordinary Session of the Council of Ministers held in Addis Ababa, Ethiopia from 21 October to 4 November 1966', CM/Res 78 (VII), paragraph 2.

111 Nkala, *The United Nations, International Law and the Rhodesian Independence Crisis*; Gowlland-Debbas, *Collective Responses to Illegal Acts in International Law*, 17–23; Robert O. Matthews, 'Talking without Negotiating: The Case of Rhodesia' (1979–1980) 39 *International Journal* 91; Stephen J. Stedman, *Peacemaking in Civil War: International Mediation in Zimbabwe, 1974–1980* (Boulder, CO: Lynne Rienner, 1991).

112 Margaret Doxey, 'The Making of Zimbabwe: From Illegal to Legal Independence' (1982) 36 *Year Book of World Affairs* 150, 161.

satisfy the international community but would not hand over the country to majority rule. In 1978 it signed an 'internal settlement' with three Black political leaders, Bishop Abel Muzorewa, Reverend Ndabaningi Sithole and Chief Jeremiah Chirau. Smith claimed that the three represented 85 per cent of the black population.[113] The settlement was entrenched in a 1979 constitution for Rhodesia/Zimbabwe. The Patriotic Front (PF, a loose alliance of ZAPU and ZANU) labelled the internal settlement 'treacherous' and threatened those involved in it with death.[114] Security Council Resolution 423 (14 March 1978) denounced the internal settlement as illegal. When Muzorewa was elected prime minister of 'Zimbabwe/Rhodesia', the Security Council declared the results of the elections null and void because they had been held under the auspices of the illegal racist regime.[115]

In December 1979, the British government convened a conference in Lancaster House in another attempt at a negotiated settlement. This conference resulted in an agreement which comprised a constitution for independent Zimbabwe, modalities for the transition to independence and terms for a ceasefire.[116] Following the signing of the Lancaster House Agreement, the Security Council terminated the measures of enforcement against Rhodesia.[117]

The success of the Lancaster House Conference in producing an agreement is attributed in large measure to the parties' sense of impending military and political defeat. The Muzorewa/Smith regime was worn out by the combined economic weight of the sanctions and the military weight of combating Zimbabwean freedom fighters. The PF feared that following the victory of the Conservative Party in the UK in May 1979, British

[113] Nkala, *Rhodesian Independence Crisis*; Gowlland-Debbas, *Collective Responses to Illegal Acts in International Law*, 23.

[114] Eddison J. M. Zvobgo, 'ZANU Death List' (Information and Publicity Department, Maputo, 13 November 1978), reproduced in Hudson, *Triumph or Tragedy?*, 226.

[115] UNSC Resolution 448 (30 April 1979).

[116] United Kingdom, 'Southern Rhodesia – Report of the Constitutional Conference, Lancaster House, London, September–December 1979 (Lancaster House, 21 December 1979)' (Cmnd 7802 1979). For an analysis of the negotiations and their outcome see Adolphe Lawson, *Les accords de Lancaster House en 1979: L'aboutissement de deux décennies de débats sur les conditions de l'indépendance du Zimbabwe* (Uppsala: Uppsala University, 1988); Jeffery Davidow, *A Peace in Southern Africa: The Lancaster House Conference on Rhodesia, 1979* (published under the auspices of the Center for International Affairs, Harvard University, Epping Bokwer, 1984).

[117] UNSC Resolution 460 (21 December 1979).

recognition of the Muzorewa government was imminent. Although the PF expected to win the military battle, it was unsure whether that victory could be achieved before its fighters lost the political, military and moral support of Rhodesia's neighbouring countries.[118]

Under the Lancaster House Agreement, Rhodesia reverted to colony status under the direct control of a governor appointed by the British government.[119] On 11 December 1979 the 'Parliament of Zimbabwe/Rhodesia' dissolved itself and provided that from the date of the governor's arrival the country, Rhodesia, 'shall cease to be an independent state and shall become part of Her Majesty's Dominions'. The governor of Southern Rhodesia reached Salisbury the following day, and the UK House of Commons was informed that 'Rhodesia has today returned to legality'.[120]

The governor, Lord Soames, had overall control of the administration of the colony until it attained independence, as well as control of the elections process. The existing administrative machinery of the territory remained in place until the new government came into power.

Elections were held in February 1980 for the bicameral parliament agreed upon in Lancaster House.[121] Seats in both houses were reserved for the White population.[122] ZANU–PF (as it became known when the PF split up, just before the elections) won fifty-seven of the eighty Black seats. Its leader, Robert Mugabe, became prime minister. On 18 April 1980, Zimbabwe became independent.[123] On 25 August 1980, it was admitted as a member state to the UN.

[118] The British government, in fact, assured the Rhodesian government that if negotiations failed on account of the PF, Britain would grant Rhodesia formal recognition under the Muzorewa government. Stedman, *Peacemaking in Civil War*, 166–171; Davidow, *A Peace in Southern Africa*, 100.

[119] Zimbabwe/Rhodesia Pre-independence Arrangements (1980) 19 *International Legal Materials* 398, paragraph 2.

[120] Peter Slinn, 'Zimbabwe Achieves Independence' (1980) 6 *Commonwealth Law Bulletin* 1038, 1050.

[121] Elections for the White seats were held on 14 February 1980, and for the Black seats on 27, 28 and 29 February 1980.

[122] Ten out of forty seats in the Senate and twenty out of a hundred seats in the House of Assembly. Zimbabwe Independence Constitution (1980), part E (Parliament), paragraphs 6, 10.

[123] This work concerns primarily the reversion of the Smith regime to colony status. However, because of the short period of time between that reversion and Zimbabwe's independence, in various contexts the transition to independence is also addressed.

2.3 Namibia

2.3.1 The South African administration

Until the First World War,[124] the territory of today's Namibia, then known as South West Africa,[125] was a German protectorate (with the exception of Walvis Bay, which belonged to the UK). During the war, the territory was occupied by South African forces. Following defeat in the war, Germany renounced all its rights to the territory.[126]

The Principal Allies and Associated Powers conferred upon the UK a mandate over Namibia, to be exercised by the government of the Union of South Africa. The mandate conferred on South Africa full powers of

[124] On the revocation of the mandate, the international stance and Namibia's transition to independence, see also Roger S. Clark, 'The International League for Human Rights and South West Africa 1947–1957: The Human Rights NGO as Catalyst in the International Legal Process' (1981) 3 *Human Rights Quarterly* 101; Lionel Cliffe *et al.*, *The Transition to Independence in Namibia* (Boulder, CO: Lynne Rienner, 1994); Virginia Curtin Knight, 'Namibia's Transition to Independence' (1989) 88 *Current History* 225; John Dugard, 'Legal Aspects of Investment in Namibia (South West Africa)', in Roger Murray, Jo Morris, John Dugard and Neville Rubin (eds.), *The Role of Foreign Firms in Namibia: Studies on External Investment and Black Workers' Conditions in Namibia* (Uppsala: Africa Publications Trust, 1974) 183; Dugard, *Recognition and the United Nations*, 111; Linda Freeman, 'The Contradictions of Independence: Namibia in Transition' (1991) 46 *International Journal (Canadian Institute of International Affairs)* 687; Kenneth W. Grundy, 'Namibia's First Year of Independence' (May 1991) 9 *Current History* 213; Elizabeth Landis, 'Namibia in International Context: The Frustration of Independence', in Brian Wood (ed.), *Namibia 1884–1984: Readings on Namibia's History and Society* (London: Namibia Support Committee, 1984); Elizabeth Landis, 'Namibia: A Transatlantic View' (1987) 3 *South African Journal on Human Rights* 347; Bryan O'Linn, *Namibia: Sacred Trust of Civilization, Ideal and Reality* (Windhoek: Gamsberg MacMillan, 2003); Motee Persaud, 'Namibia and the International Court of Justice' (1975) 68 *Current History* 220; Edzard Schmidt-Jortzig, 'The Constitution of Namibia: An Example of a State Emerging under Close Supervision and World Scrutiny' (1991) 34 *German Yearbook of International Law* 568; M. B. Schneider (ed.), *Namibia: Views and Perspectives since Independence* (Windhoek: Konrad-Adenauer Stiftung eV in co-operation with the Namibia Institute for Democracy, 1992); Paul C. Szasz, 'Statement on the Elections Process', in Heribet Weiland and Matthew Braham (eds.), *The Namibian Peace Process: Implications and Lessons for the Future* (Freiburg: Arnold Bergstrasser Institute, 1994); Laurence Tauber, 'Legal Pitfalls on the Road to Namibian Independence' (1979–1980) 12 *New York University Journal of International Law and Policy* 375; Marinus Wiechers, 'Namibia: The 1982 Constitutional Principles and Their Legal Significance' (1989–1990) 15 *South African Yearbook of International Law* 1.

[125] In UNGA Resolution 2372(XXII) (12 June 1968), the General Assembly decided that 'South West Africa' would be known as 'Namibia'.

[126] Treaty of Versailles, Article 119.

administration and legislation over the territory, as an integral part of the Union.[127]

From the outset, South Africa placed the interests of the White minority above those of the Black peoples, in continuation of the earlier German policy.[128] With the development of South Africa's formal internal policy of racial discrimination and apartheid, that policy was extended to Namibia, where it was applied more forcefully.

When the League of Nations was dissolved and its functions transferred to the UN Trusteeship Council, the UN invited South Africa to place Namibia under trusteeship. South Africa refused, and declared it would continue to administer the territory in accordance with its obligations under the mandate.[129] At the same time, it expressed a wish to incorporate Namibia into the South African Union, a request that was refused by the UN.[130] In July 1949, the National Party, elected to office in South Africa on the platform of apartheid, responded to the criticism directed at South Africa for its policy in Namibia by declaring that it would cease to report on its administration of Namibia.[131] The UN General Assembly retaliated by requesting an advisory opinion from the ICJ on the status of Namibia and the obligations of South Africa that arose from that status.[132] In 1950 the court gave the *International Status of South West Africa Advisory Opinion*, in which it said that Namibia was still a mandate territory. It clarified that the UN charter did not impose on South Africa an obligation to place Namibia under the trusteeship system, but South Africa also could not unilaterally modify the international status of the territory. South Africa therefore continued to bear the international obligations under the Covenant of the League of Nations, including the obligation to transmit annual reports and petitions from the inhabitants of the territory. In the following years, the UN attempted to reach agreement with South Africa on the future of Namibia, but with no success. In the meantime, the General Assembly's Fourth Committee overcame the

[127] The Mandate for South West Africa, 17 December 1920, Article 1, reproduced in John Dugard (ed.), *The South West Africa/Namibia Dispute: Documents and Scholarly Writings on the Controversy between South Africa and the United Nations* (Berkeley: University of California Press, 1973), 378–379.

[128] Dugard, *The South West Africa/Namibia Dispute*, 83. For a detailed account, see Israel Goldblatt, *History of South West Africa from the Beginning of the Nineteenth Century* (Cape Town: Juta, 1971).

[129] Dugard, *The South West Africa/Namibia Dispute*, 98.

[130] UNGA Resolution 65(I) (14 December 1946).

[131] UN Doc A/929 (1949), 7–8.

[132] UNGA Resolution 338(IV) (6 December 1949).

refusal of South Africa to submit reports and petitions by producing its own reports and by hearing oral petitioners from Namibia. This led to further disputes on the powers of the UN. The General Assembly requested – and obtained – two more advisory opinions of the ICJ, on the appropriate voting procedure when dealing with reports and petitions from Namibia, and on the admissibility of hearings of petitioners by the Committee on South West Africa.[133]

In view of the failure of the UN to induce South Africa to submit to UN authority by political means, the possibility of legal action was taken up. The Committee on South West Africa proposed that former members of the League of Nations that had become members of the UN bring legal proceedings against South Africa, under the mandate's dispute settlement provisions.[134] In 1960, Ethiopia and Liberia, which had been members of the League of Nations, took up the proposal and filed concurrent applications in the ICJ, instituting contentious proceedings against South Africa. The applicants sought from the court a declaration that South Africa was accountable to the UN for the administration of Namibia, and a finding that apartheid violated Article 2 of the mandate.[135] In 1962, the court held that it had jurisdiction to adjudicate upon the merits of the dispute.[136] The merits phase then proceeded, and the judgment was delivered in 1966. Although the proceedings in this second phase were entirely directed at the merits of the dispute, the court's judgment returned to a matter which had been believed to have been disposed of in 1962 – the legal standing of the applicant states. The court reversed its finding of 1962, and held that the applicant states had failed to establish a legal right or interest in the subject matter, because the obligations of the mandatory power were related to the 'conduct' provisions of the mandate and were owed only to the League of Nations and not to its individual members.[137]

This judgment met with severe criticism, both political and legal.[138] It caused tremendous disappointment among the political organs of the UN. The General Assembly actually punished the ICJ by refusing to approve

[133] *Voting Procedure Advisory Opinion* and *Admissibility of Hearings Advisory Opinion*; Shabtai Rosenne, with the assistance of Yaël Ronen, *The Law and Practice of the International Court, 1920–2005*, 5th edn (Leiden: Martinus Nijhoff, 2006), Volume I, 1001–1004.

[134] UN Doc A/3635 (1957), paragraphs 32, 34.

[135] Dugard, *The South West Africa/Namibia Dispute*, 280.

[136] *S W Africa Case (Preliminary Objections)*.

[137] *S W Africa Case (Second Phase)*, [14].

[138] See opinions reproduced in Dugard, *The South West Africa/Namibia Dispute*, 332.

an additional budgetary appropriation.[139] But the most drastic reaction of the General Assembly was directed at South Africa.[140] It attempted to achieve through political means what it had failed to obtain through legal ones. In Resolution 2145(XXI) (27 October 1966) the General Assembly revoked the mandate and, with it, South Africa's right to administer the territory. The resolution reaffirmed the inalienable right of the people of Namibia to self-determination, freedom and independence in accordance with the UN Charter, and condemned as crimes against humanity the policies of apartheid and racial discrimination practised by the government of South Africa in Namibia. It went on to state that the administration of Namibia by South Africa had been conducted in a manner contrary to the mandate, to the Charter of the United Nations and to the Universal Declaration of Human Rights (UDHR), and that since all the efforts of the UN to induce South Africa to fulfil its obligations in respect of the administration of the territory and to ensure the wellbeing and security of the indigenous inhabitants had been to no avail, the General Assembly had the right to reclaim the administration of the mandated territory. Accordingly, the General Assembly:

> 3. *Declares* that South Africa has failed to fulfil its obligations in respect of the administration of the Mandated Territory and to ensure the moral and material well-being and security of the indigenous inhabitants of South West Africa, and has, in fact, disavowed the Mandate;
>
> 4. *Decides* that the Mandate conferred upon His Britannic Majesty to be exercised on his behalf by the Government of the Union of South Africa is therefore terminated, that South Africa has no other right to administer the Territory and that henceforth South West Africa comes under the direct responsibility of the United Nations;
>
> 5. *Resolves* that in these circumstances the United Nations must discharge those responsibilities with respect to South West Africa . . .

2.3.2 The international response to continued South African administration

During the debate surrounding the adoption of Resolution 2145(XXI), doubts were raised as to the legality of the General Assembly's action. South Africa maintained that the General Assembly had no authority to

[139] Shabtai Rosenne, with the assistance of Yaël Ronen, *The Law and Practice of the International Court, 1920–2005* 5th edn (Leiden: Martinus Nijhoff, 2006), Volume I, 445.

[140] Dugard, *The South West Africa/Namibia Dispute*, 378–379.

deprive it of the mandate unilaterally and rejected Resolution 2145(XXI) as illegal.[141]

In May 1967, the General Assembly adopted Resolution 2248(S–V), which established the UN Council for South West Africa, to administer the territory until independence. The Council (renamed UN Council for Namibia (UNCN) in 1968[142]) represented Namibia and its interests in the international sphere, and issued travel and identity documents, which many states recognized. In 1974, the Council issued Decree No. 1, which sought to forbid the exploitation of Namibia's resources under South African auspices. The decree remained largely ineffective, since the authority of UNCN to promulgate it remained controversial.[143] The Council had a number of subsidiary bodies. One of those was the United Nations Institute for Namibia (UNIN) in Lusaka, Zambia, which was established to train a professional cadre for a future independent Namibia. UNIN was dominated by leaders of the South West African People's Organization (SWAPO), and some 700 members of SWAPO were trained in it as civil servants.[144] The senior management and staff later became Namibia's leading politicians, among them the prime minister and several cabinet members.[145]

In 1968, South Africa brought criminal proceedings against a number of Namibians, mostly leaders of SWAPO. They were indicted under the Terrorism Act of 1967, which had been enacted after the revocation of the mandate but applied retroactively from 27 June 1962.[146] On the eve of the judgment on the SWAPO trial, the Security Council intervened for the first time in the Namibia dispute. It 'took note' of General Assembly Resolution 2145(XXI) and of the trial being held under

[141] Doubts were also expressed whether the General Assembly was competent to determine the compatibility of apartheid with the provisions of the mandate, and whether the League of Nations could have revoked the mandate unilaterally and, if so, whether the General Assembly could do so on the same terms. Perhaps the most crucial obstacle, however, remained the nature of General Assembly and Security Council resolutions. Dugard, *The South West Africa/Namibia Dispute*, 381–409, 505–516.

[142] UNGA Resolution 2372(XXII) (12 June 1968).

[143] H. G. Schermers, 'The Namibia Decree in National Courts' (1977) 26 *International & Comparative Law Quarterly* 81.

[144] Frank Dexter Brown, 'Under Specter of Pretoria: Namibia Moves to Independence' (June 1989) 19 *Black Enterprise* 52.

[145] Craig N. Murphy, *The United Nations Development Programme: A Better Way?* (Cambridge: Cambridge University Press, 2006), 57.

[146] John Dugard, 'Foreign Affairs and Public International Law', in *Annual Survey of South African Law* (Juta, Cape Town, 1967), 38; John Dugard, 'Criminal Procedure', in *Annual Survey of South African Law* (Juta, Cape Town, 1967), 330.

'arbitrary laws whose application has been illegally extended to the territory of South West Africa in defiance of General Assembly resolutions'. It called on the government of South Africa to discontinue the 'illegal trial'.[147] Following South Africa's intransigence, the Security Council adopted another resolution, which reaffirmed that the proceedings constituted 'an illegal act and a flagrant violation of the rights of the South West Africans concerned . . . and the international status of the Territory now under direct United Nations responsibility'; censured South Africa for its flagrant defiance of its own previous resolution; and agreed that if South Africa failed to comply with that resolution, the Council would take further 'effective steps or measures'.[148] By reaffirming that Namibia was under direct UN responsibility, that the extension of South African law to Namibia was illegal, and that the trial was 'illegal', the Security Council implicitly approved the revocation of the mandate in Resolution 2145(XXI).[149]

From 1968 onwards, the South African government accelerated the implementation of apartheid in Namibia. It also extended a considerable number of its statutes to the territory,[150] in order to integrate Namibia more closely with South Africa and to develop separate homelands for different ethnic groups. The UN General Assembly vigorously condemned the South African legislative steps.[151] In subsequent resolutions, the Security Council reiterated its position that the UN General Assembly had terminated the mandate of South Africa over Namibia. It also considered the continued presence of South Africa in Namibia to be illegal and contrary to the principles of the Charter and to previous decisions of the United Nations. Moreover, the Security Council considered South Africa's presence in Namibia to be detrimental to the interests of the population of the territory and to those of the international community.[152] It referred to

[147] UNSC Resolution 245 (25 January 1968). [148] UNSC Resolution 246 (14 March 1968).

[149] John Dugard, 'Foreign Affairs and Public International Law', in *Annual Survey of South African Law* (Juta, Cape Town, 1967), 42.

[150] Development of Self-Government for Native Nations in South West Africa Bill 1968, South West Africa Constitution 1968, South West Africa Affairs Amendment Act 1969, Proclamation No. 290, 1968; Kavango Legislative Council Proclamation of 14 August 1970; Eastern Caprivi Legislative Council Proclamation of 2 February 1972; Dugard, *The South West Africa/Namibia Dispute*, 434–435. Ellison Kahn, 'Constitutional and Administrative Law', in *Annual Survey of South African Law* (Juta, Cape Town, 1970), 65–66, 79–80.

[151] UNGA Resolution 2372(XXII) (12 June 1968); UNGA Resolution 2403(XXIII) (16 December 1968); UNSC Resolution 264 (20 March 1969).

[152] UNSC Resolution 264 (20 March 1969); UNSC Resolution 269 (12 August 1969).

'the continued occupation of the territory of Namibia by the South African authorities' and called on all states 'to refrain from all dealings with the Government of South Africa purporting to act on behalf of the territory of Namibia'.[153] The Security Council called on South Africa to withdraw its administration from Namibia by 4 October 1969. South Africa refused the call. As a consequence, the Security Council adopted Resolution 276 (30 January 1970),[154] which:

> [*d*]*eclares* that the continued presence of the South African authorities in Namibia is illegal and that consequently all acts taken by the Government of South Africa on behalf of or concerning Namibia after the termination of the Mandate are illegal and invalid.

In subsequent Resolution 284 (29 July 1970), the Security Council requested an advisory opinion of the ICJ on the legal consequences for states of the continued presence of South Africa in Namibia (South West Africa) notwithstanding Security Council Resolution 276 (1970).

On 21 June 1971, the ICJ made public its Advisory Opinion on *Legal Consequences for States of the Continued Presence of South Africa in Namibia (South West Africa) notwithstanding Security Council Resolution 276 (1970)* (*Namibia Advisory Opinion*). The greater part of the *Advisory Opinion* concerned the power of the UN, and specifically that of the General Assembly and Security Council, to revoke the mandate. It concluded that following the General Assembly and Security Council resolutions, the mandate had been terminated and an obligation of non-recognition of the legality of South Africa's presence in Namibia existed. Whether the mandate was revoked only following the Security Council Resolution remained ambiguous.[155]

According to the *Namibia Advisory Opinion*, 'the continued presence of South Africa in Namibia being illegal, South Africa is under obligation to withdraw its administration from Namibia immediately and thus put an end to its occupation of the Territory',[156] and:

> ...States Members of the United Nations are under obligation to recognize the illegality of South Africa's presence in Namibia and the invalidity of its acts on behalf of or concerning Namibia, and to refrain from any acts and in particular any dealings with the Government of South Africa implying

[153] UNSC Resolution 269 (12 August 1969), paragraph 7.
[154] UNSC Resolution 276 (30 January 1970), paragraph 3.
[155] Dugard, *The South West Africa/Namibia Dispute*, 487. [156] *Namibia Advisory Opinion*, [133(1)].

recognition of the legality of, or lending support or assistance to, such presence and administration . . . [157]

The Security Council and General Assembly endorsed the court's opinion.[158] The General Assembly also called upon all states, 'Not to recognize as legally valid any rights or interests in Namibian property or resources purportedly acquired from the South African Government after 27 October 1966'.[159] Until the conflict was resolved in 1988, not one state recognized the legal right of South Africa to administer Namibia. However, there were disputes over what non-recognition entailed, particularly in the context of concessions for exploitation of natural resources.[160]

2.3.3 The illegality of the South African administration of Namibia

By remaining in Namibia's territory, South Africa violated the obligation under Article 25 of the UN Charter to comply with the decisions of the Security Council.[161] Article 25 does not, per se, constitute a peremptory norm. However, its violation would not alone have resulted in a drastic measure such as an obligation of non-recognition of South Africa's territorial claim. It is therefore important to look behind the obligation under Article 25, to the reasons for the revocation of the mandate. The revocation was brought about by South Africa's violation of the mandate's terms, which were geared towards advancing the right of the Namibian people to self-determination. In short, South Africa's administration of Namibia was essentially in violation of its obligation to respect the right to self-determination of the Namibian people.

Furthermore, once South Africa was instructed by the Security Council to withdraw its presence from Namibia, its continued presence there could be seen as an act of aggression,[162] and a violation of the prohibition on the use of force.

157 *Namibia Advisory Opinion*, [133(2)].

158 UNSC Resolution 301 (20 October 1971).

159 UNGA Resolution 2871(XXVI) (20 December 1971), paragraph 6(c).

160 Allan D. Cooper (ed.), *Allies in Apartheid: Western Capitalism in Occupied Namibia* (Basingstoke: Macmillan, 1988); Caleb M. Pilgrim, 'Some Legal Aspects of Trade in the Natural Resources of Namibia' (1990) 61 *British Yearbook of International Law* 249; *Regional Symposium* (1984).

161 *Namibia Advisory Opinion*, [112]–[115].

162 *Namibia Advisory Opinion*, separate opinion of Judge Ammoun, [12]–[13]; UNGA Resolution 39/50 (12 December 1984).

2.3.4 The transition of Namibia to independence

Throughout the period of South Africa's administration of the territory, both before and after the revocation of the mandate,[163] South Africa and the UN conducted negotiations on the future dispensation in Namibia. In 1978, the Security Council adopted Resolution 435 (29 September 1978), which called, inter alia, for the holding of elections for an independent Namibia, under UN supervision and control, and for the cessation of all hostile acts by all parties. Although both SWAPO and South Africa accepted the resolution as a matter of principle, the implementation of the resolution was delayed for over ten years. The principal cause for this delay was a demand by South Africa to link its withdrawal from Namibia with the withdrawal of Cuban troops from Angola. In the meantime, negotiations among the Western Contact Group (the US, Canada, the UK, France and the Federal Republic of Germany), South Africa and SWAPO on the substantive content of the Namibian regime that would follow the implementation of Security Council Resolution 435 yielded in 1982 an agreement on Constitutional Principles for Namibia.[164] In 1988, the US successfully mediated a tripartite agreement between South Africa, Angola and Cuba, and a bilateral agreement between Angola and Cuba,[165] which provided for Cuban withdrawal from Angola, independence for Namibia, and withdrawal of South African armed forces from Namibia under the terms of Resolution 435.

The implementation of Resolution 435 began in April 1989, leading to elections in Namibia in November of the same year. On 6 November 1989, the South African administrator-general gazetted a proclamation providing for the establishment of a constituent assembly for independent Namibia.[166] A seventy-two-member constituent assembly adopted a new constitution for Namibia on 9 February 1990, by consensus. Namibia became independent on 21 March 1990.

[163] Henry J. Richardson, 'Constitutive Questions in the Negotiations for Namibian Independence' (1984) 78 *American Journal of International Law* 76; Sushma Soni, 'Regimes for Namibia's Independence: A Comparative Study' (1991) 29 *Columbia Journal of Transnational Law* 563.

[164] Principles Concerning the Constituent Assembly and the Constitution for an Independent Namibia, UN Doc S/15287.

[165] A number of factors converged to enable this: the costs of fighting and financing the war on the part of Angola, Cuba and South Africa; the warming relationship between the US and the USSR; South Africa's realization that it was unlikely to provide a credible alternative to SWAPO; and an internal change of wind in South Africa. Laurent C. W. Kaela, *The Question of Namibia* (Basingstoke: Macmillan, 1996); Soni, 'Regimes for Namibia's Independence', 604.

[166] Constituent Assembly Proclamation of 1989 (AG 62/1989).

2.4 The TBVC

2.4.1 The establishment of the TBVC

Between 1976 and 1981, South Africa purported to grant independence to four territorial entities within its territory:[167] Transkei, Bophuthatswana, Venda and Ciskei (the TBVC).[168]

Racial segregation had been a dominant feature of South African policy after the Union of South Africa was established in 1910, and in 1948 the South African government officially adopted an apartheid policy. The development of a new international order with regard to human rights and racial discrimination brought increasing criticism by the international community of the growing discrimination within South Africa, and the South African government realized that its policy was no longer tenable. In 1961, the prime minister informed the parliament that international pressure was such that the only way in which White South Africa could retain domination in the country was to establish separate states along racial divides.[169] South Africa accordingly endeavoured to produce a new version of segregation, seemingly more in line with contemporary international standards. The South African parliament passed internal

[167] On the establishment of the TBVC, the international reaction and the reincorporation of the TBVC into South Africa, see also Gretchen Carpenter, 'Constitutional Implications of the Reincorporation for the Homelands' (July 1990) 16(7) *South African Foundation Review* 4; A. J. Christopher, *The Atlas of Changing South Africa*, 2nd edn (London: Routledge, 2001); J. J. N. Cloete, *Parliaments of South Africa* (Pretoria: J. L. van Schaik (Pty) Ltd, 1985); Paul Daphne, 'Undoing Apartheid Is Going to Cost Us' (1994) 96 *Work in Progress* 14; Francine de Clercq, 'Bophuthatswana: At the Edge of Time' (1991) 84 *Work in Progress* 17; Donald E. De Kieffer and David A. Hartquist, 'Transkei: A Legitimate Birth' (1978) 13 *New England Law Review* 428; Dermott J. Devine, 'International Law Tensions Arising from the South African Situation 1976–1986' (1987) *Acta Juridica* 165; John Dugard, 'The Future of the TBVC "States"' (1992) 8 *South African Journal on Human Rights* iii; Georges Fischer, 'La non-reconnaissance du Transkei' (1976) 22 *Annuaire français de droit international* 63; Steven Friedman (ed.), *The Long Journey: South Africa's Quest for a Negotiated Settlement* (Johannesburg: Ravan, 1993); Donald A. Heydt, 'Nonrecognition of the Independence of Transkei' (1978) 10 *Case Western Reserve Journal of International Law* 167; Anthea A. Jeffery, *Conflict at the Crossroads in Bophuthatswana* (Johannesburg: South African Institute of Race Relations, 1993); Geoffrey E. Norman, 'The Transkei: South Africa's Illegitimate Child' (1977) 12 *New England Law Review* 585; Marinus Wiechers, 'Reincorporation of the TBVC States – International Law Practice and Constitutional Implications' (1990) 16 *South African Yearbook of International Law* 119.

[168] Transkei and Bophuthatswana were each made up of numerous enclaves.

[169] 107 House of Assembly Debates, Columns 4191–4193 (10 April 1961), quoted in John Dugard, 'Collective Non-recognition: The Failure of South Africa's Bantustan States', in *Boutros Boutros-Ghali Amicorum Discipulorumque Liber: Peace Development, Democracy* (Brussels: Bruylant, 1998) Volume 1, 286.

legislation, the Status Acts,[170] which purported to give full independence to four of the Bantu national units (Bantustans) and sever them from South Africa: Transkei in 1976, Bophuthatswana in 1977, Venda in 1979 and Ciskei in 1981. The South African government claimed that this grant of independence responded to requests by the representatives of these entities. In fact, the representatives of the TBVC were acting under diktat of the South African government. South Africa also declared the process an 'internal decolonization' as an expression of self-determination.[171] This was the ultimate extension of the South African policy of apartheid.

Upon the independence of each of the TBVC, their residents automatically became citizens of the newly created states and lost their South African citizenship. Citizenship in the TBVC, as was residence in their antecedents, the Bantu national units, was based on racial affiliation.

The leading opposition movement in South Africa, the African National Congress (ANC), was vehemently opposed to the establishment of the TBVC. There was also opposition to independence from within the TBVC, fuelled by their residents' sense of material deprivation in comparison with the rest of South Africa.[172] On several occasions in which the South African and TBVC governments acted to incorporate additional territories within the TBVC, the communities whose lands were transferred attempted to resist the incorporation. These events led to violence and bloodshed, and in some cases entire communities fled their homes in order to remain within greater South Africa rather than become citizens of any of the TBVC.[173] The TBVC were governed by civil and military dictatorships, often subject to states of emergency and always prone to coups. Their governments depended on the South African government to maintain power through repression of opposition and frequent resort to violence. Ordinarily, the TBVC governments followed policies imposed by the South African government.[174]

The South African government strove to grant independence to six other Bantu national units. Its attempts remained unfruitful, for the most

[170] Status of Transkei Act 1976, Status of Bophuthatswana Act 1977, Status of Venda Act 1979, Status of Ciskei Act 1981.

[171] Dugard, 'Collective Non-recognition', 383–387.

[172] *Race Relations Survey 1989/1990* (Johannesburg: SAIRR, 1990), 435.

[173] Clive Plasket, 'The Ciskeian State of Emergency' (1990) 6 *South African Journal on Human Rights* 60.

[174] Interview by the author with Mr Zam Titus, special adviser to the minister of provincial and local government and formerly director-general of the Ministry of Constitutional Development, administrator-general of Ciskei, participant in the MPNF (Pretoria, 7 April 2004).

part because of the resistance of the leadership within these territories, both to independence and even to self-governing status.[175]

2.4.2 The international response to the establishment of the TBVC

The grant of independence to the TBVC was condemned by the UN General Assembly as a tool for the perpetuation of apartheid and for the dispossession of the Black South African population of its right to self-determination. Following the grant of independence to Transkei in 1976, the UN General Assembly declared that it:

> 1. *Strongly condemns* the establishment of bantustans as designs to consolidate the inhuman policies of *Apartheid*, to destroy the territorial integrity of the country, to perpetuate white minority domination and to dispossess the African people of South Africa of their inalienable rights;
>
> 2. *Rejects* the declaration of 'independence' of the Transkei and declares it invalid;
>
> 3. *Calls upon* all Governments to deny any form of recognition to the so-called independent Transkei and to refrain from having any dealings with the so-called independent Transkei or other bantustans . . .[176]

When Bophuthatswana was granted independence, the General Assembly reaffirmed that it:

> 2. *Denounces* the declaration of the so-called 'independence' of the Transkei and that of Bophuthatswana and any other Bantustans which may be created by the racist regime of South Africa and declares them totally invalid;
>
> . . .
>
> 5. *Again calls* upon all governments to deny any form of recognition to the so-called 'independent' Bantustans . . .[177]

Following the independence of Venda, the Security Council issued the following statement:

> The Security Council condemns the proclamation of the so-called 'independence' of Venda and declares it totally invalid. This action by the South African régime, following similar proclamations in the case of the Transkei and Bophuthatswana, denounced by the international community, is designed to divide and dispossess the African people and establish client States under its domination in order to perpetuate apartheid . . .

[175] Tanya Woker and Sue Clarke, 'Homelands' (1991) 2 *South African Human Rights Yearbook* 104.

[176] UNGA Resolution 31/6 A (26 October 1976).

[177] UNGA Resolution 32/105 N (14 December 1977).

The Security Council calls upon all Governments to deny any form of recognition to the so-called 'independent' bantustans . . . [178]

When Ciskei was granted independence, the UN General Assembly adopted a resolution on policies of apartheid of the government of South Africa, in which it, inter alia:

14. *Again calls* upon all States and organizations to refrain from any recognition of or co-operation with the so-called 'independent' bantustans'.[179]

The TBVC were never recognized by any state other than South Africa and each other.[180]

2.4.3 The illegality of the establishment of the TBVC

The UN organs condemned the creation of the TBVC as a violation of the prohibition on apartheid,[181] and of the 'inalienable right' to self-determination,[182] in the sense that the residents of the TBVC as part of the people of South Africa were not permitted to 'freely determine their political status'.[183] Another violation implicit in the texts was that of the prohibition on racial discrimination, of which apartheid was an extreme manifestation.

The General Assembly resolutions also note that the establishment of the TBVC was designed 'to destroy the territorial integrity of the country'.[184] Dugard considered this an acknowledgement of the violation of the prohibition on the territorial fragmentation of self-determination units contained in UN General Assembly Resolution 1514(XV).[185] However, as far as the self-determination unit was the international political entity of South Africa, its fragmentation was voluntary. It is difficult to argue that either its territorial integrity or its right to self-determination were violated. A further argument was made that the creation of the TBVC was an act of aggression.[186]

[178] Note by the president of the Security Council (21 September 1979), UN Doc S/13549.

[179] UNGA Resolution 37/69 A (9 December 1982).

[180] Although, since they themselves were not recognized, they were incapable of recognizing the statehood of other entities. Devine, 'Recognition'.

[181] UNGA Resolution 31/6 A; UNGA Resolution 37/69 A.

[182] Note by the president of the Security Council (21 September 1979), UN Doc S/13549.

[183] Dugard, *Recognition and the United Nations*, 105.

[184] UNGA Resolution 31/6 A.

[185] Dugard, *Recognition and the United Nations*, 104; UNGA Resolution 32/105 N (14 December 1977).

[186] The argument was rejected by a Bophuthatswana court in *S* v. *Banda and Others, Bophuthatswana (GD)*, 1989(4) SA 519, 544, on the ground that statehood is not regulated

2.4.4 The reincorporation of the TBVC into South Africa

The 1989 elections in South Africa marked the beginning of a new era and the gradual renunciation of apartheid. This included a reassessment of the TBVC's status. By October 1989, Transkei was spearheading the demand for reincorporation of the TBVC into South Africa. On 2 February 1990, the South African government declared a series of measures that together signified a first step in the dismantling of the apartheid regime.[187] Later that year, coups took place in Ciskei and Venda aimed at removing administrations that had been equivocal about reunification.[188]

The South African government announced that reincorporation of the TBVC was one option among others.[189] But it soon became clear that the future of the TBVC was exclusively within the new South Africa, and that the overwhelming majority of the Black population, within the TBVC and outside it, rejected the prospect of retaining 'independence' (with the exception of Bophuthatswana's ruler, discussed below).

In February 1992, the government-initiated Convention for a Democratic South Africa (Codesa) began negotiating the transition of South Africa to democratic rule. All four TBVC governments signed the Codesa Declaration of Intent, in which they pledged their commitment 'to bring about an undivided South Africa with one nation sharing a common citizenship, patriotism and loyalty', and to set in motion a process of establishing a constitution that would ensure 'that South Africa will be a united . . . state in which sovereign authority is exercised over the whole of its territory'.[190]

Codesa Working Group 4 was tasked with addressing the future of the TBVC. Its terms of reference included making recommendations regarding the manner in which the constitutional status of the TBVC may be affected by the outcome of the Codesa negotiations, the desirability or otherwise of the reincorporation of the TBVC, and the testing of the will of the people concerned regarding the reincorporation of the TBVC.[191] If reincorporation were decided upon, the working group was to address

by peremptory norms. The issue in that judgment was the status of Bophuthatswana, but the arguments were equally applicable to the other TBVC states.

187 *Race Relations Survey 1991/1992* (Johanesburg: SAIRR, 1992), 79.

188 Although, in the case of Ciskei, the post-coup administration was also reluctant to relinquish 'sovereignty'; see below.

189 Woker and Clarke, 'Homelands' (1991), 105.

190 Codesa, 1991 Declaration of Intent, paragraphs 2, 6a.

191 Codesa Working Group 4, Terms of Reference 1.1.4(a), (b), (c).

proposals for transitional arrangements and a time frame; disposal or transfer of assets of the TBVC governments; measures to ensure minimal interruption or disruption in administration and services and daily lives of people in the affected areas; termination of agreements and treaties; servicing and repayment of TBVC debts; and specific constitutional, legal and political measures necessary to effect reincorporation. All delegations except that of Bophuthatswana accepted the principle of reincorporation,[192] although some delegations reserved their positions or proposed certain conditions. There was no decision as to how or when the reincorporation was to occur.[193]

The Codesa process broke down in June 1992. In March 1993 another process began, the Multi-party Negotiation Forum (MPNF). This process culminated in November 1993, with an agreement on a new interim constitution to take effect after the elections. By then, reincorporation was a foregone conclusion.[194]

The leaders of Bophuthatswana and Ciskei oscillated between insisting on independence, campaigning for self-government in a federative state structure, and resigning themselves to total reincorporation.[195] Particularly adamant in his opposition to reincorporation was President Mangope of Bophuthatswana. His opposition manifested itself not only in public statements but also in the persistence of the Bophuthatswana government in passing legislation that was inconsistent with that of South Africa, at a time when Transkei, Venda and Ciskei were expressing their support for establishing a uniform legal regime for the whole country.[196]

[192] *Race Relations Survey 1992/1993* (Johannesburg: SAIRR, 1993) 506.

[193] Firoz Cachalia, 'A Report on the Convention for a Democratic South Africa' (1992) 8 *South African Journal on Human Rights* 249, 261.

[194] Interview by the author with Mr Rolf Meyer, South Africa's minister of defence, of communication and of constitutional affairs, 1991–1996 (Pretoria, 8 April 2004); interview by the author with Prof. François Venter, University of Potchefstroom, participant in the MPNF (Potchefstroom, 6 April 2004); interview by the author with Mr Zam Titus, special adviser to the minister of provincial and local government and formerly director-general of the Ministry of Constitutional Development, administrator-general of Ciskei, participant in the MPNF (Pretoria, 7 April 2004).

[195] Woker and Clarke, 'Homelands' (1991), 117.

[196] Tanya Woker and Sue Clarke, 'Homelands' (1992) 3 *South African Human Rights Yearbook* 106, 106–107. The government's position was largely Mangope's personal position. In November 1990, while Mangope was in Germany, the Bophuthatswana government reversed its stance, and stated that it intended to hold a referendum to decide the issue of reincorporation. Woker and Clarke, 'Homelands' (1992), 109. This intention (ruled out by Mangope when he returned) never materialized.

In September 1993, the Bophuthatswana government gave formal notice to the MPNF that it would not allow the operation in its territory of the Transitional Executive Council (TEC) – the South African body charged with administering South Africa in the period preceding the April 1994 elections[197] – nor facilitate the conduct of elections.[198] This resulted in strikes, rioting, looting, a mutiny of security forces and violent rampage by Mangope's Afrikaner allies. Events in Bophuthatswana came to a head in March 1994. The TEC deployed troops of the South African Defence Force, who enforced order in Bophuthatswana and on 12 March 1994 deposed Mangope. The South African government and the TEC assumed emergency powers, and two days later they appointed joint administrators for Bophuthatswana.[199]

A decree issued by the joint administrators partially suspended the constitution of Bophuthatswana. It replaced the Bophuthatswana government with the joint administrators as the executive and legislative authority. The decree also extended to Bophuthatswana the application of various South African legislative instruments, in order to enable Bophuthatswana residents to participate in the elections.[200]

Less than a fortnight after the Bophuthatswana takeover, the military leader of Ciskei, Oupa Gqozo, sensing impending mutiny in his security forces, resigned from office, and requested the TEC to take over.[201] On 26 April 1994, the joint administrators of Ciskei adopted a decree which provided for the 'termination of the sovereign independence of Ciskei and the reintegration of its territory in the national territory of South Africa with effect from 27 April 1994' (i.e. the day of general elections and entry into force of the interim constitution). The Constitution of Ciskei and other decrees governing its administration were repealed, and the then-existing Constitution of South Africa was made applicable to Ciskei.

197 Dugard, 'Collective Non-recognition', 395.

198 UN Doc E/CN.4/1994/15, paragraph 91.

199 See also George N. Barrie, 'The "Absorption" of Bophuthatswana March 1994: Extinction of State Personality from a South African Perspective, Irrelevancy from an International Perspective' (1994) *Tydskrif Vir Die Suid-Afrikaans Reg* (Journal of South African Law) 348; Andries Cilliers, 'Reincorporation of Bophuthatswana and Certain Other States into the Republic of South Africa' (1993–1994) 19 *South African Yearbook of International Law* 93.

200 Administration of Bophuthatswana Decree 1994, Articles 4(2), 5, 6, and 7 (applying to Bophuthatwana the Independent Electoral Commission Act 1993, the Transitional Executive Council Act 1993, the Independent Broadcasting Authority Act 1993 and the Electoral Act 1993).

201 Norm Dixon, 'Butcher of Bisho Bopped', *Green Left Weekly*, 30 March 1994; Jobst Bodenstein, 'Elections' (1995) 6 *South African Human Rights Yearbook* 74, 78.

On 27 April 1994, elections were held throughout South Africa, including in the TBVC. Immediately afterwards, the interim constitution came into force, and with it the repeal of the provisions granting independence to the TBVC.[202] The interim constitution was later replaced by the Constitution of the Republic of South Africa.

The national territory of the Republic of South Africa comprises nine newly defined provinces.[203] The territories of the former TBVC no longer constitute distinct units, and are subsumed into a number of different provinces. The elimination of the TBVC as separate entities was no different, in this respect, from the redefinition of the provincial boundaries within South Africa. Although Bophuthatswana and Ciskei 'lost' their independence before 27 April 1994, their status was regulated internally in the same way as that of Transkei and Venda.

2.5 Timor-Leste

2.5.1 The annexation of Timor-Leste by Indonesia

The island of Timor is situated in the Indian Ocean, about 400 miles north-west of Darwin, Australia.[204] The western regions of the island were part of the Dutch East Indies and were incorporated into the Indonesian Republic in 1949. The eastern regions of the island were, until the mid-1970s, a colony of Portugal, known as Timor-Leste. In 1960 Timor-Leste was placed on the UN list of non-self-governing territories.[205]

Until 1974 Portugal had refused to relinquish its hold over Timor-Leste or any of its other overseas territories, contending that they were all part of its metropolitan territory rather than non-self-governing territories. In 1974 a new government came to power in Portugal, and began a process of decolonization, which included the territory of Timor-Leste. Internal

[202] Interim Constitution, Article 230. Schedule 7 of the Interim Constitution repealed the Status Acts and the constitutions of the TBVC.

[203] Interim Constitution, Article 1(2), Part 1 of Schedule 1.

[204] See generally Lauri Hannikainen, 'The Case of East Timor from the Perspective of Jus Cogens', in *International Law and the Question of East Timor* (London: CIIR-IPJET, 1995); Sharon D. Korman, *The Right of Conquest: The Acquisition of Territory by Force in International Law and Practice* (Oxford: Clarendon Press, 1996), 281–292; Grayson J. Lloyd, 'The Diplomacy on East Timor: Indonesia, the United Nations and the International Community', in James J. Fox and Dionisio Babo Soares (eds.), *Out of the Ashes: Destruction and Reconstruction of East Timor* (Adelaide: Crawford House, 2003); Conflict, Security and Development Group, International Policy Institute, King's College London, *A Review of Peace Operations: A Case of Change* (London: King's College, 2003), 215–323.

[205] UNGA Resolution 1542(XV) (15 December 1961).

controversy ensued in Timor-Leste over the political form which the exercise of the right to self-determination should take. Three political parties emerged, each seeking to direct the decolonization process to a different end. Frente Revolucionária de Timor Leste Independente (Fretilin) advocated independence after a short transitional period, Associação Popular Democrática de Timor (Apodeti) advocated integration with Indonesia, and União Democrática de Timor (UDT) desired 'progressive autonomy' with continued Portuguese presence. By 1975, Fretilin appeared to be the leading party.[206]

Indonesia opposed independence for Timor-Leste. It commented on the territory's backwardness and lack of economic viability. It presented Fretilin as a left-wing party that planned to deliver the country to the Communists, an event which would have allegedly undermined regional security.[207]

On 11 August 1975, UDT seized power in Timor-Leste, with tacit support from Indonesia. Fighting between UDT and Fretilin broke out. The Portuguese administration, already in the process of dismantling, could not control the situation and by 29 August had withdrawn to the nearby island of Atauro. By mid-September, Fretilin had control of a substantial part of the territory. On 28 November 1975, in an attempt to muster international support, Fretilin declared the independence of the Democratic Republic of Timor-Leste. Two days later, a coalition of Apodeti, UDT and other parties rejected this declaration and declared the integration of Timor-Leste into the Republic of Indonesia.[208]

On 7 December 1975, Indonesian forces entered Timor-Leste and occupied it. On 18 December the foreign minister of Indonesia announced the establishment of a 'provisional government' in Timor-Leste. On 31 May 1976, the provisional government convened the first Regional Popular Assembly in Dili, which adopted a resolution requesting the integration of Timor-Leste into Indonesia. A week later the Assembly sent a delegation of 'representatives of the people of East Timor', which submitted to the

[206] Roger S. Clark, 'The "Decolonization" of East Timor and the United Nations Norms on Self-Determination and Aggression' (1995), updated and corrected version of article which appeared in (1980) 7 *Yale Journal of World Public Order* (on file with the author), 4.

[207] Clark, 'The "Decolonization" of East Timor', 7, 19–43.

[208] The declaration of the coalition has various versions. In the one published by the UN (UN Doc A/C.4/808) the coalition declared 'independence and integration'. For a discussion of the significance of the various versions see Akihisa Matsuno, paper on the Balibo Declaration prepared for the Closing Sessions of the 2nd Course on Indonesia and East Timor, Lisbon (March 1995), www.hamline.edu/apakabar/basisdata/1995/04/16/0003.html.

president of Indonesia a petition requesting integration of Timor-Leste into Indonesia. Indonesia dispatched a mission to Timor-Leste, ostensibly to ascertain the wishes of the people. Following a favourable report of the mission, the Indonesian parliament approved a bill for the integration of Timor-Leste into Indonesia as its twenty-seventh province.[209] Fretilin's military resistance to Indonesian rule continued on a significant scale until 1979, when it began to decline.[210]

2.5.2 The international response to the annexation of Timor-Leste

Portugal claimed that Indonesia was occupying Timor-Leste illegally.[211] Other states generally accepted the Portuguese contention,[212] although few concrete measures were taken to sanction the delinquency.[213] Exceptionally, on 20 January 1978, Australia granted de facto recognition to the incorporation of Timor-Leste into Indonesia by 'accept[ing] East Timor as a part of Indonesia', although it said that it deplored the previous developments, above all the use of force.[214] On 14 February 1979, Australia announced that it recognized the incorporation of Timor-Leste into Indonesia de jure. Later it claimed that other states had also recognized the annexation.[215]

The UN General Assembly adopted Resolution 3485(XXX), which:

209 Law 7/76 on the Legalization of the Integration of East Timor into the Unitary State of the Republic of Indonesia and the Formation of the Province of East Timor.

210 Clark, 'The "Decolonization" of East Timor', 11. For general references on the annexation of East Timor, see Mari Alkatiri, 'The Democratic Republic of East Timor (Statement in the Fourth Committee of the United Nations General Assembly)' (1977) 7 *Journal of Contemporary Asia* 280; James Dunn, *East Timor: A People Betrayed* (Milton: Jacaranda, 1983); Geoffrey C. Gunn, *East Timor and the United Nations: The Case for Intervention* (Lawrenceville: Red Sea, 1997).

211 E.g. *note verbale* dated 19 May 1997 from the Permanent Mission of Portugal to the United Nations addressed to the Secretary-General, UN Doc A/52/152, paragraph 1.

212 For the UK, see statement of the minister of state, Foreign and Commonwealth Office (Mr John Battle), that 'East Timor was invaded by Indonesia in 1975', Hansard HC Volume 334, Column 764 (15 February 2000).

213 Thomas D. Grant, 'East Timor, the UN System, and Enforcing Non-recognition in International Law' (2000) 33 *Vanderbilt Journal of Transnational Law* 273, 298–299.

214 (1978–1980) 8 *Australian Yearbook of International Law* 279.

215 *East Timor Case*, Counter-memorial of the Government of Australia (1 June 1992), [175]–[176]; *East Timor Case*, Rejoinder of the Government of Australia (1 July 1993), [44]–[54]. In the *East Timor Case*, Judge Skubiszewski opined that the following states may have recognized the annexation de facto: Bangladesh, India, Iran, Iraq, Jordan, Malaysia, Morocco, Papua New Guinea, the Philippines and the US. *East Timor Case*, dissenting opinion of Judge Skubiszewski, [26]. For relevant texts see Heike Krieger (ed.), *East Timor and the International Community: Basic Documents* (Cambridge: Cambridge University Press, 1997).

4. *Strongly* deplores the military intervention of the armed forces of Indonesia in Portuguese Timor;

5. *Calls upon* the Government of Indonesia to desist from further violation of the territorial integrity of Portuguese Timor and to withdraw without delay its armed forces from the territory in order to enable the people of the Territory freely to exercise their right to self-determination and independence . . . [216]

Although the resolution did not refer expressly to the prohibition on the use of force, the reference to the violation of the 'territorial integrity' of Portuguese Timor indicated that General Assembly regarded the use of force as having been illegal. The resolution was also an implicit determination that the right to self-determination had been violated.

The Security Council was less explicit. In its Resolutions 384 (22 December 1975) and 389 (22 April 1976), adopted immediately following the occupation, it:

1. *Calls upon* all States to respect the territorial integrity of East Timor as well as the inalienable right of its people to self-determination in accordance with General Assembly resolution 1514(XV);

2. *Calls upon* the Government of Indonesia to withdraw without delay all its forces from the Territory . . .

Although the resolutions do not mention any violation of international law, the call on states 'to respect the territorial integrity of East Timor as well as the inalienable right of its people to self-determination' indicates that the Security Council considered Indonesia to have compromised those.

The few other UN resolutions on Timor-Leste refer to the illegality of the Indonesian intervention only indirectly. Following the Indonesian legislation incorporating Timor-Leste, the General Assembly reaffirmed Resolution 3485(XXX), repeated the call for withdrawal, and added that the General Assembly:

5. *Rejects* the claim that East Timor has been integrated into Indonesia, in as much as the people of the Territory have not been able to exercise freely their right to self-determination and independence . . . [217]

Gradually, objection to the Indonesian intervention became mute. In 1977, the General Assembly affirmed Resolution 3485(XXX) and rejected the claim of integration, but no longer expressly called for an Indonesian

216 UNGA Resolution 3485(XXX) (12 December 1975).
217 UNGA Resolution 31/53 (1 December 1976), paragraph 5.

withdrawal.[218] In 1978, it again affirmed Resolution 3485(XXX), but did not even reject the claim of integration.[219] Subsequent resolutions neither reaffirmed Resolution 3485(XXX) nor rejected the claim of integration,[220] thus abandoning even the indirect reference to the illegality of the intervention or to its legal consequences. From 1982 until 1999, the General Assembly repeatedly deferred consideration of the question of Timor-Leste.

The last UN resolution on Timor-Leste was adopted in 1983 by the Commission on Human Rights, which reaffirmed the inalienable right of the people of Timor-Leste to self-determination and independence.[221] Until 1999, there was no further statement on the status of Indonesia in Timor-Leste by any organ of the UN.

2.5.3 *The illegality of the annexation of Timor-Leste*

Although some Timorese were enthusiastic about annexation, there was no internal consensus on the matter, and the parties which led the incorporation into Indonesia were not regarded as representative of the Timorese people. The annexation of Timor-Leste into Indonesia without proper consultation was a violation of the right of the people of Timor-Leste to self-determination under the law applicable to decolonization,[222] and as confirmed in the General Assembly resolutions and ICJ judgment.[223]

There is no doubt that the Indonesian invasion of Timor-Leste was carried out by force. However, it has been argued that because Timor-Leste was not a state, the use of force against it was not a violation of Article 2(4) of the UN Charter. Such a narrow construction of the prohibition on the use of force has long since been rejected. Furthermore, the Indonesian annexation was in violation of Article 1 of the UN Charter, which prohibits all acts of aggression and is not restricted in its applicability to states.[224]

Indonesia attempted to justify its use of force against Timor-Leste on four grounds: self-defence, invitation by the Timorese, the need to protect the future stability of Indonesia and South East Asia, and humanitarian

[218] UNGA Resolution 32/34 (28 November 1977).

[219] UNGA Resolution 33/39 (13 December 1978).

[220] UNGA Resolution 34/40 (21 November 1979); UNGA Resolution 35/27 (11 November 1980); UNGA Resolution 36/50 (24 November 1981); UNGA Resolution 37/30 (22 November 1982).

[221] UNCHR, Resolution 1983/8, (1983) UN Doc E/CN.4/1983/60 at 129.

[222] UN Doc S/PV.1864 (15 December 1975), statement of the representative of Portugal, paragraph 59; UNGA Resolution 31/53 (1 December 1976); Cassese, *Self-Determination of Peoples*, 226.

[223] *East Timor Case*, [37].

[224] Clark, 'The "Decolonization" of East Timor', 37.

purposes. However, none of these claims was sustainable as a matter of fact or of law: at no time was Indonesia threatened by forces from Timor-Leste; as pointed out with respect to the expression of interest in joining Indonesia, to the extent that Indonesia was permitted entry into Timor-Leste by forces that favoured annexation, that permission was not given by a representative government; concern for the future stability of the region, to the extent that the latter was endangered, did not permit use of force; as for humanitarian grounds, Indonesia did not take any steps that would support its claim that this was its motive or purpose.[225]

In February 1991, Portugal instituted proceedings in the ICJ against Australia,[226] with respect to a treaty which the latter had concluded with Indonesia for exploitation of natural resources in the Timor Sea, off the coast of Timor-Leste. Portugal maintained that in concluding the treaty and acting to implement it, Australia had infringed upon the rights of the people of Timor-Leste to self-determination and to permanent sovereignty over its natural resources, and upon the rights of Portugal as the administering power, and had contravened Security Council Resolutions 384 and 389.[227] Australia challenged the jurisdiction of the court, arguing that in order to decide on Portugal's application the court would have to determine the rights and obligations of Indonesia with regard to Timor-Leste, something the court could not do without Indonesia's consent to the proceedings.[228] In a majority decision, the ICJ accepted Australia's objection and ruled that it had no jurisdiction to hear the case.

225 Clark, 'The "Decolonization" of East Timor', 37–43.

226 Pursuant to their respective acceptances of compulsory jurisdiction under Article 36(2) of the ICJ Statute.

227 *East Timor Case*, [19].

228 *East Timor Case*, [33]. The proceedings and the ruling have generated extensive literature, notably Judith Bello Hippler and Peter H. F. Bekker, 'East Timor (Port v Austl)' (1996) 90 *American Journal of International Law* 94, 94–98; Roger S. Clark, 'Timor Gap: The Legality of the "Treaty on the Zone of Cooperation in an Area between the Indonesian Province of East Timor and Northern Australia"', in Peter Carey and G. Carter Bentley (eds.), *East Timor at the Crossroads: The Forging of a Nation* (London: Cassell, 1995); Roger S. Clark, 'Obligations of Third States in the Face of Illegality – Ruminations Inspired by the Weeramantry Dissent in the Case Concerning East Timor', in Anthony Anghie and Gary Sturgess (eds.), *Legal Visions of the 21st Century: Essays in Honour of Judge Christopher Weeramantry* (The Hague: Kluwer Law International, 1998); James Crawford, 'The General Assembly, the International Court and Self-Determination', in James Crawford, *International Law as an Open System* (London: Cameron May, 2002); Catriona Drew, 'The East Timor Story: International Law on Trial' (2001) 12 *European Journal of International Law* 651; Grant, 'East Timor, the UN System, and Enforcing Non-recognition'; Brandi J. Pummell, 'The Timor Gap: Who Decides Who Is in Control' (1998) 26 *Denver Journal of International Law and Policy* 655; Iain G. M. Scobbie and Catriona J. Drew, 'Self-Determination Undetermined: The Case of East Timor' (1996) 9 *Leiden Journal of International Law* 185.

Judge Weeramantry, in dissent, thought that the court could have ruled whether the right of Timor-Leste to self-determination was violated, including its permanent sovereignty over natural resources, without an enquiry into the legality of Indonesia's conduct. In his opinion, Australia had violated the obligation to respect this right.[229] His opinion did not directly address the question of recognition of the Indonesian annexation, although he pointed out the inconsistency between Australia's recognition of Indonesia's sovereignty over Timor-Leste and its recognition of the Timorese people's right to self-determination.[230] Judge Skubiszewski, also in dissent, also thought that the court's jurisdiction was not precluded by Indonesia's non-participation, because a finding on the legality of Australia's acts did not depend on a determination of the wrongfulness of Indonesia's control over Timor-Leste. However, when testing Australia's conduct against its obligation to treat Timor-Leste as a non-self-governing territory,[231] he relied on the obligation of non-recognition, which he considered to be a self-executing consequence of the 'unlawful use of force' and 'irregular acquisition of territory' by Indonesia. He also reiterated Australia's duty to respect Timor-Leste's right to self-determination.[232] Nevertheless, he stopped short of declaring that Australia's entry into negotiations with Indonesia on the treaty was a violation of international law.

2.5.4 The transition of Timor-Leste to independence

Until Indonesia's withdrawal, the UN maintained Timor-Leste on the list of non-self-governing territories, with Portugal formally designated the administering power. Portugal and Indonesia carried out negotiations on Timor-Leste in the 1980s and 1990s under UN auspices, but with little success. A sea change occurred following an internal political transformation in Indonesia, which led Indonesia's President Habibie to agree to the holding of a referendum in Timor-Leste to determine the territory's political future. On 5 May 1999, the governments of Portugal and Indonesia signed an agreement on holding a popular consultation in Timor-Leste,[233] to decide between a proposal for special autonomy for

229 *East Timor Case*, dissenting opinion of Judge Weeramantry, 154.
230 *East Timor Case*, dissenting opinion of Judge Weeramantry, 201.
231 *East Timor Case*, dissenting opinion of Judge Skubiszewksi, [96].
232 *East Timor Case*, dissenting opinion of Judge Skubiszewksi, [125], [129], [134]–[141].
233 1999 Agreement between the Republic of Indonesia and the Portuguese Republic on the Question of East Timor.

Timor-Leste within the unitary state of the Republic of Indonesia and separation from Indonesia.[234]

In the popular consultation that took place on 30 August 1999, close to half a million persons exercised their right to vote. Over 78 per cent of them voted in favour of independence.[235] Within days of the release of the results of the vote, pro-integration militia groups went on a violent rampage, killing more than a thousand people and demolishing most of the country's infrastructure. An International Force for East Timor (INTERFET), led by Australian forces, moved into Timor-Leste to restore order. On 25 October 1999, the UN Security Council established the United Nations Transitional Administration in East Timor (UNTAET) to administer the country before handing it over to an elected Timorese government. On 30 August 2001, Timor-Leste held its first elections. The elected political representatives convened the constituent assembly and drew up the country's constitution. On 20 May 2002, Timor-Leste became sovereign. That day is celebrated as Restoration of Independence Day (referring back to the 28 November 1975 declaration of independence by Fretilin).[236]

2.6 The TRNC

2.6.1 The establishment of the TRNC

The population of the island of Cyprus, all together some 780,000 persons, comprises approximately 82 per cent Christian Greek Cypriots and 18 per cent Muslim Turkish Cypriots.[237] In 1960, Cyprus gained independence from British rule. Its status was established in its constitution as well as in three international instruments: the 1960 Treaty Concerning the Establishment of the Republic of Cyprus and the 1960 Treaty of Guarantee of the Independence of Cyprus, to both of which the UK, Greece, Turkey and Cyprus are parties, and the 1960 Treaty of Alliance, to which Greece, Turkey and Cyprus are parties.

[234] 1999 Agreement Regarding the Modalities for the Popular Consultation of the East Timorese through a Direct Ballot.

[235] UN Secretary-General Press Release (3 September 1999), UN Doc SG/SM/7119 SC/6722.

[236] The Government of Timor-Leste, 'History', http://timor-leste.gov.tl/?p=29&lang=en.

[237] For general references on the establishment of the TRNC, on the international reaction and on proposals for solutions, see also Rauf R. Denktaş, 'The Crux of the Cyprus Problem' (1999) 4 *Perceptions* 5; Zaim M. Necatigil, *Our Republic in Perspective* (Lefkoşa 1985); Zaim M. Necatigil, 'The Turkish Republic of Northern Cyprus: Statehood and Recognition' (1996) 2 *Journal of Cyprus Studies* 3; Zaim M. Necatigil, 'The Legal System of the Turkish Republic of Northern Cyprus' (1998) 4 *Journal of Cyprus Studies* 213.

The constitution of Cyprus aimed at balancing the interests of the island's two communities. However, division between the two communities, which pre-dated independence, persisted. In 1963, Greek Cypriot President Makarios proposed fundamental changes to the Cypriot constitution, including abolishing Turkish Cypriot veto powers, changing the quotas of Turkish Cypriots employed in the civil service, and eliminating Turkish Cypriot communal rights. Turkish Cypriots walked out of the parliament in a protest which led to the first post-independence period of intercommunal conflict. During this period, approximately 25 per cent of the Turkish Cypriot population fled from their villages into armed enclaves. In 1964, the UN established a peacekeeping force in Cyprus (UNFICYP).[238] Between 1963 and 1974, almost 80 per cent of Turkish Cypriots lived in closed militarized communities. In 1967 the Turkish Cypriot community set up a Provisional Cyprus Turkish Administration.

Tensions escalated again in July 1974, following a coup d'état by Greek Cypriots favouring a union of Cyprus with Greece. In response to the coup, Turkey invaded Cyprus. It claimed that it was exercising its rights under the 1960 Treaty of Guarantee to protect the Turkish Cypriot population. By late August 1974, Turkish military forces had advanced to occupy the northern part of the island.[239] During the military conflict, which continued until early 1975, 183,000 Greek Cypriots fled their homes in the northern part of the island and moved to the south, while over 40,000 Turkish Cypriots fled their homes in the southern part of the island, moving north.[240]

On 1 October 1974, the Turkish Cypriot community proclaimed the creation of the Autonomous Cyprus Turkish Administration. On 13 February 1975, it declared itself the Turkish Federated State of Cyprus (TFSC), an autonomous entity within the Republic of Cyprus. The TFSC adopted a constitution by referendum on 8 June 1975.[241] It made no formal claim to independence from the Republic of Cyprus, although in 1982 the attorney-general of the TFSC noted that although the TFSC had until then refrained from asking for international recognition, it 'has gained the essential

[238] UNSC Resolution 186 (4 March 1964).

[239] Since then UNFICYP has, in addition to its earlier mandate, been maintaining the ceasefire under UNSC Resolution 355 (1 August 1974).

[240] S. K. N. Blay, 'Self-Determination in Cyprus: The New Dimensions of an Old Conflict' (1981–1983) 10 *Australian Yearbook of International Law* 67.

[241] Sosyal Mümtaz, 'Inequality of Status: Impediment to a Solution in Cyprus', in Reşat Arim (ed.), *Cyprus and International Law* (Ankara: Bilknet University Foreign Policy Institute, 2002), 132.

characteristics of Statehood in international law i.e., people, territory, government'.[242]

The establishment of the TFSC was intended to serve as a bargaining chip in negotiating a higher degree of autonomy for the Turkish Cypriot community, but subsequent negotiations under UN auspices were unsuccessful. The Turkish Cypriot community felt that the UN was adopting a pro-Greek position. This sentiment, coupled with the fear that a moderate government in Turkey would persuade the Turkish Cypriots to accept a UN solution, drove the Turkish Cypriot community to declare independence.[243] On 15 November 1983, the TFSC was dissolved and replaced by the Turkish Republic of Northern Cyprus (TRNC). The declaration of independence of the TRNC, issued by the Turkish Cypriot parliament, describes the events and reasons that led to the establishment of the TRNC from the Turkish Cypriot perspective.[244] These include the usurpation of the legislature, executive and judiciary by Greek Cypriots; the domination and exploitation of Turkish Cypriots by their Greek Cypriot compatriots; and the discrimination to which Turkish Cypriots were subject. The Declaration states that the 'Turkish Cypriot People' has no allegiance to the 'Greek Cypriot Administration'. The Declaration then addresses the right to self-determination and its consequences:

> 20. . . . The Turkish Cypriot People believe that there must be in the world:
>
> '. . . peaceful and friendly relations based on respect for the principles of equal rights and self-determination of all peoples . . . '
>
> The Turkish Cypriot People have as much right to live in freedom and independence as the Greek Cypriots.
>
> Confirmation of an Existing Reality
>
> 21. The Turkish Cypriot People have in fact exercised this right a long time ago; they have established their own State with all its organs. All that is being done today is the confirmation and declaration of an existing reality and the re-naming of our State.

[242] Zaim M. Necatigil, *The Cyprus Conflict – A Lawyer's View*, 2nd edn (Lefkoşa: A-Z Publications, 1982), 118, 119. While Necatigil's analysis of the legal situation is fraught with inaccuracies, its significance lies in that it constitutes an assertion of statehood by the highest legal officer of the TRNC (then the TFSC). Since Necatigil followed the declaratory theory, it mattered little for the strength of his argument that the TFSC had never requested international recognition.

[243] Blay, 'Self Determination in Cyprus', 78–80.

[244] UN Doc A/38/586-S/16148 (16 November 1983); Necatigil, *Our Republic in Perspective*, 78.

At the same time, the TRNC called for a partnership with the 'Greek Cypriot People' within the framework of a genuine federation.[245] In 1985, the TRNC adopted a new constitution. Apart from the international claim to independence that formally began only in 1983, the TFSC and TRNC were one continuous unit,[246] as evidenced by the reference in the declaration of independence of 1983 to an 'existing reality' which was merely being confirmed.

2.6.2 The international response to the establishment of the TRNC

The TRNC was immediately recognized as an independent state by Turkey, but by no other state. The international community continues to recognize the Republic of Cyprus as the only state on the island, for all Cypriots.

In response to the proclamation of the establishment of the TRNC, the Security Council adopted Resolution 541(1983), which:

> 1. *Deplores* the declaration of the Turkish Cypriot authorities of the purported secession of part of the Republic of Cyprus;
>
> 2. *Considers* the declaration . . . as legally invalid and calls for its withdrawal . . .
>
> 6. *Calls upon* all States to respect the sovereignty, independence, territorial integrity and non-alignment of the Republic of Cyprus;
>
> 7. *Calls upon* all States not to recognise any Cypriot State other than the Republic of Cyprus . . .[247]

Following the exchange of ambassadors between Turkey and the TRNC, the Security Council:

> 1. *Reaffirms* its Resolution 541 (1983) and calls for its urgent and effective implementation;
>
> 2. *Condemns* all secessionist actions, including the purported exchange of ambassadors between Turkey and the Turkish Cypriot leadership, declares them illegal and invalid and calls for their immediate withdrawal;

[245] Declaration of Independence, paragraph 22.

[246] This is also implied in the opinion of Sir (then Mr) Eli Lauterpacht CBE QC, 'Turkish Republic of Northern Cyprus, the Status of the Two Communities in Cyprus', attached to letter dated 7 August 1990 from the Permanent Representative of Turkey to the UN, addressed to the Secretary-General (9 August 1990), UN Doc A/44/968-S/21463, paragraph 33.

[247] UNSC Resolution 541 (18 November 1983).

> 3. *Reiterates* the call upon all States not to recognise the purported State of the 'Turkish Republic of Northern Cyprus' set up by secessionist acts and calls upon them not to facilitate or in any way assist the aforesaid secessionist entity ...[248]

Other international organisations also rejected the declaration of independence. The European Community declared that the

> ten Member States of the European Community are deeply concerned by the declaration purporting to establish a 'Turkish Republic of Northern Cyprus' as an independent State. They reject this declaration, which is in disregard of successive resolutions of the United Nations. The Ten reiterate their unconditional support for the independence, sovereignty, territorial integrity and unity of the Republic of Cyprus. They continue to regard the Government of President Kyprianou as the sole legitimate Government of the Republic of Cyprus. They call upon all interested parties not to recognize this act, which creates a very serious situation in the area.[249]

The Commonwealth Heads of Government issued a press communiqué stating, inter alia, that the

> Heads of Government condemned the declaration by the Turkish Cypriot authorities issued on 15 November 1983 to create a secessionist state in northern Cyprus, in the area under foreign occupation. Fully endorsing Security Council Resolution 541, they denounced the declaration as legally invalid and reiterated the call for its non-recognition and immediate withdrawal. They further called upon all States not to facilitate or in any way assist the illegal secessionist entity. They regarded this illegal act as a challenge to the international community and demanded the implementation of the relevant UN Resolutions on Cyprus.[250]

2.6.3 The illegality of the establishment of the TRNC

In Resolution 541(1983) the Security Council declared that it considered the declaration of independence incompatible with the 1960 Treaty of Establishment and the 1960 Treaty of Guarantee, and that therefore 'the attempt to create a "Turkish Republic of Northern Cyprus" is invalid'.

Security Council Resolution 550(1984) reaffirms Resolution 541(1983) and reiterates the condemnation of 'all secessionist actions'.[251] In both resolutions, the Security Council calls upon 'all States to respect the sovereignty, independence, territorial integrity and non-alignment of the

[248] UNSC Resolution 550 (11 May 1984).
[249] EC Bulletin 11-1983 (16 November 1983), point 2.4.1.
[250] Issued on 29 November 1983, cited in ECtHR, *Loizidou* v. *Turkey (Merits)*, [23].
[251] UNSC Resolution 550 (11 May 1984), paragraph 1.

Republic of Cyprus.'[252] These resolutions give the impression that the illegality with which the Security Council was concerned constituted the violation of the 1960 treaties, and possibly the secession. Neither, however, is a sufficient ground for an obligation of non-recognition. The 1960 treaties apply among particular states. Their violation, if such took place,[253] does not give rise to a universal obligation of non-recognition. Secession as such is not unlawful under international law,[254] and also clearly does not give rise to a legal obligation of non-recognition.

In contrast, what is significant is that the TRNC was established following the use of force by Turkey in 1974. This fact was not expressly mentioned in the resolutions but is only implied in the calls 'upon all States to respect the sovereignty, independence, territorial integrity and non-alignment of the Republic of Cyprus'.[255] Necatigil argues that because the establishment of the TRNC did not take place at the same time as the Turkish intervention, it cannot be said to have been established as a result of the use of force. He does recognize, however, that the 1983 declaration of independence was 'the culmination of a process of political and administrative evolution which began in December 1963'.[256] That process would not have culminated in independence had it not been for the Turkish intervention.[257]

As to the permissibility of the use of force, the TRNC argues that Turkey's recourse to force was within its right – and obligation – under the Treaty of Guarantee, to protect the Turkish Cypriot population.[258] However, it is not clear that the Treaty of Guarantee allows the guarantor powers to intervene on behalf of only part of the population, rather than for the protection of Cyprus as a whole. Moreover, even if the Treaty of Guarantee purports to allow such intervention, and even if it purports to allow

252 UNSC Resolution 541 (18 November 1983), paragraph 4; UNSC Resolution 550 (11 May 1984), paragraph 6.

253 A point disputed by the TRNC. See e.g. Zaim M. Necatigil, *The Cyprus Question and the Turkish Position in International Law*, 2nd edn (Oxford: Oxford University Press, 1993), 324.

254 James Crawford, 'State Practice and International Law in Relation to Succession' (1998) 69 *British Yearbook of International Law* 85, 86–87. ICJ, *Kosovo Declaration of Independence Advisory Opnion*, Written Contribution of the Authors of the Unilateral Declaration of Independence regarding the Written Statements, [4.06]–[4.13].

255 This is not a call on the TRNC, which is not recognized as a 'state'.

256 Necatigil, *The Cyprus Question*, 324–325.

257 As pointed out by Cyprus in the debate preceding the adoption of UNSC Resolution 541(1983). UN, 'Chapter VIII Mediterranean – Cyprus Question' (1983) 37 *Yearbook of the United Nations*, 255.

258 Necatigil, *The Cyprus Question*, 324.

the use of force for this purpose,[259] it cannot override the peremptory prohibition on the use of force embodied in the UN Charter.[260] Cyprus's apparent consent under the Treaty of Guarantee should not be regarded as legalizing the use of force against it at a later stage, when it no longer expresses such consent. Otherwise, i.e. if a potentially injured party can waive its right, the peremptory character of a prohibition becomes a hollow term. Nor can the Treaty of Guarantee be construed as an expression of consent to the use of force even in specific circumstances. If there is no consent while the force is being used (and clearly there was not), prior consent is irrelevant. Even a state which consents to the placing of forces on its territory may demand at any time that they leave.[261] The Turkish use of force was therefore illegal,[262] and the establishment of the TRNC was a consequence of the violation of the prohibition on the use of force.[263]

2.6.4 The Annan Plan

At the time of writing, the situation in the TRNC has not yet been resolved. Negotiations have been taking place at intervals, primarily through UN mediation,[264] but also directly between the two communities. Until the 1990s, the parties' entrenched and divergent positions and the Cold War environment obstructed attempts to achieve an overall settlement, or,

[259] Christian Heinze, 'Recognition of the Turkish Republic of Northern Cyprus as a State', in Emel Doğramaci, William Haney and Güray König (eds.), *Proceedings of the First International Congress on Cypriot Studies Gazimağusa 20–23 November '96* (Eastern Mediterranean University, 1996), 281–282; Michael Stephen, 'The European Court of Human Rights and Cyprus: The Loizidou Case', in Republic of Turkey, Ministry of Foreign Affairs, *The Loizidou Case – A Dead End* (1999), 3.

[260] VCLT Article 53. The validity of the Treaty of Guarantee arose – inconclusively – in UN debates as early as 1963, while the VCLT was still being negotiated. Egon Schwelb, 'Some Aspects of International *Jus Cogens* as Formulated by the International Law Commission' (1967) 61 *American Journal of International Law* 946, 952. For the debate over the Treaty of Guarantee see Natalino Ronzitti, *Rescuing Nationals Abroad through Military Coercion and Intervention on Grounds of Humanity* (Dordrecht: Martinus Nijhoff, 1985), 130–134; Clement H. Dodd, *The Cyprus Imbroglio* (Huntingdon: Eothen, 1998), 80; Necatigil, *The Cyprus Conflict*, Chapter 4.

[261] ICJ, *Case Concerning Armed Activities on the Territory of the Congo* (Democratic Republic of the Congo v. Uganda), Judgment of 19 December 2005, [47].

[262] E.g. PACE Recommendation 974 (1983), paragraph 12(c).

[263] Dugard, *Recognition and the United Nations*, 110. This aspect of the affair is entirely absent from the opinion of Sir (then Mr) Elihu Lauterpacht CBE QC, 'Turkish Republic of Northern Cyprus, the Status of the Two Communities in Cyprus'.

[264] Oliver P. Richmond, *Mediating in Cyprus: The Cypriot Communities and the United Nations* (London: Frank Cass Publishers, 1998).

alternatively, to introduce interim confidence-building measures.[265] In 1995, the European Union (EU) decided to begin negotiations for the accession of Cyprus to the Union.[266] This triggered renewed international interest in settling the Cyprus question by means of direct talks between the two communities. It was widely perceived that EU accession negotiations would facilitate a Cyprus settlement, although towards the end of 1999 it became apparent that the Republic of Cyprus's application to become an EU member state could be successful independently of whether the Cyprus problem was resolved or not.[267] Against this background, with co-operation from Turkey facilitating the holding of talks, the UN Secretary-General, Kofi Annan, launched in 1999 a new initiative. This initiative culminated in a draft Comprehensive Settlement of the Cyprus Problem (the 'Annan Plan').[268]

The plan proposed a 'new state of affairs in Cyprus', based on the Swiss cantonal model. A United Cyprus Republic (UCR) would be formed, with a federal government and two constituent states: one predominantly Greek Cypriot, eventually comprising about 71 per cent of the area of Cyprus, and the other predominantly Turkish Cypriot, comprising about 29 per cent of the area. Cypriots would be citizens both of the UCR and of the appropriate constituent state. The representation of both communities would be ensured in the federal government, parliament and supreme court. Turkish and Greek military forces would withdraw to a minimum by 2019. All Greek Cypriot and Turkish Cypriot forces would be dissolved.

The Annan Plan contained, inter alia, proposals for a foundation agreement, constitutions of the Greek Cypriot and Turkish Cypriot constituent states, a treaty on matters related to the new state of affairs in Cyprus, and a draft act of adaptation of the terms of accession of the UCR to the EU.

[265] Claire Palley, *An International Relations Debacle: The UN Secretary-General's Mission of Good Offices in Cyprus 1999–2004* (Oxford: Hart, 2005), 15–16; see also e.g. UN Doc S/24472.

[266] Council of the European Union, General Affairs and External Relations, Decision on Cyprus Accession (6 March 1995).

[267] The Helsinki Presidency Conclusions of 10 and 11 December 1999 read:

> 9(b) The European Council underlines that a political settlement will facilitate the accession of Cyprus to the European Union. If no settlement has been reached by the completion of accession negotiations, the Council's decision on accession will be made without the above being a precondition. In this the Council will take account of all relevant factors.

European Parliament, 'Helsinki Presidency Conclusions (10 and 11 December 1999) paragraph 9(b), www.europarl.europa.eu/summits/hel1_en.htm.

[268] The discussion in this work is based, unless otherwise noted, on the fifth and final version of the Annan Plan, of 31 March 2004.

The Annan Plan does not spell out the legal status of the TRNC, but offers concrete arrangements that do not depend on one legal narrative or another.[269] This is an obvious consequence of the attempt to satisfy both Greek and Turkish Cypriots. The plan declares its neutrality. For example, Main Article 12 of the Foundation Agreement, entitled 'Past Acts', provides for legal continuity between the TRNC and the UCR. An observation appended to Main Article 12 indicates, 'This reference, like the whole draft Article, is without prejudice to the question of the legitimacy or status of the relevant authorities under international law.'

On 24 April 2004, a week before the accession of Cyprus to the EU, the plan was put to simultaneous referenda in the government-controlled part of Cyprus and in the TRNC. The question put to the populations in both sides was:

> Do you approve the Foundation Agreement with all its Annexes, as well as the constitution of the Greek Cypriot/Turkish Cypriot State and the provisions as to the laws to be in force to bring into being a new state of affairs in which Cyprus joins the European Union united?

Voters' turnout was high – over 89 per cent in the government-controlled part of Cyprus and over 84 per cent in the TRNC. In the TRNC, almost 65 per cent of voters approved the Foundation Agreement. In government-controlled Cyprus, almost 76 per cent of voters rejected it. Without acceptance on both sides, the plan did not materialize.

The rejection of reunification by the Greek Cypriot population should not be regarded as a waiver of the claim of illegality, or as acquiescence in the division of the island. The question put to the electorate was very specific. It is therefore appropriate to read the Greek Cypriot refusal as a rejection of the specific terms offered for reunification, rather than as a rejection of reunification in principle. That said, international censure of the TRNC has diminished since it demonstrated its willingness to resolve the conflict. This is evident from the tangible aid that has been offered to the TRNC in order to relieve its economic isolation.[270] On the political

[269] For an analysis of the implied stand of the plan on this issue as it arises from its provisions regarding succession to international organizations, continuation of treaty relation, allocation of state debts and state property, see Ahmet Sözen and Kudret Özersay, 'The Annan Plan: State Succession or Continuity' (2007) 43 *Middle Eastern Studies* 125.

[270] 'EU mulls Turk-Cypriot trade link', *Kathimerini*, 19 May 2004, www.ekathimerini.com/4dcgi/_w_articles_politics_100012_19/05/2004_42965; 'The Outlook for Cyprus after the Failure of the Referendum', *European Parliament News Report*, 27 April 2004; 'American Business Delegation to North Cyprus', press release, *US*

level, the designation since 2005 of 'the area administered by Turkish Cypriots' as a separate section within the US Department of State's annual human rights report on Cyprus indicates that the US attributes a certain degree of responsibility to the TRNC for the guarantee and protection of human rights in the area under its control.[271] While these are a far cry from recognition, they are a step towards some legitimization of the TRNC as an international actor. Similar tentative steps have been taken by the European Court of Human Rights (ECtHR).[272]

Although the TRNC continues to function, and the Annan Plan has no formal status, this book considers the Annan Plan as an approximation of the prospective framework for unification of Cyprus. This approach is based on a number of factors. First, in 2008, direct negotiations resumed between the two communities, for which the Annan Plan serves as the unprofessed basis.[273] Second, the Annan Plan constitutes an indication of what the international community in general, and European institutions in particular, consider an acceptable compromise.[274] A concrete expression of this support was given in the ECtHR decision in *Demopoulos and Others* v. *Turkey* in March 2010, where the court elaborated on the political context in which it gave its decision, including a detailed description of the pertinent provisions of the Annan Plan.[275] The ECtHR did not explain how the Annan Plan was relevant to its ruling, but it implicitly used the principles in the plan as a yardstick by which to assess the adequacy of TRNC legislation as remedies. The plan therefore appears to be a blueprint not only for political negotiators, but also, to an extent, for the legal analysis by the ECtHR.

Department of State Daily Briefing, 18 February 2005, http://2001-2009.state.gov/r/pa/prs/dpb/2005/42480.htm.

[271] US Department of State, Bureau of Democracy, Human Rights, and Labor, 'Country Reports on Human Rights Practices', www.state.gov/g/drl/rls/hrrpt/index.htm.

[272] See discussion of *Demopoulos and Others* v. *Turkey* in Chapter 3 below.

[273] Interview by the author with Dr Kudret Özersay, Eastern Mediterranean University (Lefkoşa, 27–28 February 2008).

[274] European Parliament, 'Prospects for the Unification of Cyprus' – Resolution of the European Parliament (21 April 2004).

[275] ECtHR, *Demopoulos and Others* v. *Turkey*, [10]–[16].

3 The obligation of non-recognition

3.1 Introduction

In order to assess the implications of the illegality of the regime and of the obligation of non-recognition for the law and policy governing transition, it is necessary to begin by ascertaining the consequences of illegality and non-recognition during the period of the illegal regime's existence, as these consequences set the legal scene into which the post-transition regime enters and the background against which it operates.

There exists a wealth of literature on the circumstances that give rise to the obligation of non-recognition of territorial regimes, and various writers have examined the obligation with regard to specific norms.[1] But few authors link the normative aspects of the obligation with its practical consequences.[2] One approach to this link is that the obligation not to recognize the legal effect of an act does not necessarily extend to all consequences of that act.[3] A different approach, which puts greater

[1] An extensive bibliography can be found in Stefan Talmon, *Recognition in International Law: A Bibliography* (The Hague: Martinus Nijhoff, 2000).

[2] There are a handful of exceptions: John Dugard (ed.), *The South West Africa/Namibia Dispute: Documents and Scholarly Writings on the Controversy between South Africa and the United Nations* (Berkeley: University of California Press, 1973), 524–530; John Dugard, 'Legal Aspects of Investment in Namibia (South West Africa)', in Roger Murray, Jo Morris, John Dugard and Neville Rubin (eds.), *The Role of Foreign Firms in Namibia: Studies on External Investment and Black Workers' Conditions in Namibia* (Uppsala: Africa Publications Trust, 1974) 183; Frederick A. Middlebush, 'International Affairs: The Effect of the Non-recognition of Manchukuo' (1934) 28 *American Political Science Review* 677; Vera Gowlland-Debbas, *Collective Responses to Illegal Acts in International Law: United Nations Action in the Question of Southern Rhodesia* (Dordrecht: Martinus Nijhoff, 1990), 298–319.

[3] James Crawford, *The Creation of States in International Law* (Oxford: Clarendon Press, 1979), 123–124; Robert Y. Jennings, 'Nullity and Effectiveness in International Law', in *Cambridge Essays in International Law (Essays in Honour of Lord McNair)* (London: Stevens, 1965), 75.

emphasis on the non-derogability of peremptory norms,[4] suggests that the practical consequences of the illegality are extensive.

A useful point of departure is the *Namibia Advisory Opinion*, which continues to be the most authoritative text on the content of the obligation of non-recognition under customary international law.[5] The bulk of the *Advisory Opinion* addresses the preliminary question of whether the revocation of the South African mandate was lawful and whether it was binding upon states. Only at the very end of the *Advisory Opinion* does the court actually address the implications of the illegality of South Africa's presence in Namibia. Paragraph 133(2) of the *dispositif* states the obligation of non-recognition attaching to an illegal situation:

> States Members of the United Nations are under obligation to recognize the illegality of South Africa's presence in Namibia and the invalidity of its acts on behalf of or concerning Namibia, and to refrain from any acts and in particular any dealings with the Government of South Africa implying recognition of the legality of, or lending support or assistance to, such presence and administration . . .

This text is amplified in paragraphs 121–125:

> 121. The Court will in consequence confine itself to giving advice on those dealings with the Government of South Africa which, under the Charter of the United Nations and general international law, should be considered as inconsistent with the declaration of illegality and invalidity made in paragraph 2 of resolution 276 (1970), because they may imply a recognition that South Africa's presence in Namibia is legal.
>
> 122. For the reasons given above, and subject to the observations contained in paragraph 125 below, member States are under obligation to abstain from entering into treaty relations with South Africa in all cases in which the Government of South Africa purports to act on behalf of or concerning Namibia. With respect to existing bilateral treaties, member States must abstain from invoking or applying those treaties or provisions of treaties concluded by South Africa on behalf of or concerning Namibia which involve active intergovernmental co-operation. With respect to multilateral treaties, however, the same rule cannot be applied to certain general conventions such as those of a humanitarian character, the non-performance of which may adversely affect the people of Namibia. It will be for the competent international organs to take specific measures in this respect.

[4] Alexander Orakhelashvili, *Peremptory Norms in International Law* (Oxford: Oxford University Press, 2006), 205–223.

[5] For the circumstances in which the *Namibia Advisory Opinion* was given see Chapter 2 above.

123. Member States, in compliance with the duty of non-recognition imposed by paragraphs 2 and 5 of resolution 276 (1970), are under obligation to abstain from sending diplomatic or special missions to South Africa including in their jurisdiction the Territory of Namibia, to abstain from sending consular agents to Namibia, and to withdraw any such agents already there. They should also make it clear to the South African authorities that the maintenance of diplomatic or consular relations with South Africa does not imply any recognition of its authority with regard to Namibia.

124. The restraints which are implicit in the non-recognition of South Africa's presence in Namibia and the explicit provisions of paragraph 5 of resolution 276 (1970) impose upon member States the obligation to abstain from entering into economic and other forms of relationship or dealings with South Africa on behalf of or concerning Namibia which may entrench its authority over the Territory.

125. In general, the non-recognition of South Africa's administration of the Territory should not result in depriving the people of Namibia of any advantages derived from international co-operation. In particular, while official acts performed by the Government of South Africa on behalf of or concerning Namibia after the termination of the Mandate are illegal and invalid, this invalidity cannot be extended to those acts, such as, for instance, the registration of births, deaths and marriages, the effects of which can be ignored only to the detriment of the inhabitants of the Territory.

These paragraphs were neither preceded nor followed by any elaboration; as often with pronouncements by the court, they proceed *ex cathedra*. Their content is nonetheless illuminated by the separate opinions, as well as by the pleadings before the court.

3.2 The obligation of non-recognition with respect to treaty and diplomatic relations

Paragraph 122 of the *Namibia Advisory Opinion* stipulates the obligation of non-recognition with respect to treaty relations in which the illegal regime purports to act on behalf of the territory in dispute. The impermissibility of treaty relations is one of the few non-controversial elements of the customary obligation of non-recognition.[6] Treaty relations are a function that is generally reserved for sovereign states and that is therefore inapplicable when the status of sovereignty is denied.[7]

[6] Hans M. Blix, 'Contemporary Aspects of Recognition' (1970-II) 130 *Recueil des cours de l'Académie de droit international de la Haye* 589, 655.

[7] Even this statement requires some qualification, since occasionally non-state actors can also be parties to treaties.

According to paragraph 122, states may not enter into treaty relations with the illegal regime when the latter purports to act on behalf of the territory. In light of paragraph 125, which provides that 'official acts performed by the Government of South Africa on behalf of or concerning Namibia after the termination of the Mandate are illegal and invalid', such treaties, if purportedly entered into despite the prohibition, are void *ab initio*.[8] Where the illegal regime consists of an illegal annexation by an existing state, the prohibition should be read more carefully: treaties concluded by the government of the annexing state are only invalid insofar as they purport to extend to the territory under illegal annexation; they are not invalid with respect to sovereign territory. The UN Secretary-General addressed this: 'international treaties or agreements, or amendments thereof, concluded with South Africa, or the illegal South African administration of Namibia, subsequent to the termination of the Mandate, have no legal application to Namibia'.[9] By using the term 'no legal application to Namibia', rather than 'invalid', the Secretary-General indicated that although South Africa could enter into valid treaties, those would have applied only with respect to its own territory, and not with respect to Namibia.

Article 122 also prohibits states from invoking or applying existing treaties or provisions of treaties ('prior treaties') concluded by South Africa on behalf of or concerning Namibia which involve active intergovernmental co-operation. This prohibition does not always constitute a practical obstacle for illegal regimes. It could have affected South Africa's attempt to continue invoking prior treaties applicable to Namibia. In contrast, neither the USSR nor Indonesia ever attempted to implement prior treaties in the Baltic states or Timor-Leste respectively. The difference is not surprising: the USSR and Indonesia took over foreign territory and claimed that the responsibility for international relations transferred from the previous sovereign to them. Under the laws of state succession with respect to treaties, which purportedly applied in those instances, the treaties of an international entity terminate when that entity is absorbed into another. In contrast, South Africa was refusing to relinquish the territory of Namibia and claimed that the international responsibility for the territory continued to lie with itself. A successful invocation of prior treaties was important for consolidating its claim. Also, unlike in the

[8] The entry into relations under such circumstances may give rise to international responsibility, as it is a violation of the obligation to refrain from such action.

[9] *Namibia Advisory Opinion*, ICJ Pleadings Volume I, 105 [120], emphasis added.

Baltic states and Timor-Leste, the fact that there was no change on the ground in Namibia enabled South Africa to implement prior treaties: the governmental machinery already in place in Namibia made the implementation of prior treaties technically possible, while the convergence of the legal and illegal regimes made it difficult for other states to establish in specific instances whether South Africa was implementing a treaty on its own behalf or purporting to act on behalf of Namibia.

With respect to Rhodesia, the TBVC and the TRNC,[10] the stance with respect to prior treaties would not have been conclusive evidence of the regime's status: continued implementation of prior treaties could be an application of the law of state succession with respect to treaties, or, on the contrary, an indication that there is no new state and that the territory continues to be governed by the ousted sovereign. Non-application of prior treaties, on the other hand, could reflect a clean-slate policy on the part of a new purported state with respect to treaties of the previous sovereign. For this and other reasons, the illegal regimes had no particular interest in invoking prior treaties.

The prohibition on invocation or application of existing treaties is qualified with respect to 'certain general conventions such as those of a humanitarian character, the non-performance of which may adversely affect the people of Namibia'. The *Advisory Opinion* does not elaborate the terms of this exception. Its wording resembles that of the Vienna Convention on the law of Treaties (VCLT) Article 60(5), on the exception to suspension of a treaty on the ground that there has been a material breach. Article 60(5) provides that such suspension does not apply to provisions that relate to 'the protection of the human person contained in treaties of a humanitarian character'.[11] There are differences in the scope of coverage of the two regimes. VCLT Article 60(5) sets an exception to suspension of both bilateral and multilateral treaties, while the exception in paragraph 122 is limited to 'general' conventions. On the other hand, under Article 60(5), non-suspendable treaty provisions are only those relating to the

[10] In the case of Rhodesia, in addition to succession to treaties concluded by the UK and extended to Southern Rhodesia, the question could have arisen of succession to certain treaties that Southern Rhodesia had been party to in its own capacity as a colony, separately from the UK, e.g. the Agreement Revising the Telecommunications Agreement Signed at Bermuda 4 December 1945, annexed to the Final Act of the United States–Commonwealth Telecommunications Meeting (signed 12 August 1949) 87 UNTS 131.

[11] VCLT Article 60(5) is mentioned in the *Namibia Advisory Opinion* expressly only in paragraph 96, in the context of the power of the UN General Assembly to revoke the mandate.

protection of the human person, while paragraph 122 excludes from suspension a wider category of 'general conventions', of which humanitarian ones are only an example. This latter difference may reflect the wider concern of the *Advisory Opinion*, that suspension of treaties should not adversely affect the people of Namibia not only individually but also as a people on the path to statehood.

The reference in paragraph 122 to conventions of a 'humanitarian character' immediately brings to mind the 1949 Geneva Conventions and their precursors, the 1907 Hague Conventions and their annexed regulations. Indeed, the direct trigger for the Security Council debate that resulted in the request for the *Namibia Advisory Opinion* was the detention and trial of SWAPO fighters under the South African Terrorism Act 1967, which the General Assembly considered to be in violation of Geneva Conventions III and IV of 1949.[12] It is thus possible that the court was alluding to these conventions as those that are exceptionally invocable.

There was, however, no need for an exception in order to provide for the protection of Namibian inhabitants under these instruments. South Africa's responsibility towards the inhabitants of Namibia under the laws of armed conflict, both customary and conventional, was already engaged by virtue of its acceptance of the laws of armed conflict on its own behalf, because by definition the laws of armed conflict have extraterritorial application. In other words, if the exception concerns only treaties on the laws of armed conflict, it is superfluous. It is therefore reasonable to interpret the phrase 'general conventions such as those of a humanitarian character' as referring to a more general set of instruments, which South Africa may have concluded on behalf of Namibia and which would not have otherwise applied only on Namibian territory. A possible category is human rights treaties. At the time when the *Namibia Advisory Opinion* was given, the application of human rights treaties was perceived as territorially bound. Without special provisions, South Africa would not have been held accountable under such treaties – or even under customary human rights law – outside its own territory. Interpreting 'conventions of a humanitarian character' as extending to human rights treaties purportedly entered into on behalf of annexed territory effectively bridged this gap.[13] For

[12] UNGA Resolution 2678(XXV) (9 December 1970).

[13] See also Office of the Legal Adviser of the UN Secretariat, suggesting that in addition to the Geneva Conventions, 'general conventions of a humanitarian character' include also 'international human rights instruments', Legal Adviser of the UN Secretariat, 'Treaties Concluded by South Africa', 144 para 6.

example, the ICJ may have alluded to human rights treaties prohibiting racial discrimination and genocide, which only a short time earlier it had declared to contain obligations *erga omnes*.[14] As a matter of fact, however, South Africa had not even become a signatory to the then-existing major human rights instruments, other than the 1926 Slavery Convention,[15] let alone extended them to Namibia. It had joined and extended to Namibia two treaties deposited with the International Labour Organization,[16] the 1937 Protocol Relating to Certain Cases of Statelessness,[17] and four conventions for suppression of traffic in persons.[18] However, the court may simply have been making a general statement of no concrete application, unaware of the exact stock of treaties which South Africa had entered into on behalf of Namibia.[19]

The obligation in paragraph 123 echoes Security Council Resolution 283(1970), which requested all states 'to refrain from any relations – diplomatic, consular or others – with South Africa implying recognition of the authority of the South African Government over the territory of Namibia' and 'to terminate existing diplomatic and consular representations as far as they extend to Namibia and to withdraw any diplomatic or consular mission or representative residing in the territory'.[20] As with treaties, the prohibition on diplomatic relations is a clear element of

14 ICJ, *Barcelona Traction Case*, [33], [34].

15 There is conflicting information on whether the 1953 Protocol amending the Convention had been expressly extended to Namibia. UN Doc S/10288 (12 August 1971), 6, 9.

16 ILO conventions often concern the 'protection of the human person' as suggested by the reference to VCLT Article 60(5), but are not usually referred to as 'humanitarian'. South Africa was party to two ILO conventions on behalf of Namibia: ILO Convention No. 42, and ILO Convention No. 89. Neither refers expressly to the protection of the human person.

17 Protocol Relating to Certain Cases of Statelessness.

18 1921 International Convention for the Suppression of Traffic in Women and Children, 1933 International Convention for the Suppression of Traffic in Women of Full Age, 1950 Convention for the Suppression of Traffic in Persons and of the Exploitation of the Prostitution of Others, and the 1950 Final Protocol to the Convention for the Suppression of Traffic in Persons and of the Exploitation of the Prostitution of Others. The classification of these four conventions as 'humanitarian' is somewhat difficult, as they contain provisions not only for protection of individuals by states, but also for extensive co-operation between states in matters such as extradition and transfer of information on offenders.

19 The Security Council later requested the UN Secretariat to make a study of these treaties, which were listed in UN Doc S/10288 (12 August 1971). For further discussion see Chapter 4 below.

20 UNSC Resolution 283 (29 July 1970), paragraphs 1 and 3.

the customary obligation of non-recognition, because such relations are reserved to sovereign states.

3.3 The obligation of non-recognition with respect to other dealings with the illegal regime

Paragraph 124 of the *Advisory Opinion* provides that the obligation of non-recognition also imposes upon states the obligation 'to abstain from entering into economic and other forms of relationship or dealings with South Africa on behalf of or concerning Namibia which may entrench its authority over the Territory'. The majority opinion is silent on what constitutes these 'forms of relationship or dealings', other than implicitly distinguishing them from international treaty relations.[21] In addition, it is not clear whether the 'authority' which must be prevented from becoming entrenched is formal status or actual control. The differentiated use in the *Advisory Opinion* of 'entrenchment of authority' and 'legality' suggests that the authority to which the majority referred is concrete, in the sense of 'control', rather than formal status, which is already denied to the illegal regime. Unlike treaties and diplomatic relations, which entrench the formal authority of the illegal regime and *ipso facto* also the illegal regime's factual hold, with respect to relationships of other types the criterion of entrenchment has to be express.

Further insight as to the majority opinion may be gained from the separate opinions. Judges Onyeama, Petrén and Dillard advocated a formal approach towards dealings, according to which those are prohibited only if they are carried out at a level which implies recognition of governmental authority, rather than if they entrench the actual hold of South Africa over Namibia. Judge Onyeama opined that the de facto control of South Africa over Namibia was actually a basis of the *validity* of some of its acts:

> while I agree that there is on States an obligation of non-recognition of the legality of the presence of South Africa and of its administration in Namibia, I do not agree that this obligation necessarily extends to refusing to recognize the validity of South Africa's acts on behalf of or concerning Namibia in view of the fact that the administration of South Africa over Namibia (illegal though it is) still constitutes the de facto government of the Territory.[22]

[21] See also writtten statement of the Secretary-General, *Namibia Advisory Opinion*, ICJ Pleadings Volume I, [120]–[148].

[22] *Namibia Advisory Opinion*, separate opinion of Judge Onyeama, 149.

A similar position was taken by Judge Petrén, who emphasized the need to distinguish dealings carried out on a governmental level from those carried out on a lower, administrative level:

> although the notion of non-recognition excludes official and ostentatious top-level contacts, customary usage does not seem to be the same at the *administrative level*, since necessities of a practical or humanitarian nature may justify certain contacts or certain forms of co-operation.
>
> A similar approach seems to prevail in regard to international agreements. While non-recognition seems not to permit the formal conclusion of treaties between governments, agreements between administrations, for instance on postal or railway matters, are considered to be possible . . . [I]n the international law of today, non-recognition has obligatory negative effects in only a very limited sector of governmental acts of a somewhat symbolic nature.[23]

Judge Petrén expressly rejected the possibility that the criterion for denying recognition of South African acts should be that they support its factual control of Namibia, arguing that

> [a]s for the prohibition of acts which would constitute lending support or assistance to the presence and administration of South Africa in Namibia, this vague and general formula gives no very clear idea of the specific acts it is intended to cover.[24]

Similarly, Judge Dillard emphasized that the doctrine of non-recognition 'permits of flexibility in application *at such governmental levels* as do not imply recognition of legitimacy'.[25] The fact that the judges regarded themselves as dissenting on this issue from the majority opinion indicates that the majority interpreted the prohibition on 'dealings' more widely, possibly including any act that might entrench South Africa's effective control in Namibia, rather than merely formal authority. The three judges' statements suggest that there are three categories of international interaction: treaty relations, which are entirely prohibited; 'dealings', which imply recognition of governmental authority and are therefore prohibited; and other relations, which do not imply governmental authority and are therefore permitted. An example of the distinction between dealings that imply governmental authority and other relations that do not is offered by the *Steinberg* affair (1979), concerning a potential request by the US for the surrender by Rhodesia of an individual residing in Rhodesia. Keeping in

23 *Namibia Advisory Opinion*, separate opinion of Judge Petrén, 134, emphasis added.

24 *Namibia Advisory Opinion*, separate opinion of Judge Petrén, 137.

25 *Namibia Advisory Opinion*, separate opinion of Judge Dillard, 166, emphasis added.

mind its obligations under Security Council Resolution 277(1970), which imposed a prohibition on recognition of the Rhodesian regime's official acts, the US did not make a formal request to the Rhodesian government for Steinberg's return. Instead it made an informal inquiry through other governments, concerning the possibility of obtaining Steinberg's expulsion from Rhodesian territory. Such 'dealings' were considered by the US permissible as they did not amount to recognizing Rhodesia's authority. Rhodesia indicated some willingness to consider the US's request; but then attached conditions which, in the opinion of State Department officials, would have amounted to recognition of the Rhodesian regime in violation of Security Council Resolution 277(1970). The US therefore did not pursue the matter any further.[26]

3.4 The exception to the prohibitions relating to international interaction

The prohibition on relations with South Africa as an illegal regime in Namibia was not without qualification. The first sentence of paragraph 125 prescribes a limit to the obligation of non-recognition: it should not result in depriving the people of Namibia of any advantages derived from international co-operation. The use of the term 'people of Namibia' is noteworthy in contradistinction to the use in the subsequent sentence of 'the inhabitants of the Territory'. By implication, the 'advantages derived from international cooperation' were such as benefited the Namibian people collectively.[27]

The collective interest in question may have been the realization of the right to self-determination. This was the ultimate aim of international co-operation through the UN with respect to Namibia, and its violation was the ground for the adoption of a policy of non-recognition. South Africa acknowledged, albeit not very clearly, that it was still in the position of a mandatory power, a status which entailed obligations to advance the Namibian people's right to self-determination. In fact, South Africa's obligations under the mandate had already been the subject of earlier

[26] *United States of America* v. *Louis Steinberg*.

[27] See also the written statement of the Netherlands: *Namibia Advisory Opinion*, ICJ Pleadings Volume I, 350: 'the non-recognition of South Africa's *de facto* administration of the territory should not result in depriving the peoples of Namibia from any advantage derived from international co-operation'. Written statement of the Government of the Kingdom of the Netherlands, *Pleadings* Volume I, 352.

proceedings in the ICJ,[28] and the court may have referred to the need to maintain contacts with South Africa insofar as those were necessary for achieving the goal of self-determination. Judge Onyeama expressly recalled South Africa's obligations as a mandatory power, noting that 'South Africa is under a legal obligation to end its unlawful occupation by withdrawing from Namibia its presence and its administration, but while it remains in the Territory it must act in conformity with its obligations under the Mandate and the Charter'.[29] Nevertheless, it is odd for the court to have referred to 'international cooperation' without a direct mention of the right to self-determination and of South Africa's international obligation to promote it.

A different interpretation of 'international cooperation' was given by the Office of Legal Affairs of the UN Secretariat, which considered that continuing the advantages deriving from international co-operation would provide a basis for the exceptional accession of Namibia to constituent instruments of international organizations through UNCN action.[30] However, the *Advisory Opinion* was restricted to the customary international legal consequences of South Africa's illegal status. Thus, while it may have served as a political basis for promoting UNCN, it could not be interpreted as referring directly to it, because the operation of UNCN was by no means based on customary international law.

3.5 The obligation of non-recognition with respect to internal acts

3.5.1 Introduction

The *Namibia Advisory Opinion* does not directly address the status of internal acts of South Africa in Namibia. That it concerns these acts at all can only be inferred from the second sentence of paragraph 125, which provides:

> In particular, while official acts performed by the Government of South Africa on behalf of or concerning Namibia after the termination of the Mandate are illegal and invalid, this invalidity cannot be extended to those acts, such as, for instance, the registration of births, deaths and marriages, the effects of which can be ignored only to the detriment of the inhabitants of the Territory.

28 *International Status of South West Africa Advisory Opinion*; *Voting Procedures Advisory Opinion*; *Admissibility of Hearings Advisory Opinion*; *South West Africa Case (Preliminary Objections)*; *South West Africa Cases (Second Phase)*.

29 *Namibia Advisory Opinion*, separate opinion of Judge Onyeama, 148.

30 Legal Adviser of the UN Secretariat, 'Treaties Concluded by South Africa', 144, paragraph 9.

Despite the vague formulation of paragraph 125, from the use of 'registration of births, deaths and marriages' as an example of 'official acts performed by the Government of South Africa on behalf of or concerning Namibia', it is evident that insofar as other states are concerned, paragraph 125 provides not only the exception, but also the rule on the invalidity of official internal acts of illegal regimes.

Internal acts constituted the bulk of activities carried out by South Africa with respect to Namibia, and were the means by which South Africa violated the Namibians' right to self-determination. As noted above, it was post-revocation enforcement of criminal law that triggered the Security Council's debate that finally led to the request for the *Advisory Opinion*.[31]

Historically, too, it is also internal acts that have created difficulties in situations of non-recognition. The status of internal acts arises before the authorities of other states in a variety of situations. Often it arises in the context of recognition and enforcement of foreign judgments and administrative acts, and the resolution of conflicts in civil matters.[32] However, it may also arise in contexts of public law or criminal law.[33] The validity of internal acts may also arise before international institutions. For example, internal measures may be invoked as local remedies which must be exhausted before international proceedings are instituted;[34] a grant of nationality is also relevant to the adoption of international claims.

In view of the different contexts in which the validity of internal acts can arise, it is odd that it received only an indirect reference in the court's delineation of the consequences of illegality and non-recognition. But the *Namibia Advisory Opinion* is not the first instance in which non-recognition

[31] Blix, 'Contemporary Aspects of Recognition', 666; Dugard, *The South West Africa/Namibia Dispute*, 413–423; *Yearbook of the United Nations* (1968), 766–775; *Yearbook of the United Nations* (1970), 734–740.

[32] E.g. in the US: *Horn* v. *Lockhart*; *Werenjchik and Others* v. *Ulen*; *Petrogradsky Bank* v. *The National City Bank of New York*; *Salimoff* v. *Standard Oil Company*; *Crist* v. *Turkey*. In the UK: *Carl Zeiss Stiftung* v. *Rayner & Keeler (No. 2)*; *Ndhlovu and Other* v. *the Queen*; *In re James*; *Emin* v. *Yeldag*; *Madzimbamuto and Baron* v. *Lardner-Burke and Another (PC)*; *Kuwait Airways Corporation (Consolidated Appeals)*, [113]–[118]. *Crist* v. *Turkey*; In New Zealand: *Bilang* v. *Rigg*. See also US statement, *Namibia Advisory Opinion*, ICJ Pleadings Volume I, 883; ECJ, *The Queen* v. *Minister of Agriculture* (ex parte *Anastasiou)*.

[33] The grant of nationality affects refugee status-determination procedures, e.g., in the UK, *Veysi Dag* v. *The Secretary of State for the Home Department*, [24]; law enforcement measures taken by the illegal regime may be pertinent for deciding double-jeopardy claims in extradition procedures, although extradition is likely to be prohibited as it constitutes the invocation of an international treaty.

[34] ECtHR, *Cyprus* v. *Turkey (Fourth Interstate Case)*; ECtHR, *Xenides-Arestis* v. *Turkey (Admissibility)*; ECtHR, *Demopoulos and Others* v. *Turkey*.

on the grounds of illegality of the regime has been extended to internal acts. Security Council Resolution 277(1970), concerning Rhodesia, issued shortly before the *Advisory Opinion* was given, called on member states

> to take appropriate measures, at the national level, to ensure that any act performed by officials and institutions of the illegal regime in southern Rhodesia shall not be accorded any recognition, official or otherwise, including judicial notice, by the competent organs of their States . . .

This resolution expressly mentions measures 'at the national level', including, without doubt, domestic judicial decisions to which the prohibition on according 'judicial notice' refers. Notably, Resolution 277(1970) was adopted under Chapter VII; its content may exceed the customary principle of non-recognition, and it is therefore not necessarily indicative of the content of the customary obligation elaborated in the *Namibia Advisory Opinion*.

3.5.2 The prohibition and the Namibia *exception*

Paragraph 125 concerns the consequences of non-recognition of internal acts *ex post facto*. This is hardly surprising, given that states had no control over South Africa's conduct within Namibia, but could only react to such conduct. The guidance of the ICJ on internal acts differs from its *ex ante* instructions on international interaction with South Africa, which could (if states obey) prevent the prohibited consequences of the illegal regime's conduct from materializing in the first place. Nonetheless, by declaring that the exceptional recognition of internal acts of South Africa in Namibia is a 'particular' instance of the rules governing international relations, paragraph 125 implies uniformity between the *ex ante* rules governing international interaction and the *ex post facto* rules governing the internal conduct of the illegal regime. As noted above, under the majority opinion, the permissibility of recognizing the illegal regime's acts depends on whether these acts entrench that regime's actual control of the territory. The internal conduct of a regime is eminently relevant to this control.

This interpretation of paragraph 125 emerges when it is read against the pleadings. Paragraph 125 closely resembles the pleadings by the US, which argued:

> In determining whether or not to give effect within their own territories to particular acts of administration performed in Namibia by the illegal occupant, States should examine a particular act *in light of the interest of the inhabitant or inhabitants of Namibia with respect to whom it was taken.*

Thus, by way of illustration, it would seem that municipal courts should generally be permitted to admit into evidence *birth, marriage or death certificates* issued by South Africa in Namibia on the same basis as documents emanating from other territorial authorities despite the unlawful character of South Africa's occupation.[35]

The US argument, in turn, echoes a doctrine applied by US courts following the American Civil War. In *Texas* v. *White* (1868) the US Supreme Court formulated the following rule on the extent of non-recognition of acts of the Confederate governments:

It may be said, perhaps with sufficient accuracy, that acts necessary to peace and good order among citizens, such for example, *as acts sanctioning and protecting marriage and the domestic relations, governing the course of descents*, regulating the conveyance and transfer of property, real and personal, and providing remedies for injuries to person and estate, and other similar acts, which would be valid if emanating from a lawful government, must be regarded in general as valid when proceeding from an actual, though unlawful government.[36]

On this basis, the US Supreme Court was explicit that:

No one that we are aware of seriously questions the validity of judicial or legislative acts in the insurrectionary States touching these and kindred subjects, *where they were not hostile in their purpose or mode of enforcement to the authority of the National government*, and did not impair the rights of citizens under the Constitution.[37]

A slightly different distinction between acts that may be given effect and those that may not was suggested in the *Namibia Advisory Opinion* by Judge de Castro:

A distinction must be made between the private and the public sector. It would seem that the acts of the *de facto* authorities relating to the acts and rights of private persons should be regarded as valid (validity of entries in the civil registers and in the Land Registry, validity of marriages, validity of judgments of the civil courts, etc.). On the other hand, other States should not regard as valid any acts and transactions of the authorities relating to public property, concessions, etc. States

[35] US statement, *Namibia Advisory Opinion*, ICJ Pleadings Volume I, 883, emphasis added.

[36] *Texas* v. *White*, 733, emphasis added.

[37] *Horn* v. *Lockhart*, 580, emphasis added. A similar distinction was suggested in English case law. In *Carl Zeiss Stiftung* v. *Rayner & Keeler (No. 2)*, Lord Wilberforce in an *obiter dictum* expressed support for the *Texas* v. *White* rule. In his view, non-recognition 'cannot be pressed to its ultimate logical limit, and ... where private rights, or acts of every-day occurrence, or perfunctory acts of administration are concerned (the scope of these exceptions has never been precisely defined) the courts may, in the interest of justice and common sense ... give recognition to the actual facts or realities found to exist in the territory in question'. Lord Denning in the UK, *Hesperides* v. *Aegean Turkish Holidays*, 218; and *in re James*, 61. With regard to *B* v. *B* and *Emin* v. *Yeldag*, see below.

will thus not be able to exercise protection of their nationals with regard to any acquisitions of this kind.[38]

Most acts that directly contribute to entrenching the regime are also likely to belong to the public sphere.[39] This overlap is illustrated in the case law. In *Caglar* v. *Billingham* (1996), the UK Special Commissioners, in reviewing a tax appeal, concluded that the exception to non-recognition covers 'the enforcement of laws relating to commercial obligations or matters of *private law* between individuals or matters of *routine administration* such as the registration of births, marriages or deaths'.[40] In *B* v. *B* (2000), the English High Court suggested that non-recognition concerned a spectrum of activities, ranging from treason against the illegal regime, which would clearly not be recognized, and a decision concerning a dog licence which obviously would be recognized.[41] It then proceeded to locate marriage and divorce decrees along this spectrum. The court found that it could not recognize a divorce decree from the TRNC because such a decree 'cannot be handled without the blessing' and the involvement of the state. It is not entirely clear whether the court intended to apply the entrenchment/routine acts distinction (suggested by the example of treason), or the public/private distinction (suggested by the reference to the involvement of the state). In practice it seems to have applied neither, given that it disregarded the explicit exception relating to registration of marriages (which presumably includes divorces as well).[42]

If one adopts the entrenchment/routine test for recognition, the question arises whether entrenchment is examined by reference only to the direct consequence of the specific act, or in a wider context. The US post-Civil War jurisprudence regarded acts of the Confederate states as invalid only if they patently furthered the rebellion of the Confederacy. In other words, the test of entrenchment is carried out with respect to the direct consequences of the specific act in question. However, application of post-Civil War jurisprudence to regimes that are illegal under international law is problematic. This jurisprudence considered the acts of the

[38] *Namibia Advisory Opinion*, separate opinion of Judge De Castro, 218–219.

[39] For a discussion of changes to property rights in the territory under the illegal regime see Chapter 7 below.

[40] UK, *Caglar* v. *Billingham*, [121], emphasis added. In this decision the exception was not applied because the matter concerned diplomatic status and not a private transaction.

[41] UK, *B* v. *B*, 715.

[42] This seems to have been rectified a year later, when a UK Court refrained from taking a position on the exact scope of the exception, but confirmed that it covered recognition of divorce decrees. UK, *Emin* v. *Yeldag*, [62].

purportedly seceding states in terms of US constitutional law, all the while refusing to acknowledge the secession. Thus at issue was neither the territorial status of the seceding states nor the status of the governments whose acts were in question, but only the constitutionality of their conduct. There was no dispute that the Confederate state governments had legal status and powers under the law of the Union. The only flaw in their acts was when they advanced the rebellion and thus exceeded their constitutional powers. Accordingly, there was no reason to deny the validity of these governments' acts beyond those that directly advanced the rebellion. Where the very existence of the territorial entity and its government is illegal, giving effect to *any* act of the illegal regime would contribute to its entrenchment because it would legitimize the regime's existence. A more appropriate analogy for illegal regimes under international law would be from the stance taken towards acts of the Confederacy's federal government, the very existence of which was illegal under US law. Indeed, the acts of the Confederacy's federal government were *all* denied all recognition.[43]

Another difference between the situation before the US Supreme Court and the *Namibia Advisory Opinion* is that the US Supreme Court formulated its rule only after the rebellion had ended, while the *Namibia Advisory Opinion* concerned the consequences of illegality during the existence of the illegal regime. This difference was emphasized in the partly dissenting joint opinion in *Cyprus* v. *Turkey* (2001), suggesting that non-recognition during the existence of the illegal regime should be more extensive than after its termination,[44] and not necessarily be limited to acts which directly entrench the regime. A third difficulty in analogizing from post-Civil War jurisprudence to paragraph 125 of the *Namibia Advisory Opinion* is that if the obligation of non-recognition covers only acts which further the illegal regime in a direct and concrete manner, the exception in paragraph 125 becomes superfluous, because perfunctory acts of administration, such as the registration of marriages, do not fall within the prohibition in the first place. Moreover, perfunctory acts of administration and acts which should be exceptionally recognized are not mutually exclusive categories: prevention of detriment might call for exceptional recognition of non-perfunctory, public acts, and there may be

[43] E.g. US, *Williams* v. *Bruffy*; US, *Ford* v. *Surget*.

[44] ECtHR, *Cyprus* v. *Turkey (Fourth Interstate Case)*, partly dissenting opinion of Judge Palm joined by Judges Jungwiert, Levits, Panţîru, Kovler and Marcus-Helmons, 102.

perfunctory and private acts that do not call for exceptional recognition. In conclusion, the post-Civil War interpretation is excessively narrow with respect to both the obligation of non-recognition and its exception.

Instead of the post-Civil War interpretation, the *Namibia Advisory Opinion* should be read as providing a wide obligation of non-recognition. According to this reading, preventing the illegal regime from obtaining the status it seeks necessitates denial of any act capable of furthering this goal, regardless of its specific purpose or form. Indeed, the prohibition in the *Advisory Opinion* on 'dealings' with the illegal regime and the exception to non-invocation of treaties is formulated not in terms of the purpose or form of the act but in terms of its consequences. A priori, no act is deserving of recognition, because any recognition, direct or indirect, entrenches the illegal regime. At the same time, any act can be exceptionally recognized, if this is necessary to prevent detriment to the inhabitants of the territory. This interpretation is both wider and more flexible than the previous ones. It can also be seen as a very broad reading of the entrenchment/routine distinction. The prohibition on recognition is wider because it extends to all acts of the illegal regime. In this vein, Judge Ammoun regarded any act of co-operation with South Africa as an entrenchment of the illegal regime, even if indirectly. He said that

> the General Assembly has adopted resolution upon resolution in order to dissuade member States of the United Nations from giving any assistance whatsoever to South Africa, even such as is not expressly intended to consolidate its presence in Namibia . . . It is in this sense that the court's Opinion is to be understood.[45]

On the basis of the same understanding of paragraph 125, Judge Petrén voted against paragraph 133(2) of the *dispositif*.[46] The exception is more flexible because it allows exceptional recognition of any of the illegal regime's acts, if circumstances require, even those that do entrench the illegal regime.

The wide interpretation of the prohibition also underlies the UN Secretary-General's statement to the ICJ in the pleadings on the *Namibia Advisory Opinion*, when he noted:

[45] *Namibia Advisory Opinion*, separate opinion of Vice-President Ammoun, 99–100. Judge Ammoun's reliance on Security Council and General Assembly resolutions nonetheless raises the question of the applicability of his opinion to the customary international legal obligation.

[46] *Namibia Advisory Opinion*, separate opinion of Judge Petrén, 135.

> It will be the prerogative of the future Legislative Assembly of Namibia . . . to decide whether, and to what extent, to recognize or validate any act undertaken under void laws during the illegal South African presence, or to grant retroactive validation to any such law having an otherwise acceptable content.[47]

This statement is premised on the invalidity of the South African internal acts, regardless of their specific content. Later practice relying on the *Namibia Advisory Opinion* also supports the wide interpretation of the prohibition and its exception. For example, in a series of cases the ECtHR ruled that Article 159 of the TRNC Constitution was illegal, without inquiring whether that article had a visible effect of entrenching the regime.[48] It thus applied a broad prohibition. Conversely, the flexibility of the exception is demonstrable in another series of cases, where the ECtHR examined whether decisions of TRNC judicial organs could be regarded as valid domestic remedies that must be exhausted before approaching the ECtHR.[49] Under a narrow interpretation of the exception, there would have been no room for such exceptional recognition, because local judicial organs are not a perfunctory tool of administration, and in the specific circumstances they reinforce the factual changes that the illegal regime put into effect in the territory (allocation of land to Turkish settlers in the TRNC). Nonetheless, the ECtHR was of the opinion that considerations of the immediate wellbeing of the population justified regarding TRNC judicial organs as local remedies. Again, it disregarded the question whether the acts entrenched the regime.

3.5.3 *The effect of international human rights law on the* Namibia *exception*

The increasingly voluminous body of human rights law has had an important effect on the obligation of non-recognition and on the exception to it. One aspect of this phenomenon is the increasing willingness to recognize, under the *Namibia* exception, the authority of the illegal regime, rather than only the consequences of its acts. This authority accompanies the responsibility under international human rights law. To appreciate the import of this recognition, it is necessary first to note the difference between purported annexations and purportedly independent states: it

47 *Namibia Advisory Opinion*, Written Statement of the Secretary General, ICJ Pleadings Volume I, [146].

48 *Loizidou* v. *Turkey (Merits)*; *Cyprus* v. *Turkey (Fourth Interstate Case)*. In fact, the act concerned was a public one which was capable of entrenching the regime (expropriation of property).

49 *Cyprus* v. *Turkey (Fourth Interstate Case)*, [98]; *Demopoulos and Others* v. *Turkey*.

is hardly disputed any more that a state is responsible under international human rights law towards the population of any territory under its effective control, regardless of its formal status in that territory.[50] An illegally annexing state is, accordingly, responsible under international human rights law towards the population in the territory under its control. The scope of rights for which it is responsible is controversial. Some consider that the state is responsible for the entire array of rights that apply in its sovereign territory,[51] while others contend that the extent of responsibility depends on the particular circumstances and type of control that the state exercises. As for purportedly independent states, which are a particular type of non-state actor, scholarly opinion differs, on both theoretical and practical grounds.[52] Some commentators consider that non-state actors are not bound by international human rights law. Another strand of thought emphasizes that human rights norms reflect the legitimate expectations of the international community as a whole. It is therefore appropriate and feasible to call on non-state groups to respect human rights norms when they exercise significant control over territory and population and have identifiable political structures, without thereby affecting the legitimacy of those actors.[53] Arguably, non-state actors are bound at most by customary human rights law. This body of law, however, is constantly expanding and becoming more detailed. In addition, non-state actors may be specifically permitted to join relevant treaties, and at times they voluntarily undertake a commitment to conventional rights.[54]

However, whatever the theoretical merits of holding non-state actors responsible under international human rights law, the difficulty in imposing obligations on non-state actors derives from their limited capacity to discharge such obligations. This gap between power and obligation has led scholars to different conclusions. Some commentators argue against imposing human rights obligations on non-state actors because of the futility of holding the latter responsible under standards that they cannot

[50] ICJ, *Wall Advisory Opinion*, [107]–[113]; ECtHR, *Loizidou* v. *Turkey (Merits)*, [52].

[51] By implication, so does the ICJ, e.g. *Wall Advisory Opinion*, [127]–[137].

[52] Andrew Clapham, 'Human Rights Obligations of Non-state Actors in Conflict Situations' (2006) 88 *International Review of the Red Cross* 491, and sources therein.

[53] E.g. advocated by Philip Alston, UN Special Rapporteur on Extrajudicial, Summary or Arbitrary Executions, Report on Sri Lanka (27 March 2006), UN Doc E/CN.4/2006/53/Add.5.

[54] On consensual undertakings of human rights obligations by non-state entities see Michael Schoiswohl, *Status and (Human Rights) Obligations of Non-recognized De Facto Regimes in International Law: The Case of 'Somaliland'*, especially 214–287.

fulfil.[55] Others suggest that human rights obligations can be imposed that are commensurate with the power of the non-state actor.[56] Clapham notes that the notion of a differentiated extent of obligations is already recognized in conventional human rights law,[57] relating to social and economic rights, and in armed conflict. For example, the obligations of non-state actors are limited to 'general principles common to international human rights law' with which they are held capable of complying.[58] Applying this non-state-actor framework to illegal regimes nonetheless presents a particular challenge: unlike armed groups, international organizations and other non-state actors, illegal regimes have the technical capacity of a state. What they lack is the legal capacity. There is therefore no *practical* reason to limit the scope of human rights by which they are bound, but a *normative* one. In other words, if non-state actors are held capable of being responsible under international human rights law in a manner which corresponds with their power, their responsibility should encompass the entire gamut of customary or voluntarily undertaken obligations, because they have the ability to discharge these obligations. Under this approach, putative states as well as annexing states can be held responsible under international human rights law.

While this conclusion is not problematic in itself, it leads to a further question, namely whether in order to enable illegal regimes to discharge their obligations, the normative bar to exercising the corresponding authority should be lifted. In other words, should the legal authority of illegal regimes be recognized when it is required for them to discharge their human rights obligations?[59] Authority is necessary for compliance with positive obligations, which are most commonly associated with the obligation to ensure and protect (rather than merely respect) human rights. Such authority could be given effect through an expansive interpretation of the *Namibia* exception. But the notion that an illegal regime

55 Lindsay Moir, *The Law of Internal Armed Conflict* (Cambridge: Cambridge University Press, 2002), 194.

56 Eyal Benvenisti, 'Responsibility for the Protection of Human Rights under the Interim Israeli–Palestinian Agreements', (1994) 28 *Israel Law Review* 297, 314–316.

57 Clapham, 'Human Rights Obligations of Non-state Actors', 502, citing ICESCR Article 2(1).

58 Common Article 3 to the Geneva Conventions; Commission for Historical Clarification, 'Guatemala Memory of Silence' (Guatemala City, 1999), also annexed to 'Letter dated 23 April 1999 from the Secretary General to the President of the General Assembly' (27 April 1999), UN Doc A/53/928.

59 In cases of purported annexation that constitute occupation, Article 43 of the Hague Regulations sets the relevant legal framework.

is responsible and authorized to respect, ensure and protect the human rights of the population entails a paradigmatic shift. It means that the conduct of an illegal regime may have legal validity not only *ex post facto* but also *ex ante*. For example, the obligation to protect the rights to life and security of persons requires the illegal regime to adopt criminal legislation prohibiting bodily assault. For such legislation to be an effective deterrent, it must be given legal validity irrespective of its prospective application in a specific instance. By implication, the necessity for exceptional *ex ante* recognition in order to prevent detriment to the population must be examined not by reference to a specific individual but with respect to the population at large.

This paradigmatic change carries some risk: acknowledgement of the authority *ex ante* presupposes that the governmental apparatus is acting for the benefit of the population.[60] Where the regime is not sovereign, this presumption has no basis. In the case of illegal regimes, it is particularly ill-based, since the very illegality of the regime suggests a conflict of interests between the governing authority and the population. Since the regime does not enjoy the legitimacy of a sovereign state authority, its authority to discharge its human rights obligations should be recognized discriminatorily, so as to ensure that it does not abuse its powers.

The expansion of the *Namibia* exception to include positive measures by an illegal regime to ensure and protect the human rights of the population under its control has found expression in the practice of the ECtHR. In 1996 the question arose whether the TRNC could expropriate property of Greek Cypriots who have fled to the south of the island. In *Loizidou* v. *Turkey (Merits)*, Turkey argued that the need to provide housing for displaced Turkish Cypriots fleeing from the south of the island justified the taking of property, despite the fact that there were immediately identifiable individuals who were injured by such taking. This position found favour with some of the judges.[61] Even the majority opinion did not exclude the possibility that taking of property could be justifiable in principle, but in the circumstances found that it was disproportionate.[62] A clear expansion of the *Namibia* exception to validate authority to take positive measures for the discharge of human rights obligations re-emerged in

[60] Granted, even in a sovereign state, the governmental apparatus may operate other than to the benefit of the population. But from an international legal perspective, sovereignty reflects a (rebuttable) presumption of legitimate goals.

[61] *Loizidou* v. *Turkey (Merits)*, dissenting opinions of Judges Baka and Pettiti.

[62] *Loizidou* v. *Turkey (Merits)*, 2235, 2242.

2008 in *Foka* v. *Turkey* and in 2009 in *Protopapa* v. *Turkey*. Although this jurisprudence relates specifically to the application and interpretation of the ECHR, it is premised on principles common also to the universal conventions on human rights, such as the obligation on states not only to respect human rights but also to ensure them.[63] It is therefore instructive for other contexts. This jurisprudence provides such a wide exceptional validity under the *Namibia* exception, that little remains of the obligation of non-recognition insofar as internal acts are concerned.

In *Foka* v. *Turkey*, the applicant was a Greek Cypriot residing in the TRNC at the time of events alleged in the application. She was returning from government-controlled Cyprus to the TRNC when she was subject to a short period of detention and interrogation. The question arose whether in the circumstances the detention was a legitimate interference with the right to liberty of the applicant. Under ECHR Article 5, the interference must be 'prescribed by law', a term which essentially refers back to national law. The applicant and the government of Cyprus argued that since the TRNC was invalid and unrecognized, no deprivation of liberty imposed by its agents could be regarded as lawful. The ECtHR rejected this argument and ruled that in light of Turkey's accountability for violations of the ECHR in the TRNC,

> it would not be consistent if the adoption by the authorities of the 'TRNC' of civil, administrative or criminal law measures, or their application or enforcement within that territory, were to be denied any validity or regarded as having no 'lawful' basis in terms of the Convention.[64]

The court accordingly considered that when the TRNC authorities act in compliance with laws in force within the TRNC,[65] those acts should in principle be regarded as having a legal basis in domestic law for the purposes of the Convention. In other words, it recognized the validity of TRNC legislation on the ground that it constituted an element in the discharge by the TRNC (or Turkey) of its human rights obligations towards that population and therefore was beneficial to the population. The court emphasized that this conclusion did not in any way put in doubt either the view adopted by the international community regarding the establishment of the TRNC or the fact that the government of the Republic of Cyprus remains the sole legitimate government of Cyprus. On the facts,

63 ICCPR Article 2(1), 'to respect and ensure'; ECHR Article 1, 'to secure'.
64 *Foka* v. *Turkey*, [80], [81], [83].
65 Specifically in that case, the TRNC Customs and Excise Law, No. 37 of 1983.

it found that the conditions of detention did not constitute a violation of ECHR Article 5.[66]

In *Protopapa* v. *Turkey*, the Greek Cypriot applicant was arrested by TRNC authorities after she took part in a demonstration at the UN Buffer Zone 1989 which the TRNC authorities regarded as potentially being an 'unlawful assembly'. She was then subject to criminal proceedings in the TRNC.[67] She, too, alleged that she had been deprived of her liberty in contravention of ECHR Article 5, because the law authorizing the detention was a product of an illegal entity, the TRNC. Similarly, the government of Cyprus argued that the applicant had been convicted in respect of an offence that was not provided for by law and thus in violation of ECHR Article 7, because TRNC law did not constitute 'national law' under the ECHR.[68] Turkey, as the respondent, argued that the detention and conviction were in compliance with TRNC law.[69] The court noted that the applicant had committed an offence under TRNC laws relating to 'unlawful assembly' and entry into TRNC territory without permission and other than through an approved port. The court followed the *Foka* ruling with respect to both the detention and the criminal proceedings, namely that acts carried out in compliance with TRNC law should be regarded as 'lawful' for the Convention's purposes.[70] Again it emphasized that recognition of the legal validity of the criminal law enforcement measures was necessary in order to secure the human rights of the local population, i.e. such recognition was beneficial to the population in terms of the *Namibia* exception.

In both cases, the ECtHR assumed the applicability of the *Namibia* exception to specific TRNC legislation. It did not examine whether those specific acts were indeed taken in pursuit of securing the human rights of the population. Foregoing such enquiry is acceptable only if there is a presumption that every act of the regime is in pursuit of respecting, securing or protecting the human rights of the population. Obviously, there is no ground for such a presumption, which would render any act of the illegal regime exceptionally valid. First, as noted above, the presumption that the government operates for the benefit of the population has no place in an illegal regime. Second, and conversely, governmental policy – in a sovereign state or under an illegal regime – may go beyond binding human rights obligations. With respect to an illegal regime, where recognition of acts is exceptional, recognition should be

66 *Foka* v. *Turkey*, [84], [89].
67 *Protopapa* v. *Turkey*, [32].
68 *Protopapa* v. *Turkey*, [92].
69 *Protopapa* v. *Turkey*, [55].
70 *Protopapa* v. *Turkey*, [60], [61], [94].

limited to acts that are necessary for discharging human rights *obligations*, and should not extend to *voluntary* acts. Accordingly, the court should have examined whether the measures taken in the specific instances were truly required for the illegal regime's discharge of its human rights obligations.

Had the court undertaken this enquiry, its conclusion may well have been in the negative. The detention and legal proceedings in the two cases were carried out in order to enforce the TRNC's border control. These acts were not necessary for the securing of human rights obligations; they were directly related to the existence of the TRNC separately from Cyprus, and further entrenched it. The disregard by the ECtHR of the significance and the effect of these individual acts may be explained by the fact that, as noted above, the ECtHR maintained that the exceptional legal effect could extend not only to the enforcement or implementation of regulatory measures, but also to the civil, administrative and criminal measures themselves, namely the legislation. If the entire body of criminal law is regarded as valid under the *Namibia* exception, it is not surprising that the effects of specific instances of its application (e.g. to enforce border controls) are immaterial. The leniency of the court is particularly striking in *Protopapa* v. *Turkey* with respect to the application of TRNC immigration law to Greek Cypriots, which has no purpose other than to entrench the illegal regime. This body of law differs from the prohibition on unlawful assembly (which formed the basis for Protopapa's conviction), which is in itself a valid measure for the protection of public order, even if in the specific instance it was used to protect the existence of the illegal regime. Immigration law applied by an illegal regime against entrants from the lawful regime has no redeeming feature. Particularly given its furtherance of the illegal regime, there was no reason for the court to recognize the validity of this law, not even exceptionally. Moreover, the court could have partly avoided the question of the validity of TRNC law, because the TRNC authorities acted on the basis of the pre-1983 Cypriot Criminal Code. The court could have relied on that code not on the basis of the *Namibia* exception, but on the basis of its continued validity as the law of the lawful sovereign.

In part, the expansion of the *Namibia* exception is an inevitable consequence of the expansion of international human rights law, which was not fully envisaged in 1971. Yet the ECtHR's interpretation validates more than is unavoidable. The court could have carried out a more rigorous examination of the acts of the illegal regime, not all of which are called for by human rights considerations. However, these nuances were lost in the court's blanket recognition of the legal effect of TRNC legislation, despite the fact that it benefited not the population at large but the purported sovereign existence of the regime. By disregarding these nuances, the ECtHR effectively emptied the obligation of non-recognition of any meaning insofar as internal acts of the illegal regime are concerned. If this approach is followed, non-recognition can be implemented only at the inter-state level.

The willingness of the ECtHR to give effect to acts of the TRNC in a manner which benefits the purported sovereignty of the illegal regime, rather than the population, reached a peak in early 2010 in *Demopoulos and Others* v. *Turkey*, when the court ruled, for the first time, that an application against Turkey was inadmissible because of non-exhaustion of local TRNC remedies.[71] The Greek Cypriot applicants complained that they had been deprived of the enjoyment of their possessions in the TRNC. Turkey, the respondent, argued that the application was inadmissible since the applicants had not approached the Immovable Property Commission (IPC) and therefore had not exhausted local remedies. The IPC is a local TRNC body, set up to resolve claims to property that had been expropriated under the TRNC constitution on the ground that it had been abandoned in 1974. The applicants argued that requiring exhaustion of TRNC remedies lent legitimacy to an illegal occupation.[72] The court examined the TRNC legislation, and concluded that the IPC constituted an accessible and effective framework of redress in respect of complaints of interference with property owned by Greek Cypriots. It said that a key consideration in the prevention of detriment to those subject to the illegal regime, as required under the *Namibia* exception, was to avoid a legal vacuum in which victims of human rights violations cannot have redress. It therefore found the applicants' complaints inadmissible for non-exhaustion of domestic remedies. By ruling on the obligation to approach the commission rather than the validity of any of its decisions, the court reaffirmed the shift described above, of giving broad *ex ante* effect to norms of the TRNC, rather than exceptional recognition *ex post facto* to specific acts based on these norms.

The reliance of the ECtHR on the *Namibia* exception to give effect to domestic remedies as a bar to access to the ECtHR is a stretch of the doctrine by any standard. In essence, the court confused the role of domestic

[71] Earlier jurisprudence envisaged this possibility but did not apply it on the merits: *Cyprus* v. *Turkey (Fourth Interstate Case)*; *Xenides-Arestis* v. *Turkey (Admissibility)*.

[72] *Demopoulos and Others* v. *Turkey*, [92].

remedies to ensure that the government complies with its human rights obligations, with their role as a bar to international adjudication; or, in other words, the right to domestic remedies under ECHR Article 13 with the obligation to exhaust them under ECHR Article 35. The obligation under ECHR Article 13 to secure the population's human rights requires the TRNC (or Turkey) to provide domestic remedies in case of human rights violations. The establishment of the IPC constitutes such a remedy, and, indeed, decisions adopted by the commission might merit exceptional recognition under the *Namibia* exception, for the benefit of individuals or segments of the population relying on the mechanism or on its decisions. However, the court gave effect to the domestic remedies not as a guarantee of human rights but as a procedural bar to international adjudication, under ECHR Article 35. The court's statement, that an appropriate domestic body, with access to the properties, registries and records, is the more appropriate forum for deciding on complex matters of property ownership and compensation than an international one,[73] only means that the population should have *access* to a domestic body. The obligation to *exhaust* domestic remedies is not beneficial to the population. It is – in the TRNC, as in any state – an obstacle to every individual seeking redress at the international level. Such an obstacle is usually justified by other considerations, primarily maintenance of the international tribunal's subsidiarity to the national systems,[74] and protection of the international tribunal from case overload. That, however, is not a consideration that falls within the purview of the *Namibia* exception. Previously, in *Cyprus* v. *Turkey (Fourth Interstate Case)* (2001), the minority judges dissented precisely on whether the wellbeing of the population made it necessary to give legal effect to the courts of the TRNC, noting that the 'Court should not assume too readily that it is acting for the benefit of the local population in addressing the legality of such arrangements'.[75] The obligation to exhaust domestic remedies derives from deference to the states' sovereignty, giving them an opportunity to put matters right through their own legal system. Where sovereignty is denied, there is no justification for such deference. In short, there is no reason to give effect to legislation of an illegal regime as a domestic remedy which must be

[73] *Demopoulos and Others* v. *Turkey*, [97].

[74] Pieter Van Dijk, Fried van Hoof, Arjen van Rijn and Leo Zwaak (eds.), *Theory and Practice of the European Convention on Human Rights*, 4th edn (Antwerp: Intersentia, 2006), 126.

[75] *Cyprus* v. *Turkey (Fourth Interstate Case)*, partly dissenting opinion of Judge Palm joined by Judges Jungwiert, Levits, Panţîru, Kovler and Marcus-Helmons, 102.

exhausted before recourse is had to an international tribunal. At best, the decisions of a domestic remedial institution merit exceptional recognition *ex post facto*.

One might ask whether a ruling such as in *Demopoulos and Others* v. *Turkey* would have been given (if a tribunal had been available) if at issue were not Turkey, the TRNC and Greek Cypriots but, for example, South Africa and Namibians, or, to bring the matter to modern-day conflicts, Israelis and Palestinians in East Jerusalem. More likely, the illegal regime would have been condemned for adding insult to injury by purporting to offer remedies for violations that it was in a position to commit only because of its illegal conduct. To appreciate the *Demopoulos and Others* v. *Turkey* ruling, it must therefore be read in its political context. This judgment was the first time in which the ECtHR made reference to the passage of time and the non-reversibility of changes in the TRNC as relevant factors in its legal determination.[76] The court also described the political dimensions of the conflict, including the failure in 2004 to resolve the dispute. In this context it mentioned the rejection of the Annan Plan by the Greek Cypriots.[77] The judgment also describes in detail the property provisions of the Annan Plan, and while it does not elucidate the relevance of the plan, it seems to use the plan as a yardstick by which to measure the appropriateness of the Immovable Property Commission mechanism.[78] In short, the ECtHR appears to have regarded the situation in the TRNC almost as a fait accompli, with little sympathy for the party with which the applicants were associated. Against this background, it was willing to give broad legal effect to the TRNC's acts. At the same time it is noteworthy that in *Demopoulos and Others* v. *Turkey* the ECtHR for the first time referred to Turkey's status in the TRNC as an 'illegal occupation', and reiterated that its conclusion 'does not in any way put in doubt the view adopted by the international community regarding the establishment of the "TRNC" or the fact that the government of the Republic of Cyprus remains the sole legitimate government of Cyprus'.[79] Formally, then, it did not retract from the illegality of the TRNC.

Also surprising is the court's rebuke of the applicants for attempting to use their individual rights 'as a vehicle for the vindication of sovereign rights or findings of breaches of international law between Contracting States'.[80] As long as applicants do not abuse the process (and given that

[76] *Demopoulos and Others* v. *Turkey*, [83]–[86], [115]. [77] *Demopoulos and Others* v. *Turkey*, [9].
[78] See Chapter 7 below. [79] *Demopoulos and Others* v. *Turkey*, [94], [96].
[80] *Demopoulos and Others* v. *Turkey*, [115].

prima facie they have been victims of human rights violations, the use of a complaint to further a political goal is not an abuse of the right[81]), it is not for the court to question their motivation. Moreover, the fact that the alleged violation is linked to a breach of general international law, namely the establishment of the TRNC, does not detract from its being a violation of a Convention right. The court should not refuse to take account of general international law if it is a factor relevant to the rights of individuals before it, particularly when at issue is the procedural access to the court, which is as much an institutional and inter-state matter as it is a human rights one. Perhaps behind the court's reluctance to deal with the vindication of breaches of international law between states lay its inability to resolve all the claims arising from an inter-state conflict. There is some hint of this in the court's statement that applicants who do not want to make use of the Immovable Property Commission 'may choose not to do so and await a political solution'.[82] It goes without saying that individuals whose applications are inadmissible for non-exhaustion of domestic remedies are not obligated to make use of the domestic remedies. It is also true that individuals can bring about changes through political processes. But it is highly unusual for the court to remind applicants of the political course of action as an alternative to legal redress.

3.5.4 The beneficiaries of the exception

The reference in the second sentence of paragraph 125 to 'inhabitants of the territory' suggests that the consequences of an act should be examined with respect to both individuals and the population at large.[83] The people who need to be protected are primarily those who live within the territory under the control of the illegal regime.[84] This was clearly the situation in Namibia, for which the formula was originally drafted.

However, the exception should be interpreted more expansively. It should cover the interests of any person affected by the illegal regime, including people outside its territory but subject to its control. A general scope of coverage along these lines was suggested in the oral pleading of the Netherlands regarding the *Namibia Advisory Opinion*, which suggested that

[81] Van Dijk *et al.*, *Theory and Practice of the ECHR*, 193.
[82] *Demopoulos and Others* v. *Turkey*, [128].
[83] US statement, *Namibia Advisory Opinion*, ICJ Pleadings Volume I, 883.
[84] US, *Baldy* v. *Hunter*, 401.

non-recognition does not exclude taking into account the fact of exercise of powers in so far as that taking into account is necessary in order to do justice to the legitimate interests of the individual which is, in fact, *subjected to that power*.[85]

This includes, for example, persons who own property which is subject to the actual control of the illegal regime. In the case of Namibia there was a significant group of foreigners invested in the territory. However, their activity in the territory was perceived as particularly injurious to the Namibian population and to the prospective independent state of Namibia,[86] so it is perhaps not surprising that the ICJ did not make any reference to the protection of such investors. Where foreign investors are not implicated in the illegality of the regime, there seems to be no reason to deny them legal protection. The jurisprudence of the ECtHR, for example, confirms that the exception applies not only to permanent inhabitants of the territory, but also to other individuals affected by the acts of the illegal regime.[87] Ironically, as criticized above, this jurisprudence now also obligates the non-resident applicants to surrender to the legal control of the illegal regime on the basis of the *Namibia* exception.[88]

The inclusion as beneficiaries of persons other than inhabitants who find themselves in the territory raises the question whether the exception protects inhabitants who have moved into the territory after the non-recognized regime had been established, particularly individuals brought in by that regime. The post-Civil War case law in the US, from which the *Advisory Opinion* appears to have borrowed, distinguished inhabitants who found themselves under the illegal regime from individuals who voluntarily subjected themselves to that regime and colluded with it.[89] The latter were held to be acting not in good faith and could not benefit from the exception to non-recognition. The majority opinion in

85 *Namibia Advisory Opinion*, ICJ Pleadings Volume II, 130, emphasis added.

86 Caleb M. Pilgrim, 'Some Legal Aspects of Trade in the Natural Resources of Namibia' (1990) 61 *British Yearbook of International Law* 249; Christopher Cosslett, 'The Economics of "Illegal" Development – International Law and Natural Resource Exploitation in Namibia 1966–1986' (1987) 41 *Journal of International Affairs* 165.

87 *Demopoulos and Others* v. *Turkey*, [94], [96]; and its precursors, *Cyprus* v. *Turkey (Fourth Interstate Case)*, *Xenides-Arestis* v. *Turkey (Admissibility)*. This is also apparent from earlier jurisprudence which concerned Greek Cypriots living in Southern Cyprus and owning property in the TRNC.

88 By having to exhaust domestic TRNC remedies; *Demopoulos and Others* v. *Turkey*.

89 US, *Lamar* v. *Micou*, 473.

the *Namibia Advisory Opinion* does not mention good faith as a condition for protection under the exception. However, a requisite of good faith was mentioned by Judge Dillard as a criterion for applying the exception:

> A detailed specification of the particular acts which may or may not be compatible with South Africa's illegal presence in Namibia cannot be determined in advance since they depend on numerous factors including not only *the interests of contracting parties who acted in good faith* but the immediate and future welfare of the inhabitants of Namibia.[90]

It is not clear if Judge Dillard's statement concerns good faith in the intergovernmental relations referred to in paragraphs 122–124 of the *Advisory Opinion*,[91] or also good faith of individuals in the context of internal acts of the South African administration, such as registration of property transfers among individuals. In *Demopoulos and Others* v. *Turkey*, the ECtHR took into account the interests of the Turkish settlers when it confirmed that the *Namibia* exception justified giving effect to the operation of the IPC. It did not tie the legitimacy of these interests with considerations of the legality or good faith involved in those settlers' residence in the TRNC.[92]

The *Namibia* exception gives effect to otherwise invalid acts in order to respond to human needs. Where those needs were created in an illegal or illegitimate manner, the justification for exceptional concessions to address them weakens. In balancing the necessity of the exceptional recognition against the detriment that would otherwise be caused to the individual, that person's conduct might come into play, for example in considering the alternative means available to him or her. In the cases examined in this book, many settlers were involuntarily transferred to the territories under dispute. Settlers also arrived voluntarily but in ignorance of the political and legal situation. This ignorance was in some cases intentionally promoted by the illegal regimes. Therefore, although their migration was voluntary, their good faith might pull towards entitling them to protection under the *Namibia* exception.

90 *Namibia Advisory Opinion*, Separate Opinion of Judge Dillard, 167, emphasis added.

91 In which case the reference to good faith may allude to the provision of VCLT Article 69(2)(b), which provides that 'acts performed in good faith before the invalidity was invoked are not rendered unlawful by reason only of the invalidity of the treaty'.

92 Compare with *Wall Advisory Opinion*, [120]–[121].

3.6 Conclusions

Some of the elements in the obligation of non-recognition are clear and relatively easy to apply. Such are the prohibitions on the conclusion of treaties, on the invocation of prior treaties, and on the maintenance of diplomatic relations. Beyond these, particularly with regard to internal acts, the scope of the obligation is vague. A joint military manoeuvre headed by chiefs of staff practising the defence of the disputed territory is clearly a prohibited dealing; states are probably also required to deny the validity of an internal law purporting to conscript residents of the disputed territory to serve in the illegal regime's military forces. These are acts that emanate from the government of the illegal regime, and contribute directly to the entrenchment of that regime. At the other end of the spectrum, co-operation with health authorities of the illegal regime in order to avoid the spread of disease is probably a permitted dealing, as would be the recognition of an internal certification by the illegal regime of the professional qualification of residents of that territory who trained as physiotherapists. Between these extremes, a host of situations remains unanswered. It is not clear whether the prohibition on recognizing the legality of an act attaches to a formal authority that the act implies; to its direct contribution to the entrenchment of the illegal regime; or perhaps it is not limited at all, because any recognition of an act *ipso facto* strengthens the effective control of the illegal regime on the territory. This chapter proposes that the obligation should be seen as encompassing all acts, regardless of their immediate purpose. However, any act can also be exceptionally recognized if failure to recognize it would cause detriment to the individuals in question, even if the act is one which contributes to the entrenchment of the regime.

The ECtHR's judgments bring to the fore the tension between the invalidity of acts of the illegal regime and the illegal regime's obligation to respect, ensure and secure the human rights of persons under its jurisdiction. This tension introduces a paradigmatically different definition of the exception to non-recognition of internal acts of the illegal regime. According to this definition, the detriment and benefit to the population have to be examined in a wider perspective, which acknowledges the authority of illegal regimes to act in order to respect, ensure and protect the human rights of the population, sometimes even to the immediate detriment of specific individuals. However, each exercise of authority must be considered individually, and there is no ground for a presumption that all acts of the illegal regime are geared towards and necessary for the pursuit of its human rights obligations. The present leniency of the ECtHR in giving effect to acts of the TRNC, while possibly stemming from the specific circumstances of the conflict in Cyprus, goes beyond the requirements of international human rights law and risks emptying the obligation of non-recognition of any effect insofar as internal acts of the regime are concerned.

4 The effect of transition on treaty relations of the territory

4.1 Introduction

Two main issues arise in regard to the effect of the territorial regime's illegality and its non-recognition on the treaty relations of the territory. One is the status of treaty relations that existed prior to the illegal regime: Do they survive the illegal regime and bind the returning sovereign, or, if the post-transition regime is a new state, can it exercise the option of succession to these treaties? Another issue is the status of treaties purportedly concluded by the illegal regime on behalf of the territory: can they be available to the post-transition regime if it wishes to 'succeed' to them? Are there any circumstances in which they may be binding upon the post-transition regime? These questions are pertinent to transition from both putative states and putative annexations, although treaties are more likely to be purportedly concluded with governments of existing states regarding illegally annexed territory, than with non-state actors.

In the international sphere, the post-transition regime is constrained by the consensual nature of inter-state relations. It is therefore not in a position to give unilateral effect to invalid acts or to terminate valid acts preceding the illegal regime, except where the law of treaties itself permits unilateral action. Thus, if a treaty purportedly entered into by the illegal regime on behalf of the territory was treated as a nullity by other parties, the post-transition regime cannot validate the treaty with respect to its territory without the consent of the other parties.[1] Conversely, the post-transition regime cannot unilaterally abrogate a treaty validly entered into on behalf of its territory. This does not mean that in all cases the legal situation which prevailed prior to the emergence of the illegal

[1] This is true prospectively as well as retroactively.

regime would be reinstated and applied to its ultimate logical end. The law of treaties itself contains mechanisms for adapting a legal situation to factual changes that have taken place through time without having been immediately reflected in the law.

The present chapter begins with a normative analysis of the status of treaties that existed prior to the illegal regime ('prior treaties'), and of treaties purportedly concluded by the illegal regime. This is followed by a study of the practice of the post-transition regimes.

4.2 Doctrine

4.2.1 Transition with respect to prior treaties

Introduction

As discussed in Chapter 3, during the existence of the illegal regime, states must not apply or invoke existing treaties other than in specific exceptions. At the heart of the non-invocability of prior treaties lies the lack of authority of the illegal regime to act on behalf of the territory. Nevertheless, the treaties themselves continue to exist and are still in force. The *Namibia Advisory Opinion* reflects this by providing that states must abstain from 'invoking' or 'applying' those treaties, terms which imply the existence of the treaties, and by qualifying the obligation of 'non-performance' of the treaties rather than their 'invalidity' or 'termination'.[2]

Given the continued existence of prior treaties, the question arises whether, when the illegal regime comes to an end, these treaties are resuscitated and once again become operative. In this context, it is necessary to distinguish post-transition regimes that are returning sovereigns from post-transition regimes that are new entities. If the post-transition regime is a returning sovereign, as the Baltic states regarded themselves, the continuity of statehood implies at least a presumption of continuity of prior treaties. The question is whether either party can rely on the existence of the illegal regime to counter the presumption of continuity.

The situation is partly governed by the law of state succession with respect to treaties. Under this law, if the post-transition regime is a new international entity, it is not bound by prior treaties,[3] irrespective of the illegal regime's intervention in the succession. Only if the post-transition

[2] See also Written Statement of the Secretary-General, *Namibia Advisory Opinion*, ICJ Pleadings Volume I, 106 [123]; Written Statement of the United States, *Namibia Advisory Opinion*, ICJ Pleadings Volume I, 885.

[3] VCST Article 16.

regime declares itself a successor to the regime that had concluded the prior treaties does the question also arise of the illegal regime's effect on the ability of the post-transition regime to succeed to the treaties. Specifically with respect to Namibia, the question also arises of succession to treaties entered into by a mandatory power. The practice of the League of Nations, the UN and new states does not provide clear guidance on whether the ordinary law of state succession applies to states emerging from a mandate or trusteeship status. The Council of the League issued a memorandum providing that new states should ensure and guarantee the maintenance in force of treaties applied to the mandate territory before independence,[4] but actual practice of post-mandate states is not uniform. It appears that having been under mandate does not distinguish Namibia in any significant way from post-colonial states, in terms of its choice whether to succeed to pre-1966 treaties or not.[5]

The content and consequences of the obligation of non-recognition should be interpreted to the extent possible as permitting a choice of action to the future legal regime rather than limiting it.[6] Accordingly, there is no reason to limit the post-transition regime's options of succession in comparison with the options available to other new states. However, the passage of time, combined with non-invocation, may create circumstances which limit the choice of the post-transition regime whether to resume the application of treaty relations by succeeding to prior treaties. First and foremost, the counterparty may have in the meantime become entitled to terminate the treaty.

The following sections explore three potential grounds for termination of treaties – impossibility of performance, fundamental change of circumstances and desuetude. They examine the extent to which these grounds apply in the circumstances that typically follow lengthy non-invocation based on an obligation of non-recognition. The circumstances giving rise to a right to terminate a treaty may actually mature much earlier than transition. The *Namibia Advisory Opinion* does not expressly prohibit states from terminating prior treaties during the period of non-recognition, and

4 PMC Minutes 20 229, reproduced in Luther H. Evans, 'The General Principles Governing the Termination of a Mandate' (1932) 26 *American Journal of International Law* 735, 750.

5 UNIN, *Independent Namibia: Succession to Treaty Rights and Obligations, Incorporating Namibian Treaty Calendar*, based on the work of Julio Faundez, Namibia Studies Series No. 13 (ed. N. K. Duggal) (Lusaka: UNIN, 1989), 34–36.

6 Written Statement of the United States, *Namibia Advisory Opinion*, ICJ Pleadings Volume I, 885.

only prohibits the 'invocation' or 'application' of treaties vis-à-vis the illegal regime. Nonetheless, it is submitted that any legal interaction that is predicated on the existence of a competent counterparty should be regarded as prohibited, including treaty termination.[7] Consequently, the treaty remains suspended,[8] and termination becomes a practical option once transition takes place.

Impossibility of performance

VCLT Article 61(1) provides:

> A party may invoke the impossibility of performing a treaty as a ground for terminating or withdrawing from it if the impossibility results from the permanent disappearance or destruction of an object indispensable for the execution of the treaty. If the impossibility is temporary, it may be invoked only as a ground for suspending the operation of the treaty.

It is not surprising if, during the lengthy period of non-invocation of a treaty, tangible objects required for the application of a treaty disappear for whatever reason.[9] Since conventional mechanisms for maintaining the operation of the treaty do not operate, this loss might at some point become irreversible.[10]

The question examined here is whether changes that are directly related to the illegality of the regime can also be considered a 'disappearance or destruction of an object' which entitle a party to terminate the treaty. Although impossibility of performance is usually relied upon when there is a physical, rather than legal, obstacle to performance,[11] in the *Gabčíkovo-Nagymaros Case* the court did not reject the possibility that the term 'object' in Article 61 could also be understood as embracing a legal regime.[12] In

[7] In the absence of effective control, it is not clear that an ousted sovereign is competent to act on behalf of the territory. But see below on UK practice, which after 1965 terminated treaties applicable to Rhodesia after recovering its right as the colonial power over Southern Rhodesia.

[8] VCLT Articles 61(1) (impossibility of performance) and 62(3) (fundamental change of circumstances).

[9] In general, see Robert Y. Jennings and Sir Arthur Watts (eds.), *Oppenheim's International Law*, 9th edn (London: Longman, 1996), Volume I, 1303–1304.

[10] E.g. the Finnish–Estonian treaty concerning property rights over submarine cables, concluded 16 April 1936, terminated as a result of the impossibility of its application because the cables no longer existed. Correspondence of the author with Ms Marja Lehto, head of the Public International Law Unit, Finnish Ministry for Foreign Affairs, 17 May 2005.

[11] Anthony Aust, *Modern Treaty Law and Practice* (Cambridge: Cambridge University Press, 2000), 240.

[12] ICJ, *Gabčíkovo-Nagymaros Case*, [103].

the case of an illegal regime, the disappearance is of a governing body with legal capacity to act on behalf of the territory. The matter can be further complicated when the emergence of the illegal regime is accompanied by the disappearance of the international personality of the previous regime. For example, even among states that did not recognize the Soviet annexation of the Baltic states, some considered the Baltic states themselves as having ceased to exist in 1940. However, when the Baltic states reverted to independence, states that had refused to recognize the annexation did not dispute the claim of the Baltic states to continuity from the pre-1940 states. At any rate, Article 61(1) distinguishes a permanent impossibility from a temporary one. Since non-recognition is intended to be a temporary situation (albeit, at times, a lengthy one), the impossibility of performance due to the illegal regime's legal incapacity allows only suspension of the treaty rather than its termination. Once the illegal regime is replaced by a legal one, the parties are, *ceteris paribus*, bound again to apply the treaty.

Fundamental change of circumstances

Political, economic, technological, social and other changes may occur during the period of non-recognition, in such a manner that by the time of transition, in the absence of appropriate amendments to the treaty, the treaty becomes obsolete.[13] According to VCLT Article 62(1):[14]

> A fundamental change of circumstances which has occurred with regard to those existing at the time of the conclusion of a treaty, and which was not foreseen by the parties, may . . . be invoked as a ground for terminating or withdrawing from the treaty . . . [only if]:
>
> (a) the existence of those circumstances constituted an essential basis of the consent of the parties to be bound by the treaty; and
>
> (b) the effect of the change is radically to transform the extent of obligations still to be performed under the treaty.

Again, the longer the period of non-recognition persists, the greater is the probability that changes occur that would fundamentally change the

[13] In general, see Jennings and Watts, *Oppenheim's International Law*, Volume I, 1304–1309; Lord Arnold D. McNair, *The Law of Treaties* (Oxford: Clarendon Press, 1961), 681–691; Akos Toth, 'The Doctrine of Rebus sic Stantibus in International Law' (1974) 19 *Juridical Review* 56, 147, 263; Detlev F. Vagts, 'Rebus Revisited: Changed Circumstances in Treaty Law' (2005) 43 *Columbia Journal of Transnational Law* 459.

[14] Which reflects customary international law: *Fisheries Jurisdiction Case (Federal Republic of Germany* v. *Iceland)*, Judgment of 2 February 1973, [1973] ICJ Rep 49, [36].

situation of the parties. The question is whether the illegality of the regime or its non-recognition can themselves be regarded as fundamental changes of circumstances. Two types of change are specifically characteristic of non-recognition of an illegal regime. One is when a non-invoking state acts in a manner which makes reactivation of the treaty impossible; the other is the emergence of the post-transition regime. These will be considered in turn.

The reality of long-term non-recognition is that states are likely, at some stage, to rely on the non-invocability of their treaty relations, and to adjust their other treaty relations accordingly. When non-recognition ends, they may be in a fundamentally and irreversibly different position from that in which they were when non-recognition began, and wish to put Article 62 into operation. Yet termination under Article 62 depends on the fundamental change having been unforeseen; that is, external to the voluntary conduct of the parties. Therefore, a non-invoking state may not rely on its own action to substantiate a claim of unforeseeable change.[15]

The other potentially fundamental change of circumstances that is characteristic of transition from an illegal regime is the emergence of the post-transition regime itself, especially if it involves significant changes to the structure and *raison d'être* of a treaty. In ordinary cases of emergence of new states, such changes form the basis of the clean-slate doctrine. The general justifications for that doctrine are no less compelling when an illegal regime intervenes in the process, and there is no reason a priori to deny the post-transition regime the prerogative granted to a new independent state. As for the counterparty, if in an ordinary case a newly independent state wishes to succeed to the treaties of its predecessor, the counterpart state is obligated to consent. There is no reason why the intervention of the illegal regime as such would exempt the counterpart state from this obligation, if reactivation of the treaty is possible in other respects.

[15] Moreover, according to Article 62(2)(b), a state also may not invoke a fundamental change if that change is the result of its own breach of an international obligation owed to any other party to the treaty. Acts tending to obstruct the resumption of the operation of the treaty are a breach of an international obligation towards another party if the treaty is suspended on grounds enumerated in the VCLT (VCLT Article 72(2)). However, since the obligation of non-recognition is not a VCLT-enumerated ground for suspension, the pre-emption of the future reactivation of a treaty during the existence of an illegal regime is not strictly speaking a breach of Article 72(2). It is therefore not in itself an obstacle to invoking Article 61(1).

In conclusion, the existence of the illegal regime, the obligation of non-recognition and transition into the post-transition regime are not, per se, fundamental changes of circumstance that permit the termination of treaties beyond the already existing exemption under the general law of state succession.

Desuetude

The doctrine of desuetude concerns discontinuance of a treaty through protracted non-use, and consequent implied mutual consent to terminate it.[16] The fact that the VCLT makes no specific reference to this doctrine may indicate that it is little more than a form of implied consent, and not an independent ground for termination.[17]

When non-invocation of a treaty is a legal obligation incumbent on a party, there is no reason to assume that compliance with such an obligation is accompanied by mutual consent to terminate the treaty. For one thing, 'mutual consent' is not possible when only one party is competent to act. Even if the stance of the incompetent party were to be examined, there is no reason to assume it wishes to terminate the treaty. As discussed in the introduction to this chapter, in some cases it can even be assumed that the illegal regime has an interest in displaying continuity in order to establish its own legitimacy, and the ousted sovereign has an interest in maintaining the treaty in force in order to reinforce its own legal existence. The non-invoking party may also be waiting for reactivation of the treaty rather than seeking to be exempt from its own commitments.

Once transition takes place, the will of the competent parties can be ascertained. To recall, the present discussion is premised on the assumption that unless grounds for termination exist, prior treaties are binding on the post-transition regime, whether because it is a returning sovereign or because it has declared itself a successor to treaties of the lawful sovereign. If, following transition, the parties continue not to invoke a treaty despite the removal of the legal obstacle to such invocation, this may in some circumstances indicate their mutual consent to terminate

16 Jennings and Watts, *Oppenheim's International Law*; McNair, *The Law of Treaties*, 516–518.

17 In the *Gabčíkovo-Nagymaros Case*, [123], the ICJ implied that the list of grounds for termination in the VCLT is not exhaustive, when it assumed that extinction of a state could lead to termination of its treaties. Phoebe N. Okowa, 'Case Concerning the Gabcíkovo-Nagymaros Project (*Hungary/Slovakia*)' (1998) 47 *International & Comparative Law Quarterly* 688, 692.

the treaty;[18] legally, however, this would be unrelated to the earlier suspension.

In conclusion, the non-use of a treaty during the period of non-recognition does not indicate consent to terminate the treaty. It therefore does not, by itself, substantiate a desuetude claim.

Conclusions

The existence of the illegal regime, the transition from it and the obligation of non-recognition do not, in themselves, fulfil the requisites of the various grounds for a unilateral termination of treaties. There is no permanent disappearance of an object that is vital for performance, there is no unforeseen change of circumstances, and mutual consent cannot be presumed. The prohibition on invocation of treaties vis-à-vis the illegal regime results only in the temporary suspension of the treaty, and upon transition the treaty is reactivated. Its survival through the process of transition is governed by the law of state succession and is unaffected by the intervention of the illegal regime. A post-transition regime which is a new state may adopt a clean-slate approach, in which case it is not bound by the treaty, regardless of the illegality of the previous regime.

4.2.2 Treaties concluded by the illegal regime

According to paragraph 125 of the *Namibia Advisory Opinion*, treaties concluded by the illegal regime are void *ab initio*. Examples of treaties purportedly concluded by an illegal regime on matters related exclusively to the disputed territory are few and far between. In contrast, there are cases where an illegally annexing state concluded treaties applicable primarily to its own sovereign territory, but purported to extend them to the annexed territory.[19] Treaties of both kinds raise three main questions.

The first is the ground for the invalidity pronounced by the ICJ. The law of treaties as codified in the VCLT does not directly regulate the effect of the obligation of non-recognition on the validity of treaties concluded by the illegal regime. It is therefore necessary to identify existing grounds

[18] Maria Lehto, 'Succession of States in the Former Soviet Union: Arrangements Concerning the Bilateral Treaties of Finland and the USSR' (1993) 4 *Finnish Yearbook of International Law* 194, 216. Compare with ICJ, *Gabčíkovo-Nagymaros Case*, [114].

[19] All the Soviet and Indonesian treaties, applied respectively to the Baltic states and to Timor-Leste, fall within this category.

with which the invalidity pronounced by the ICJ in the *Namibia Advisory Opinion* can be associated. Only then can the general law governing invalidity of treaties and its consequences be applied to such treaties. The other two questions concern the consequences of invalid treaties. One is whether an invalid treaty may nonetheless have valid consequences, binding upon the post-transition regime. The other question is the converse, namely whether the post-transition regime can succeed to treaties concluded by the illegal regime that had never been valid with respect to its territory.

With regard to the first question, the invalidity of treaties purportedly concluded by the illegal regime can be grounded in their conflict with a peremptory norm.[20] In this context two approaches are possible. Under one approach, a treaty is illegal and void if its *object* conflicts with international public order.[21] Accordingly, the *content* of a treaty is the exclusive yardstick for its compatibility with peremptory norms. Some treaty content may be intimately linked to the illegality of the regime. For example, the Timor Gap Treaty between Indonesia and Australia prejudiced the right of the Timorese to dispose of their natural resources and violated their exercise of the right to self-determination.[22] However, not every treaty concluded by an illegal regime is substantively in violation of a peremptory norm. Accordingly, under this approach, not every treaty of an illegal regime would be invalid. A different approach reflects the expansion of the notion of peremptory norm beyond the law of treaties. According to this approach, the prohibition on violating peremptory norms can serve as a yardstick for assessing the *process* of contracting into a treaty and not only the substantive content of the treaty.[23] All treaties concluded by an illegal regime (whether a putative state or the government of an existing state on behalf of an illegally annexed territory) would therefore be void, regardless of their content, because the effective control of the regime over the territory, which enables it to enter into the treaty, is grounded in a violation of a peremptory norm.

20 VCLT Article 53.

21 Report by Mr H. Lauterpacht, Special Rapporteur on the Law of Treaties: 'A treaty, or any of its provisions, is void *if its performance* involves an act which is illegal under international law', UN Doc A/CN.4/63 (24 March 1953), 155, emphasis added.

22 ICJ, *East Timor Case*, dissenting opinion of Judge Weeramantry, 113, 222.

23 Alexander Orakhelashvili, *Peremptory Norms in International Law* (Oxford: Oxford University Press, 2006), 138; Written Statement of the Secretary-General, *Namibia Advisory Opinion*, ICJ Pleadings Volume I, 105 [121]–[122].

Orakhelashvili goes even further in arguing that the consequences of a violation of a peremptory norm reach further than those of an 'ordinary' violation of law. Thus an act in consequence of the violation of a peremptory norm is itself a violation of a peremptory norm. An agreement made possible because a peremptory norm had been violated effectively constitutes an agreement to ignore the effects of the norm in the relations between the contracting parties, and is therefore itself a violation of the peremptory norm.[24] The acts of both parties, not only the illegal regime but also its counterpart, are tainted with illegality.

Where the invalidity of a treaty is based on it being in violation of a peremptory norm, not only the parties to the treaty may invoke the invalidity but also third parties.[25] The post-transition regime may therefore invoke the invalidity of treaties purportedly concluded by the illegal regime irrespective of the post-transition regime's position on succession to treaties in general.

The second question presented above is whether an invalid treaty may nonetheless generate valid consequences binding upon the post-transition regime. This question arises particularly with respect to treaties that create boundary regimes, which, under the customary law of state succession,[26] acquire existence outside their founding treaty.[27] The Vienna Convention on Succession of States in Respect of Treaties (VCST) stipulates:

> A succession of States does not as such affect:
>
> (a) a boundary established by a treaty, or
>
> (b) obligations and rights established by a treaty and relating to the regime of a boundary.

Thus, even if a treaty is no longer in effect, the practice it generated may have consolidated a boundary regime. On the other hand, this rule, as all other rules of state succession, assumes that the boundary regime had been created validly.[28] Therefore, although Article 11 reflects the

[24] Orakhelashvili, *Peremptory Norms*, 139. [25] Orakhelashvili, *Peremptory Norms*, 148–149.

[26] McNair, *The Law of Treaties*, 256; Jan Klabbers, Martti Koskenniemi, Olivier Ribbelink and Andreas Zimmermann (eds.), *State Practice Regarding State Succession and Issues of Recognition: The Pilot Project of the Council of Europe* (The Hague: Kluwer Law International, 1999), 572.

[27] ICJ, *Gabčíkovo-Nagymaros Case*, [123].

[28] VCST Article 14 stipulates that nothing in the Convention 'shall be considered as prejudging in any respect any question relating to the validity of a treaty'.

consequences of effective practice *erga omnes*, it cannot be assumed to apply automatically to boundary treaties of an illegal regime, for the same reason that the VCST does not apply directly to replacement of illegal regimes. Müllerson suggests that the balance between the illegality of the regime and the effectiveness of practice lies in the specific circumstances of each case and must take account of extra-legal factors. One of those, he suggests, is the passage of time since the illegal claim was made. The longer the time that has passed, the weightier are the arguments in favour of the recognition of existing realities.[29] According to this approach, a boundary regime created by an illegal regime may bind the post-transition regime if it operates effectively for a lengthy period of time, despite the invalidity of the treaty underlying the regime.

A final question is whether the post-transition regime may opt to succeed to treaties purportedly concluded by the illegal regime, thereby binding itself and other parties. If a treaty conflicts substantively with a peremptory norm, the illegality cannot be acquiesced in, perhaps with the exception of acquiescence by the international community as a whole.[30] The other parties may be estopped by their own lack of good faith from arguing invalidity, but the post-transition regime also may not invoke the treaty. If the flaw in the treaty is the incompetence of one of the parties (the illegal regime) in entering into it because that regime has acquired its control over the territory through a violation of a peremptory norm, then a different, competent actor may replace the incompetent one, but this replacement still requires a new treaty, because the illegal regime's treaty does not exist as a matter of law. If there is doubt as to the illegality of the previous regime, the invocation of a treaty by the post-transition regime against a counterparty may be construed as implicit acquiescence in the treaty's validity and in the legality of the previous regime.[31]

In conclusion, treaties purportedly concluded by an illegal regime are invalid and have no existence once that regime ends. With respect to treaties that establish boundary regimes, while they themselves are invalid, the regime that they created may continue to exist. In light of these conclusions, it is interesting to examine the extent to which the general rules of state succession were applied or modified by post-transition regimes with respect to prior treaties, the extent to which they have

[29] Rein Müllerson, *International Law, Human Rights and Politics: Developments in Eastern Europe and the CIS* (London: Routledge, 1994), 150.

[30] VCLT Article 45; Orakhelashvili, *Peremptory Norms*, 146–147.

[31] VCLT Article 45(b).

succeeded in entering into treaties on behalf of the territory in dispute, and how the post-transition regime regarded such treaties.

4.3 Practice

4.3.1 Rhodesia

The status of treaties during the period of non-recognition

From 1965 until 1979, treaties previously in force for Southern Rhodesia generally remained in force for it, but were not applied.[32] The status of prior treaties was nonetheless not uniform in all cases, because of different positions taken by the counterpart states. For example, in *S* v. *Oosthuizen* (1977), the South African court considered the status of an extradition treaty concluded between South Africa and Southern Rhodesia in 1963. The court proceeded on the premise that from the time of UDI, Rhodesia had been acting as an independent state, although it remained unrecognized by South Africa or internationally. Accordingly, Southern Rhodesia, with which the extradition treaty had been concluded, was no longer in existence, and the extradition treaty had lapsed.[33] The status of another pre-UDI extradition treaty was considered in the US, in *US* v. *Steinberg* (1979). In that affair, the US court ruled that the status of an extradition treaty between the US and Southern Rhodesia was governed by the obligation of non-recognition and the consequent prohibition on invocation of a still-existing treaty.

Rhodesia, under the Smith government, concluded no international treaties. The UK, being directly responsible for the international relations of the colony of Southern Rhodesia, took various treaty actions with regard to the territory, including ratification of new treaties (which remained largely inoperative)[34] and termination of treaties.[35] In certain cases, the

[32] E.g. US Department of State, *Treaties in Force, a List of Treaties and Other International Agreements of the United States in Force on January 1, 1964* and US Department of State, *Treaties in Force, a List of Treaties and Other International Agreements of the United States in Force on January 1, 1973*, with regard to the Agreement Revising the Telecommunications Agreement Signed at Bermuda on 4 December 1945, Annexed to the 1949 Final Act and Agreement for the Revision of the Telecommunications Agreement signed at Bermuda on 4 December 1945. Both list Southern Rhodesia as party.

[33] The facts of the case are summarized in John Dugard, 'Rhodesia: Does South Africa Recognize It as an Independent State?' (1977) 94 *South African Law Journal* 127, 128.

[34] It ratified the Additional Protocol of the Constitution of the Universal Postal Union, on 30 June 1972, also on behalf of Southern Rhodesia. 1972 UNTS 400.

[35] 1973 Termination of the Application of the Double Taxation Convention with the US with Respect to Its Application to Southern Rhodesia: Notification of Termination

UK included reservations in its instruments of accession to treaties, indicating that treaty law normally applicable to Southern Rhodesia would not apply to it until the UK was in a position to ensure that treaty obligations were implemented.[36] The international community saw the UK not only as competent to act on behalf of the territory but also as obligated to do so. In 1970, the UN General Assembly adopted a resolution in which it called upon the UK to ensure the application to the armed conflict in Rhodesia of Geneva Conventions III and IV.[37] As discussed in Chapter 3 above, the Geneva Conventions are not premised on the contracting party's title to the territory but rather determine a state's responsibility for the conduct of its forces outside its territory. The call to comply with the conventions despite effective control over the territory was therefore not in itself extraordinary. The situation in Rhodesia was nonetheless complicated because the UK did not have effective control over Rhodesian forces and the implementation of the treaties would have required the co-operation of the Rhodesian authorities.

Transition

Soon after independence, Zimbabwe informed the UN Secretary-General of its policy with respect to succession to treaties. With respect to bilateral treaties, Zimbabwe declared that it

> will continue to apply within its territory . . . all bilateral treaties validly concluded or recognised by the United Kingdom Government in respect of Southern Rhodesia for a period of three years from the date of independence, i.e. 18th

of the Convention and Protocol between the Government of the United Kingdom of Great Britain and Northern Ireland and the Government of the United States of America for the Avoidance of Double Taxation and the Prevention of Fiscal Evasion with Respect to Taxes on Income (signed 16 April 1945 and 6 June 1946), 928 UNTS 135 Annex A.

36 Reservation to the accession of the UK to the 1962 Convention on Consent to Marriage, Minimum Age for Marriage and Registration of Marriages (9 July 1970), 1970 UNTS 400. Compare with the qualification of Cyprus's accession to the EU in Protocol No. 10 Article 1(1), which stipulates: 'The application of the acquis shall be suspended in those areas of the Republic of Cyprus in which the Government of the Republic of Cyprus does not exercise effective control'. Protocol No. 10 to the Act Concerning the Conditions of Accession of the Czech Republic, the Republic of Estonia, the Republic of Cyprus, the Republic of Latvia, the Republic of Lithuania, the Republic of Hungary, the Republic of Malta, the Republic of Poland, the Republic of Slovenia and the Slovak Republic and the Adjustments to the Treaties on which the European Union is Founded, [2003] OJ L236/955.

37 UNGA Resolution 2652(XXV), paragraph 11.

April, 1980, unless such treaties are terminated or modified earlier by mutual consent . . .[38]

The statement further indicated that during the three-year period, Zimbabwe would review all bilateral treaties, to determine whether they require termination, revision or renegotiation, in light of Zimbabwe's sovereign status. It would negotiate with the states concerned on the possibility of the continuance, modification or termination of such treaties. At the end of that period, Zimbabwe would regard such treaties that have not been continued or modified as having terminated.

The period of review of bilateral treaties was twice extended by one year and ended on 18 April 1985. At its conclusion, the prime minister of Zimbabwe informed of the UN Secretary-General that Zimbabwe had

concluded a number of bilateral treaties with other governments with the effect that these instruments have superseded some of the earlier ones. It has become evident to [Zimbabwe] that many contracting parties prefer to enter into new arrangements with [Zimbabwe] rather than revive those treaties whose operations might have been suspended or terminated between 1965 and 1979 or which are now considered to be obsolete in the conduct of present-day international relations.[39]

Zimbabwe declared that prior bilateral treaties would expire on 18 April 1985, unless Zimbabwe or the other contracting party had communicated its intention to maintain the treaty in force, or unless the process of renegotiating its terms and provisions had been agreed upon.[40]

As regards multilateral treaties, Zimbabwe decided on a six-year review period to confirm, modify or terminate its obligations under the treaties concerned. At the expiration of that period, treaties that had not been terminated would continue fully in force. The default arrangement with

[38] In a note dated 24 February 1981, cited in US Department of State, *Treaties in Force, a List of Treaties and Other International Agreements of the United States in Force on January 1, 2004*, 311–312.

[39] Received 20 February 1985, cited in US Department of State, *Treaties in Force, a List of Treaties and Other International Agreements of the United States in Force on January 1, 2004*, 311–312.

[40] The US, for example, presented Zimbabwe with a list of international treaties that it intended to maintain in force. Certain pre-UDI treaties are still in force, such as the 1899 Convention Relating to Tenure and Disposition of Real and Personal Property, the 1936 Supplementary Convention relating to the Tenure and Disposition of Real and Personal Property, and the 1951 Consular Convention between the United States and the United Kingdom. US Department of State, *Treaties in Force, a List of Treaties and Other International Agreements of the United States in Force on January 1, 2004*, 312.

respect to multilateral treaties was the converse of the one governing bilateral treaties, namely succession rather than termination. This is hardly surprising, since Zimbabwe had no power to renegotiate multilateral treaties.[41] Had it terminated their application, its only option would have been to rejoin them under the exact same terms. Under the circumstances, it was simpler to succeed to them.

Since the Smith regime did not conclude any treaties, the status of post-UDI 'Rhodesian' treaties did not arise. Zimbabwe was willing to succeed to treaties concluded after UDI by the UK on behalf of Southern Rhodesia.[42]

In conclusion, Zimbabwe's practice was similar to that of other post-colonial states. The illegality of the regime generated factual changes that played into the application of the law of state succession, but it did not have a direct normative effect. The policy of non-recognition did not prejudice Zimbabwe's freedom of action.

4.3.2 Namibia

The status of treaties during the period of non-recognition

Pre-1966 treaties

In the absence of any provisions in the mandate for South West Africa that could be construed as providing for the continuation of treaty rights and obligations,[43] South Africa as mandatory power exercised the clean-slate approach with regard to treaties concluded by Germany as colonial power.[44] Consequently, of the German colonial period only a few boundary treaties remained in force. At the time when the South African mandate was revoked, there were some 180 treaties applicable to Namibia,[45] most of them having been entered into by South Africa acting as a mandatory power on behalf of Namibia. The status of these prior treaties does not seem to have raised any practical concern after 1966. This is not surprising, given Namibia's geographical, economic and social isolation. Also, the distinction between application of a treaty to Namibia or to South Africa was often blurred.

41 It is therefore not clear what it meant by 'modification'.

42 E.g. the 1977 Agreement between the Government of the United States of America and the Government of the United Kingdom and Northern Ireland Concerning Air Services, 28 UST 5367.

43 UNIN, *Independent Namibia*, 27.

44 Interview by the author with Dr Sackey Akweenda, Attorney-General's Office 1991–2000, Windhoek, 27 February and 2 March 2004.

45 Ninety-six bilateral ones and eighty-five multilateral ones, based on UNIN, *Independent Namibia*, 63–143.

In Resolution 283(1970), the Security Council requested the Secretary-General to undertake a detailed study of all multilateral treaties to which South Africa was a party and that might have been considered to apply to the territory of Namibia, either by direct reference or on the basis of relevant provisions of international law. The purpose of this study was to establish means for an effective implementation of the Security Council resolution in light of South Africa's refusal to withdraw from Namibia. The Secretary-General produced a list of multilateral treaties that had been deposited with him or with the Secretariat of the League of Nations, or that had been transmitted to the Secretariat of the UN for registration in accordance with Article 102 of the Charter. The study might have been overinclusive in that some of the treaties that had been transmitted for registration under Article 102 might have terminated by the time the study was conducted, without the Secretary-General having been notified.[46] Altogether the study listed ninety multilateral treaties.[47] Of those, fifty-six had been expressly extended to Namibia as a mandate territory. The others were listed as applicable 'on the basis of relevant provisions of international law'. According to the Secretary-General's report, this meant that in the absence of a territorial clause in the treaties themselves, they could be considered applicable to Namibia. However, under the mandate system, in the absence of a territorial clause the mandatory power had to make a specific declaration in order to apply a treaty to the mandate territory.[48] Thus 'relevant provisions of international law', as opposed to express undertakings, actually excluded the application of the treaties to Namibia.

Of the treaties listed in the Secretary-General's study as applicable to Namibia on the date of the revocation of the mandate, a few can be regarded as humanitarian and thus invocable under the terms of

[46] UN Doc S/10288 (12 August 1971).

[47] In view of the critique below, the data in UNIN, *Independent Namibia*, appears more reliable than that in the Secretary-General's study.

[48] Quincy Wright, *Mandates under the League of Nations* (Chicago: University of Chicago Press, 1930), 450; Quincy Wright, 'Some Recent Cases on the Status of Mandate Areas' (1926) 20 *American Journal of International Law* 768, 772, note 11. Covenant of the League of Nations Article 22 and the Mandate for South West Africa provide that in the case of Namibia and other Class C mandates, the mandatory power could administer the territories as an 'integral portion of its territory'. This was a compromise for the benefit of Australia, New Zealand and South Africa, which sought to annex their mandate territories: E. T. Williams, 'Japan's Mandate in the Pacific' (1933) 27 *American Journal of International Law* 428, 433. However, Francis B. Sayre, 'Legal Problems Arising from the United Nations Trusteeship System' (1948) 42 *American Journal of International Law* 263, 286, considers that this is meaningless in terms of sovereignty of the mandatory power.

the *Namibia Advisory Opinion*: two International Labour Organization treaties,[49] the 1926 Slavery Convention,[50] the 1930 Protocol Relating to Certain Cases of Statelessness, and four conventions for suppression of traffic in persons.[51]

The study also listed the four Geneva Conventions, although there is no indication that South Africa had ever extended their application to Namibia. These treaties nonetheless did apply to conflicts in Namibia, but, as discussed in Chapter 3 above, this was related not to the *Namibia* exception but to the Geneva Conventions' application directly to South Africa's forces wherever they operated. There is no indication that any state has ever invoked the humanitarian treaties, other than through UN resolutions that called on South Africa to treat Namibians captured during their struggle for freedom as prisoners of war in accordance with Geneva Convention III and to comply with Geneva Convention IV.[52]

Post-1966 South African treaties

The UN envisaged a systematic review of post-1966 South African treaties. In Resolution 301(1971), the Security Council endorsed the *Advisory Opinion* and requested

> the Ad Hoc Sub-Committee on Namibia to review all treaties and agreements which are contrary to the provisions of the present resolution in order to ascertain whether States have entered into agreements which recognize South Africa's authority over Namibia, and to report periodically thereon . . .[53]

No further action was taken on this issue.

In fact, after the revocation of the mandate, South Africa purported to extend to Namibia fifteen bilateral treaties and two multilateral treaties

49 ILO Convention No. 42 concerning workmen's Compensation for Occupational Diseases, and ILO Convention No. 89 concerning Night Work for Women Employed in Industry.

50 The study provides conflicting information on whether the 1953 Protocol amending the Convention had been expressly extended to Namibia, UN Doc S/10288 (12 August 1971), 6, 9.

51 1921 International Convention for the Suppression of Traffic in Women and Children, 1933 Convention for the Suppression of Traffic in Women of Full Age, 1950 Convention for the Suppression of Traffic in Persons and of the Exploitation of the Prostitution of Others, and 1950 Final Protocol to the Convention for the Suppression of Traffic in Persons and of the Exploitation of the Prostitution of Others. The classification of these four conventions as 'humanitarian' is somewhat difficult, as they contain provisions not only for protection of individuals by states, but also not only extensive co-operation between states in matters such as extradition and transfer of information on offenders.

52 UNGA Resolution 2678(XXV), paragraph 11; UNGA Resolution 2871(XXVI), paragraph 6.

53 UNSC Resolution 301 (20 October 1971), paragraph 14.

('post-1966 South African treaties') applicable to its own territory.[54] The bilateral treaties covered such topics as air services,[55] consular privileges,[56] development of water resources,[57] extradition[58] and admission to medical practice.[59] One multilateral treaty concerned customs: in 1969 South Africa signed the 1969 Customs Union Agreement with Botswana, Lesotho and Swaziland. South Africa's territory was defined in Article 1 as 'the area in respect of which the Government of the Republic of South Africa is a Contracting Party to the General Agreement on Tariffs and Trade'. That agreement, from 1948, defined the Union of South Africa as inclusive of Namibia.[60] None of the other parties to the 1969 Customs Union Agreement made any reservations or objections to the extension of the treaty to Namibia as part of South Africa.[61] The other multilateral treaty entered into by South Africa on behalf of Namibia was the 1969 Convention on the Conservation of the Living Resources of the Southeast Atlantic. South Africa signed the convention in 1969 and ratified it in October 1970. The 'Convention Area', defined in Article 1 by lines of longitude and latitude, included Namibian territorial waters. Of twelve other parties to the convention, only Italy declared that its ratification 'in no way implies recognition on the part of Italy of the legitimacy of the South African administration in Namibia'.[62]

South Africa entered into another bilateral treaty on behalf of Namibia, which, unlike the other treaties noted here, applied exclusively to Namibian territory. On 21 January 1969, the governments of South Africa and Portugal concluded the Agreement on the First Phase of Development of the Water Resources of the Kunene River Basin (the Kunene River Basin Agreement). Given the parameters of the *Namibia Advisory Opinion*, this agreement was void *ab initio*.[63]

[54] UNIN, *Independent Namibia*.

[55] 1967 Amendments to Agreement with Norway and Sweden; 1967 Agreement with Belgium.

[56] 1967 Exchange of Notes on Consular Privileges with the UK.

[57] 1969 Agreement with Portugal on the Kunene River Basin, discussed below.

[58] 1968 Treaty with Swaziland; 1969 Treaty with Botswana.

[59] 1965 Agreement with Belgium.

[60] General Agreement on Tariffs and Trade (signed 30 October 1947, entered into force 1 January 1948), 55 UNTS 189, Annex A.

[61] Hardly surprising, given the dependency of these states' economies on South Africa's.

[62] List of signatories available at www.fao.org/Legal/treaties/015s-e.htm. Other original signatories were Japan, Portugal and the USSR.

[63] On the implementation of the Kunene Agreement see Piet Heyns, 'Water-Resources Management in Southern Africa', in Nakayama Mikiyasu (ed.), *International Waters in Southern Africa* (Tokyo: UNU, 2003), 10–14, and discussion below.

Notably, South Africa had signed and ratified all seventeen post-1966 treaties before the ICJ's *Namibia Advisory Opinion* was handed down (the Convention on the Conservation of the Living Resources of the Southeast Atlantic entered into force shortly after the *Advisory Opinion* was given, but by then South Africa had completed its own acceptance procedures). Although these treaties were void *ab initio* with respect to Namibia, the parties might not have been cognizant of the obligation of non-recognition and its implications until the *Advisory Opinion* was given. Following the *Advisory Opinion*, the obligation of non-recognition against Namibia was adhered to,[64] and states refrained from entering into treaties with South Africa in which it acted on behalf of or concerning Namibia. For example, a fortnight after the revocation of the mandate, South Africa deposited with the General Secretariat of the International Telecommunications Union (ITU) an instrument of accession to the 1965 International Telecommunications Convention, on its own behalf and on behalf of Namibia. By agreement of the majority of members of the ITU, the Administrative Council of the ITU resolved that the government of South Africa no longer had the right to represent Namibia within the ITU.[65]

As with the pre-1966 treaties, and probably for the same reasons, the seventeen post-1966 treaties raised no interest while South Africa was administering Namibia. On the whole, their validity or applicability to Namibia during the period of non-recognition has never been challenged.

UNCN treaties

General Assembly Resolution 2248(S–V)[66] set up UNCN (at the time entitled the United Nations Council for South West Africa) and entrusted it with the power 'to administer South West Africa until independence, with the maximum possible participation of the people of the Territory'. This provision was understood by UNCN – and by various states and organizations – as conferring upon it the power to administer Namibia not so much in the territory (which in practice it could not and did not do), but externally, through maintenance of international relations on Namibia's behalf. The power 'to represent Namibia' wherever required

64 Despite some reservations as to the underlying premises of the request leading to it, e.g. those of the UK. 'The Question of Namibia' (1970) 24 *Yearbook of the United Nations* 734, 740.

65 ITU, Resolution No. 619, 'Question of the Territory of South West Africa'.

66 UNGA Resolution 2248(S–V) (19 May 1967).

was confirmed in various General Assembly resolutions.[67] The treaty-making power was recognized in Resolution 3031(XXVII), which requested UNCN 'to continue to examine the question of bilateral and multilateral treaties which explicitly or implicitly include Namibia, and to seek to replace South Africa as the party representing Namibia in all relevant bilateral and multilateral treaties'.[68] In 1973, the General Assembly extended a call to states to enter into consultations with UNCN for the same purpose.[69] The call for such replacement confirms that the treaties entered into by South Africa were considered to be still in force with regard to Namibia, otherwise there would have been no need to take any account of them.

Until its dissolution in 1990,[70] UNCN concluded eight bilateral treaties, on the issuance of travel and identity documents[71] and on return to Nigeria of certain Namibians.[72] It also acceded to fifteen multilateral treaties on behalf of Namibia. Of these, nine were substantively related to the situation in Namibia, and UNCN's accession was a clear assertion of Namibia's rights vis-à-vis South Africa. These treaties include the 1973 International Convention on the Suppression and Punishment of the Crime of Apartheid, the 1966 Convention on the Elimination of all forms of Racial Discrimination (CERD), the 1982 UN Convention on the Law of the Sea (UNCLOS), and the four Geneva Conventions and their Additional Protocols I and II.[73] UNCN also acceded to constituent instruments of five UN special agencies and organizations which admitted Namibia in the capacity of a state.[74]

[67] E.g. UNGA Resolution 2871(XXVI) (20 December 1971), paragraph 13(a); UNGA Resolution 3031(XXVII) (18 December 1972), paragraph 9(a).

[68] UNGA Resolution 3031(XXVII) (18 December 1972), paragraph 9(i).

[69] UNGA Resolution 3111(XXVIII) (12 December 1973), paragraph I(16).

[70] UNGA Resolution 44/243 (11 September 1990).

[71] 1970 UNCN–Zambia Travel Documents Agreement; 1970 UNCN–Uganda Travel Documents Agreement; Ethiopia, Kenya, Tanzania, Zaire and Botswana, UN Doc A/AC.131/1985. On the history of these treaties see J. F. Engers, 'The United States Travel and Identity Document for Namibians' (1971) 65 *American Journal of International Law* 571.

[72] 1972 Nigeria–UNCN Right of Return Agreement.

[73] Depositary Notification p. o.411.61.(5) of 30 November 1983.

[74] FAO, 'Report of the 19th Session of the FAO Conference' (November 1977), 74–75; ILO, 'International Labour Conference Resolution Concerning the Admission of Namibia [Selection Committee]' (23 June 1978); UNESCO, 'Resolution of the General Conference Concerning the Admission of Namibia' (30 October 1978), Records of the General Conference Twentieth Session Volume I, 20 C/Resolution 0.7; IAEA, 'Application for Membership of the Agency – Resolution Adopted during the 238th Plenary Meeting, on 20 September 1982' (18 October 1982), GC(XXVI)/RES/393; UNIN, *Independent Namibia*, 140–143. According to the ITU website, Namibia is a member since 25 January 1984. The

Since the UN acted on the premise that South Africa had already acceded to the Geneva Conventions on behalf of Namibia in 1952, the 1983 accession of UNCN to the four Geneva Conventions may have been an act of 'replacement' envisaged in Resolution 3031(XXVII), although UNCN made no statement to that effect. South Africa objected to this accession. No other state raised any objection or responded to the South African objection. With this possible exception, there was no duplication in the status of Namibia as party through UNCN accession and as party through South African pre-1966 accession.

Transition

The validity of treaties was not a major issue before the Namibian government. As noted earlier, some 180 treaties applied to Namibia before 1966. By 1990, some of those had become customary law, making succession largely irrelevant.[75] South Africa entered into only seventeen treaties after 1966. UNCN's bilateral treaties were substantively obsolete once Namibia had become independent.

Policy prior to independence

Both SWAPO and UNCN participated in the conferences which led to the adoption of the VCST in 1978, and the Vienna Convention on Succession of States in Respect of State Property, Archives and Debts (VCSPAD) in 1983. The final acts of both conferences were accompanied by specific resolutions concerning Namibia,[76] which reflect the Namibian leadership's position at the time. The resolutions exclude, expressly in 1978 and implicitly in 1983, the application of the conventions' rules to the relationship between South Africa and Namibia, on the ground of the illegality of the South African regime.

The common operative paragraph of the resolutions provides that the conference:

WHO admitted Namibia through UNCN accession as a non-self-governing territory: World Health Assembly Resolution WHA 27.23 of May 1974.

75 E.g. the Slavery Convention of 1926.

76 Final Act of the United Nations Conference on Succession of States in Respect of Treaties, Resolution Concerning Namibia (22 August 1978), UN Doc A/Conf.80/31, (1978) 17 *International Legal Materials* 1488, 1516–1517; Final Act of the United Nations Conference on Succession of States in Respect of State Property, Archives and Debts, Resolution Concerning Namibia (7 April 1983), UN Doc A/Conf.117/15, (1983) 22 *International Legal Materials* 305.

Resolves that the relevant articles of the Vienna Convention on Succession of States in Respect of [Treaties/State Property, Archives and Debts] shall be interpreted, in the case of Namibia, in conformity with United Nations resolutions on the question of Namibia . . .

The resolution attached to the Final Act of the VCST further resolves 'that South Africa is not the predecessor State of the future independent State of Namibia'. In 1983, the resolution attached to the Final Act of the VCSPAD was worded less strongly:

Resolves that, in consequence, all the rights of the future independent State of Namibia should be reserved.

The conventions were adopted at the height of SWAPO's international struggle against South Africa, and it is not surprising that they were so blunt and legalistic. However, the resolutions reflected no more than intended policy. Final acts are not binding instruments, and Namibia did not become party to either convention.

A similar approach was taken by a 1989 UNIN study on succession of independent Namibia to treaty rights and obligations created by prior administrations – German colonial rule, South Africa as mandatory power, the South African post-1966 administration and UNCN.[77] The study, endorsed by SWAPO, adopted a strict formalistic interpretation of the obligation of non-recognition and invalidity of post-1966 South African treaties on the basis of the *Namibia Advisory Opinion*. Although it recognized potential benefits for Namibia from succession to treaties concluded by South Africa, it sought means of achieving this result without compromising the principles set out in the *Advisory Opinion* on the invalidity of post-1966 South African treaties.

But UNIN also offered other approaches. A 1979 study on constitutional options for Namibia, representative of the general mindset in UNIN, suggested:[78]

The dependent territory may, on independence, opt for universal succession, no succession or a middle course in the rejection and acceptance of the inherited rights and obligations. Treaties that are clearly technical will pose no serious problems but political and economic treaties may require critical examination . . . Not all rights and obligations can, however, be discarded without creating a vacuum

[77] UNIN, *Independent Namibia*.

[78] UNIN, *Constitutional Options for Namibia: A Historical Perspective*, based on the work of M. D. Bomany and C. Ushewokunze, Namibia Studies Series No. 2 (ed. N. K. Duggal) (Lusaka: UNIN, 1979), 53.

and some of the rights may indeed be in favour of the new state. Further, some of the obligations may not be discarded without prompting legitimate complaints by the other party or parties. Many newly independent states therefore choose to review the treaties.

This study and others compared Namibia with Tanganyika and Zambia, implying that, in due course, the situation of Namibia would be akin to that of post-colonial states, rather than a unique case of transition from an illegal regime.[79] The 'middle course' between blanket rejection and total acceptance of treaties was intended to serve as a balance between the clean-slate and the universal-succession theories, rather than between concepts of legality and effectiveness.

The Namibian Constitution

The Namibian Constitution contains a presumption of succession to treaties, partially subject to review. The category of treaties for which succession is provided and the category of treaties subject to approval or rejection by parliamentary review are not identical, resulting in a complex framework for determining validity of treaties. Article 143 of the Namibian Constitution stipulates: 'All existing international agreements binding upon Namibia shall remain in force, unless and until the National Assembly acting under Article 63(2)(d) otherwise decides.' This formulation begs the question of what were the agreements that were 'binding upon Namibia' on the eve of independence, when the constitution came into force. From the analysis above it emerges that binding agreements include prior treaties as well as treaties entered into by UNCN. According to Article 143, all such treaties remained in force, unless otherwise decided by the National Assembly.

Article 143 is complemented by Article 63(2), which provides:

> The National Assembly shall further have the power and function, subject to this Constitution:...
>
> d) to consider and decide whether or not to succeed to such international agreements as may have been entered into prior to Independence by administrations within Namibia in which the majority of the Namibian people have historically not enjoyed democratic representation and participation...

This provision could apply to treaties entered into by the German colonial rulers and by South Africa as mandatory power. Such treaties therefore

[79] UNIN, *Toward a New Legal System for Independent Namibia*, based on the work of Mengo D. F. Sichilongo, Namibia Studies Series No. 5 (ed. N. K. Duggal) (Lusaka: UNIN, 1981), 53.

remain in force unless the National Assembly decides otherwise. Article 63(2) does not apply to UNCN treaties, because UNCN was not an administration 'within Namibia'. UNCN treaties therefore remain in force and are not subject to review.

However, soon after independence the Namibian attorney-general adopted an interpretation according to which Article 63(2)(d) could also expand the scope of binding treaties beyond Article 143: the National Assembly could not only reject succession to prior treaties, but could also approve succession with regard to post-1966 South African treaties.[80] Such an interpretation is supported by the terminology 'decide whether or not to succeed', indicating that there was no default arrangement, and decisions of two types were envisaged, namely opting out of succession and opting into it. The indirect reference in one constitutional provision to both prior and post-1966 South African treaties is peculiar, but it is in line with the intention of the constitution's drafters to leave matters obscure.[81] As pointed out earlier, South Africa attempted to extend treaties to Namibia after 1966 only in rare cases, providing little scope for testing this issue.

The Namibian government requested South Africa to provide it with a list of treaties that had been in force with respect to Namibia prior to independence, for the purpose of implementing the constitutional provisions. The cut-off date ('prior to independence') suggests that Namibia was entertaining the possibility of giving effect also to post-1966 South African treaties. However, by the time this list had been examined, a debate over parliamentary treaty review developed in another context,[82] making the attorney-general reluctant to bring any international agreement to parliament.[83] No further action was taken on the status of the treaties listed by South Africa, nor has the Namibian National Assembly ever held any debate under Article 63(2)(d).

[80] Interview by the author with Dr Sackey Akweenda, Attorney-General's Office 1991–2000, Windhoek, 27 February and 2 March 2004.

[81] Interview by the author with Prof. François Venter, University of Potchefstroom, participant in the MPNF, Potchefstroom, 6 April 2004.

[82] There was a constitutional debate at the time on the respective competences of parliament and government with regard to entering into executive and non-executive agreements. The attorney-general was trying to establish a distinction between executive and non-executive agreements which does not appear in the constitution, and argued that only non-executive agreements needed ratification by parliament.

[83] Interview by the author with Dr Sackey Akweenda, Attorney-General's Office 1991–2000, Windhoek, 27 February and 2 March 2004.

Namibian practice

Pre-1966 treaties Even if state succession is considered self-executing as a matter of law, in practice it is not. A state must notify its intention to succeed to treaties, and a general notification such as a constitutional provision is not usually considered sufficient.[84] With two exceptions, Namibia has never given notification of its succession to treaties. Accordingly, it is not surprising that despite the constitutional provisions, depositaries of treaties to which South Africa had been party also on behalf of Namibia prior to 1966 do not usually record Namibia as party today unless it has formally acceded to the treaty since 1990. This matter is unrelated to the status of South Africa in Namibia from 1966 until 1990.

The first exceptional notification of a succession concerned is the 1949 Convention on Road Traffic, which South Africa accepted in 1952 and extended to Namibia. In 1993 Namibia deposited an instrument of succession to this convention with effect from 21 March 1990, the date on which it became independent and assumed responsibility for its international relations.[85]

The other instance in which Namibia notified its succession is with regard to the four Geneva Conventions, to which South Africa acceded in 1952.[86] On 1 August 1991, Namibia informed the depositary, Switzerland, that Namibia considered these conventions to be binding upon it by succession.[87] It explained:

> Regarding your request on Namibia's position . . .
>
> [t]he Government of the Republic of Namibia considers these conventions which were acceded to by the Republic of South Africa and extended to Namibia prior to the cancellation by the General Assembly of the United Nations Organisation

[84] UN Secretary-General, 'Summary of Practice of the Secretary-General as Depositary of Multilateral Treaties, Prepared by the Treaty Section of the Office of Legal Affairs' (1999) UN Doc ST/LEG/7/Rev.1, paragraphs 303–306.

[85] Instrument of succession, 13 October 1993, Depositary Notification C. N.434.1993. TREATIES-3 of 18 January 1994 entitled 'Convention on Road Traffic Signed at Geneva on 19 September 1949 Succession by Namibia'.

[86] South Africa ratified the Conventions on 31 March 1952. The Conventions entered into force with respect to South Africa on 30 September 1952. See www.eda.admin.ch/etc/medialib/downloads/edazen/topics/intla/intrea/depch/warvic.Par.0019.File.tmp/mt_080303_49conv4part_f.pdf.

[87] Namibian Ministry of Foreign Affairs ref. PE/INFO/11 of 1 August 1991 containing attorney-general ref. AG/mk of 19 July 1991 (on file with the author). In Depositary Notification p. o.411.61.(5) of 25 October 1991 the Swiss Federal Department of Foreign Affairs noted that Namibia deposited 'a declaration of succession' for the four Geneva Conventions, without further details.

of the mandate for South West Africa on 27th October 1966, to be binding upon Namibia by virtue of the doctrine in regard to treaty succession and more particularly in accordance with the provisions of Articles 143 and 144 of the Namibian Constitution.

This notification is noteworthy for a number of reasons. First, it is a response to a query from the depositary. It can only be speculated whether Namibia would have regarded itself (and would have been regarded by other states) as bound by the treaties had it not been for this query. Second, the Geneva Conventions are the only instances where there was apparent duplication in the accession on behalf of Namibia: South Africa, according to the attorney-general's letter, had acceded on behalf of Namibia prior to 1966; UNCN acceded on behalf of Namibia in 1983, without expressly claiming to replace the government of South Africa as representative of Namibia. The choice to succeed to South Africa's accession to the Geneva Conventions rather than to UNCN's is interesting given that Namibia became party to the Additional Protocols on the basis of UNCN accession, contained in the same document as UNCN's accession to the Geneva Conventions.[88] Namibia's choice is particularly vexing since it is not even clear on what basis it was asserted that South Africa had extended its own accession to the Geneva Conventions to Namibia. There is no indication of such extension in Swiss documentation concerning the South African instrument of accession or elsewhere. This was, however, the premise of Namibia's action, and was accepted by the depositary. The choice to succeed to South Africa's accession may reflect some doubt within the Namibian government as to the status of UNCN accessions (doubt that was apparently even greater than that as to whether South Africa has acceded to the conventions with respect to Namibia),[89]

[88] On 17 June 1994 the Republic of Namibia deposited the following declaration with the Swiss Federal Council, as depositary of the Protocols (Depositary Notification of 27 July 1994):

> The Ministry of Foreign Affairs wishes to inform that the Protocols are binding on Namibia, in accordance with Article 143 of the Namibian Constitution, which provides that
>
> 'all existing international agreements binding upon Namibia shall remain in force, unless and until the National Assembly acting under Article 63(2)(d) hereof otherwise decides'.
>
> On 18 October 1983, the United Nations Council for Namibia acceded to the Protocols.

[89] This is understandable, given that there had been controversies over the powers of UNCN. See Lawrence L. Herman, 'The Legal Status of Namibia and of the United Nations

leading it to avoid reliance on UNCN action where there was an alternative.

Post-1966 South African treaties **General** A straightforward application of the guidelines given in the *Namibia Advisory Opinion* meant that the few instances where South Africa purportedly extended its treaties to Namibia after 1966 had no legal effect. As noted, Namibian constitutional law nonetheless allows the National Assembly to decide on succession to post-1966 treaties, thereby possibly giving them some effect. In practice, Namibia has not implemented these constitutional provisions.

Kasikili/Sedudu Island The matter of post-1966 South African treaties arose in a case before the ICJ in 1996. Namibia and Botswana submitted an application to the court to determine the boundary around, and legal status of, an island in the Chobe River on the border between Namibia and Botswana (referred to as Kasikili in Namibia, Sedudu in Botswana), on the basis of the Anglo-German Treaty of 1890 and rules and principles of international law.[90]

In interpreting the 1890 treaty, the court took account of practice subsequent to the treaty. One of the events that Botswana raised as relevant was a joint survey carried out at the beginning of July 1985 at the request of the Botswana and South African authorities. Namibia disputed the claim that the survey represented a substantive agreement,[91] but, more importantly, it claimed that an agreement between South Africa and Botswana could not have been validly concluded in 1985, given the incompetence of both states to act with respect to Namibia.[92] The court accepted Namibia's position on the facts, and then added:

Council for Namibia' (1975) 13 *Canadian Yearbook of International Law* 306; Nico J. Schrijver, 'The Status of Namibia and of Its Natural Resources in International Law', in *Proceedings of the Regional Symposium on International Efforts to Implement Decree No 1 for the Protection of the Natural Resources of Namibia, Geneva, Switzerland (27–31 August 1984)*, 17–52; Government of the United States (in its capacity as depositary to the International Atomic Energy Agency), 'Circular Note Sent to the States Parties to the Statute of the International Atomic Energy Agency Concerning the Instrument of Acceptance Tendered by the UNCN – Question of the Accession to Multilateral Treaties by Namibia, as represented by the UNCN' (1983) *United Nations Juridical Yearbook* 192, 192–193.

90 The reference to the 1890 treaty confirms that Namibia considered itself bound by colonial boundary treaties.

91 ICJ, *Kasikili/Sedudu Island Case*, [68].

92 *Kasikili/Sedudu Island Case*, Counter-Memorial of the Republic of Namibia Volume I, [108]–[126]. See www.icj-cij.org/docket/files/98/8578.pdf.

> This is in itself sufficient to dispose of the matter. It is unnecessary to add that in 1984 and 1985 the two States had no competence to conclude such an agreement, since at that time the United Nations General Assembly had already terminated South Africa's Mandate over South West Africa by resolution 2145 (XXI) of 27 October 1966, and the Security Council had approved that measure by resolution 276 (1970) of 30 January 1970. The Court itself, in its Advisory Opinion of 21 June 1971 on the Legal Consequences for States of the Continued Presence of South Africa in Namibia (South West Africa) notwithstanding Security Council Resolution 276 (1970), stated the following in this regard:
>
> '. . . States Members of the United Nations are under obligation to recognize the illegality of South Africa's presence in Namibia and the invalidity of its acts on behalf of or concerning Namibia, and to refrain from any acts and in particular any dealings with the Government of South Africa implying recognition of the legality of . . . such presence and administration'.
>
> Furthermore, the evidence indicates that the Botswana Government's preliminary contacts with the President of the United Nations Council for Namibia and the United Nations Commissioner for Namibia with a view to obtaining their approval prior to the Pretoria meeting of 19 December 1984 were not pursued further, and did not have the result sought by Botswana.[93]

This *obiter dictum* confirmed that agreements purportedly concluded by South Africa after the revocation of the mandate could not have had any validity with regard to Namibia. It also hinted that if UNCN, as a competent authority, had approved the negotiations between Botswana and South Africa, the outcome might have been different. The special character of boundary treaties did not arise in this case, because no treaty had in fact been concluded. If agreement between South Africa and Botswana had been reached and implemented, its invalidity would have been in conflict with the extra-treaty existence of a boundary regime.

The Kunene River Basin Agreement After independence it was suggested that the Kunene River Basin Agreement be brought to parliament to be given force under Article 63(2)(d) of the constitution. The suggestion supports the interpretation of Article 63(2)(d) as permitting the validation of post-1966 South African treaties, despite the difficulties involved in such validation from an international legal perspective. As noted above, no discussion was held in parliament. In addition, there was a tacit understanding that silence on the matter of validity implied acquiescence in the agreement. A permanent joint technical commission established by Namibia and Angola (Portugal's successor), which was tasked with

[93] ICJ, *Kasikili/Sedudu Island Case*, [69], reference omitted, ellipses mine.

reviewing all existing bilateral agreements on water allocation, declared it had no intention of changing the 'existing' legal situation – in which it included the 1969 agreement. Finally, the Namibian and Angolan ministers of agriculture 'validated' the agreement. This was considered sufficient to give force to the agreement despite its having been concluded by South Africa during its illegal administration of Namibia.[94]

Practice regarding the Kunene River Basin Agreement can be reconciled with the earlier invalidity of the treaty, if the 'validation' of the treaty by the two parties is regarded as the conclusion of a new agreement, with terms identical to those of the 1969 one. The content of the agreement was not itself objectionable from an international legal perspective, but only the identity of one of its original parties. That party had been replaced by competent Namibia, and since the 'validation' was carried out by consultation and agreement of the two parties, there was no risk of adverse effect on the non-Namibian party.

An important factor in the stance taken by Namibia with regard to the Kunene Agreement is that it was (together with the other agreements concluded with Portugal and later Angola on water issues) advantageous to Namibian interests. Namibia therefore had an interest in maintaining it in force, rather than insisting on legal formalities that some considered minutiae. This is in contrast to the Kasikili/Sedudu Island controversy, where Namibia had no interest in pursuing the process that had supposedly begun in 1984–1985 and therefore argued forcefully on the basis of the illegality of South Africa's actions.

Practice with respect to UNCN treaties UNCN's bilateral treaties concerned the issuance and recognition of travel and identity documents for Namibian refugees and exiles. Upon independence they became superfluous, and no issue of succession arose.[95]

In contrast, international practice with respect to multilateral treaties concluded by UNCN suggests not only that these treaties continued to exist, but that Namibia did not even need to succeed to them in order to maintain its membership. Instead, there appears to be continuity in

[94] Interview by the author with Dr Sackey Akweenda, Attorney-General's Office 1991–2000, Windhoek, 27 February and 2 March 2004.

[95] Paul C. Szasz, 'Succession to Treaties under the Namibian Constitution' (1989–1990) 15 *South African Yearbook of International Law* 65, 73, suggested that these treaties should be distinguished from the multilateral ones, in that UNCN concluded them not on behalf of Namibia but in its own capacity as a UN administering body.

the presentation of Namibia between UNCN and the Namibian government. This is exemplified by the date of accession recorded by the UN Secretary-General as depositary. Normally, the date on which a treaty enters into force for a successor state is the date of that state's independence (or other critical date for change of responsibility of international relations).[96] However, in all those cases where UNCN acceded on behalf of Namibia to multilateral treaties deposited with the UN Secretary-General, Namibia is recognized today as party from the date of UNCN's accession rather than from the day on which Namibia became independent or notified its succession.[97] Another element of continuity between UNCN and the Namibian government is the absence of a succession notification: the UN Secretary-General generally requires a specific notification in order to consider a state successor to a treaty. In the case of Namibia's succession to UNCN treaties, he forewent this requirement. Finally, the absence of a succession or accession notification is particularly striking in the case of international organizations, where membership is dependent on admission by the organization, and therefore even a clear notification of succession or accession would not normally suffice.[98] Nonetheless, Namibia has been regarded as a member on the basis of UNCN accession without needing to be admitted upon independence by the organization.

It appears that although Namibia was not recognized as independent until February 1990, UNCN was likened to a government of an existing state, the acts of which require no confirmation by a subsequent government.[99] This raises the question whether UNCN's inaction also affects Namibia. Specifically, UNCN's inaction in the area of succession

[96] Compare with VCST Article 17(1).

[97] IAEA: since 1983, www.iaea.org/About/Policy/MemberStates/index.html; FAO: since 1983, www.fao.org/Legal/member-e.htm; UNESCO: since 1978, http://erc.unesco.org/cp/MSList_alpha.asp?lg = E; ITU: since 1984, www.itu.int/cgi-bin/htsh/mm/scripts/mm.list?_search = ITUstates. The UN Secretary-General records Namibia as party, from the date of UNCN's ratification or accession, to the International Convention on the Suppression and Punishment of the Crime of Apartheid, http://untreaty.un.org/ENGLISH/bible/englishinternetbible/partI/chapterIV/treaty9.asp; CERD, Office of the United Nations High Commissioner for Human Rights, 'Status of Ratifications of the Principal International Human Rights Treaties as of 16 June 2006', http://www2.ohchr.org/english/bodies/docs/RatificationStatus.pdf, 8; and UNCLOS, *Law of the Sea Bulletin* No. 43 (NY Division for Ocean Affairs and the Law of the Sea, Office of Legal Affairs UN 2000), 6.

[98] Konrad G. Bühler, *State Succession and Membership in International Organizations, Legal Theory* versus *Political Pragmatism* (The Hague: Kluwer Law International, 2001).

[99] Szasz, 'Succession to Treaties', 72.

from prior treaties may be construed as an implicit adoption of a clean-slate policy. However, it should be borne in mind that UNCN's goal was to advance Namibia's future options without prejudicing them. Its mandate extended to measures that South Africa was incompetent to make on Namibia's behalf, and were deemed necessary for practical or symbolic reasons. There was no need for UNCN to precipitate normative changes that would have eventually taken place without its intervention. It must therefore be assumed that even if certain results emanate from positive action by UNCN, the converse results cannot be inferred from its inaction. In other words, the fact that UNCN did not succeed to prior treaties should not be regarded as an obstacle to Namibian succession to them.

4.3.3 The Baltic states

The status of treaties during the period of non-recognition

International practice relating to prior treaties of the Baltic states was not uniform. Some states, such as the US[100] and France,[101] regarded pre-1940 treaties with the Baltic states as remaining in force, even if not always invocable. States that had recognized the Soviet annexation as valid, and those that had not recognized the annexation but considered that the Baltic states had ceased to exist, such as Switzerland and the UK, considered pre-1940 treaties to have terminated.

Between 1940 and 1990 the USSR entered into numerous treaties. Insofar as the treaties had territorial application, they purported to cover the Baltic states. During that period there was little discussion of the legal status of the Baltic states. States that had refused to recognize the annexation may have considered it unnecessary to reiterate their position with respect to every treaty. The positions of other states were ambiguous.

Transition

Pre-1940 treaties

Most states accepted the Baltic states as continuators of the pre-1940 states and, as a matter of principle, the consequent presumption that

[100] US Department of State *Treaties in Force* issues contain the following statement in the entries of Estonia, Latvia and Lithuania, reproduced every year from the annexation until 1991: 'The United States has not recognized the incorporation of Estonia, Latvia, and Lithuania into the Union of Soviet Socialist Republics. The Department of State regards treaties between the United States and those countries as continuing in force'.

[101] In *Gerbaurd* v. *Meden* (1951) 18 *International Law Reports* 288, the Franco-Latvian Treaty of 1937 was applied.

pre-1940 treaties were still in force.[102] Nonetheless, developments during the fifty years of annexation had rendered many of the treaties obsolete or impracticable.

In many cases, the Baltic states and their treaty partners agreed on a review of individual pre-1940 treaties.[103] Some treaties were subsequently replaced.[104] Others were simply terminated, usually through an official declaration.[105] An example is the protocol which Latvia signed with Norway in 1994. In this protocol, the Governments of Norway and of Latvia, '[p]redicating the non-recognition of the illegal incorporation of Latvia into the former Soviet Union', '[r]ecognizing the continued validity of bilateral treaties entered into between Norway and Latvia in the period between 1920 and 1940', and '[t]aking into account that the agreements entered into in the period between 1920 and 1940 do not fully reflect the new state of affairs in the bilateral Norwegian–Latvian relations', agreed that four agreements 'are considered to have lapsed'.[106] In similar terms, the 1994 protocol between Norway and Lithuania provides that two prior

[102] Succession to treaties is the focus of most of the literature addressing the consequences of continuity of statehood of the Baltic states. See Yolanda Gamarra, 'Current Questions of State Succession Relating to Multilateral Treaties', in Jan Klabbers, Martti Koskenniemi, Olivier Ribbelink and Andreas Zimmermann (eds.), *State Practice Regarding State Succession and Issues of Recognition: The Pilot Project of the Council of Europe* (The Hague: Kluwer Law International, 1999), 424; Rytis Satkauskas, 'États Baltes: Succession ou identité?', memoire de DÉA Université de Paris I Panthéon-Sorbonne (1999–2000).

[103] US–Estonia Diplomatic Relations Memorandum, Article III; US–Latvia Diplomatic Relations Memorandum, Article III; for Polish practice, see Klabbers *et al.*, *State Practice Regarding State Succession*, 773. Finland and Estonia maintained in force only one pre-1940 treaty (on cultural co-operation). Klabbers *et al.*, *State Practice Regarding State Succession*, 772.

[104] United States of America and Latvia 1922 Convention for the Exchange of Money Orders, replaced by the 1993 Postal Money Order Agreement between the United States Postal Service and the Postal Administration of Latvia; United States of America and Lithuania 1923 Convention for the Exchange of Money Orders, replaced by the 1993 Postal Money Order Agreement between the United States Postal Service and the Postal Administration of Lithuania; Renata Szafarz, 'The Practice of Poland as the "Other State Party" and as a Depositary – as Regards Succession of Recently Established States in Respect of Treaties' (1995–1996) 22 *Polish Yearbook of International Law* 221, 223.

[105] Lehto, 'Succession of States in the Former Soviet Union', 217.

[106] On commerce and navigation of 14 August 1924, on abolition of legalization of certificates of origin of 13 May 1929, on reciprocal recognition of tonnage certificates of 10 June 1925 and on extradition and mutual assistance in criminal matters of 12 September 1927, cited in the 1994 Protocol between the Government of the Kingdom of Norway and the Government of the Republic of Latvia on the Agreements governing Bilateral Norwegian–Latvian Relations.

treaties 'are considered to have terminated'.[107] Other declarations on the status of other pre-1940 treaties are much more laconic. The exchanges of notes between the Slovak Republic and Lithuania,[108] as well as between the Czech Republic and Lithuania,[109] declare the 'invalidity' of agreements concluded by Czechoslovakia and Lithuania. These exchanges do not indicate when the termination took place.[110] In none of the termination agreements or exchanges was a legal (as opposed to political or historical) ground for termination specified. Since the termination had no retroactive effect, there was no issue of violating any acquired rights, and mutual consent of the parties was sufficient.

As for multilateral treaties, the three Baltic states consider pre-1940 treaties to continue to be in force. This position was accepted by the UN Secretary-General[111] and by other depositaries.[112]

Post-1940 treaties

All three Baltic states made clear their position that they did not succeed to treaties purportedly entered on their behalf by the USSR. The Lithuanian

[107] On commerce and navigation of 1923, and on reciprocal exemption from road duties on automobiles and other motor vehicles of 1930, cited in the 1994 Protocol between the Government of the Kingdom of Norway and the Government of the Republic of Lithuania on the Agreements governing Bilateral Norwegian–Lithuanian Relations.

[108] 2004 Exchange of Notes between the Slovak Republic and Lithuania concerning the 1923 trade agreement, the 1930 agreement on conciliation and arbitration, the 1931 agreement on abolition of visa requirements, and the 1931 agreement on legal assistance.

[109] 1999 Exchange of Notes between the Czech Republic and Lithuania.

[110] Czechoslovakia's position was that the Baltic treaties had ceased to exist in 1940 – correspondence of the author with Mr Jan Čižek, director of the International Law Department, Ministry of Foreign Affairs, Czech Republic, 18 and 25 April 2005. Slovakia, which relied on its succession to treaties from Czechoslovakia, found it appropriate in 2004 to exchange the notes mentioned above. Since neither of the successor states of Czechoslovakia had the power to terminate treaties that had ceased to exist prior to their independence, the purpose of exchanges was probably only to remove doubts as to the legal situation rather than to create a new one – correspondence of the author with Mr Rytis Satkauskas, Legal and International Treaties Department, Lithuanian Ministry of Foreign Affairs, 30 March–8 August 2005.

[111] Satkauskas, 'États Baltes: Succession ou identité', 59; Estonia, for example, was recorded on the UN treaty database as party from 18 August 1938 to the 1936 International Convention Concerning the Use of Broadcasting in the Cause of Peace.

[112] E.g. the Belgian Ministry of Foreign Affairs. The list of parties to the International Convention for the Unification of Certain Rules of Law Relating to Assistance and Salvage at Sea and Protocol of Signature of 1910, as provided by the depositary, the Ministry of Foreign Affairs of Belgium, lists Estonia as party from 20 February 1930 and Lithuania as party from 26 September 1932. See http://diplomatie.belgium.be/en/binaries/i1_tcm312-79719.pdf.

statement is the most explicit in rejecting Soviet treaties on the ground of the Soviet regime's illegality, informing the UN Secretary-General:

> The Republic of Lithuania was occupied by the USSR on the 15th of June 1940. Many Western countries did not recognize the incorporation of the Republic of Lithuania into the USSR.
>
> Having restored its independence on the 11th of March 1990, the Republic of Lithuania neither is nor can be the successor state of the former USSR. The Republic of Lithuania can not take the responsibility for the treaties concluded by the former USSR, for it neither participated in making those treaties nor influenced them. Therefore the Republic of Lithuania can not take the responsibility for the past treaties concluded by the USSR.[113]

The Estonian and Latvian positions are less explicit on the grounds for, but equally explicit on the invalidity of, post-1940 treaties. Estonia informed the UN Secretary-General:

> Estonia does not regard itself as a party by virtue of the doctrine of treaty succession to any bilateral or multilateral treaties entered into by the USSR. The Republic of Estonia has begun careful review of multilateral treaties in order to determine those to which it wishes to become a party. In this regard it will act on a case-by-case basis in exercise of its own sovereign right in the name of the Republic of Estonia.[114]

Latvia, too, informed the Secretary-General that 'Latvia does not regard itself as party by virtue of the doctrine of treaty succession to any bilateral or multilateral treaties entered into by the former USSR.'[115]

The position of other states was, as issues of potential succession usually are, variable and not uniform.[116] Some states proceeded from the same position as that of the Baltic states, namely that Soviet treaties are invalid

[113] Letter dated 22 June 1995, cited in *Multilateral Treaties Deposited with the Secretary-General, Status as at 1 April 2009, Volume II, Part I, Chapters VIII to XI* (New York: United Nations, 2009), xxxi.

[114] Letter dated 8 October 1991, cited in *Multilateral Treaties Deposited with the Secretary-General, Status as at 1 April 2009, Volume II, Part I, Chapters VIII to XI*, xv; Hanna Bokor-Szegõ, 'Questions of State Identity and State Succession in Eastern and Central Europe', in Mojmir Mrak (ed.), *Succession of States* (The Hague: Martinus Nijhoff, 1999), 99–100.

[115] Letter dated 26 February 1993, cited in *Multilateral Treaties Deposited with the Secretary-General, Status as at 1 April 2009, Volume II, Part I, Chapters VIII to XI*, xxxi.

[116] Hague Academy of International Law, Center for Studies and Research in International law and International Relations, *State Succession: Codification Tested against the Facts* (Dordrecht: Martinus Nijhoff, 1996), 116.

in their respect.[117] Others declared that they considered the clean-slate doctrine to apply, thereby avoiding the question of invalidity.[118]

The Baltic states understood that it would be a long time before new agreements could replace the complete network of post-1940 treaties vis-à-vis states with which relations were particularly close prior to their regaining independence, such as neighbouring states. Yet the legal vacuum that would have been created if the invalidity of post-1940 treaties were upheld strictly was too great to be ignored. Accordingly, pragmatic arrangements were made for such treaties to continue to apply on a provisional basis. For example, in 1992 Finland and Estonia exchanged notes on the temporary application of thirteen agreements concluded by Finland and the USSR. The exchange provided that the agreements would not enter into force, but that only their operative paragraphs would be applied 'for practical reasons *ad interim*', for a period not exceeding three years, pending new agreements.[119] These agreements concerned co-operation in taxation, environmental protection, legal assistance, fishing and maritime delimitation. By 1997, nine bilateral agreements had been concluded to replace the ones applied provisionally. Provisional arrangements were also considered in negotiations between Finland and the other two Baltic states, but the idea was abandoned due to lack of interest on all sides.[120] Likewise, Latvia and Lithuania agreed with Poland on the provisional application of the 1957 Polish–Soviet Agreement on Legal Assistance. Estonia, on the other hand, informed Poland in 1993 that the

117 For the US, see Lucinda Love, 'International Agreement Obligations after the Soviet Union's Break-up: Current United States Practice and Its Consistency with International Law' (1993–1994) 26 *Vanderbilt Journal of Transnational Law* 373; for Norway, see the 1994 Protocol between the Government of the Kingdom of Norway and the Government of the Republic of Lithuania on the Agreements Governing Bilateral Norwegian–Lithuanian Relations; 1994 Protocol between the Government of the Kingdom of Norway and the Government of the Republic of Latvia on the Agreements Governing Bilateral Norwegian–Latvian Relations; For Czechoslovakia and the Czech Republic, correspondence of the author with Mr Jan Čižek, Director of the International Law Department, Ministry of Foreign Affairs, Czech Republic, 18 and 25 April 2005.

118 E.g. the Netherlands, correspondence of the author with Ms Tamara Jaspers, Treaties Division, Legal Affairs Department, Ministry of Foreign Affairs, 1 and 4 April 2005. Dutch policy was in line with the interpretation of its earlier conduct as an implicit recognition of the annexation; see Chapter 2 above.

119 Finland–Estonia Exchange of Notes of 9 January 1992; Lehto, 'Succession of States in the Former Soviet Union', 214–215. Estonia and Finland later agreed to continue the provisional application of five of these agreements and part of a sixth agreement, until 1997.

120 Correspondence of the author with Ms Marja Lehto, head of the Public International Law Unit, Finnish Ministry for Foreign Affairs, 17 May 2005.

same agreement did not apply in their mutual relations.[121] The various provisional arrangements allowed for an organized process of transitional treaty-making. By 2005, none of the post-1940 treaties were being applied (even provisionally) any longer.

The refusal of all three Baltic states to accept the legal force of post-1940 Soviet treaties raises the question of boundary regimes based on such treaties. Between 1940 and 1990 the USSR concluded a number of treaties regarding territorial and maritime delimitation with Sweden, Finland and Poland, and concerning, inter alia, the territories of the Baltic states.

The Act on the Re-establishment of the State of Lithuania states:

> The State of Lithuania stresses its adherence to universally recognized principles of international law, recognizes the principle of inviolability of borders as formulated in the Final Act of the Conference on Security and co-operation in Europe in Helsinki in 1975 . . .

This statement has been read as affirmation that Lithuania accepted as a matter of fact the changes to its borders effected during the period of Soviet rule, both with the Russian Federation and with third states.[122] However, since Lithuania did not digress from the principle that Soviet treaties are invalid in its respect, a basis for accepting these borders has to be identified. The Act can be interpreted as an acknowledgement by Lithuania that in the conflict between invalidity of treaties and the boundary regimes created by them, the latter prevail because of subsequent practice. An example is its position regarding the border with Poland. In 1945 Poland and the USSR concluded a boundary treaty concerning the Polish–Soviet border, covering, inter alia, the boundary between the Soviet Republic of Lithuania and Poland.[123] Once the independence of the Baltic states was restored, Poland accepted that the Baltic states' separation from the USSR was the end of illegal occupation, and considered the three states identical to the pre-war states. Nonetheless, Poland considered Lithuania a successor to the 1945 treaty.[124] Lithuania did not object to preservation of that boundary (by which it gained territories in excess

[121] Szafarz, 'The Practice of Poland', 224.

[122] This reading vindicates the critique that the Helsinki Final Act was an implicit recognition of the annexation; see Chapter 2 above.

[123] For a detailed description of the history of the Lithuanian–Polish boundary, see Wladislaw Czapliński, 'International Legal Aspects of Polish–Lithuanian Relations' (1991–1992) 19 *Polish Yearbook of International Law* 31.

[124] Szafarz, 'The Practice of Poland', 223–224.

of its pre-1940 area), although it did not refer to 'succession' to the 1945 treaty. It allowed the implementation of the boundary regime to trump invalidity, as reflected in a 1994 Treaty on Friendly Relations and Good Neighbourly Cooperation, which stipulates:

remembering the complicated history of the two nations as well as the long term closeness of Lithuanians and Poles and taking into account the possibility for the two nations to interpret the common history of the two states in different ways . . .

with both sides formally ratifying now and for the future the integrity of the current territories, with capitals in Vilnius and Warsaw, *not taking into account how the borders were formed in the past . . .*

Article 2

1. The Contracting parties recognize the inviolability of the existing border between them marked in the territory and mutually commit themselves to respect without any conditions the other's sovereignty and territorial integrity.

2. The parties confirm that they do not have any territorial claims and also will not make any such claims in the future.[125]

The definition of the borders as 'marked in the territory' regardless of 'how the borders were formed' allowed preservation of the 1945 boundary by reference to practice irrespective of the formal status of the 1945 treaty, thus avoiding potential controversy.[126]

The Lithuanian acknowledgement of the boundaries may also have deflected a controversy with Sweden, which held a legal position that was diametrically opposed to that of the Baltic states, having recognized de jure the annexation of the Baltic states by the USSR.[127] In 1988, Sweden and the USSR concluded a maritime delimitation agreement.[128] In 1993,[129] the Swedish government held, 'According to principles of public

125 In the Preamble and Article 2, emphasis added.

126 In 1996 a new boundary treaty was concluded between Lithuania and Poland. It differed slightly from the earlier one, and superseded it. Correspondence of the author with Mr Rytis Satkauskas, Legal and International Treaties Department, Lithuanian Ministry of Foreign Affairs, 30 March–8 August 2005.

127 William J. H. Hough III, 'The Annexation of the Baltic States and Its Effect on the Development of Law Prohibiting Forcible Seizure of Territory' (1985) 6 *New York Law School Journal of International & Comparative Law* 303, 440–443.

128 Agreement Concerning the Delimitation of the Continental Shelf and of the Swedish Fishing Zone and the Soviet Economic Zone in the Baltic Sea.

129 In a bill requesting parliamentary ratification of a bilateral agreement on fisheries, concluded between the Governments of Sweden and Estonia. The policy set out in the bill applied to all three Baltic states.

international law the agreements on territorial delimitation concluded between Sweden and the USSR . . . remain fixed between Sweden and the four new States [the Russian Federation and Baltic states]'.[130] Given that Sweden regarded the annexation as valid and considered the Baltic states successors to the USSR,[131] it is not surprising that it considers the 1988 agreement to be binding upon the Baltic states, in accordance with principles of state succession to boundary treaties under VCST Article 11. Lithuania, for its part, continued to apply the agreement without acknowledging its de jure applicability. It later concluded a treaty with Sweden to replace it.[132]

Similarly, Estonia and Finland only agreed on temporary application of four post-1940 treaties concluded between the USSR and Finland concerning maritime delimitation and boundary regimes.[133] These treaties have since been replaced in part.[134] This arrangement avoided taking a stance on the relationship between the invalidity of the treaty and the resulting boundary regime. The Estonian and Latvian policy of refusing to accept existing boundary treaties with third parties may have been influenced by their dispute with the Russian Federation both over their status and over particular adjustments made to their territories during the period of Soviet rule. Lithuania does not share a border with the Russian Federation other than in Kaliningrad Oblast, and therefore its relation with third states had no direct bearing on its position vis-à-vis the Russian Federation.

Both Estonia and Latvia had concluded boundary treaties with the Russian Federation which allocated to the Russian Federation territory that

130 Pierre Michel Eisemann and Martti Koskenniemi (eds.), *State Succession: Codification Tested against the Facts* (Dordrecht: Martinus Nijhoff, 2000), 96, 314–315 Doc S/66.

131 An earlier text in the same bill explicitly said that, from a Swedish point of view, the Baltic states had acceded to the rights and obligations on fisheries of the USSR. Eisemann and Koskenniemi, *State Succession*, 313.

132 Satkauskas, 'États Baltes: Succession ou identité', 65.

133 1965 Finland–USSR Agreement on the Gulf of Finland; 1967 Finland–USSR Agreement on the North Eastern Part; 1980 Finland–USSR Jurisdiction Agreement and 1985 Finland–USSR Economic and Fishing Zone Agreement; Finland–Estonia Exchange of Notes of 9 January 1992; Lehto, 'Succession of States in the Former Soviet Union', 214–215.

134 1996 Agreement on the Delimitation of the Maritime Zones in the Gulf of Finland and in the Northern Baltic Sea. Another treaty, on the trilateral point of the maritime zones and continental shelves of Finland, Estonia and Russia, in the Gulf of Finland, has been drafted but has not been signed, pending the signature of a bilateral border agreement between Estonia and Russia. Correspondence of the author with Ms Marja Lehto, head of the Public International Law Unit, Finnish Ministry for Foreign Affairs, 17 May 2005.

until 1940 had been under Estonia or Latvia's sovereignty. Latvia pushed for drafting that would confirm the existing border as a matter of practice without recognizing the legal validity of the Soviet annexation. Russia objected to this drafting.[135] Moreover, in their internal legislation relating to the treaties, Estonia and Latvia gave declarations referring to the 1920 Tartu and Riga Peace Treaties, which imply that the two states maintain their territorial claims to the areas in question.[136] In reaction, the Russian Federation refused to ratify the new boundary treaties. Eventually, Latvia amended its ratifying law, so that it only mentions a previous legislative instrument in which the 1920 Riga Peace Treaty is mentioned. In this way, Latvia maintained its legal claims formally, but sufficiently discretely for the Russian Federation to accept the situation.[137] The Latvian–Russian boundary treaty was finally signed and ratified in 2007. The Russian Federation still refuses to ratify the treaty concluded with Estonia.

4.3.4 The TBVC

The TBVC present three unique aspects of the consequences of illegality with respect to treaty relations. One is the purported renouncement by the legal regime (South Africa) of international responsibility for the territory; the second is the purported devolution of this responsibility to an illegal regime (the TBVC) which could not exercise such a responsibility; the third is the existence of purported international treaties between the legal regime and the illegal one, namely between South Africa and the TBVC. These are discussed in turn.

When the TBVC were established, each of the Status Acts provided that 'South Africa shall cease to exercise any authority' over the territories concerned.[138] By this, South Africa purportedly renounced its

135 Vladimir Socor, 'Kremlin Assails Baltic states', *Eurasia Daily Monitor*, issue 93, 12 May 2005; Vladimir Socor, 'Moscow Signs Border Agreement With Estonia', *Eurasia Daily Monitor*, issue 99, 20 May 2005; Vladimir Socor, 'Moscow Refuses to Ratify Border Treaty with Estonia', *Eurasia Daily Monitor*, issue 122, 23 June 2005, all at http://jamestown.org/edm/byregion.php#rid_12. For the Latvian declaration, see www.am.gov.lv/en/policy/bilateral-relations/statement/Declaration.

136 E.g. Act on the Ratification of the State Border Treaty between the Republic of Estonia and the Russian Federation and the Treaty on the Delimitation of Maritime Areas of Narva Bay and the Gulf of Finland between the Republic of Estonia and the Russian Federation.

137 LETA, 'Saeima Conceptually Approves Draft Law on Ratification of Latvia–Russia Border Treaty', 26 April 2007, www.mfa.gov.lv/en/news/DomesticNews/2007/april/26-1/.

138 E.g. Status of Transkei Act, Article 2.

international responsibility for each of the TBVC. The Status Acts also provided for devolution of treaty relations from South Africa to the TBVC.[139] But a devolution agreement is not sufficient for succession, which requires the consent, express or otherwise, of counterparties to the treaties.[140] For such consent, those counterparties must recognize the aspirant successor as an entity capable of succession. Since states were not willing to extend such recognition to the TBVC, the TBVC could not succeed to South African treaties.[141]

Since South Africa and the TBVC were conscious that this devolution was rejected internationally, they concluded a myriad of bilateral and multilateral agreements, ostensibly to facilitate the application, on a purportedly inter-state level, of treaties that had 'previously' applied to the TBVC as internal units of South Africa. For example, South Africa–TBVC agreements provided that South Africa would be responsible for the implementation in the TBVC of the Southern African Customs Union;[142] nationals of the TBVC continued to use South African documents in their travels abroad. In light of these arrangements, the purported devolution never raised any practical problems, because South Africa continued to represent the TBVC internationally, albeit on a purportedly new legal basis, i.e. of delegation of international competence rather than simple sovereignty. The South Africa–TBVC arrangements were regarded, from an international perspective, as domestic law. In addition, following the economic sanctions against South Africa, the opportunities for conflict between the international and the South African approaches were limited. In short, internationally, South Africa's claim not to represent the TBVC was almost inconsequential.[143]

Insofar as multilateral treaties were concerned, South Africa did not notify the depositaries of the treaties to which it was party that the territorial application of the treaties had changed. As a matter of law, it could have advocated that the rule of moving treaty boundaries applied,

139 E.g. Status of Transkei Act, Article 4.

140 VCST Article 17; Sir Arthur Watts, *The International Law Commission 1949–1998* (Oxford: Oxford University Press, 1999), 1078–1084.

141 For a discussion based on the TBVC being states, albeit not recognized ones, see Dermott J. Devine, 'Maritime Conventions and the Reincorporation of the Coastal Homelands into South Africa' (1992–1993) 18 *South African Yearbook of International Law* 127.

142 Interview by the author with Dr Michèle Olivier, University of Pretoria, Pretoria, 7 April 2004.

143 See UK, *Gur Corporation* v. *Trust Bank of Africa*, 624, on non-treaty-related matters.

according to which the territorial reach of treaties follows the boundaries of the state as they change from time to time, with no need for any notification.[144] Under the South African interpretation, once it ceded the territories to the TBVC states, its treaties no longer applied in those territories. As for succession of the TBVC states to these treaties, whether a treaty applies in the ceded territory depends on the law applicable to the international entity to which the territory is ceded.[145] As a practical matter, South Africa did not inform of the purported devolution because it knew that such notification would be rejected.[146] As far as international law and the international community were concerned, South Africa's renunciation through its domestic law had no effect. It remained responsible for its entire territory, and therefore all treaties to which it was party, whether entered into before or after the establishment of each of the TBVC, were applicable to the entire territory of South Africa, including the TBVC.

By repealing the Status Acts and the TBVC constitutions,[147] the South African parliament retracted the grant of independence and the 'devolution' arrangements. This repeal aimed to bring domestic law in line with international law, rather than to effect direct changes under international law. Even according to the rule of moving treaty boundaries, once the TBVC were reincorporated, South African treaties automatically extended back to their territories.

The TBVC have never entered into a treaty as defined in the VCLT with any state other than South Africa. They only concluded non-governmental agreements with Taiwan and with multinational corporations, which stipulated that they were governed by domestic law rather than by international law.[148] Responsibility for TBVC agreements with multinational companies was subrogated under domestic law to the South African

144 VCST Article 35, chapeau; see also Article 14 concerning predecessors of newly independent States; Watts, *The ILC*, 1180.

145 VCST Articles 14, 34.

146 Devine, 'Maritime Conventions', 128. Another route that South Africa might have followed in order to exclude the application of its treaties to the TBVC, at least with regard to treaties that it accepted after granting independence to the TBVC, was to register their non-applicability to the territories of the TBVC as a reservation. However, apart from the doubtful validity of such a reservation, at least with respect to international human rights law (ECtHR, *Ilascu* v. *Moldova and Russia*, [324]), it would have been an implicit admission of sovereignty over the TBVC, which is what South Africa sought to avoid.

147 1993 Interim Constitution Schedule 7.

148 Interview by the author with Dr Michèle Olivier, University of Pretoria, Pretoria, 7 April 2004.

government.[149] The internal allocation of competence within South Africa was not a matter of international law but of constitutional law.

As for South Africa–TBVC treaties, these became extinct upon the reincorporation of the TBVC. Under the pre-1994 South African approach to international law, this was the consequence of the extinction of the international legal personality of a party to a treaty.[150] As far as the international community was concerned, this was an internal matter governed by domestic law.

In theory, the termination of a South Africa–TBVC treaty could have raised a problem, if it infringed upon acquired rights or individual interests based on the treaty. In practice these purportedly international treaties had not been incorporated into South African or TBVC law. Therefore no individual rights had been created that could be violated.[151]

Another potential difficulty could have arisen with respect to outstanding liabilities between the TBVC and South Africa. Article 231 of the Interim Constitution, on continuation of international agreements, stipulates:

> (1) All rights and obligations under international agreements which immediately before the commencement of this Constitution were vested in or binding on the Republic within the meaning of the previous Constitution, shall be vested in or binding on the Republic under this Constitution, unless provided otherwise by an Act of Parliament.

This section was not related to succession of treaties, given that the international personality of South Africa did not change. Rather, it confirmed that treaties to which South Africa was a party before 27 April 1994 continued to be in force, despite the illegitimacy of the previous government.[152] Article 231 was also not intended to address the status of agreements between South Africa and the TBVC. Initially, the provision concerned 'international agreements . . . vested in or binding on the Republic'. This wording clearly excluded agreements between South Africa and the TBVC,

[149] Interview by the author with Dr Michèle Olivier, University of Pretoria, Pretoria, 7 April 2004. For an example of an interest of Bophuthatswana being transferred to South Africa, see US, *Achievers* v. *South Africa Intervenor*.

[150] Aust, *Modern Treaty Law*, 251; McNair, *The Law of Treaties*, 518. But see Phoebe N. Okowa, 'Case Concerning the Gabcíkovo-Nagymaros Project (*Hungary/Slovakia*)' (1998) 47 *International & Comparative Law Quarterly* 688, 692.

[151] Interview by the author with Prof. Neville Botha, Unisa, Pretoria, 8 April 2004.

[152] Michèle Olivier, 'The Status of International Law in South African Municipal Law: Section 231 of the 1993 Constitution' (1993–1994) 19 *South African Yearbook of International Law* 1, 4.

because under the Interim Constitution the TBVC were already part of the republic, and the republic could not be bound by agreements with itself.[153] However, during the technical refinement process, the addition of 'within the meaning of the previous Constitution' was inserted. This modification complicated matters, because under 'the previous Constitution' the republic did not include the TBVC. The constitution thus appeared to preserve agreements between South Africa and the extinct TBVC.[154] Despite this inadvertent anomaly, treaties between South Africa and the TBVC were deemed to have ceased to exist. The allocation of liabilities that had accrued under these agreements was regulated under constitutional law.[155]

4.3.5 Timor-Leste

General

As Indonesia took over the administration of Timor-Leste, Portugal's treaties ceased to be implemented. Formally, however, they remained in force and even to date certain depositaries consider Timor-Leste party to treaties on the basis of Portugal's accession to, and extension to Timor-Leste of, treaties in the beginning of the twentieth century.[156]

Indonesia extended its own treaties to Timor-Leste.[157] This does not appear not have raised any interest, probably since Timor-Leste was a small, secluded and underdeveloped region, which Indonesia maintained inaccessible.[158] Since there was no formal and express refusal to recognize the Indonesian annexation of Timor-Leste, the question of applicability of Indonesian treaties to Timor-Leste was easily brushed aside, with the exception of the Timor Gap affair, discussed below.

153 1993 Interim Constitution, Schedule 1.

154 Olivier, 'The Status of International Law in South African Municipal Law', 6.

155 1993 Interim Constitution, Article 239(3), (4).

156 E.g. the list of parties to the International Convention for the Unification of Certain Rules of Law Relating to Assistance and Salvage at Sea and Protocol of Signature of 1910, as provided by the depositary, Belgium, lists 'Timor' as party (under 'Portugal') since 1914 (available at http://diplomatie.belgium.be/fr/binaries/i2a_tcm313-79745.pdf). The insistence on Portugal's status as administering power throughout the Indonesian administration probably combined with an oversight of Timor-Leste's clean-slate approach, discussed below.

157 ICJ, *East Timor Case*, [32].

158 Lauri Hannikainen, 'The Case of East Timor from the Perspective of Jus Cogens', in *International Law and the Question of East Timor* (London: CIIR-IPJET, 1995); Geoffrey C. Gunn, *East Timor and the United Nations: The Case for Intervention* (Lawrenceville: Red Sea, 1997), 15–21.

Transition

Section 158 of Timor-Leste's constitution stipulates that

> 1. Confirmation, accession and ratification of bilateral and multilateral conventions, treaties, agreements or alliances that took place before the entry into force of the present Constitution shall be decided upon by the respective competent bodies on a case-by-case basis.
>
> 2. The Democratic Republic of East Timor shall not be bound by any treaty, agreement or alliance entered into prior to the entry into force of the Constitution which is not confirmed or ratified or adhered to, pursuant to item 1 above.

This provision effectively adopts the clean-slate approach with respect to both Portuguese and Indonesian treaties, while reserving the right of Timor-Leste to become party to specific treaties if it finds this appropriate, on the basis of previous acts. The reservation of the right to adhere unilaterally to treaties entered into by Indonesia implies that they are not regarded as invalid *ab initio*. In practice, Timor-Leste did not draw on prior action by Portugal or Indonesia, but acceded independently to various treaties.[159]

The Timor Gap affair

Background In 1972, Australia and Indonesia agreed on the delimitation of the waters between their respective coasts.[160] This followed years of controversy over delimitation of the continental shelf, during which Indonesia argued that the two states shared a continental shelf which should be divided along the equidistance line, while Australia maintained that the Timor Trough, a steep cleft extending in an east–west direction about forty nautical miles from the island of Timor and 250–350 nautical miles from Australia, breaks the continental shelf between Australia and the island, so that there are two distinct shelves. Accordingly it demanded that the Trough constitute the boundary.[161] The two states eventually agreed on a boundary that passes roughly one-third of the way north of the Timor Trough towards the line of equidistance, significantly closer to

[159] E.g. CAT, CEDAW, CRC, ICESCR, ICCPR and the Genocide Convention, to which it acceded on 16 April 2003; Geneva Convention, for which it deposited the instrument of accession on 8 May 2003, Depositary Notification P.242.512-Mali/Mauri/Timor.

[160] 1972 Australia–Indonesia Seabed Boundaries Agreement.

[161] Gillian Triggs and Dean Bialek, 'The New Timor Sea Treaty and Interim Arrangements for Joint Development of Petroleum Resources of the Timor Gap' (2002) 3 *Melbourne Journal of International Law* 322, 324.

the Indonesian coast than to that of Australia.[162] In this, Indonesia partly conceded the demand to rely on Australia's definition of the continental shelf.

The delimitation stopped short on either side of the Timor Sea opposite the coast of Timor-Leste, which was then under Portuguese law, thereby creating the Timor Gap. Australia and Portugal did not negotiate maritime boundaries in this area because Australia wished first to secure Indonesian consent to its definition of the boundary, while Portugal awaited the conference on the law of the sea to bolster its own position, which resembled Indonesia's original equidistance claim.[163]

Soon after Indonesia's annexation of Timor-Leste, the matter of negotiating a boundary with Australia across the Timor Gap arose; negotiations began following Australia's recognition of Indonesia's de jure sovereignty over Timor-Leste in February 1979. It has been suggested that Australia's willingness to recognize Indonesia's control over Timor-Leste de facto and later de jure was intended to elicit Indonesian support for Australia's interests in that region.[164]

By then the concept had developed of the exclusive economic zone and the principle of equitable delimitation of overlapping claims to it and to the continental shelf.[165] Indonesia sought to benefit from the new state of the law so that at least the Timor Gap would be delimited in accordance with the equidistance principle, enabling it to exercise authority in the seabed beyond its otherwise narrowly defined continental shelf. Australia maintained its earlier position, and the boundary negotiations over the Timor Gap did not come to fruition. However, exploratory surveys indicating the potential for oil and gas exploitation in the Timor Sea induced the two states to negotiate an agreement on resource exploitation in the area. In 1989 Australia and Indonesia concluded the Timor Gap Treaty (TGT), whereby a 'Zone of Cooperation' was created 'in an area between

162 Robert King, 'Certain Maritime Arrangements in the Timor Sea, the Timor Sea Treaty and the Timor Gap, 1972–2007', submission to the Australian Parliament's Joint Standing Committee on Treaties Inquiry into the Treaty on Certain Maritime Arrangements in the Timor Sea (March 2007), 6.

163 King, 'Certain Maritime Arrangements', 12.

164 King, 'Certain Maritime Arrangements', 18–21; Christine Chinkin, 'Australia and East Timor in International Law', in *International Law and the Question of East Timor* (London: CIIR/IPJET, 1995); Quinton Temby, 'The Blessed Curse' (October 2003) *New Internationalist* 361. For a detailed account of the Australian policy and statements in this regard, see King, 'Certain Maritime Arrangements'.

165 UNCLOS Articles 55, 74, 83.

the Indonesian Province of East Timor and Northern Australia' within which exploitation of petroleum resources could take place.

The zone of co-operation was a joint development area (JDA), a common mechanism used to regulate exploitation of natural resources as an alternative to boundary delimitation.[166] The character of JDAs as provisional alternatives to boundary delimitation is reinforced by Articles 74 and 83(3) of UNCLOS, which provide, with regard to the delimitation of the exclusive economic zone and the continental shelf respectively,

> Pending agreement as provided for in paragraph 1 [on delimitation], the States concerned, in a spirit of understanding and co-operation, shall make every effort to enter into provisional arrangements of a practical nature and, during this transitional period, not to jeopardize or hamper the reaching of the final agreement. Such arrangements shall be without prejudice to the final delimitation.

JDAs sometimes replace boundary delimitation altogether, as in the case of Antarctica.[167] In other cases they serve as interim arrangements,[168] either while boundary delimitation negotiations are under way or when boundary delimitation is deferred,[169] as was the case of the TGT. In some instances a JDA proves a useful prelude to a final agreement on the boundary, because as the extent of exploitable resources becomes known, the question of the ultimate delimitation becomes either easier to settle in a new environment of co-operation or a moot issue, particularly when the resources are depleted.[170]

The zone of co-operation covered the area where the Australian and Indonesian maritime claims overlapped. The benefits of exploitation were to be shared equally between Indonesia and Australia, so as to achieve

166 Francisco Orrego-Vicuña, 'Regional Co-operation in Nonliving Resources: Joint Management Zones', in Peter Bautista Payoyo (ed.), *Ocean Governance: Sustainable Development of the Seas* (Tokyo: UNU, 1994).

167 Sir Arthur Watts, *International Law and the Antarctic Treaty System* (Cambridge: Grotius, 1992), 140.

168 Memorandum of Understanding between Thailand and Malaysia on the Establishment of a Joint Authority for the Exploitation of the Resources of the Seabed in a Defined Area of the Continental Shelf of the two Countries in the Gulf of Thailand (signed 21 February 1979); Agreement between Japan and the Republic of Korea Concerning Joint Development of the Southern Part of the Continental Shelf Adjacent to the Two Countries (signed 30 January 1974, entered into force 22 June 1978) 1225 UNTS 113.

169 Ibrahim F. I. Shihata and William T. Onorato, 'Joint Development of International Petroleum Resources in Undefined and Disputed Areas', in Gerald H. Blake, Martin Pratt, Clive Schofield and Janet Allison Brown (eds.), *Boundaries and Energy: Problems and Prospects* (London: Kluwer Law International, 1998), 434.

170 Shihata and Onorato, 'Joint Development of International Petroleum Resources', 443.

'optimum commercial utilization' of the petroleum resources.[171] This division also aimed at confirming the sovereignty-neutral character of the TGT.[172] It has been suggested that although Indonesia refused to accept the Timor Trough as a boundary line, its consent to Australia's demand that the Trough serve as the basis for delineating the zone of co-operation was a quid pro quo for Australian support of Indonesia's position with regard to boundary delimitation in archipelagic waters.[173]

East Timor Case (Portugal v. Australia) In February 1991 Portugal instituted proceedings in the ICJ against Australia.[174] It maintained that in negotiating and concluding the TGT, initiating its performance, taking internal legislative measures for its application, and continuing to negotiate with Indonesia, Australia had acted illegally: it had infringed upon the rights of the people of Timor-Leste to self-determination and to permanent sovereignty over its natural resources, infringed upon the rights of Portugal as the administering power, and contravened Security Council Resolutions 384 and 389.[175]

As discussed in Chapter 2 above, in a majority decision the ICJ ruled that it had no jurisdiction to hear the case, on the grounds that in order to decide Portugal's claims it would have had to rule on the legality of Indonesia's entry into and continued presence in Timor-Leste, and that it could not do so without Indonesia's consent.

Judge Skubiszewski, in dissent, who considered that the court could have exercised jurisdiction, addressed the significance of Australia's entering into the TGT in terms of Australia's recognition of Indonesia's annexation. He implied that it was a violation by Australia of the obligation of non-recognition, which could have been addressed irrespective of Indonesia's position.[176] Judge Skubiszewski compared the TGT with treaties on the avoidance of double taxation, which Indonesia had successfully concluded, arguably acting also on behalf of Timor-Leste. He made the following distinction:

171 TGT Article 2. 172 Triggs and Bialek, 'The New Timor Sea Treaty', 329.

173 Prof. José Ramos Horta, Timor-Leste's minister of foreign affairs, lecture at Cambridge University, 10 June 2004 (notes on file with the author).

174 Pursuant to their respective acceptances of compulsory jurisdiction under ICJ Statute Article 36(2).

175 *East Timor Case*, [19].

176 *East Timor Case*, dissenting opinion of Judge Skubiszewksi, [126].

no recognition can be implied from the tax treaties. They do not deal with territorial problems, and they do not refer explicitly to East Timor, but concern Indonesian territory under Indonesian legislation for tax purposes alone. This is an issue that could be regulated by the contracting parties without detracting from the posture of non-recognition (if it was adopted) or without entailing recognition. On the other hand, the Timor Gap Treaty refers to 'the Indonesian Province of East Timor' and is based on the assumption of Indonesian sovereignty over that area, which sovereignty Australia has recognized.[177]

This statement suggests that the entry into a treaty with an illegal regime is a violation of the obligation of non-recognition only if the treaty deals with a territorial problem or refers explicitly to territory. However, Judge Skubiszewski's statement should be read in the context of discussing the ICJ's jurisdiction. Judge Skubiszewski suggested that the taxation treaties were not *patently* in violation of the obligation of non-recognition because they did not deal with territorial problems and did not refer explicitly to Timor-Leste. In contrast, the TGT was patently a violation of the obligation, being both expressly applicable to Timorese territory and substantively in violation of the right to self-determination. On this basis he opined that Australia's responsibility for entering into it could be considered without its counterparty (Indonesia) being party to the proceedings.

The Timor Sea Treaty and subsequent agreements The TGT applied unhindered until Indonesia's withdrawal from Timor-Leste. When UNTAET took over the administration of Timor-Leste in 1999, it was granted treaty-making power, in order to enable it to confirm the continued operation of the TGT, and to negotiate an alternative arrangement. Australia was interested in maintaining the TGT regime not only to preserve its generous share of the revenues, but also so that its boundary with Indonesia on both sides of the Timor Gap did not become renegotiable.[178] Representatives of the Timorese people maintained that the TGT was illegal.[179] At the same time, they recognized that the TGT regime should be maintained to ensure legal security for investments in petroleum activities in the Timor Gap.[180] They therefore advocated an agreement on

[177] *East Timor Case*, dissenting opinion of Judge Skubiszewksi, [122].
[178] King, 'Certain Maritime Arrangements', 37.
[179] Triggs and Bialek, 'The New Timor Sea Treaty', 328.
[180] Frank Brennan, 'The Timor Sea's Oil and Gas: What's Fair' (North Sydney Catholic Social Justice Series, No. 51, 2004); J. R. V. Prescott, 'Australia – United Nations Transitional Administration in East Timor (UNTAET)' in Jonathan I. Charney and

a transitional period, following which the share of revenues should be changed so as to grant the lion's share to Timor-Leste, in whose maritime area the majority of oilfields lay.[181] UNTAET and Australia therefore agreed in an exchange of notes of the year 2000 to continue the 'terms' of the TGT, so that while the TGT itself was at an end, its basic provisions continued to apply.[182]

Australia and the intended leadership of Timor-Leste could not reach agreement on a maritime boundary. The Timorese therefore emphasized that any replacement treaty to the TGT would be an administrative arrangement and not a boundary delimitation, which they hoped would be negotiated on different terms. Australia, on the other hand, objected to a 'renegotiation of boundaries'.[183] To pre-empt the risk that Timor-Leste open adversarial legal proceedings, Australia deposited on 21 March 2002 a declaration excluding from its acceptance of the compulsory jurisdiction of the ICJ 'any dispute concerning or relating to the delimitation of maritime zones, or arising out of, concerning, or relating to the exploitation of any disputed area of or adjacent to any such maritime zone pending its delimitation'.[184] It also made a declaration under UNCLOS that it did not accept any of the mechanisms for dispute resolution 'with respect to disputes concerning the interpretation or application of articles 15, 74 and 83 relating to sea boundary delimitations as well as those involving historic bays or titles'.[185]

Upon Timor-Leste's independence, on 20 May 2002, Australia and Timor-Leste signed the Timor Sea Treaty (TST) on the joint development of petroleum resources of the Timor Sea. The Treaty created a Joint Petroleum Development Area (JPDA) that covered the same area as the zone of co-operation under the TGT.[186] The revenue sharing was changed, however, from 50%–50% to 90%–10% in favour of Timor-Leste, applicable

Robert W. Smith (eds.), *International Maritime Boundaries* (The Hague: Martinus Nijhoff, 2002), Volume IV, 2758.

181 King, 'Certain Maritime Arrangements', 40.

182 This practice is similar to that of the Nordic and Baltic states.

183 King, 'Certain Maritime Arrangements', 48–49.

184 Declaration of 22 March 2002, http://www.icj-cij.org/jurisdiction/index.php?p1=5&p2=1&p3=3&code=AU.

185 *Law of the Sea Bulletin*, No. 48 (NY Division for Ocean Affairs and the Law of the Sea, Office of Legal Affairs, UN, 2002), 16.

186 Compare with Parliament of the Commonwealth of Australia, Joint Standing Committee on Treaties, 'Report 49 The Timor Sea Treaty' (Canberra, November 2002), point 3.10.

retroactively from the date of Timor-Leste's independence.[187] Until the new agreement came into effect,[188] an exchange of notes, also of 20 May 2002, maintained the less-favourable terms of the TGT, while the TGT itself was considered terminated.

The TST envisaged the signing of an International Unitization Agreement (IUA) of the Greater Sunrise Oilfield, which straddles the JPDA.[189] Timor-Leste was reluctant to sign the IUA, because it regards the entire Greater Sunrise Oilfield as falling within its own maritime boundaries, while the revenue sharing to which Australia agreed under the IUA was 79.9%–20.1% in Australia's favour. However, Australia threatened not to ratify the TST until Timor-Leste consented to the IUA.[190] Without ratification of the TST, the less-beneficial division of profits from the JDA would have continued, as provided under the 2002 exchange of notes. In addition, exploitation of another oilfield (Baya Udan) was likely to collapse, depriving Timor-Leste of urgently needed short-term funds. Timor-Leste therefore reluctantly signed the IUA in March 2003. At the same time the Australian parliament ratified the TST.[191]

Disagreement over boundary delimitation continued. Timor-Leste declared that it would not ratify the IUA until boundary delimitation negotiations were under way, while Australia maintained that such negotiations would not begin until Timor-Leste ratified the IUA.[192] After Timor-Leste had expressed interest in 'creative' solutions, Australia proposed that Timor-Leste put the issue of permanent maritime boundary delimitation on hold for a number of decades, and in return Australia would accept changes to the system of revenue sharing, from 79.9%–20.1% in its own favour, under the IUA, to 50%–50%. Timor-Leste consented, and on 12 January 2006 the two states signed the Treaty on Certain Maritime Arrangements in the Timor Sea (CMATS), under which they would share equally in the revenues under the IUA, and put on hold their claims to jurisdiction and maritime boundaries in the Timor Sea for fifty years.[193] The CMATS expressly provides that the parties shall not be under an obligation to negotiate permanent maritime boundaries for the duration of

187 TST Article 25.

188 Timor-Leste ratified the TST on 17 December 2002. Following Australian ratification, it came into force on 2 April 2003.

189 TST Annex E.

190 King, 'Certain Maritime Arrangements', 52.

191 The IUA was signed on 6 March 2003. The TST was presented to the Australian Parliament for ratification on 5 March 2003.

192 King, 'Certain Maritime Arrangements', 57.

193 CMATS Articles 4, 5, 12.

the treaty. This provision pre-empts any Timorese claim that Australia's refusal to conduct such negotiations is a show of bad faith.[194] The parties will also not commence any dispute settlement proceedings against the other that would raise the delimitation of maritime boundaries in the Timor Sea.[195] Timor-Leste ratified the IUA and the CMATS on 20 February 2007. The two agreements entered into force on 23 February 2007.

The effect of the TGT on Timor-Leste's subsequent obligations The TGT was concluded by a party which acquired its treaty-making power through a violation of a peremptory norm. The TGT's content was itself in violation of a peremptory norm, depriving the Timorese of the right to dispose of their natural resources. In short, the TGT should have been treated as an invalid treaty. It nonetheless had consequences beyond the period of Indonesian administration.

Formally, the post-independence instruments are not related to the TGT. The 2002 exchange of notes, for example, expressly provides that in agreeing to continue the pre-independence arrangements until the entry into force of the TST, Timor-Leste did not recognize the validity of the TGT or the validity of the 'integration' of Timor-Leste into Indonesia.[196] Yet in fact, the existence of the TST is a direct consequence of the existence of the TGT, and except for the revenue sharing, the TST duplicates the TGT. This is acknowledged, for example, in the preamble to the TST, which recalls that the parties are 'aware of the need to maintain security of investment for existing and planned petroleum activities in an area of seabed between East Timor and Australia'. One might argue that Timor-Leste was coerced into concluding the TST in order to ensure continuity from the TGT. Most of the pressure originated from threats of the oil companies to withdraw their investments.[197] There was also substantial

[194] CMATS Article 3(7). CMATS Article 3(1) even suggests that Timor-Leste is prohibited from making direct requests for negotiations, as it provides that neither party 'shall . . . pursue . . . by any means in relation to the other Party its claims to sovereign rights and jurisdiction and maritime boundaries for the period of this Treaty'.

[195] CMATS Article 4. [196] 2002 Exchange of Notes Article 8.

[197] E.g. John Phaceas, 'Darwin Gas Pipeline back on as East Timor Backs off', *Weekend Australian*, 22 December 2001, www.etan.org/et2001c/december/16–22/22darwin.htm. This pressure continued with regard to ratification of the IUA; see e.g. David King and Agence France Presse, 'Woodside Taps Timor over Treaty', *Australian*, 14 April 2004, www.etan.org/et2004/april/15–21/14woodsd.htm.

political pressure by Australia.[198] But this was not a case of coercion which gives rise to a right to terminate the treaty. There was no personal coercion of a representative of Timor-Leste, nor any use of force,[199] and the oil companies were legally entitled to withdraw their investments.

A separate question is whether the TGT has prejudiced Timor-Leste's maritime boundary delimitation. The TGT and all subsequent agreements between Timor-Leste and Australia explicitly and meticulously deny any possibility of relying on them or on subsequent practice in any manner relating to boundary delimitation. They provide that

1. Nothing contained in this Treaty shall be interpreted as:

(a) prejudicing or affecting Timor-Leste's or Australia's legal position on, or legal rights relating to, the delimitation of their respective maritime boundaries;

(b) a renunciation of any right or claim relating to the whole or any part of the Timor Sea; or

(c) recognition or affirmation of any right or claim of the other Party to the whole or any part of the Timor Sea.

2. No act or activities taking place as a result of, and no law entering into force by virtue of, this Treaty or the operation thereof, may be relied upon as a basis for asserting, supporting, denying or furthering the legal position of either Party with respect to maritime boundary claims, jurisdiction or rights concerning the whole or any part of the Timor Sea.[200]

While Timor-Leste's interests in the short term are better served under the CMATS than under the TGT (in terms of revenues), it is likely that had it not been for the TGT in the first place, it would have had much greater leverage against Australia. Indeed, had it not been for the TGT, Timor-Leste's rights over the Timor Gap might have been recognized to the complete exclusion of Australia. Australia's reservations to the international tribunals' jurisdiction and its reluctance to negotiate maritime delimitation with Timor-Leste suggest that it does not consider that it has a good claim to maintain the existing line as a maritime boundary.[201]

198 King, 'Certain Maritime Arrangements'; Hamish McDonald, 'Timor Gas Billions All at Sea', *Sydney Morning Herald*, 27 March 2002, www.etan.org/et2002a/march/24-31/27smh.htm, last accessed 13 April 2010.

199 VCLT Articles 51, 52.

200 CMATS Article 2. Similar provisions are TGT Article 2(3), TST Article 2, IUA Article 1.

201 Australia resisted holding negotiations until November 2003. It then wished to hold meetings no more than twice yearly, while Timor-Leste wishes to hold them monthly. (March 2004) 5 *La'o Hamutuk Bulletin* 5; House of Representatives, Congressional Records – Extensions of Remarks E1423 (20 July 2004) (Mr Dennis J Kucinich).

However, the fifty-year moratorium on recourse to third-party dispute resolution[202] and Australia's reservations distance Timor-Leste from any legal forum in which to raise arguments on maritime delimitation. If an eventual boundary agreement is reached through bilateral negotiations, Australia's greater political power may compensate for its legal disadvantage.

In conclusion, the conduct of the illegal regime left the rights of the post-transition regime hostage to the power of a third party. The obligation of non-recognition failed to protect the ousted sovereign or the interests of the post-transition regime, because it was ignored by a party (Australia) strong enough to influence both the illegal regime and, later, the post-transition regime.

4.3.6 The TRNC

Treaties applicable to the Republic of Cyprus prior to 1983 are still applied with respect to the government-controlled part of the island,[203] but are not applied in the TRNC.[204] There are agreements between Turkey and the TRNC that the two parties consider international treaties. In view of the policy of non-recognition, internationally these are considered instruments of a non-international character. There are no treaties between the TRNC and other states.

The current situation in the TRNC is partly comparable with that of the TBVC in that the TRNC has agreements with the only state recognizing it; the similarity goes further in that there is an alternative legal argument to the law of treaties which permits international law to regard such agreements as valid despite the obligation of non-recognition. In the case of the TBVC, they were regarded as domestic legal instruments. In the case of the TRNC, they are regarded as agreements between the occupying power and an indigenous government.[205] However, there the similarity ends between the TRNC and the TBVC, because the expected resolution of the conflict is different. The TBVC were reincorporated into the state with which they had agreements. For this reason it was clear that South Africa–TBVC treaties became extinct or at most became a matter of domestic law. In contrast, there is no serious prospect of the TRNC

202 CMATS Article 3.

203 Unless their subject matter is the northern part of the island – the author is not aware of any such treaties.

204 ECJ, *The Queen* v. *Minister of Agriculture* (ex parte *Anastasiou*), 3116.

205 Geneva Convention IV, Article 47; Eyal Benvenisti, *The International Law of Occupation* (Princeton, NJ: Princeton University Press, 1993), 99.

being incorporated into Turkey. Therefore the prospective status of existing agreements between the TRNC and Turkey remains a pertinent issue. To regulate the situation, Annex V of the Foundation Agreement contains a list of treaties that would be preserved as international treaties binding upon the UCR, including fifty-six agreements between the TRNC and Turkey. Other treaties will terminate upon reunification. This can be justified by their invalidity *ab initio*, or, according to international law as perceived by the TRNC, by the extinction of one of the concluding parties, the TRNC.

4.4 Conclusions

4.4.1 Transition with respect to prior treaties

Whether the illegal regime claimed to succeed to prior treaties or not depended on whether continuity supported its territorial claim. South Africa had an interest in invoking prior treaties with regard to Namibia, to support its claim that no change had taken place with regard to its rights in that territory. In contrast, continuity of treaty relations would have conflicted with the claims of annexing states, namely the USSR and Indonesia. In cases of purported statehood, i.e. Rhodesia and the TRNC, continuity of treaty relations is inconclusive evidence of international status. It could have been interpreted either as an acknowledgement that the incoming regime is a successor to the previous regime, or that it is an illegal regime but the treaties continued to exist because the ousted regime continues to exist in law. Accordingly, practice of the illegal regimes was not uniform.

Doctrinal analysis suggests that prior treaties, namely treaties that preceded the illegal regime, survive the duration of the illegal regime, and are reactivated once the illegal regime withdraws. Practice of the post-transition regime largely follows this analysis. In many cases, the protracted non-invocation of bilateral treaties during the period of non-recognition made the reactivation difficult, and arrangements were made to replace the treaties. But this replacement itself demonstrates the premise that the prior treaties survive the illegal regime and should be addressed through the general laws of treaties and state succession. The policies and practice of Rhodesia and Namibia towards prior treaties is comparable with that of post-colonial, newly independent states. Neither the illegality nor the non-recognition of the illegal regimes seem to have had any discernible bearing on the matter.

Perhaps surprisingly, the lengthy existence of an illegal regime has even facilitated the process of transition with regard to treaties. It was sufficiently long to have rendered various prior treaties so outdated that it was not difficult to reach mutual consent on terminating them, irrespective of their precise status under international law. The period of non-recognition generated facts relevant for the application of the law of state succession (and continuity).

The same applied with respect to multilateral treaties, although in respect to those, the willingness of the post-transition regime to succeed to prior treaties was greater. This is unsurprising given that individual states have no power to renegotiate multilateral treaties. If the post-transition regime wanted to be party to the multilateral treaties in question, it had nothing to gain by terminating its membership in them. Under the circumstances, it was simpler to succeed to them.

4.4.2 Treaties concluded by the illegal regime

Treaties purportedly concluded by an illegal regime are invalid *ab initio*. Under the law of state succession, the post-transition regime does not have a choice whether to succeed to them or not. Nonetheless, the constitutional instruments of Namibia and Timor-Leste provide for such an option, even if this option has never been acted upon. Namibia adopted a pick-and-choose policy, succeeding to and validating treaties that were beneficial to it, and refusing to do so when they were not. The circumstances governing the Kunene River Basin Agreement, the only post-1966 South African treaty that Namibia attempted to validate, demonstrate the importance of a consensual process beyond the formal constitutional authorization. The Annan Plan also envisages an endorsement of TRNC treaties with Turkey, which is not likely to argue that the treaties are invalid due to the illegality of the TRNC.

A number of factors led to the adoption of a flexible, pragmatic approach towards treaties of the illegal regime. One is the tremendous political changes that took place in the post-transition regimes, which made the status of treaties of the illegal regimes a minor issue. Particularly in Namibia, the receptiveness to treaties of the illegal regime reflected a change of mindset, namely the abandonment of discourse on the illegality of the South African regime, and a self-perception of Namibia as a state emerging from ordinary colonial rule. Another factor is perhaps the indeterminate legal status of the treaties, given the ambiguous positions adopted by counterpart states on the illegality of the exiting regime. The pragmatic approach also avoided disputes over legal issues where all parties had similar substantive interests. The post-transition regimes' matter-of-fact attitude may also have been motivated by their limited political clout. Mälksoo notes the reservation of the international community to entertain territorial claims against the Russian Federation.[206] This lack of support may have discouraged the Baltic states from taking issue with third states, towards which there was even less international censure than towards the Russian Federation. Timor-Leste's political and economic inferiority, too, prevented it from presenting a strong opposition to continuation of the terms of the TGT with Australia.

In conclusion, where states acknowledged the illegality of the annexation, the consequences of non-recognition are hardly disputed. Where states express themselves equivocally on the legality of the annexation, the struggle of the post-transition regimes to assert their principled position was more difficult. In this sense, the consequences of non-recognition appear to be largely in the hands of third states.

This conclusion is reinforced by an examination of the situation in South Africa. Non-recognition led the South African and TBVC governments to make arrangements to circumvent the non-recognition of the TBVC. Prima facie, non-recognition fulfilled its role of preventing the consequences of recognition from taking effect. In practice, however, the illegality became invisible to the international community, and the illegal regimes could operate unhindered, instead of being paralysed by the international community's refusal to co-operate with them.

206 Lauri Mälksoo, *Illegal Annexation and State Continuity: The Case of the Incorporation of the Baltic States by the USSR* (Leiden: Martinus Nijhoff, 2003), 250.

5 The effect of transition on the domestic law of the territory

When pleading the case for an obligation of non-recognition of South Africa's acts in Namibia, the UN Secretary-General noted that

> It will be the prerogative of the future Legislative Assembly of Namibia . . . to decide whether, and to what extent, to recognize or validate any act undertaken under void laws during the illegal South African presence, or to grant retroactive validation to any such law having an otherwise acceptable content.[1]

The present chapter examines whether the Secretary-General's statement, that the post-transition regime enjoys the prerogative of validating acts of the illegal regime or rejecting them, was correct as a matter of law and practice. Like the Secretary-General, this chapter focuses on law of the illegal regime which has acceptable content and would have been valid if it were not for the illegality of the regime.[2]

5.1 Doctrine

5.1.1 The post-transition regime's freedom of action

The obligation of non-recognition is aimed at preventing the consolidation of the illegal regime in the territory. Its *raison d'être* disappears once the illegal regime comes to an end. Since the underlying rationale for the obligation is ultimately the protection of the rights of the lawful regime, it is untenable that these rights should be prejudiced by the illegality of the previous regime any more than they should be prejudiced by its

[1] *Namibia Advisory Opinion*, Written Statement of the Secretary General, ICJ Pleadings Volume I, [146].

[2] In this chapter the terms 'law', 'norms' etc. indicate purported law of an illegal and non-recognized regime. The legal validity of that law is the subject matter of this chapter.

effectiveness. Accordingly, the obligation of non-recognition per se should not have any effect binding upon the post-transition regime. The post-transition regime should be free to decide whether, and to what extent, to reverse the consequences of the acts of the illegal regime in order to bring them into line with the invalidity of the illegal regime's acts. It should also be free to decide whether, and to what extent, to give legal effect to norms or acts of the illegal regime in order to bring its domestic law into line with factual changes that have taken place. In this respect, transition under international law from an internationally illegal regime differs from transition under domestic law from a domestically illegal regime, such as was the post-Civil War situation in the United States. In the latter case, where the illegality derives from domestic law and the constitutional system remains intact, the post-transition regime acts within that same constitutional system which regards the previous regime as illegal, and therefore its law must follow the consequences of that illegality to its logical end. In the former case, where the illegality derives from international law, the post-transition regime and the illegal regime do not share the same ground norm,[3] and therefore the post-transition regime is not, in principle, legally bound in any way to the consequences of the illegality. If the post-transition regime voluntarily endorses the acts of the illegal regime, the legal effect of those acts derives from the post-transition regime's free sovereign will. The previous violation of a peremptory norm is no longer the basis of the acts, and therefore the previous illegality becomes immaterial.

The freedom of the post-transition regime to reverse the consequences of the acts of the illegal regime should not be confused with, or analogized from, the clean-slate doctrine of state succession. State succession is a forward-looking doctrine, premised on the validity of actions of the previous regime, and concerned with the maintenance of this validity under the new legal order. In contrast, transition from an illegal regime is premised on the invalidity of the actions of the previous regime. The question is whether this difference has any practical implications. Although the post-transition regime is not bound by the obligation of non-recognition or by the acts of the illegal regime as such, it may be obligated under norms of international law, other than those relating to territorial status, to give legal effect to the consequences of the acts of the illegal regime. In that case, the difference between transition from

[3] Hans Kelsen, *General Theory of Law and State* (New Brunswick: Transaction Publishers, 2006; originally published Cambridge, MA: Harvard University Press, 1949) 111.

an illegal regime and state succession diminishes considerably. One set of such constraints on the freedom of the post-transition regime which is particularly relevant to acts under domestic law is international human rights law.

5.1.2 Retroactive effect of criminal norms of the illegal regime

At the time of transition, the validity of the illegal regime's norms (as opposed to the validity of its acts under the norms) is of little practical significance. One area of law where exceptionally the validity of the norms themselves arises, and therefore requires particular attention, is criminal law, which includes the prohibition on retroactive penalization.

The prohibition on retroactive penalization, namely that no one should be held guilty of a criminal offence on account of an act which did not constitute a criminal offence under domestic or international law at the time it was committed,[4] has been part of domestic criminal legal systems from as early as the thirteenth century.[5] Today it is a basic tenet of international human rights law, embodied in various international and regional human rights treaties,[6] although it may have emerged as such only subsequent to some of the events examined in this book.[7] The essence of the prohibition of retroactive penalization is to provide a safeguard against arbitrary prosecution, conviction and punishment. It places a general duty on states to define criminal offences precisely and by law,[8] so that individuals know what acts and omissions will make them criminally liable. For this, the law must also be accessible.

The foreseeablilty of law is measured in light of actual legal practice, rather than by reference to formal applicability alone. Thus, for example, the ECtHR has ruled that the enforcement of unwritten norms of common law, where such enforcement was foreseeable, did not violate the

[4] ICCPR, Article 15; ECHR, Article 7.

[5] Emilio von Hofmannsthal, 'War Crimes Not Tried under Retroactive Law' (1947) 22 *New York University Law Quarterly Review* 93, 93–96.

[6] ICCPR Article 15; ECHR Article 7; UDHR Article 9; Banjul Charter Article 7(2).

[7] In *Eichmann* v. *Attorney-General of Israel*, Case No. 336/61, Supreme Court Judgment of 29 May 1962 (1962) 36 *International Law Reports* 277, 281–282, the Supreme Court of Israel held that there was no prohibition in international law on retroactive penal legislation, quoting Julius Stone, *Legal Controls of International Conflict: A Treatise on the Dynamics of Disputes- and War-Law*, 2nd edn (Sydney: Maitland Publications, 1959); and Hans Kelsen, *Peace through Law* (Chapel Hill: University of North Carolina Press, 1944).

[8] Manfred Nowak, *U.N. Covenant on Civil and Political Rights: CCPR Commentary*, 2nd edn (Kehl: N. P. Engel, 2005), 359–361.

prohibition on retroactive penalization.[9] Under the same logic, the fact that the illegal regime's law is invalid under international law is less significant than its actual enforcement in the territory. Holding a person criminally responsible under the norms of the illegal regime for acts committed during the existence of that regime and while its norms were enforced is permissible, irrespective of the formal status of those norms. In fact, recourse to that law is even mandated (if the post-transition regime wishes to apply criminal law at all), because while the illegal regime enforces its law effectively, individuals in the territory have no reason to expect to be held to account under any other law. It does not matter whether individuals are aware of the illegality of the regime and of the legal implications of this illegality.

The ECtHR has treated this matter peripherally. Under its jurisprudence, the effective enforcement of an illegal regime's criminal norms – even those that entrench its control over the territory – entails that they be regarded as *valid* law for ECHR purposes during the regime's existence.[10] If the criminal norms of the illegal regime are regarded as valid during the existence of the illegal regime, their application by the post-transition regime is clearly not retroactive. Replacing them by any other law, including prior law of the territory, would violate the qualitative requirements of accessibility and foreseeability, and would constitute prohibited retroactive penalization.[11] It follows that if the post-transition regime wishes to exercise its powers under domestic criminal law with respect to acts committed during the existence of the illegal regime, it may only apply the criminal norms of the illegal regime that were enforced during that period.

5.1.3 Prospective validity of acts of the illegal regime

The principal question facing the post-transition regime is the future of acts carried out by the illegal regime under its own law. The post-transition regime may opt for validation of such past acts. Harder questions arise if the post-transition regime attempts to reverse or ignore the effect of

[9] *SW* v. *the United Kingdom*, Application No. 20166/92, Judgment of 22 November 1995 (1995) Series A No. 335-B, [34]–[36]. This is also the common interpretation of ICCPR Article 7. Nowak, *CCPR Commentary*, 360 marginal 3.

[10] *Protopapa* v. *Turkey*, [94].

[11] At issue here are norms emanating from domestic law and not customary international criminal law, which may be enforceable even if they did not form part of the illegal regime's written domestic law.

the illegal regime's acts. To what extent is the post-transition regime permitted to do so?

A distinction has to be made between giving effect to an illegal regime's acts as a matter of law, and taking account of these acts as a matter of fact. The acts of the illegal regime have a direct normative value only if they are valid under the *Namibia* exception, and only if this normative value survives the transition. Acts which are invalid *ab initio* have no normative value in themselves. However, they may generate factual changes, and those may eventually carry normative consequences for the post-transition regime. In other words, even if the post-transition regime is free to ignore the purported normative changes made by the illegal regime, it might not be free to ignore the effect of these changes on the ground. The constraints on the post-transition regime in this respect derive primarily from international human rights law, and must be considered with respect to each area of law separately.

The following review demonstrates that, by and large, post-transition regimes have opted for continuity in the law that had previously been enforced by the illegal regime (albeit under a new constitutional order), implicitly giving effect to acts carried out under that law. Exceptionally, in particular areas the post-transition regime rescinded the acts of the illegal regime on the basis of the latter's illegality. These areas of law are considered in subsequent chapters.

5.2 Practice

5.2.1 Rhodesia

Rhodesia under the Smith regime maintained the law that was applicable prior to UDI, with some constitutional changes ensuing from its transformation into a republic. Rhodesian courts faced the question of the validity of acts of the Smith regime in a series of cases concerning detention orders issued under emergency legislation promulgated after UDI.[12] While concurring in the validity of the orders, the judges differed as to the basis of that validity. For some, the validity of the orders hinged upon the legal order that applied prior to UDI;[13] others relied on the de

[12] Rhodesia, *Madzimbamuto and Baron* v. *Lardner-Burke (GD)*, Rhodesia, *Madzimbamuto and Baron* v. *Lardner-Burke (AD)*, UK, *Madzimbamuto and Baron* v. *Lardner-Burke and Another (Privy Council)*; *Ndhlovu and Other* v. *the Queen*; *Dhlamini and Others* v. *Carter and Another (No. 3)*. For a review of the entire series of cases, see J. M. Eekelaar, 'Rhodesia: The Abdication of Constitutionalism' (1969) 32 *Modern Law Review* 19.

[13] *Madzimbamuto and Baron* v. *Larder-Burke (GD)*, 166.

facto existence of independent Rhodesia to justify the validity of the specific legislation,[14] or on its de jure recognition by the courts themselves.[15] These judgments closed the door on raising within Rhodesia any further challenge to the validity of Rhodesian acts.

Continuity of the legal order, particularly with regard to land allocation, was a vital component of the Smith regime's consent to withdraw from power. Since the UK parliament was aware of the potential controversy over the validity of Rhodesian law, it defined the government's powers broadly. It empowered the governor to 'make laws for the peace, order and good government of Southern Rhodesia, including . . . the continuation, with such adaptations, qualifications, exceptions and modifications as he may deem appropriate, of provisions purporting to have effect as law immediately before the appointed day'.[16] The order also authorized the governor to validate transactions entered into during the period since 11 November 1965.[17] This authorization avoided any statement as to the validity of the norms enforced until the governor's re-entry.

The governor's first ordinance concerned prospective law, and provided that 'all laws in Southern Rhodesia immediately before . . . the Governor assumed office . . . shall have full force and effect as law on and after the appointed day'.[18] In light of the terminology of the authorizing order, the unqualified reference to 'laws' (rather than to 'provisions purporting to have effect as law') might suggest an implicit admission of the validity of Rhodesian legislation prior to 1980. However, the emphasis in the ordinance was prospective, and it would be imprudent to attach to it great significance with respect to pre-1980 law. The governor did not make any legal provision on pre-1980 law, and the validity of Rhodesian norms between 1965 and 1980 does not seem to have arisen at a later stage.

There were few exceptions to the continued effect of Rhodesia's law. One was an amnesty law adopted by the governor, which pardoned persons

[14] Judges AJA Fieldsend and AJA Jarvis in *Madzimbamuto and Baron* v. *Lardner-Burke (AD)*.

[15] Judges JP Quénet and JA Macdonald in *Madzimbamuto and Baron* v. *Lardner-Burke (AD)*.

[16] Southern Rhodesia Constitution (Interim Provision), Order 1979, Section 4, approved by the House of Commons on 12 December 1979, and by the House of Lords on 17 December 1979.

[17] The Lord Privy Seal Sir Ian Gilmour in Hansard, HC Volume 975, Column 1485 (12 December 1979); Lord Trefgane in Hansard HL Volume 403, Column 1515 (17 December 1979).

[18] Southern Rhodesia Constitution (Interim Provisions), Ordinance 1979, Section 4.

acting in 'furtherance of or designed to frustrate the rebellion', satisfying both sides of the liberation war.[19]

5.2.2 Namibia

The revocation of the mandate had no discernible effect on the law that was enforced in Namibia. South Africa continued legislating for Namibia, and enforced its law through the executive and judicial authorities, making no distinction between pre-revocation and post-revocation acts.

The validity of South African law in Namibia was considered by domestic courts on two occasions. *S* v. *Tuhadeleni and Others* concerned the validity of the Terrorism Act of 1967, under which SWAPO members were arrested and convicted in 1968, and which triggered the Security Council's action which eventually led to the request for the *Namibia Advisory Opinion*. The defendants argued that the South African parliament was incompetent to enact the Terrorism Act, because the legislative competence of the parliament had been extended to Namibia only under the mandate; and at the time that the Terrorism Act was enacted, the mandate had already been revoked. The court of first instance and the court of appeal rejected this plea on the ground that under the then-South African constitution they had no jurisdiction to inquire into the validity of an Act of parliament.[20]

A similar ruling was given in *Binga* v. *Administrator-General, South West Africa and Others*. The applicant challenged the extension of compulsory military service in Namibia to non-white inhabitants of the territory. He argued, inter alia, that following the revocation of the mandate, the South African parliament was incompetent to legislate for Namibia. The majority in the South West Africa Supreme Court (a South African court) ruled that since the government of South Africa had internal sovereignty over the territory of Namibia, the matter was non-justiciable before a domestic court.[21] Justice Mouton added in a separate opinion that Resolution 276(1970) was not binding, and that any findings in the *Namibia Advisory*

[19] Rhodesia Amnesty Ordinance of 1979, Section 3, General Amnesty Ordinance of 1980.

[20] Article 59 of the 1961 South African Constitution, *S* v. *Tuhadeleni and Others (T)*; *S* v. *Tuhadeleni and Others (AD)*, 177. For an analysis of this matter, see John Dugard, 'South West Africa and the "Terrorist Trial"' (1970) 64 *American Journal of International Law* 19.

[21] Namibia, *Binga* v. *Administrator General, South West Africa and Others*, 969. The case went on appeal to the South Africa Supreme Court, on different grounds.

Opinion concerning the illegality of acts by South Africa must be considered *obiter dicta*.[22]

The working assumption of the Namibian state-makers was, from an early stage, that norms that had been enforced under South Africa's administration, post- as well as pre-1966, would be adopted as law by independent Namibia, with the obvious exception of racially discriminatory norms.[23] The attitude dominating the Constituent Assembly during the debate on the drafting of the constitution was that the legality or recognition of South Africa's administration was no longer at issue, and that Namibian independence would follow the 'standard procedure of taking over from a colonial power'.[24] This approach was embodied in Article 140(1) of the Namibian constitution, which provides:

> Subject to the provisions of this Constitution, all laws which were in force immediately before the date of Independence shall remain in force until repealed or amended by Act of Parliament or until they are declared unconstitutional by a competent Court.

The use of the term 'in force' with respect to both previous and prospective law, when for the latter 'in force' necessarily means 'legally valid', implies admission of the validity of post-1966 law. Alternatively, the phrase 'all laws *which* were in force' may altogether exclude post-1966 legislation from adoption as prospective law (because it was invalid under international law). This ambiguous drafting is not accidental. Since it was not clear what sort of issues may arise, the drafters of the constitution, South African professors of international and constitutional law recruited by

22 Namibia, *Binga* v. *Administrator General, South West Africa and Others*, 964.

23 UNIN, *Constitutional Options for Namibia: A Historical Perspective*, based on the work of M. D. Bomany and C. Ushewokunze, Namibia Studies Series No. 2 (ed. N. K. Duggal) (Lusaka: UNIN, 1979), 52; UNIN, *Namibia: Legal Framework and Development Strategy Options for the Mining Industry*, based on the work of M. D. Bomani, Harbans S. Aulakh, Wilfred W. Asombang and C. Ushewokunze, Namibia Studies Series No. 10 (ed. N. K. Duggal) (Lusaka: UNIN, 1987), 150; Statement by SWAPO secretary for legal affairs Dr E. N. Tjiriange (later Namibia's first minister of justice) at the Preparatory Seminar on Law Drafting for Independent Namibia held at UNIN, Lusaka, Zambia, 11–15 April 1989; interview by the author with Prof. Marinus Wiechers, Unisa, constitutional drafter for Namibia 1988–1990, Pretoria, 9 April 2004.

24 *Namibian Constituent Assembly Debates*, Volume I, 94–95 (21 November 1989–31 January 1990) (Justus Garoëb, United Democratic Front); *Namibian Constituent Assembly Debates*, Volume II, 33 (1 February 1990–16 March 1990) (Vekuii Rukuoro, Namibia National Front), 34 (1 February 1990–16 March 1990) (Dirk Mudge, DTA, Chairman Dr Hage Geingob, subsequently first prime minister of Namibia).

the Constituent Assembly,[25] intentionally left the matter unresolved so as to leave the state a free hand in the future.[26]

The Namibian constitution also regulates the attribution of administrative acts of the South African administration to the new authorities. Article 140(3) of the Namibian constitution directly addresses the consequences of South African norms. It provides:

> Anything done under such laws [which were in force immediately before the date of Independence] prior to the date of Independence by the Government, or by a Minister or other official of the Republic of South Africa shall be deemed to have been done by the Government of the Republic of Namibia or by a corresponding Minister or official of the Government of the Republic of Namibia, unless such action is subsequently repudiated by an Act of Parliament...

This provision effectively endorses the consequences of South African acts, while again remaining silent on the validity of the norms from which these acts originated.

However, Article 145 of the constitution provides:

> (1) Nothing contained in this Constitution shall be construed as imposing upon the Government of Namibia:
>
> ...
>
> b) any obligations to any person arising out of the acts or contracts of prior Administrations which would not otherwise have been recognised by international law as binding upon the Republic of Namibia.
>
> (2) Nothing contained in this Constitution shall be construed as recognising in any way the validity of the Administration of Namibia by the Government of the Republic of South Africa or by the Administrator-General appointed by the Government of the Republic of South Africa to administer Namibia.

Article 145 could have created a conflict with the attribution of South African acts to the Namibian government under Article 140(3). Under an expansive reading, Article 145(2) upholds the invalidity of the South African administration. Consequently, post-1966 laws were not 'in force immediately before the date of independence', as stipulated in Article 140(1), and acts carried out under them were not attributable to the Namibian government under Article 140(3). Article 145 was nonetheless

[25] Prof. Arthur Chaskalson (later chief justice, Supreme Court of South Africa), Prof. Marinus Wiechers and Prof. Gerhard Erasmus.

[26] Interview by the author with Prof. Marinus Wiechers, Unisa, constitutional drafter for Namibia 1988–1990, Pretoria, 9 April 2004.

adopted by the Constituent Assembly without discussion.[27] The potential for conflict was soon removed, in *Minister of Defence* v. *Mwandinghi* (1991). The case concerned a claim of damages against the South African minister of defence, for an injury caused by South African forces operating in Namibia prior to independence. When Namibia became independent, the plaintiff sought to replace the respondent, the South African minister, with the Namibian minister. He relied on Article 143 to attribute the South African minister's conduct to the Namibian minister. The Namibian minister of defence objected, arguing that Article 145 did not allow attribution of alleged delicts. The Supreme Court rejected this argument, and went on to clarify that Article 145 excluded attribution of South African acts to the Namibian government only if their *substantive* content contravened international law, for example if they created an obligation arising under apartheid laws.[28] The illegality of the South African administration per se did not obstruct the continuity provided by Article 140(3).

Alongside the general validation and adoption of South African norms, the Namibian constitution maintains an escape clause in Article 140(3), which permits the Namibian parliament to repudiate acts of the South African government. The Namibian parliament has acted upon this authority in only one instance. The case concerned a non-profit organization, Cultura 2000, incorporated in February 1989 with the object, inter alia, of preserving and promoting the language and culture of 'communities of European descent'. In March 1989 the Representative Authority for Whites operating under the South African administration sold Cultura 2000 a farm, gave it a donation and also granted it a substantial loan. In February 1990, shortly before Namibian independence, the loan was converted into a donation. In December 1991 the Namibian parliament enacted the State Repudiation (Cultura 2000) Act of 1991, which repudiated the donations and provided that monies paid to Cultura 2000, and any property transferred to it, vested in the government of Namibia. In the proceedings that ensued, the Supreme Court first reiterated its ruling in *Minister of Defence* v. *Mwandinghi* that the invalidity of the South African administration under international law was not a bar to the adoption of its law as Namibian law. The court said:[29]

[27] Interview by the author with Prof. Marinus Wiechers, Unisa, Constitutional drafter for Namibia 1988–1990, Pretoria, 9 April 2004.

[28] *Minister of Defense* v. *Mwandinghi*, 72 at H and 74 at G-H.

[29] *Government of the Republic of Namibia* v. *Cultura 2000*, 181.

> Clearly many of the laws enacted by the South African government during its administration of Namibia and many of the acts performed by that administration during that time were plainly inconsistent with the ethos and express provisions of the Constitution and therefore unacceptable to the new Namibia. But there were clearly other acts with no ideological content such as the registration of births, deaths and marriages, for example, which did not fall into that category and there would clearly be chaos in the administration of the country by a future government if all such acts, regardless of their character or content, were to be considered invalid simply on the 'logical' ground that they were performed by an administration considered to be invalid.

This statement resembles the post-Civil War US jurisprudence. It distinguishes the formal invalidity, referring in this case to international rather than to constitutional law, from the substantive flaw in the legislation. This is similar to the entrenchment interpretation of the *Namibia* exception.

The court then explained that repudiation under Article 140(3) did not render an act void but merely reversed the fiction that the act had been carried out by the government of Namibia or its officials.[30] The court did not set any guidelines on the types of act that may be repudiated, other than note that the constitution expresses 'the strongest revulsion of the new State to the policies and actions of the previous administration based on the policy of apartheid'.[31]

This raises a question as to why only the Cultura 2000 transaction was repudiated, while other acts carried out by the South African administration that were based on the policy of apartheid remained untouched. The Cultura 2000 affair was the result of a governmental probe into land transfers initiated by the ethnic administrations in the six-month period prior to independence. These transfers were suspect as pre-emptive action to benefit Whites prior to majority rule[32] and to frustrate the results of the first free elections.[33] The fact that the transaction was carried out in an attempt to perpetuate the illegal policy underlying the illegal regime was a particular affront to the rule of law and to the transition to a legal regime. Although the court rejected the proposition that the illegality of the South African administration was in itself a ground for repudiation, the political context of the

30 *Government of the Republic of Namibia* v. *Cultura 2000*, 190.

31 *Government of the Republic of Namibia* v. *Cultura 2000*, 179.

32 Lionel Cliffe *et al.*, *The Transition to Independence in Namibia* (Boulder, CO: Lynne Rienner, 1994), 228–229.

33 *Government of the Republic of Namibia* v. *Cultura 2000*, 178–179.

Cultura 2000 transaction appears to have been significant to the court's ruling.[34]

In conclusion, the approach of the Namibian constitution was, in general, one of validity of South African legislation and acts, subject to the possibility of repudiation on grounds of unconstitutionality. Once the goal of independence was achieved, good relations with South Africa, itself in a state of transformation, were important to Namibia, and it was no longer felt necessary to pursue the means previously adopted under international law to deny legitimacy to the South African administration.

5.2.3 The Baltic states

In 1940, the USSR substituted its law for the laws of the pre-1940 states. Upon transition, all three states reverted to their pre-1940 constitutional law as the basic norm of their legal systems, thereby reinforcing their claims to be continuators of the pre-1940 states rather than new states. In June 1992 Estonia adopted a constitution by referendum, in compliance with Article 1 of its 1938 constitution, which was in turn recognized in the preamble of the 1992 constitution. This link between the two constitutions served to uphold constitutional continuity from pre-1940 Estonia.[35] Latvia's 1990 Declaration on the Restoration of Independence re-established the authority of its 1922 constitution. At the same time it suspended that constitution (except for a few articles that, under that constitution's provisions, could only be amended by referendum) until the adoption of a revised constitution. In the interim, the declaration called for the implementatiuon of 'those constitutional and other legal acts of the Latvian SSR which are in effect in Latvia when this Declaration is adopted' insofar as they do not contradict the remaining provisions of the 1922 constitution.[36] A similar process took place in Lithuania: on 11 March 1990 the Supreme Council of Lithuania reinstated the 1938 constitution, and the validity of the constitutions of the USSR and Lithuanian Soviet Republic were terminated. However, this reinstatement did not affect the legal system as a whole. The Law on the Reinstatement of the 1938 Constitution clarified that 'the reinstatement of the Constitution of

[34] For further discussion of the *Government of the Republic of Namibia* v. *Cultura 2000* with respect to land, see Chapter 7 below.

[35] Continuity of the law was provided in a 1992 Law on the Application of the Constitution Article 2(1).

[36] Latvia, Supreme Council's 1990 Declaration on the Restoration of Independence, Articles 3, 4, 6.

Lithuania does not in itself re-establish other laws in effect in the Republic of Lithuania prior to 15 June 1940'.[37] It also stipulated that laws and acts in force would remain in force, unless they contradicted the Provisional Basic Law of Lithuania, which was enacted on the same day and which suspended the 1938 constitution in order to harmonize its provisions 'with the altered political economical and other social relations which have developed through the years'.[38] In all three states, the significance of the reversion to the pre-1940 constitutions was largely symbolic. All three states were resigned, as a practical exigency, to the continued application of laws enacted by local parliaments, until the post-transition authorities had adopted all necessary laws.

The legislative instruments in the Baltic states defined the prospective body of law by reference to existing norms. As argued above with regard to the Namibian constitution, the reference to those norms should be taken as a pragmatic working definition rather than as a statement on their legal status. The qualifying terminology referring to Soviet legislation – 'in force', 'implement', 'in effect' – emphasized the factual enforcement of the purported law rather than its normative validity.

In two areas of law, the Baltic states took immediate legislative steps to rescind the effects of Soviet legislation. One is the grant of nationality, with respect to which post-1990 instruments provided for reversion to the legislation that applied prior to the annexation. The other is rights in real property. Post-1990 instruments revoked the nationalization orders of 1940. The law and practice in these two areas of law are discussed below in Chapters 6 and 7.

5.2.4 The TBVC

The constitutions of the TBVC provided for continuity of the law between the pre-independence Bantustans and the independent states. The Republic of Transkei Constitution Act 1976, Article 60(1), for example, provided that:

> (a) all laws which immediately prior to the commencement of this Act were in operation in any district of Transkei . . .

[37] Lithuania, Law on the Reinstatement of the 12 May 1938 Constitution of Lithuania, Article 4.

[38] Continuity of law was again stipulated when the Provisional Basic Law was replaced by the constitution in 1992, through the Law on the Procedure for the Enforcement of the Constitution, Article 2.

shall continue in operation and continue to apply except in so far as such laws are superseded by any applicable law of Transkei or are amended or repealed by Parliament in terms of this Act . . .

Legislation in the TBVC was amended from time to time, often following and replicating changes in South African law. The resulting uniformity enabled smooth interaction between the TBVC and South Africa. Since the TBVC were considered by South Africa to be independent states rather than separate provinces, their competences were wider than those of the provinces and paralleled those of the national South African legislature.[39]

While politically it was clear to the negotiators of South Africa's transition to democracy that the TBVC were illegitimate entities, it was decided to treat them as legally valid, both as a symbolic gesture of reconciliation and as a practical measure to ensure legal stability.[40] Article 229 of the South African Interim Constitution provided for the continuity of existing laws:

> Subject to this Constitution, all laws which immediately before the commencement of this Constitution were in force in any area which forms part of the national territory, shall continue in force in such area, subject to any repeal or amendment of such laws by a competent authority.

This provision applied to the TBVC as areas which form 'part of the national territory'. Their legislation continued to apply until replaced by 'rationalizing' legislation, i.e. legislation providing uniformity across South Africa in matters within the competence of the national government. The status of TBVC norms was formally similar to the status of norms of the former provinces of South Africa, although TBVC norms stood out because of the previously wide competence of the TBVC, which was sometimes closely connected with the racial segregation underlying the establishment of the TBVC. An example is the Transkei Marriage Act of 1978, which legalized polygamy through customary marriages, alongside a single civil marriage.[41] Although this law did not expressly apply to any

[39] E.g. Transkei Territorial Waters Act of 1978 and Ciskei Territorial Waters Act of 1986.

[40] Interview by the author with Mr Zam Titus, special advisor to the minister of provincial and local government and formerly director-general of the Ministry of Constitutional Development, administrator-general of Ciskei, participant in the MPNF, Pretoria, 7 April 2004.

[41] Transkei Marriage Act of 1978, Section 3. Cedric B. Mndaweni, 'Limping Marriages in the New South Africa?' (1991) 24 *Comparative & International Law Journal of South Africa* 215, 216.

specific ethnic group, in practice it only applied to Blacks, to whom customary law was applicable. The Transkei Marriage Act continued to apply in the territory previously under Transkei's rule (incorporated since 1994 in the Eastern Cape Province), but only to Blacks. This only changed in 1998 when the Act was replaced by the all-South African Recognition of Customary Marriages Act.

Post-1994 legislation is silent on whether the TBVC are previously autonomous territories within South Africa or formerly independent states. Dugard considered that the repeal of the Status Acts by the Interim Constitution[42] intentionally avoided any suggestion of former statehood.[43] Yet the language used in legislation that repealed or amended TBVC legislation is not uniform. Some instruments avoid mentioning the TBVC by name. This is most noticeable in the Interim Constitution itself, which uses terminology such as 'any area forming part of the national territory'.[44] Other Acts refer to the 'former Republics of Transkei, Bophuthatswana, Venda and Ciskei'.[45] As the status of the TBVC became a less sensitive issue, the drafting gradually grew less careful.[46]

In two areas of law, South African legislation provides for a reversion of apartheid legislation. One area is nationality, which in 1993, even before the final step towards democracy, was restored to individuals deprived of it under apartheid law. The other area is rights in real property. The South African constitution provides for restitution of property to persons who had been dispossessed since 1913 of their property on discriminatory grounds. The law and practice in these two areas of law are considered below in Chapters 6 and 7.

42 South African Interim Constitution, Article 230 and Schedule 7.

43 John Dugard, 'Public International Law' (1993) *Annual Survey of South African Law* 61, 70; interview by the author with Prof. François Venter, University of Potchefstroom, participant in the MPNF, Potchefstroom, 6 April 2004. But compare with Andries Cilliers, 'Reincorporation of Bophuthatswana and Certain Other States into the Republic of South Africa' (1993–1994) 19 *South African Yearbook of International Law* 93, 100–104.

44 E.g. Interim Constitution, Articles 229 and 235(1)(c), covering both provinces and homelands, and Article 224(2)(b), concerning areas that had military forces of their own, where this terminology is reserved for the TBVC.

45 E.g. Plant Breeders' Rights Amendment Act, 1996 (South Africa); Mineral and Energy Laws Rationalization Act, 1994 (South Africa); Imprint Amendment Act, 1994 (South Africa); Independent Broadcasting Authority Amendment Substitution of Section 79 of Act 153 of 1993, 1996 (South Africa); Admission of Advocates Amendment Act, 1994 (South Africa); Estate Agents Amendment Act, 1996 (South Africa); Customs and Excise Amendment Act, 1994 (South Africa); Stamp Duties Act, 1968; Income Tax Act, 1995 (South Africa); National Forests Act, 1998 (South Africa).

46 Interview by the author with Mr Gerritt Grove, parliamentary drafter, South Africa, Pretoria, 7 April 2004.

5.2.5 Timor-Leste

With the annexation of Timor-Leste to Indonesia, Indonesian legislation was extended to the territory.[47] Indonesian law governed the territory exclusively until 1999. Upon taking control of Timor-Leste, UNTAET was immediately confronted with the need to determine the law of the territory. Security Council Resolution 1272(1999), which established UNTAET, conferred upon it legislative powers. This did not obviate the need to identify a subsidiary legal system to complement UNTAET legislation, in order to avoid a legal vacuum in the initial phase of the transitional administration. The resolution authorized a special representative of the UN Secretary-General 'to enact new laws and regulations and to amend, suspend or repeal existing ones'.[48] There is no reference in the resolution or in the debate preceding its adoption to the source or content of these 'existing' laws and regulations,[49] e.g. whether they are those actually enforced (Indonesian law) or those applied to the territory previously (Portuguese and customary Timorese law). Both Timorese customary law and customary international law were clearly insufficient to regulate many spheres of life. The Timorese political elite expressed a clear preference for the adoption of Portuguese law, with which it was familiar from its long exile in the former Portuguese colonies in Africa. However, Portuguese law had not been utilized in Timor-Leste for twenty-four years and was unfamiliar to the local population and professionals.

UNTAET soon decided to apply Indonesian law as the subsidiary law of Timor-Leste. This decision was made solely for a practical reason: to avoid a situation whereby local lawyers, virtually all of whom had obtained their law degrees at Indonesian universities, had to be introduced to an entirely foreign legal system.[50] UNTAET Regulation 1999/1 provided, inter alia, that:

[47] Law 7/76 on the Legalization of the Integration of East Timor into the Unitary State of the Republic of Indonesia and the Formation of the Province of East Timor, Elucidation, general part, item 4.

[48] UNSC Resolution 1272(1999), paragraph 6. [49] UN Doc S/PV.4057 (25 October 1999).

[50] Hansjörg Strohmeyer, 'Policing the Peace: Post-conflict Judicial System Reconstruction in East Timor' (2001) 24 *University of New South Wales Law Journal* 171, 174; Hansjörg Strohmeyer, 'Collapse and Reconstruction of a Judicial System: The United Nations Missions in Kosovo and East Timor' (2001) 95 *American Journal of International Law* 46, 58. Strohmeyer was the acting principal legal adviser at the time when Regulation 1999/1 was promulgated. Wayne Hayde, 'Ideas and Realties of the Rule of Law and Administration of Justice in Post Conflict East Timor' (2004) 8 *International Peacekeeping: The Yearbook of International Peace Operations* 65.

> 3.1 Until replaced by UNTAET regulations or subsequent legislation of democratically established institutions of East Timor, the laws applied in East Timor prior to 25 October 1999 shall apply in East Timor . . .

UNTAET intentionally avoided identifying Indonesian law as the laws that 'shall apply'.[51] This was a lesson learnt from the UN experience only a short time earlier, in Kosovo. The UN Mission in Kosovo (UNMIK), an international administration similar to UNTAET, had been faced with a similar dilemma, namely whether to adopt as subsidiary law Serb law, which had been enforced on the eve of the entry of international forces to the territory in March 1999; or Kosovar law, which had been applied until March 1989, when Serbia annulled Kosovo's autonomous status. Guided by pragmatic considerations, UNMIK chose to apply Serb law, referring to it as 'the laws in force in Kosovo prior to 24 March 1999'.[52] This decision was met with resentment and outrage by Kosovar judges and prosecutors, who retaliated by interpreting UNMIK's regulation as including only pre-1989 Kosovar law.[53] Eventually, UNMIK amended its regulation so as to fall in line with the practice of the courts.[54] Conscious of the sensitivity of this issue, UNTAET drafted Regulation 1999/1 in a manner that would not make the application of Indonesian law entirely obvious. Nonetheless, UNTAET's intention was clear to all those involved.

In practice, Indonesian law was not uniformly applied in all spheres of law. The difficulties in applying it and the need to establish the relationship between it and international standards led to piecemeal application and unsuccessful attempts at conducting a systematic revision of law.[55] As a result, criminal law, for example, was only sporadically enforced until

[51] The term 'shall apply' is ambiguous and can be interpreted as establishing de jure applicability or a de facto arrangement. The Portuguese text, which is also an official UNTAET language (UNTAET Regulation 1991/1 Section 5.2), uses the term *manter-se-ão válidas*, i.e. 'shall remain valid'. This formulation is also problematic, because it expressly identifies prospective law through previously valid law, the scope of which may be controversial. Under Regulation 1999/1, the English version prevails over the Portuguese.

[52] UNMIK, Regulation 1999/1 on the Authority of the Interim Administration in Kosovo (25 July 1999), UN Doc UNMIK/REG/1999/1.

[53] Roger F. M. Lorenz, 'The Rule of Law in Kosovo: Problems and Prospects' (2000) 11 *Criminal Law Forum* 127, 128–130.

[54] UNMIK, Regulation 1999/24 on the Law Applicable in Kosovo (12 December 1999), UN Doc UNMIK/REG/1999/24.

[55] UN Doc S/1999/1024, paragraph 54; Jonathan Morrow and Rachel White, 'The United Nations in Transitional East Timor: International Standards and the Reality of Governance' (2002) 22 *Australian Yearbook of International Law* 1, 10.

September 2000, when a new code of criminal procedure was adopted.[56] The pragmatic ambition of Regulation 1999/1 to provide legal certainty and continuity by applying Indonesian law was severely curtailed.[57]

The arrangement under UNTAET Regulation 1999/1 was carried through to independent Timor-Leste via a constitutional provision on continuity. As Section 165 of Timor-Leste's constitution stipulates, 'Laws and regulations in force in East Timor shall be applicable to all matters except to the extent that they are inconsistent with the Constitution or the principles contained therein.' This provision was given effect by an interpretative law, which provided that 'legislation applicable in Timor-Leste on 19 May 2002 shall remain in force' subject to the constitution and necessary modifications.[58] This incorporated UNTAET regulations into the law of independent Timor-Leste.

Regulation 1999/1 was adopted on 27 November 1999, and was given retroactive effect from 25 October 1999.[59] Together with all subsequent legislation referring to it, it only regulated the *prospective* law of Timor-Leste; that is, from October 1999 onwards. UNTAET did not attempt to determine what the law of Timor-Leste was prior to October 1999. Regulation 1999/1 takes account of the fact that Indonesian law was *enforced* in that period as a matter of *fact*, but is silent on whether that practice was lawful or not under international law. That was considered a political issue, to be decided in due course by the sovereign authorities of Timor-Leste.

However, UNTAET could not avoid addressing the law applicable to pre-October 1999 events altogether, as it was tasked with setting up the Special Panels for Serious Crimes (SPSCs) in the Dili District Court, to try international and other serious crimes committed during the 1999 riots.[60] UNTAET's regulations provided that 'the courts in East Timor shall apply the law of East Timor as promulgated by Section 3 of UNTAET Regulation No. 1999/1'.[61] Unlike Regulation 1999/1 and the constitution,

[56] Regulation 2000/30.

[57] Morrow and White, 'The UN in Transitional East Timor', 10–11.

[58] Law No. 2/2002, Interpretation of Applicable Law on 19 May 2002, Article 1.

[59] UNTAET Regulation 1999/1, Section 8.

[60] UNTAET Regulation 2000/15, Sections 1, 4; UNTAET Regulation 2001/25, Section 9. Jurisdiction over non-international crimes was limited to crimes allegedly committed between 1 January 1999 and 25 October 1999.

[61] UNTAET Regulation 2000/11, Section 5.1; UNTAET Regulation 2000/15, Section 3.1. These regulations were later replaced by Regulation 2001/25, Section 5.1, which reproduces the jurisdiction provisions.

this provision did not determine the territorial law of Timor-Leste; rather, it determined the law governing specific cases adjudicated by the courts of Timor-Leste, relating to pre-October 1999 events. Courts routinely applied Indonesian law on the basis of this provision until July 2003, when the question of the applicable law arose for the first time in *Public Prosecutor* v. *Armando dos Santos*.[62]

Dos Santos had been indicted for murder and other inhumane acts as crimes against humanity, with regard to acts committed in April 1999. In September 2002 he was convicted by the SPSC of murder under Indonesian law, and was sentenced to twenty years' imprisonment.[63] The prosecution appealed the decision, submitting that dos Santos should have been convicted of crimes against humanity (under Indonesian law) rather than murder. Although the prosecution's appeal did not raise the question of the law governing the case, this was the first issue which the Court of Appeal chose to address. The court did not explain why that issue suddenly arose and why it had not arisen before. As a point of departure it took the constitution, which maintains the applicability of 'laws and regulations in force in East Timor'. Since this referred to UNTAET Regulation 1999/1, the court proceeded to examine whether the common understanding of the phrase 'laws applied prior to 25 October 1999' in Regulation 1999/1 as referring to Indonesian law was correct.

The majority of the court noted that Indonesia's annexation of Timor-Leste was illegal under international law and therefore invalid *ab initio*. Thus, it said, under international law the law of Timor-Leste remained Portuguese law throughout the period of Indonesian annexation. Emphasizing that the 'laws applied in East Timor prior to 25 October 1999' could only be those which had legitimately been in force in accordance with the principles of international law, the court concluded that Regulation 1999/1 referred to Portuguese law. Finally, the court considered that if UNTAET had intended to adopt Indonesian law despite its invalidity, it would have done so explicitly. The majority then proceeded to quash the conviction under Indonesian law, and declared dos Santos guilty of 'crimes against humanity in the form of genocide' under the Portuguese Penal Code (despite the fact that dos Santos had not been indicted for genocide).

62 Timor-Leste, *Public Prosecutor* v. *Armando dos Santos*.

63 On the *dos Santos* affairs see David Cohen, *Indifference and Accountability* (Honolulu: East–West Center, 2006), 83.

The Timorese Judge, Jacinta Correia da Costa, dissented.[64] She opined that although Indonesia's presence in Timor-Leste was not recognized de jure, it was recognized de facto, and the application of its laws could not be denied. Furthermore, while conceding that Regulation 1999/1, Section 3.1, could be considered ambiguous if read in isolation, she argued that when read as a whole, Section 3 referred more evidently to Indonesian law. this was because Sections 3.2 and 3.3 of the regulation repealed various legislative acts that existed only under Indonesian law and not under Portuguese law, so these sections could only be meaningful if Section 3.1 were interpreted as adopting Indonesian law.[65]

The Court of Appeal repeated its ruling that Portuguese law was the law of Timor-Leste in twenty-three other cases, most of them on criminal matters.[66] These judgments caused confusion and division in the Timorese legal and political communities. Timor-Leste's prime minister Mari Alkatiri described the decision as 'incompetent and unconstitutional'.[67] The prosecutor-general of Timor-Leste filed an application with the Supreme Court of Justice requesting a declaration clarifying the issue of applicable law in Timor-Leste. He argued that the mistaken rulings of the Court of Appeal rendered illegal the decisions of the courts in all the criminal cases heard in the preceding three years. Furthermore, they would have far-reaching implications and consequences for the system of justice in Timor-Leste and for the governance of Timor-Leste as a whole.[68] The majority of the legal community operating in Timor-Leste, both international and local, also rejected the *dos Santos* decision.[69] The SPSCs and the Dili District Court continued to apply Indonesian law. The SPSC rejected the argument based on the illegality of the Indonesian

64 In *dos Santos* she only appended her opinion that the law governing the case was Indonesian law. On the circumstances of this statement see Cohen, *Indifference and Accountability*, 85. Judge Correia da Costa elaborated her position in the following case, *Agustino da Costa* v. *the Prosecutor General*.

65 *Agustino da Costa* v. *the Prosecutor General*, Judgment of 18 July 2003, [5], [8]. Section 3.2 repealed the Laws on Anti-Subversion, Social Organizations, National Security, National Protection and Defense, Mobilization and Demobilization, and the Law on Defense and Security. Section 3.3 abolished capital punishment.

66 In *Foo Hau Kuin* v. *JJ McDonald*, an appeal was made to the Court of Appeal to apply Portuguese law in a civil case.

67 Quoted in Jill Jolliffe, 'Old European Tongue Brings Chaos to Newest Asian Nation', *Sydney Morning Herald*, 26 July 2003, www.etan.org/et2003/july/18–21/26oldeur.htm.

68 Office of the Prosecutor-General, Information Release of 24 July 2003, www.etan.org/et2003/july/18–21/23prosec.htm. Timor-Leste's Supreme Court has not yet been established, and its functions are performed by the Appeals Court.

69 JSMP, 'Dili District Court, Final Report 2003'.

occupation as inconclusive with respect to the applicable law,[70] and interpreted Regulation 1999/1 as referring to Indonesian law on the basis of arguments similar to those of Judge Correia da Costa.[71]

In order to clarify the situation, Timorese parliamentarians tabled a bill in parliament, stating expressly that Indonesian law was the subsidiary law under Regulation 1999/1, and accordingly under the Timorese constitution. Although the move proposed by the Court of Appeal was not anticipated and took the legal community by surprise, when the matter came to parliamentary debate, opinions were divided. The debate was charged with political tension, focusing on the ramifications of the legislation for relations with Portugal and with Indonesia, and on the message that the proposed legislation conveyed regarding the legacy left to Timor-Leste by Portuguese and Indonesian rulers. Timorese judges, public prosecutors and public defenders, most of whom had graduated from Indonesian universities and studied Indonesian law, threatened to resign from their positions unless parliament voted in favour of Indonesian law.[72] They underlined the fact that few Timorese police or court officials were fluent in the Portuguese language or knew Portuguese law, making the application of Portuguese law unfeasible.[73] Advocates of the Portuguese option, including the president of the Court of Appeal, countered by pointing out the dangerous juridical dependence that Timor-Leste could face in relation to its powerful neighbour if Indonesian law were adopted.

70 The SPSC noted that 'the UN also branded the continued Portuguese occupation as illegal', *Public Prosecutor* v. *João Sarmento and Domingos Mendonça*, Decision of 24 July 2003, 12–13, [40]. In fact, none of the UN organs and subsidiary bodies have ever labelled either the Portuguese or the Indonesian occupation illegal. It only deplored and condemned various aspects of the Portuguese administration (UNGA Resolution 1699(XVI) (19 December 1961), UNGA Resolution 1807(XVII) (14 December 1962)), and deplored the Indonesian intervention. Nor did the Court of Appeal in *dos Santos* claim that the UN had declared the Indonesian occupation illegal, but said that 'the UN never recognized that military occupation'. *Public Prosecutor* v. *Armando dos Santos*, 4. In fact, the UN maintained Timor-Leste on the list of non-self-governing territories as a Portuguese territory, on the one hand, but, on the other, did not clearly reject the annexation by Indonesia.

71 *Public Prosecutor* v. *João Sarmento and Domingos Mendonça*, [35]–[39].

72 KESTA, 'Parliament Passed Law on Applicable Law', *Selected Postings from East Timor*, 1 October 2002, www.etan.org/et2003/october/01-6/00parlmnt.htm.

73 Portuguese and Tetum are the official languages of Timor-Leste. In 2009, only 37 per cent of the Timorese population spoke Portuguese, mainly people aged between ten and twenty-four. Tetum is known at some level to some 86 per cent of the population, since it is the language used in church services. However, Tetum is primarily an oral language and not a written one. Marie Quinn, 'Letting go of Indonesian' (April–June 2009) 96 *Inside Indonesia*, http://insideindonesia.org/content/view/1191/47/.

Proponents of applying Indonesian law prevailed, and in October 2003 the Timorese parliament adopted Law 10/2003 (Interpretation of Section 1 of Law 2/2002 of 7 August, and Sources of Law), expressly declaring Indonesian law to be the subsidiary law in Timor-Leste. The Law provides:

> Interpreting a law literally, outside its context and system, aloof from reality, and in violation of the most elementary rules of legal hermeneutics, leads to an absurdity, which may undermine the country's stability, as it tends to bring about a situation of institutional crisis that would otherwise not exist.
>
> ...
>
> Section 1: Authentic interpretation
>
> Under the terms of the provision of section 1 of Law No. 2/2002, of 7 August, applicable legislation in East Timor on 19 May 2002 means all Indonesian legislation that was applied and was in force 'de facto' in East Timor, prior to 25 October 1999, as provided by UNTAET Regulation No. 1/1999.[74]

The law was made applicable retroactively to Timor-Leste's Restoration of Independence Day, 20 May 2002.[75] This confirmed definitively that Indonesian law was the subsidiary law of Timor-Leste.

The Court of Appeal's majority opinion contained a series of errors: framing the question as one of the territorial law of Timor-Leste rather than of the law applicable to acts tried by the SPSCs; relying on a faulty and non-authoritative translation of Regulation 1999/1 into Portuguese;[76] and interpreting Regulation 1999/1, Section 3.1, in disregard of its legislative and historical context.[77] But most importantly for present purposes, the Court of Appeal mistakenly gave paramount importance to the principle that the acts of an illegal regime, including its laws, cannot have legal consequences. It ignored the fact that the choice of domestic law of a state, even when emerging from an illegal regime, is grounded in the constitutional law of that state, not in international law. The only imperative ground for rejecting a choice of the post-transition regime to maintain the law of the illegal regime would be if it violated principles of international

[74] '[T]oda a legislação indonésia que era aplicada e vigorava "de facto" em Timor-Leste, antes do dia 25 de Outubro de 1999'.

[75] Portugal's state secretary for foreign affairs and co-operation expressed 'some disappointment' over the decision but said that it would not affect bilateral relations. Lusa (Agência de Notícias de Portugal, Portugal's news agency), 'Lisbon Says Adoption of Indonesian Law No Threat to Relations', Dili, 2 October 2002, www.etan.org/et2003/october/01-6/02lisbon.htm.

[76] Cohen, *Indifference and Accountability*, 84–85.

[77] JSMP, 'East Timor Court of Appeals', 14–19, 22–26.

human rights. Indeed, the majority in the Court of Appeal justified its decision on the basis of the *nullum crimen sine lege* principle. It argued that since Portuguese law was the governing law, convicting dos Santos on the basis of other law would amount to retroactive penalization.[78] But after twenty-four years of Indonesian rule, exclusively under Indonesian law, there was no anticipation by individuals that Portuguese law would be enforced against them. The use of Portuguese law in these circumstances was contrary to the fundamental principle of legal certainty, which the prohibition on retroactive penalization guarantees. Avoidance of retroactive penalization required the court to take account of Indonesian law, which had been foreseeable, accessible and enforced in practice, in order to ensure that the law enforced was that which the defendant could have known and acted upon. In short, it was the application of any criminal law *other* than Indonesian law that would have resulted in a violation of international human rights law.

The *dos Santos* ruling can simply be attributed to professional inadequacy on the part of the judges.[79] But it seems crucial that the controversial ruling by the Court of Appeal was decided by a majority vote of the international members of the bench. The judges were 'international', but they were not disinterested parties. They reportedly said that the issue was 'a matter of politics',[80] and they opted for a political statement on the illegality of the previous regime, even while compromising the observance of international human rights standards to which their office was immanently committed. It is neither surprising nor exceptional that international judges in hybrid courts rely on their acquaintance with the law under their own domestic jurisdictions.[81] But rarely do judges have

[78] In the case of indictment under international criminal law, the question may seem immaterial, as the prohibiting norms are deemed to have existed whether or not incorporated into domestic law. *Public Prosecutor* v. *João Sarmento and Domingos Mendonça*, [11]–[34]. In fact, dos Santos was indicted for crimes against humanity, which formed part of customary international law at the time of their commission; there should therefore not have been any issue of retroactivity. Nonetheless, since the mandate of the domestic courts in Timor-Leste is not limited to international crimes, the general question of the applicable law remains pertinent. In addition, the application of international criminal law by the domestic courts was subject to severe criticism. JSMP, 'East Timor Court of Appeals', 9; Cohen, *Indifference and Accountability*, 86.

[79] Suzanne Katzenstein, 'Hybrid Tribunals: Searching for Justice in East Timor' (2003) 16 *Harvard Human Rights Journal* 245; Cohen, *Indifference and Accountability*, 83–87, Morrow and White, 'The UN in Transitional East Timor'.

[80] Cohen, *Indifference and Accountability*, 85.

[81] Daniel Terris, Cesare P. R. Romano and Leigh Swigart, *The International Judge* (Lebanon: Brandeis University Press, 2007), 168–170.

an opportunity to openly impose their national law on the post-conflict states. The Portuguese-trained judges had this opportunity in Timor-Leste, and their 'politics' were the advancement of Portuguese culture in Timor-Leste, even at the cost of the principle of legality. Both majority judges had received their legal training in Portugal and were recruited there (although the president of the Court of Appeal, who led the campaign to apply Portuguese law, is Timorese by ethnicity).[82]

By the same token, the dissenting Timorese judge's preference for Indonesian law can be explained by her own familiarity with Indonesian rather than Portuguese law. But it is no less significant that her opinion was led by considerations of stability and pragmatism, which called for consideration of the fact that these norms were used in practice, rather than for a formal upholding of international law.

Indonesian law has been gradually replaced by UNTAET and Timorese legislation with prospective effect, by implication giving effect to acts carried out under Indonesian law prior to 1999. In two notable areas, exceptions have been made. One is the legislation on nationality, which not only disregards status granted under Indonesian law (practice that is characteristic of new states), but, more importantly, contains particular provisions regarding naturalization based on residence in the territory during the Indonesian annexation. The other area is regulation of conflicting claims to real property, where pre-1976 titles have been taken into account despite their annulment under Indonesian law. These areas of law are considered below in Chapters 6 and 7 respectively.

5.2.6 The TRNC

The 1975 constitution of the TFSC maintained the 1960 constitution of Cyprus and certain other legislation in force insofar as they were not inconsistent with the 1975 constitution itself.[83] However, the TFSC constitution was so comprehensive that it almost replaced the 1960 one.[84] The 1985 constitution of the TRNC also provides for continuity: 'The legislation in force on the date of the coming into operation of this Constitution shall continue to be in force, in so far as such legislation is not contrary to

[82] Although they failed even in applying that law. Cohen, *Indifference and Accountability*, 83–87.

[83] Constitution of the TFSC, Transitional Article 1.

[84] Zaim M. Necatigil, 'The Legal System of the Turkish Republic of Northern Cyprus' (1998) 4 *Journal of Cyprus Studies* 213, 243–244.

or inconsistent with the provisions of this Constitution'.[85] Some pre-1974 legislation of the Republic of Cyprus therefore continues to apply in the TRNC.[86]

Article 12 of the Foundation Agreement, entitled 'Past Acts', stipulates:

> (1) Any act, whether of a legislative, executive or judicial nature, by any authority in Cyprus whatsoever, prior to entry into force of this Agreement, is recognised as valid and, provided it is not inconsistent with or repugnant to any other provision of this Agreement or international law, its effect shall continue following entry into force of this Agreement. No-one shall be able to contest the validity of such acts by reason of what occurred prior to entry into force of this Agreement.

An observation appended to Article 12 indicates:

> The criterion of inconsistency with or repugnance to international law refers to any act which by its nature is contrary to international law. This reference, like the whole draft Article, is without prejudice to the question of the legitimacy or status of the relevant authorities under international law.

In stark contrast to the previous cases reviewed, the transitional provision lays down the legal situation expressly: the effects of norms that were applied in the TRNC would be considered valid with respect to the period prior to reunification, and (with some exceptions noted below) shall continue to have effect.

Similarly to the Namibian constitution as interpreted by the Namibian Supreme Court, conformity with international law is a yardstick for the *substantive* content of existing law. The non-recognition or illegality of the TRNC, being 'what occurred prior to entry into force' of the Agreement, may not be raised as an argument against the validity of the consequences of such norms.

A potential obstacle to ensuring the continuity provided for in Article 12 is that it was not incorporated into prospective United Cyprus Republic (UCR) domestic law. The draft constitution for the UCR, which would have deemed certain parts of the Foundation Agreement to have been adopted under it,[87] does not mention the Main Articles of the Foundation Agreement, where Article 12 is located. Article 12 is therefore not entrenched in

[85] TRNC Constitution, Part VII, Transitional Provisions, Validity of Existing legislation and Allegation of Inconsistency of Such Legislation with the Constitution, Transitional Article 4(1).

[86] E.g. the Criminal Code, mentioned in ECtHR, *Protopapa* v. *Turkey* [25]–[28] and in ECtHR, *Christodoulidou* v. *Turkey*, [69].

[87] Annan Plan, draft constitution of the UCR, Article 49(1).

the proposed internal law of Cyprus or its constituent states.[88] In view of the bitter and legalistic dispute in Cyprus over the status of the TRNC and its acts, the transitional provisions of any future reunification plan should be anchored more accurately, e.g. by ensuring that a provision along the lines of Article 12 is properly incorporated in the UCR constitution.

The continued validity of TRNC acts has notable exceptions. Another observation appended to Article 12 provides:

> Matters of citizenship, immigration, and properties affected by events since 1963 are dealt with in a comprehensive way by this Agreement; any validity of acts prior to entry into force of this Agreement regarding these matters shall thus end unless they are in conformity with the relevant provisions of this Agreement.

The law and practice in these areas of law are considered below in Chapters 6 and 7.

5.3 Conclusions

A feature common to all the cases studied here is the acquiescence of the post-transition regimes in the validity of the acts of the illegal regime. The Annan Plan is explicit on this, while other transitional arrangements left it implied.

By and large, this policy generated little controversy. This can be attributed to the fact that legal changes in the post-transition regime have been so sweeping that the illegality of the preceding regime's law and its preservation became a marginal issue. In the TRNC the situation may prove different, because the change of regime is not expected to be as revolutionary as in the other cases, and because the legal situation has not remained frozen in time, but has been considered by the ECtHR (with respect to both the status of the legal system and specific acts) in decisions which bind both Cyprus and Turkey.

All post-transition regimes have faced an unavoidable tension between the symbolic value of the principled rejection of the illegal regime's law, on the one hand, and the need to maintain that law in use in order to ensure legal and social stability, on the other. In most cases, the overriding criterion in deciding which body of law to adopt as post-transition law was

[88] A similar problem was flagged with respect to devolution and agreement legislation for the British colonies in the 1950s and 1960s (Daniel P. O'Connell, *State Succession in Municipal Law and International Law* (London: Stevens and Sons, 1967), Volume I, 108), which formally lapsed upon independence. In practice, no dispute over the validity of these provisions has even been raised in the newly independent states.

clearly pragmatic, namely the need to provide stability and certainty. Thus the choices of the post-transition regimes were generally characterized by a smooth, straightforward transition.

In addition, upholding the symbolic value of reverting to prior law has its own drawbacks, which might render this choice less than attractive. One factor is the relative legitimacy of the illegal regime's law and the law preceding it, particularly in the eyes of the local population. Where the preceding law also suffered from illegitimacy, the incentive to cause upheaval in order to reinstate it is smaller than in situations where that law enjoys legitimacy on the part of the local population in terms both of origin and content. For example, in Zimbabwe, Namibia and Timor-Leste, rejection of the illegal regime's law would have meant reversion to earlier colonial law. This hardly generated enthusiasm among the population. The situation was different in the Baltic states (and Kosovo), where the law preceding that of the illegal regime enjoyed strong formal and substantive legitimacy on the part of the local population, although in the Baltic states it was acknowledged that pre-Soviet law was ill-equipped to regulate modern life in a democratic society. This prevented reversion to it as a practical measure. Kosovar law had been in disuse for only a single decade, so the reversion to pre-1989 law might have appeared feasible. Even there it proved a harmful choice in practice, which resulted in a morass of uncertainty and confusion.[89]

At the same time, in specific areas of law, pragmatic continuity gave way to a different approach, of reversion to the *status quo ante*. This took various forms: express repeal of the legislation of the illegal regime, reinstatement of previous law, new legislation with specific provisions regarding the period of the illegal regime, and more. These actions focused almost exclusively on two areas: residence (and nationality), and rights in land. In these, the post-transition regimes compromised on stability and certainty in favour of other, less instrumental, considerations. The first area of law – residence – is considered in the next chapter; the other – rights in land – is addressed in Chapter 7.

[89] Lorenz, 'The Rule of Law in Kosovo: Problems and Prospects', 129–130.

6 The effect of transition on settlers implanted by illegal regimes

6.1 Introduction

Illegal regimes characteristically take measures to change the demographic composition of the territory under their control. One common strategy is the forced removal of local inhabitants from the territory. The other main strategy is the transfer into the territory of a settler population loyal to the illegal regime's government, and the subsequent granting of residence or nationality in the territory to this population.[1] This chapter concerns the response of the post-transition regime to this second strategy, which was prevalent to different extents in most of the case studies.

At the time of transition from the illegal regime to the new, lawful regime, it is not surprising that there are calls, at various levels, for the physical removal or expulsion of settlers from the country, or at least for their exclusion from the body politic. These calls represent a variety of interests and sentiments. Common to most situations is resentment towards the settlers as representatives of the exploiting regime, and a quest for retribution. This sentiment is not limited to situations where an illegal regime ends; it is common to many regimes following political conflict. Another motive for advocating expulsion is the concern of the post-transition regime that despite formal withdrawal, the previous, illegal regime will utilize its diaspora to continue dominating the territory under the new regime.

[1] The terms 'nationality' and 'citizenship' are used here interchangeably. Generally, 'nationality' reflects the international dimension of the relationship between a state and the individual, while 'citizenship' reflects the domestic, constitutional dimension of the same relationship. In some cases, the phenomenon of secondary citizenship or nationality (for example in federated states) complicates this delineation. In the cases examined in this article this matter does not arise.

The legal power of the post-transition regime to reverse the acts of the illegal regime by removal of settlers may be limited in various ways. One possibility is that the formal status which the illegal regime had conferred upon the settlers survives the transition. In addition, international human rights law may limit the ability of the post-transition regime to expel the settlers, regardless of their formal status in the territory.[2]

The first section of this chapter examines two doctrinal issues. One is whether status granted to settlers by the illegal regime survives the process of transition in light of the law governing illegal regimes. The other is the constraints on expulsion of settlers arising from international human rights law. The doctrinal analysis is followed by a review of the policy and practice of the various post-transition regimes.

6.2 Doctrine

6.2.1 Status granted to settlers under an illegal regime

International law protects individuals of certain categories from expulsion on the basis of their status under the state's law. First and foremost, the expulsion of nationals is almost absolutely prohibited under both universal[3] and regional instruments,[4] and the prohibition is considered part of customary international law. Long-term residence is also gaining

2 Limitations on expulsion of settlers may emanate from a variety of sources. The Special ILC Rapporteur on the expulsion of aliens (hereafter Special Rapporteur) catalogues, in addition to limitations based on human rights law, limitations inherent in the international legal order and limitations relating to the procedure of expulsion. UN Doc A/CN.4/581 (19 April 2007), paragraph 27. The latter category is generally unaffected by the identity of potential expellees or the circumstances of expulsion (except with respect to national security grounds for expulsion, e.g. ICCPR Article 13; ECHR Protocol 7, CETS 155 (opened for signature 22 November 1984, entered into force 1 November 1998), Article 1(2)). Therefore it is of limited interest in the present context. Moreover, procedural guarantees, around which a large part of jurisprudence revolves, usually affect the legality of individual acts of expulsion rather than general policies.

3 ICCPR Article 12(4). The prohibition in Article 12(4) is limited to 'arbitrary' denial of the right to enter one's country that is unreasonable in the circumstances; the HRC nonetheless 'considers that there are few, if any, circumstances in which deprivation of the right to enter one's own country could be reasonable'. Furthermore, Article 12(4) has been interpreted as not only permitting entry into one's own country, but also as prohibiting expulsion from one's own country, see *Stewart* v. *Canada*, individual opinion of Committee Member Bhagwati (dissenting). For a discussion of the prohibition on expulsion of nationals see UN Doc A/CN.4/581 (19 April 2007).

4 ECHR Protocol 4, Article 3(1); ACHR, Article 22(5); Arab Charter on Human Rights, reprinted in (1997) 18 *Human Rights Law Journal* 151, Article 22.

ground as a protected status,[5] although it is not yet formally recognized as such under any of the major human rights instruments.

In order to establish whether settlers under an illegal regime can benefit from the protection against expulsion on the basis of nationality or residence purportedly granted to them by the illegal regime, the validity of that status must be considered. Even if status granted by the regime is valid under either of these bodies of law, a second question is whether this validity survives the transition from the illegal regime to the legal one.

The obligation of non-recognition prevents states from giving validity to acts of the illegal regime. However, the *Namibia* exception allows exceptional recognition of acts of the illegal regime when that is required in order to prevent detriment to the inhabitants of the territory. The applicability of the exception to status granted to settlers depends on a number of factors. The first is whether the exception applies to settlers *ad personam*, i.e. whether it protects non-indigenous inhabitants of the territory. The reference in the *Namibia Advisory Opinion* to the 'inhabitants of the Territory' was clearly to the indigenous population, as in Namibia there was no significant settler population to speak of. However, as discussed in Chapter 3 above, eligibility for protection under the *Namibia* exception should also be extended to non-local individuals acting in good faith who find themselves under the control of the illegal regime. This may apply in some cases to settlers, depending on the circumstances of their arrival in the territory.

A second question is whether the grant of civic status falls within the substantive scope of the *Namibia* exception. The regulation of population movement is the epitome of entrenchment of the regime, and the grant of nationality is a power specifically reserved to sovereign states. It is, therefore, even under the narrowest interpretations of the obligation of non-recognition,[6] an act which should not be recognized as having legal

5 EU law is gradually assimilating permanent residents (nationals of third countries) to nationals of member states. Directive 2003/109 prohibits expulsion of long-term lawful residents in member states except when their presence constitutes an actual and sufficiently serious threat to public policy or public security. The legality of presence in the country depends on domestic law. Council Directive (EC) 2003/109 concerning the Status of Third-Country Nationals Who Are Long-Term Residents [2004] OJ L16/44. Judgments for failure to interpose have already been given in Case C-5/07 *Commission* v. *Portugal*, [2007] ECR I-00120; Case C-59/07 *Commission* v. *Spain*, [2007] ECR I-161; Case C-34/07 *Commission* v. *Luxemburg*, [2007] ECR I-175. See also ECtHR, *Üner* v. *the Netherlands*, [37].

6 Namely acts which entrench the illegal regime or acts in the public sphere which involve the exercise of powers reserved only to states. See Chapter 3 above.

effect. The grant of residence, too, is aimed at changing the demographic character of the territory so as to entrench the illegal regime in it.[7] While only nationality reflects the formal authority of the illegal regime, the concrete effect of residence on the entrenchment of the illegal regime is no less severe than that of nationality, and prima facie there is no justification for recognizing its legal effect. The interpretation of the *Namibia* exception according to which, a priori, no act of any kind should be recognized, whether or not it visibly entrenches the illegal regime,[8] calls for a case-by-case examination whether, under the specific circumstances, non-recognition of nationality or residence would be detrimental to the individuals.

The claim that nationality granted by the illegal regime should be recognized on the basis of the *Namibia* exception was made in *Veysi Dag* (2001), an asylum request made in the UK by a Turkish Cypriot claiming to be a national of the TRNC and alleging to be persecuted by its authorities. The Immigration Appeal Tribunal first rejected the relevance of the *Namibia* exception to the TRNC, noting that unlike South Africa, which had been recognized as a sovereign state albeit over less extensive territory than it claimed, the TRNC is not recognized as a state at all. The tribunal assumed that the *Namibia* exception would have been formulated differently had the ICJ had in mind a purportedly independent state rather than a purported annexation. Furthermore, the Immigration Appeal Tribunal considered that 'nobody has identified any disadvantage which would accrue to the appellant by reason of the international non-recognition of the "Turkish Republic of Northern Cyprus"'.[9] Accordingly it found that the *Namibia* exception was inapplicable. This statement seems to be based on a mistaken framing of the question. The non-recognition of the TRNC's statehood was not at issue. What the *Namibia* exception required was an assessment of the potential detriment to TRNC inhabitants, and to Mr Dag specifically, as a result of the non-recognition of the legal validity of his purported TRNC *nationality*. In asylum requests, for example, to deny refuge from persecution on the ground that the persecuting entity is not a state of nationality, despite the fact that it operates

[7] Within ordinary states, the grant of residence is formally more easily reversible than the grant of nationality, although this reversibility diminishes as the immunity to expulsion of long-term residents grows. See e.g. European Convention on Nationality Article 20(a). However, this immunity is irrelevant in the context of the recognition by other states of residence as a status.

[8] *Namibia Advisory Opinion*, separate opinion of Vice-President Ammoun, 99–100.

[9] UK, *Veysi Dag v. the Secretary of State for the Home Department*, [23].

as such to the exclusion of all other states, could be detrimental to the inhabitant.[10]

In those instances where there is justification for giving legal effect to status (nationality or residence) granted by the illegal regime on the basis of the *Namibia* exception, the question arises whether this validity survives transition to the lawful regime. An analogy can be made from the law of state succession with respect to nationality,[11] which is premised on the validity of the acts of the previous regime. The law of state succession does not obligate a successor state to grant its nationality to former nationals of the predecessor state.[12] By analogy, even exceptionally valid status granted by an illegal regime does not survive transition (at least not if the post-transition regime is a new state). The consequences of this rather arcane perception of individuals as pawns which states can move about may nonetheless be mitigated by other bodies of law, such as international human rights law.

6.2.2 Limitations on expulsion of settlers based on international human rights law

Introduction

The previous analysis indicates that the post-transition regime is not obligated to recognize any formal status of the settlers in its territory. However, the factual presence of settlers may generate legal consequences, embodied in international human rights law, that limit the post-transition regime's right to expel them despite the illegality of their arrival in the territory.

Various international human rights may be implicated in measures of expulsion. These include the right to a hearing, the prohibition on racial and other discrimination, the right to property,[13] the right to family and private life, the prohibition on inhuman treatment, and more. The

[10] In *Veysi Dag* v. *the Secretary of State for the Home Department*, [33], the UK Immigration Appeal Tribunal pointed out that in the circumstances, even if TRNC nationality were recognized, the appellant would not have succeeded in his asylum request.

[11] As codified in ILC, *Draft Articles on Nationality of Natural Persons in Relation to the Succession of States*.

[12] Even the European Convention on Nationality Article 20(a), provides that states are obligated to grant only the right to remain in that state, to nationals of a predecessor state habitually resident in the territory over which sovereignty is transferred to a successor state and who have not acquired its nationality.

[13] E.g. when the freedom of ownership is conditional upon residential status, or when expulsion is carried out in a manner that prevents individuals from benefiting from their property.

present discussion focuses on certain norms which are particularly pertinent to expulsion of long-term settlers implanted under an illegal regime. It also focuses on two international instruments: the 1966 International Covenant on Civil and Political Rights (ICCPR), which is binding on all post-transition regimes examined here,[14] and the European Convention on Human Rights and Fundamental Freedoms (ECHR), which is binding upon the Baltic states and is expected to be binding upon the UCR.[15] These legal instruments are independent of each other both institutionally and substantively. The existence (or otherwise) of any right under one of them does not affect the existence (or otherwise) of any right under the other. Accordingly, the rights of settlers have to be examined separately under each instrument as may be relevant to the specific post-transition regime. At the same time, there is undoubtedly some cross-fertilization between the work of the ECtHR and the Human Rights Committee (HRC) overseeing the implementation of the ICCPR, which affects the interpretation of various provisions within the two instruments.

Protection of a person's attachment to the territory

When the illegal regime lasts over two decades, as has happened in the cases examined here, there are likely to be many members of the settler community who consider the territory their home both geographically and socially, having lived there a large part of their life or even all of it. They may have never been to their state of origin (possibly their state of nationality, but not necessarily). This long-term residence is a fact which generates legal consequences and may be protected under international human rights instruments.

ECHR Article 8

ECHR Article 8 stipulates:

1. Everyone has the right to respect for his private and family life, his home and his correspondence.
2. There shall be no interference by a public authority with the exercise of this right except such as is in accordance with the law and is necessary in a

[14] ICCPR, to be binding upon the UCR according to the Annan Plan, Foundation Agreement, Annex V, Item 112 in the multilateral treaty list binding upon the UCR.

[15] Annan Plan, Foundation Agreement, Annex V, Item 204 in the multilateral treaty list binding upon the UCR. The rights to privacy and to the home are also guaranteed by the Constitution of Estonia, Article 33; Constitution of Latvia, Article 96; Constitution of Lithuania, Article 24; Constitution of Timor-Leste, Article 37; Annan Plan, Draft Constitution for the UCR, Article 11(1), enshrining the ECHR in the constitution.

> democratic society in the interests of national security, public safety or the economic well-being of the country, for the prevention of disorder or crime, for the protection of health or morals, or for the protection of the rights and freedoms of others.

Under ECtHR jurisprudence, the concept of 'private life' within the meaning of Article 8 encompasses the totality of social ties between individuals and the communities in which they live.[16] The right to private life protects 'the right to establish and develop relationships with other human beings and the outside world' and 'can sometimes embrace aspects of an individual's social identity'.[17] The expulsion of long-term integrated residents therefore constitutes an interference with their right to respect for private life.[18]

The criteria for assessing a person's integration within the state were developed mostly with respect to expulsion of criminal convicts, but are applicable *mutatis mutandis* to expulsion on other grounds, including settlement under an illegal regime. The extent of integration is measured through the solidity of social, cultural and family ties with the state of residence and with the state of origin (usually the state of nationality).[19] Those depend on the length of the person's stay in the country from which he or she is to be expelled, the nationalities of other persons affected, the person's family situation and the seriousness of the difficulties which family members are likely to encounter in the candidate expellee's country of origin. The ECtHR has recognized that the longer a person has been residing in a particular state, the stronger would his or her ties with that country be, and the weaker would the ties with the state of nationality be. Therefore the court has regard for the special situation of foreigners who have spent most, if not all, of their childhood in the state of residence, were brought up there and received their education there.

16 ECtHR, *Üner* v. *Netherlands*, [59].

17 ECtHR, *Pretty* v. *United Kingdom*, Application No. 2346/02 ECHR 2002-III [61]; cf ACHR Article 11(2). According to the jurisprudence of the Inter-American Commission on Human Rights, 'The requirements of art 11 encompass a range of factors pertaining to the dignity of the individual, including, for example, the ability to pursue the development of one's personality and aspirations, determine one's identity, and define one's personal relationships'. Report No. 4/01 Case 11.625 María Eugenia Morales de Sierra, Guatemala (19 January 2001), [46].

18 *Üner* v. *the Netherlands*, [59], uses the term 'settled' in the sense of 'integrated', which is more common in Council of Europe documents and ECtHR judgments.

19 ECtHR, *Üner* v. *the Netherlands*, [58].

ECtHR judges have in a number of cases proposed that long-term residents should be treated similarly to nationals, rendering them practically immune to expulsion.[20] In *Üner* v. *the Netherlands*, however, the majority opinion squarely rejected the proposition that this assimilation should be read into Article 8, insisting that states should be permitted to maintain the functionality of Article 8(2). Thus an 'integrated alien' is not a separate category of persons enjoying immunity from expulsion by virtue of quasi-status alone.[21]

ICCPR Article 12(4)

The universal human rights instruments do not protect long-term residents as such. This matter was considered in *Stewart* v. *Canada* in 1996 with respect to ICCPR Article 12(4), which stipulates, 'No one shall be arbitrarily deprived of the right to enter his own country'. The applicant was a British citizen who had resided in Canada since the age of seven but had never acquired Canadian nationality. He was facing deportation from Canada on grounds of his criminal activity, and complained that this was a violation of his right under Article 12(4). Article 12(4) had been interpreted as protecting, first and foremost, nationals.[22] In line with earlier interpretations, the majority in the HRC held the view that the term 'his own country' in Article 12(4) 'applies to individuals who are nationals and to certain categories of individuals who, while not nationals in a formal sense, are also not "aliens" within the meaning of article 13 [which prohibits the arbitrary expulsion of aliens lawfully in the country], although they may be considered as aliens for other purposes'.[23] The Committee added that the concept 'his own country'

[20] Judge Martens in ECtHR, *Beldjoudi* v. *France*; also his dissenting opinion in ECtHR, *Boughanemi* v. *France*; Judge Morenilla partly dissenting and Judge Wildhaber concurring in ECtHR, *Nasri* v. *France*; Judge Baka dissenting in ECtHR, *Boughanemi* v. *France*, and in ECtHR, *Boujlifa* v. *France*; Judge Morenilla dissenting in ECtHR, *Boujlifa* v. *France*; joint dissenting opinion of Judges Baka and van Dijk in *Boujlifa* v. *France*; Joint Dissenting Opinion of Judges Costa, Zupančič and Türmen in ECtHR, *Üner* v. *the Netherlands*, [5].

[21] ECtHR, *Slivenko* v. *Latvia*, [95]. ECtHR, *Üner* v. *the Netherlands*, [56]–[58], which examines this issue in light of the Committee of Ministers Recommendation Rec (2000) 15 and PACE Recommendation 1504 (2001).

[22] The prohibition in Article 12(4) is not absolute but is limited to 'arbitrary' denial of the right to enter one's county that is unreasonable in the circumstances; the HRC nonetheless 'considers that there are few, if any, circumstances in which deprivation of the right to enter one's own country could be reasonable' (HRC General Comment 27: Freedom of movement (Article 12), in 'Compilation of General Comments', UN Doc HRI/GEN/1/Rev.9 Volume I, paragraph 21).

[23] *Stewart* v. *Canada*, [12.3].

embraces, at the very least, an individual who, because of his special ties to or claims in relation to a given country cannot there be considered to be a mere alien. This would be the case, for example, of nationals of a country who have there been stripped of their nationality in violation of international law and of individuals whose country of nationality has been incorporated into or transferred to another national entity whose nationality is being denied them . . . The language of article 12, paragraph 4, permits a broader interpretation, moreover, that might embrace other categories of long-term residents, particularly stateless persons arbitrarily deprived of the right to acquire the nationality of the country of such residence.[24]

Since Mr Stewart's failure to acquire Canadian nationality was attributed to his own inaction, the HRC found that he was not protected by Article 12(4). In *Madafferi* v. *Australia* the Committee summarized its jurisprudence thus:

a person who enters a State under the State's immigration laws, and subject to the conditions of those laws, cannot normally regard that State as his 'own country', when he has not acquired its nationality and continues to retain the nationality of his country of origin. An exception might only arise in limited circumstances, such as where unreasonable impediments are placed on the acquisition of nationality.[25]

Accordingly, under the HRC's jurisprudence, attachment to the territory through long-term presence does not suffice to protect a person from expulsion. What is required is a formal link to the state of residence, such as nationality, or special circumstances that justify substitution of that formal link, generally linked to victimization of the person by that state with respect to formalizing the relationship, or by the state of origin with respect to the enjoyment of its own nationality. Persons holding a foreign nationality who have not been unfairly denied the possibility of naturalization in the state of residence are therefore not protected by Article 12(4).[26]

[24] *Stewart* v. *Canada*, [12.4]. See also *Madafferi* v. *Australia*.

[25] HRC, *Madafferi* v. *Australia*, [9.6]. The Committee may have limited the scope of Article 12(4) further than member states had expected it to. In 1981 Canada claimed that the right under Article 12(4) was available to nationals or permanent residents. HRC, *AS* v. *Canada*, Decision on Admissibility, Communication No. 68/1980 (31 March 1981) UN Doc CCPR/C/12/D/68/1980, [5.1]. But in HRC, *Canepa* v. *Canada*, [9.2], Canada claimed that a person cannot acquire a right under Article 12(4) by virtue only of long-term residence. HRC, *Madafferi* v. *Australia* followed *Stewart* v. *Canada*.

[26] In other words, a person can only have one 'own country'. It is not a matter of comparative strength of links but of one attachment excluding another. In HRC, *Toala et al.* v. *New Zealand*, [11.4], the Committee went even further in restricting recourse to Article 12(4), this time on factual grounds, by suggesting that nationals who have no effective links with the state of nationality cannot claim the right under Article 12(4) with respect to that State.

This jurisprudence was criticized by a minority of Committee members, in *Stewart* v. *Canada* and subsequently.[27] The dissenting view on this point (held by at least six members of the HRC[28]) was that the ICCPR is concerned with the 'strong personal and emotional links an individual may have with the territory where he lives and with the social circumstances obtaining in it'. Therefore a state should be regarded as 'one's own country' not by virtue of one's formal ties, but by virtue of 'the web of relationships that form his or her social environment'.[29] The dissenting committee members opined that even in the absence of a formal link or quasi-link of nationality, Article 12(4) invites consideration of such matters as long-standing residence, close personal and family ties and intentions to remain, as well as the absence of such ties elsewhere.[30] The minority view in *Stewart* thus attached to Article 12(4) a meaning similar to that of ECHR Article 8. This approach may be preferable to the majority opinion, which implies that a state of residence becomes a person's 'own country' only through the cumulative failures of itself and of the state of nationality. In addition, it is difficult to imagine that the drafters of Article 12(4) intended to attach to a very general terminology the specific meaning attributed to it by the majority opinion. On the other hand, it is also difficult to read the phrases 'his own country' or 'arbitrarily' as incorporating the protection

27 HRC, *Canepa* v. *Canada*, individual opinions by Committee Members Evatt and Medina Quiroga (dissenting), and Chanet (dissenting).

28 HRC, *Stewart* v. *Canada*, individual dissenting opinion by Committee Members Evatt, Medina Quiroga, Aguilar Urbina [5]–[7], and dissenting opinions by Committee Members Bhagwati, Chanet and Prado Vallejo. Committee Member Klein's opinion does not address the matter expressly but his agreement with the other dissenting judges may be inferred from his dissatisfaction with the delineation of the relationship between Articles 12(4) and 13.

29 Both quotes from the dissenting opinion by Committee Members Evatt, Medina Quiroga, Aguilar Urbina, [5].

30 Dissenting opinion by Committee Members Evatt, Medina Quiroga, Aguilar Urbina, [5]–[6]. See also Manfred Nowak, *U.N. Covenant on Civil and Political Rights: CCPR Commentary*, 2nd edn (Kehl: N. P. Engel, 2005), 287–288; Stig Jagerskiold, 'The Freedom of Movement', in Louis Henkin (ed.), *The International Bill of Rights: The Covenant on Civil and Political Rights* (New York: Columbia University Press, 1981), 180–181; Jean-Marie Henckaerts, *Mass Expulsion in Modern International Law and Practice* (The Hague: Martinus Nijhoff, 1995), 83; Hurst Hannum, *The Right to Leave and Return in International Law and Practice* (Dordrecht: Martinus Nijhoff, 1987), 59–60. See also 'The Right to Leave and the Right to Return: A Declaration Adopted by the Uppsala Colloquium, Sweden, June 21, 1972', reprinted in (1973) 7 *International Migration Review* 62–66. Under Article 12 of the declaration, states may refuse re-entry of long-term residents who are not nationals only in the most exceptional circumstances.

of a social environment.[31] Furthermore, it is unlikely that the status of a person which creates international obligations for that state should be defined by factors entirely outside that state's control. It is true that the majority's interpretation also takes account of factors outside the state of residence's control, such as illegally created statelessness by other states, but it does not allow the individual unilaterally to create obligations upon the state of residence. In *Canepa* v. *Canada*, Mr Scheinin, in critique of the majority opinion in *Stewart* as overly limited, added other potential categories of persons entitled to protection under Article 12(4), namely 'if the person is stateless or if it would be impossible or clearly unreasonable for him or her to integrate into the society corresponding to his or her de jure nationality'.[32] Mr Scheinin's formula remains distinct from the minority view in that it requires some impediment to integration in the state of nationality, and does not bar expulsion on the sole ground of integration in the state of residence. But like the minority, this formula expands this 'inability', from formal obstacles to practical obstacles that result from strong integration in the state of residence.[33] This modification bridges some of the gap between the minority and the majority views, by shifting slightly from reliance on formal status alone to accommodation of factual considerations.

Although the majority's limited interpretation was incorporated in the HRC's General Comment on Article 12(4) adopted in 1999, the Committee did attach some weight to the candidate expellee's factual link with the state of residence. It noted that 'other factors may in certain circumstances result in the establishment of close and enduring connections between a person and a country', and requested states to report on the rights of permanent residents to return to their country of residence.[34] This implies that long-term residence may be not entirely without consequences.

Status versus circumstances and settlers under an illegal regime

There is a striking difference between the protection from expulsion available under ICCPR Article 12(4) and that offered under ECHR Article 8.

[31] See also Amnesty International, 'The Right to Return: The Case of the Palestinians, Policy Statement, Amnesty International's Position on Forcible Exile and the Right to Return' (30 March 2001), MDE 15/013/2001, [7].

[32] HRC, *Canepa* v. *Canada*, individual opinion by Committee Member Scheinin.

[33] Compare with ECtHR, *Üner* v. *the Netherlands*, [58].

[34] HRC General Comment 27, in 'Compilation of General Comments', UN Doc HRI/GEN/1/Rev.9 Volume I, paragraph 20.

Protection under Article 12(4) depends on formal status, while under ECHR Article 8 it depends on the factual situation. Interestingly, in both the HRC and the ECtHR there have been attempts to move from one type of protection to the other. In the ECtHR it was proposed to regard long-term residence as a quasi-status which generates immunity to expulsion. A trend in the opposite direction was discernible in the HRC, namely the attempt to base protection under Article 12(4) on factual circumstances rather than on a formal status. As noted above, these attempts have generally failed.

The difference in approach between ECHR Article 8 and ICCPR Article 12(4) is potentially crucial for settlers under an illegal regime. Under ECHR Article 8, the illegality of these settlers' arrival in the territory and the lack of formal status under the post-transition regime's law are two factors among many that need to be considered. As the calls gain ground to apply to long-term residents the same legal standards that are applied to nationals,[35] the weight of these factors may become even less significant. In contrast, under ICCPR Article 12(4) status remains a decisive criterion for protection against expulsion. Settlers' attachment to the territory of the post-transition regime will be a relevant factor only if the 'other factors' that create 'enduring connections' with the state of residence are given weight. For this reason, the potential shift in interpretation of ICCPR Article 12(4) is of paramount importance.

The mention in *Stewart* v. *Canada* of the applicability of Article 12(4) to long-term residents who become stateless following state succession in their country of origin is acutely relevant to settlers in the Baltic states.[36] Many of them had become stateless as a result of the USSR's break-up and the gaps created by the lack of co-ordination of the domestic legislation between the Russian Federation, the various newly independent states and the Baltic states. Article 12(4) can cover situations of loss of nationality following changes of sovereignty in the state of origin, but, under the HRC's jurisprudence, only if the loss is linked to conduct in bad faith by that state or by the state of residence. If protection under Article 12(4) is contingent upon nationality being 'denied', then inadvertently stateless persons such as Soviet-era settlers in the Baltic states are not protected. These persons are also not protected under the latter part of the HRC's

35 Through EU law, which admittedly distinguishes lawful residents from unlawful ones, a distinction which will not be eliminated easily.

36 See also HRC General Comment 27, in 'Compilation of General Comments', UN Doc HRI/GEN/1/Rev.9 Volume I, paragraph 20.

opinion in *Stewart*, which prohibits expulsion of stateless persons arbitrarily deprived of the right to acquire the nationality of the state. Since states are not obligated to grant nationality to stateless persons, the refusal of the post-transition regime to do so does not, in itself, constitute arbitrary conduct.

The right to family life

ICCPR Article 17 protects everyone from 'arbitrary or unlawful interference with his privacy, family, home'. The term 'privacy' has been interpreted narrowly, in the sense of isolation from society and the public, rather than the forging of social ties.[37] It thus differs from 'private life' under the ECHR.

Some protection of social ties is nonetheless available under Article 17 through the protection of the family. The term 'family' has originally also been interpreted narrowly, protecting individuals from expulsion only when expulsion would entail separation from immediate family relations, rather than from a social environment. This changed in *Winata* v. *Australia*. The matter concerned an Indonesian couple facing deportation from Australia after residing there illegally for many years. The couple had a thirteen-year-old child, a citizen of Australia who was thereby entitled to remain in the country. The HRC noted that expulsion of the parents would have compelled the family to choose between leaving the child alone in Australia and having him accompany them while removing him from his state of nationality and familiar social environment. The majority found this to be an 'interference' with the 'family', because 'substantial changes to long-settled family life would follow' whatever choice the parents made. The Committee found this interference to be arbitrary with respect to all family members. It took into consideration the fact that the complainants' son 'has grown in Australia from his birth 13 years ago, attending Australian schools as an ordinary child would and developing the social relationships inherent in that'.[38] Similar circumstances were presented in *Madafferi* v. *Australia*. There the Committee noted that the state's reasons for the removal of a person must be weighed against the degree of hardship that the family and its members would encounter as a consequence of such removal. In the assessment of this hardship the Committee took account of the alien environment that the spouse and children would have faced in moving from the state of residence to the

[37] Nowak, *CCPR Commentary*, 379. [38] HRC, *Winata* v. *Australia*, [7.2]–[7.3].

state of nationality, the language barrier for the children, and the difficulty in caring under such circumstances for the expellee, whose mental health had been seriously troubled, in part by acts that could be ascribed to the state wishing to expel him.[39]

Together, the *Winata* and *Madafferi* jurisprudence applies to the family of the candidate expellee the criteria employed under ECHR Article 8: the totality of social ties between the family and the society in which it lives, and the difficulties that the family would face in the state of nationality. The protection of the family from arbitrary interference as interpreted by the HRC may prohibit the expulsion of settlers under an illegal regime, if they are integrated within local society or have children who are nationals of the post-transition regime. This assimilation of ICCPR Article 17 to ECHR Article 8 led several members of the Committee to dissent.[40] The two provisions still differ with respect to adult second-generation immigrants who are attached to the state of residence, but have no formal family relationships there.[41] They would be protected from expulsion under ECHR Article 8 but not under ICCPR Article 17.

The ECtHR has in a number of cases faced situations similar to that of *Winata*, namely where expulsion would have created difficulties for the family in the candidate expellee's country of origin and was therefore an interference with the right to respect for 'family life'. However, once Article 8 was expanded to cover a person's social environment, the need to rely on the right to respect for family life was reduced to rare situations where the only link that an individual has to the state of residence is marriage to one of its nationals or to a long-term resident.[42]

Protection of the home

ICCPR Article 17 also protects the individual from interference with the 'home'. The use of 'home' rather than 'dwelling', abode' and so on may suggest that the intention was to take account of the sociological notion of 'home', namely the emotional link of a person to his or her place of residence, in which case 'home' could reasonably be interpreted as encompassing the social environment of a person, and to assimilate Article 17 to

[39] HRC, *Madafferi* v. *Australia*, [9.7]–[9.8]. Compare with *Nasri* v. *France*, partly dissenting opinion of Judge Morenilla.

[40] HRC, *Winata* v. *Australia*, individual opinion by Committee Members Bhagwati, Khalil, Kretzmer and Yalden (dissenting); individual opinion of Committee Member Wedgewood in HRC, *Madafferi* v. *Australia*.

[41] E.g. HRC, *Canepa* v. *Canada*.

[42] As was the case in ECtHR, *Boultif* v. *Switzerland*.

ECHR Article 8. However, the jurisprudence of the HRC does not approve of this approach. In *Canepa* v. *Canada*, a candidate expellee invoked his right to protection of the home. After establishing that expulsion of the complainant would not cause disruption of immediate family relations, the Committee concluded that '[t]here appear to be no circumstances particular to the author [of the complaint] or to his family which would lead the Committee to conclude that his removal from Canada was an arbitrary interference with his family, nor with his privacy or home'.[43] It thus attached no weight to social ties as 'home' for the purpose of Article 17. The HRC's General Comment on Article 17 also suggests that the acceptable interpretation is limited to 'home' as a tangible structure rather than as a social institution.[44] Support for this approach is also available in the ruling of the ECtHR, which said, in the context of ECHR Article 8, that a particular place and property is a 'home' if one has 'concrete and persisting links with the *property* concerned', and emphasized that the term was not synonymous with 'family roots', which is 'a vague and emotive concept'.[45] It therefore appears that settlers cannot successfully challenge their expulsion on the ground that it constitutes a violation of their home.

The prohibition on inhuman treatment

In a number of cases, the ECtHR considered the claim that expulsion of long-term residents, particularly second-generation ones, violated the prohibition on inhuman treatment, codified in ECHR Article 3.[46] In *Beldjoudi* v. *France*, Judge de Meyer said that expulsion of the applicant, who 'would be ejected, after over forty years, from a country which has always in fact been "his" since birth, even though he does not possess its "nationality"', would constitute inhuman treatment.[47] This statement suggests that long-term residence – from birth in this case – renders expulsion *ipso facto* a violation of the prohibition on inhuman treatment. It does not seem to matter whether that residence was lawful or not. In *Nasri* v. *France*, Judge de Meyer qualified this categorical statement when, reiterating his

43 ECtHR, *Canepa* v. *Canada*, [11.5]. There were no individual opinions on this issue.

44 HRC General Comment 16: Article 17 (Right to Privacy) (23 March 1988) in 'Compilation of General Comments', UN Doc HRI/GEN/1/Rev.9 Volume I.

45 ECtHR, *Demopoulos and Others* v. *Turkey*, [136], emphasis added.

46 ICCPR, Article 7; CAT, Article 2.

47 ECtHR, *Beldjoudi* v. *France*, separate opinion of Judge de Meyer.

position, he added that he did so 'in particular in view of Mr Nasri's disability' (deaf-mutism).[48] Accordingly, settlers may need to demonstrate particular hardships in integration in their state of nationality.

Judge Morenilla in *Nasri* v. *France* provided another rationale for reliance on ECHR Article 3. First, he concurred that expulsion would have been a violation of Article 3 because of the sensory and social isolation to which the applicant would have been exposed to if expelled to his state of nationality.[49] However, he suggested that Article 3 might be applicable regardless of the future awaiting the candidate expellee. He considered the general question which underlies the application of Article 3 to be

> the limits to be imposed on administrative measures – or sanctions – of deportation to the country 'of origin', on account of criminal or antisocial behaviour on the part of 'second generation' aliens, including those who, like the applicant, came as children accompanying their migrant worker parents.[50]

He noted:

> A State which, for reasons of convenience, accepts immigrant workers and authorizes their residence becomes responsible for the education and social integration of the children of such immigrants as it is of the children of its 'citizens'. Where such social integration fails, and the result is antisocial or criminal behaviour, the State is also under a duty to make provision for their social rehabilitation instead of sending them back to their country of origin, which has no responsibility for the behaviour in question and where the possibilities of rehabilitation given the foreign social environment are virtually non-existent.

Unlike Judge de Meyer, Judge Morenilla attached significance to the conduct of the state of long-term residence. It remains unclear whether he interpreted Article 3 as protecting all second-generation immigrants born to lawful residents, only those whom the state has failed to integrate or those who in addition face hardship in their state of origin for the same reasons for which they failed to integrate in the state of residence.

Judge Wildhaber interpreted the statements of Judges de Meyer and Morenilla as extending protection under Article 3 to all second-generation immigrants. For this reason he objected to the reliance on Article 3, and commented that it 'might have implied that no balancing of public interests can take place but rather that immigrants of the "second generation"

[48] ECtHR, *Nasri* v. *France*, partly dissenting opinion of Judge de Meyer.
[49] ECtHR, *Nasri* v. *France*, partly dissenting opinion of Judge Morenilla, [1].
[50] ECtHR, *Nasri* v. *France*, partly dissenting opinion of Judge Morenilla, [2].

cannot be expelled at all'.[51] Judge Wildhaber alluded to the fact that the prohibition on inhuman treatment bears no exception or balancing mechanism among the hardship of expulsion, the interests of the state of residence and the circumstances of the individual's arrival in it. Had the two judges suggested that any expulsion of a second-generation immigrant was inhuman treatment, Judge Wildhaber's criticism would have been justified. But the two judges qualified the application of Article 3 by taking into account factors such as the history of the candidate expellees, what those persons were expected to face in the states of origin and the conduct of the state of residence. Thus, while protection under Article 3 is absolute once its applicability in a particular case is established, entering within its scope, particularly when the risk to the individual is not physical, is not necessarily guaranteed to all second-generation immigrants. At the same time, Judges de Meyer and Morenilla did go beyond the ordinary interpretation of Article 3, which assumes that only human interference constitutes inhuman treatment, at least where no clear physical risk is expected.[52]

Insofar as settlers under an illegal regime are concerned, the liberal interpretation of Judge Morenilla of the prohibition on inhuman treatment is unlikely to provide protection from expulsion. Since the post-transition regime is not responsible for the presence of the settlers in its territory, the dislocation itself is unlikely to be considered severe enough to trigger the prohibition, although in individual cases there may be particular hardship.

The prohibition on discrimination

The ICCPR only prohibits discrimination in the enjoyment of treaty rights.[53] The ECHR prohibits discrimination as a free-standing concept, irrespective of other rights. Discrimination is the unreasonable inequality in treatment of individuals or groups, which has the purpose or effect of nullifying or impairing their exercise of human rights and fundamental freedoms on an equal footing with others.[54] A distinction among persons

[51] ECtHR, *Nasri* v. *France*, concurring opinion of Judge Wildhaber.

[52] Pieter van Dijk, Fried van Hoof, Arjen van Rijn and Leo Zwaak (eds.), *Theory and Practice of the European Convention on Human Rights*, 4th edn (Antwerp: Intersentia, 2006), 440.

[53] ICCPR, Articles 2, 26.

[54] ECHR, Article 14; Protocol No. 12 to the Convention for the Protection of Human Rights and Fundamental Freedoms (signed 4 November 2000, entry into force 1 April 2005) ETS 177; CERD, Article 1(1); ACHR, Article 1(1); UDHR, Article 7; HRC General Comment 18: Non-discrimination (9 November 1989), in 'Compilation of General Comments', UN Doc HRI/GEN/1/Rev.9 Volume I, paragraph 1.

is not discriminatory if the criteria used are reasonable and objective and their effect is proportionate to the aim pursued.[55] At the same time, distinctions based on race, colour, descent and national or ethnic origin are deemed absolutely prohibited.[56]

In considering whether the distinction between settlers and nationals of the post-transition regime is a legitimate criterion for expulsion, it should be borne in mind that expulsion of foreign nationals is not prima facie discriminatory merely because nationals may not be expelled under similar circumstances.[57] But where vulnerability to expulsion hinges on eligibility for nationality, the question whether the state has acted in a discriminatory manner shifts from the criteria for expulsion to the criteria of eligibility for nationality.

It is generally accepted that states may lay out conditions for the acquisition of nationality, provided that these do not discriminate against any particular national origin.[58] However, an apparently neutrally drafted distinction is prohibited if it is merely a cover-up for an exclusion of a specific ethnic or national origin. Therefore when the post-transition regime establishes criteria for nationality that are dependent on affiliation with the illegal regime, the question is whether this is a legitimate differentiation or a discriminatory one. For example, naturalization is often dependent on a certain period of legal residence in the country. Such a provision might prevent settlers from relying on their residence in the territory during the existence of the illegal regime. Prima facie, this provision is not discriminatory because it also excludes other illegal residents and does not impair the settlers' enjoyment of any human right on an equal footing with other foreigners. If, however, only residence under the illegal regime is excluded but not other instances of illegal residence, the post-transition regime's conduct may be suspect of discrimination. The question would then be whether the distinction between illegal residence under the illegal regime and other illegal residence is justifiable or arbitrary.

55 HRC General Comment 18: Non-discrimination (9 November 1989), in 'Compilation of General Comments', UN Doc HRI/GEN/1/Rev.9 Volume I, paragraph 13.

56 CERD, Article 2(1). The prohibition on racial discrimination is often referred to as a peremptory norm.

57 CERD, Article 1(2); UN Doc A/CN.4/565 (10 July 2006), paragraph 280.

58 CERD, Article 1(3). The term 'nationality' used in the Convention should be read as 'national origin', which is similar but not clearly identical to 'ethnic origin'. Natan Lerner, *The UN Convention on the Elimination of All Forms of Racial Discrimination* (Alphen aan den Rijn: Sijthoff & Noordhoff, 1980), 29–30.

The prohibition on collective expulsion

If the post-transition regime is contemplating the removal of a large number of individuals on the basis of their group affiliation, namely their being settlers brought in by an illegal regime, the collective character of removal becomes pertinent. Collective expulsion has been understood by the ECtHR,[59] and subsequently by the ILC Special Rapporteur on the Expulsion of Aliens, as

> any measure by the competent authorities compelling aliens, as a group, to leave a country, except where such a measure is taken after and on the basis of a reasonable and objective examination of the particular case of each individual alien of the group.[60]

In other words, collective expulsion is defined by the lack of individual review. It is prohibited by Article 4 of ECHR Protocol 4, and by other regional instruments.[61] The ICCPR contains no specific provisions on collective expulsion, but Article 13 (which prohibits arbitrary expulsion of aliens lawfully within the territory of a state) has been interpreted as requiring an inspection of the circumstances of each individual. Henckaerts argues that collective expulsion is qualitatively similar to individual expulsion, because the requirement of a review process exists also with respect to individual expulsions. Nonetheless, collective expulsion merits a separate prohibiting provision because the massive scale of expulsions

[59] ECtHR, *Sultani* v. *France*; see also ECtHR, *Becker* v. *Denmark* (Admissibility), quoted in Henckaerts, *Mass Expulsion*, 12, footnote 35: the decision to expel must be based on 'a reasonable and objective examination of the particular cases of each individual alien of the group'. See also ECtHR, *Conka* v. *Belgium*, [56].

[60] UN Doc A/CN.4/581 (19 April 2007), paragraph 107.

[61] Article 22(9) ACHR provides: 'The collective expulsion of aliens is prohibited'; Article 12(5) of the Banjul Charter provides: 'The mass expulsion of non-nationals shall be prohibited. Mass expulsion shall be that which is aimed at national, racial, ethnic or religious groups'. The preparatory memorandum of the UN Secretariat for the ILC distinguished collective expulsion from mass expulsion, which it defined by the quantitative element. According to the memorandum, mass expulsion is prohibited (even if it is not collective) where it imposes an excessive burden on the receiving state or when it constitutes an abuse of rights. UN Doc A/CN.4/565 (10 July 2006), paragraphs 993–994. In the context of settlers under an illegal regime, it is appropriate to speak of 'collective expulsion', because prima facie the issue is that of targeting a group without considering the particulars of each individual. At any rate, it is doubtful whether the distinction proposed by the memorandum is reflected in the international instruments. The ILC Special Rapporteur, for example, considered Article 12(5) of the Banjul Charter as prohibiting collective expulsion, contrary to the article's express wording. Indeed, Article 12(5) prohibits the discriminatory nature of the expulsion, rather than the number of expellees.

creates a presumption that certain norms have been violated, particularly the prohibition on discrimination and the right to review.[62] The ILC Special Rapporteur concludes that 'it seems reasonable to suggest that there is a general principle of international law on this matter that is "recognized by civilized nations" and prohibits collective expulsion'.[63]

Expulsion by the post-transition regime of settlers under an illegal regime because of their status would appear to be a collective expulsion. This shifts the burden of proof onto the post-transition regime to show that the expulsion is lawful. The post-transition regime may discharge this burden by providing each individual with a genuine process of review, of the ground for expulsion and of the proportionality of the expulsion as a response to that ground. Group affiliation alone would not be a legitimate ground for expulsion unless the post-transition regime can point to a detriment to it that is associated with that group. Such detrimental factors are considered in the following section.

Grounds for interference with protected rights

The fact that an act of expulsion interferes with a person's family or private life does not mean that it is impermissible. ECHR Article 8 provides an exhaustive list of grounds that would justify interference with one's private life: 'national security, public safety or economic well-being of the country, for the prevention of disorder or crime, for the protection of health or morals, or for the protection of rights and freedoms of others'.[64] The justification for expulsion is assessed in relation to the aim and effects of the measure under consideration. The interference must be justified by a pressing social need, and there must be a 'reasonable relationship of proportionality between the means employed and the aim sought to be realized'.[65] Of the various international instruments, only the ECHR sets out an exhaustive list of grounds for expulsion, as well as other specific limitations, thereby setting the highest threshold for permissible interference with rights.[66] If an aim is legitimate and proportionate for

62 Henckaerts, *Mass Expulsion*, 14–15.

63 UN Doc A/CN.4/581 (19 April 2007), paragraph 115.

64 ACHR Article 30 allows a wider scope of restriction, requiring that restrictions be placed only in accordance with law, for reasons of general interest and in accordance with the purpose for which such restrictions have been established.

65 ECtHR, *Case Relating to Certain Aspects of the Laws on the Use of Languages in Education in Belgium (Merits)*, [10], cited by Henckaerts, *Mass Expulsion*, 24; see also ECtHR, *Üner* v. *the Netherlands*, [55].

66 See also UDHR Article 29.

the purpose of ECHR Article 8, it would likely also be non-discriminatory under the ECHR. It would probably also be regarded as non-arbitrary for the purposes of ICCPR Articles 12(4), 13 and 17, which are drafted in more general terms than ECHR Article 8.

The present section examines whether the illegality of the regime and of the settlement under it, as well as the characteristic circumstances surrounding its termination, can be considered legitimate grounds for a general policy on the expulsion of settlers. But the determination whether expulsion serves a legitimate aim and whether it is a proportionate means of achieving that aim must ultimately be made by reference to each individual potential expellee's circumstances and cannot be exhausted *in abstractu*. Accordingly, the present examination is unavoidably generalized.

Illegality of the settlers' presence in the post-transition regime's territory

The expulsion of settlers may formally fall within the ECHR Article 8 category of 'prevention of disorder and crime', which under ECtHR jurisprudence entitles the state to take dissuasive measures such as expulsion against persons who have violated immigration law.[67] This jurisprudence clearly refers to domestic immigration law. But although the transfer of the illegal regime's settlers is likely to be prohibited under the immigration law of the ousted regime,[68] the weighty violation of law generated by the transfer of settlers is not of domestic law but of international law. Where the illegal regime consists of an annexation, it is also governed by the law of occupation.[69] Article 49 of the Fourth Geneva Convention prohibits the occupying power from deporting or transferring parts of its own civilian population into the territory it occupies. This prohibition constitutes customary law.[70]

Maintenance of the international legal order may be a goal justifying restrictions on rights, particularly if the violation is a serious one. But dissuasive measures such as expulsion are valuable against people who act in bad faith with knowledge that they are violating the law. This is not

67 ECtHR, *Shevanova* v. *Latvia*, [74]; ECtHR, *Kaftailova* v. *Latvia*, [66].

68 It is questionable whether the domestic law of the ousted regime should be regarded as even applicable at the time that the settlers arrived.

69 On the Baltic states, Timor-Leste and the TRNC, see Eyal Benvenisti, *The International Law of Occupation* (Princeton, NJ: Princeton University Press, 1993), 67–72, 153–159, 177–181.

70 Jean Marie Henckaerts and Louise Doswald-Beck (eds.), *Customary International Humanitarian Law Volume I: Rules* (Geneva: ICRC, 2005), 462–463, Rule 130 and sources cited.

clearly the case of settlers. Not only does their knowledge of the actual situation differ from one individual to another; but the legal status of the territory may have been sufficiently indeterminate that it might be excessive to hold them in full knowledge of the implications of their conduct. The expulsion of persons who had not exercised any choice in relocating to the territory (whether they knew of the illegality or not) or were born in it carries even less weight for ensuring order and preventing crime.[71] Even when individuals knowingly and patently violate domestic immigration law, state interests often give way to individual circumstances.[72] Such an outcome is all the more expected when the individual acts in good faith.

Furthermore, under international law the responsibility for the transfer of settlers does not attach directly to the settlers, but to the illegal regime. Although Additional Protocol I and the ICC Statute designate the transfer by the occupying power of parts of its own civilian population into the territory it occupies as a war crime,[73] it is unlikely that criminal responsibility rests with every individual settler. Rather, it should rest with the facilitators of settlement.[74] Individuals should not be held accountable for the illegal regime's action, even when that accountability is reflected in the imposition of 'mere' administrative measures such as expulsion.

Protection of the right to self-determination

The 'protection of the rights and freedoms of others' includes the protection of the realization of the right to self-determination of the post-transition regime and its people. The presence of a settler population

71 In 2005, 11 per cent of the residents of Estonia were stateless. Over half of them had been born in Estonia. European Commission against Racism and Intolerance (ECRI), Third Report on Estonia (adopted 24 June 2005), paragraph 124.

72 HRC, *Winata* v. *Australia*; ECtH, *Shevanova* v. *Latvia*.

73 Additional Protocol I, Articles 85(4)(a) and 85; ICC Statute, Article 8(2)(b)(viii). None of the occupying powers discussed here are or have been parties to Additional Protocol I. The provisions of the ICC Statute are not directly applicable to any of the cases examined here, because the settlement occurred before 2002, possibly with the exception of the TRNC. Turkey is not party to the ICC Statute; Cyprus is party to it.

74 The Commentary on the ICC Statute acknowledges the challenge to the attribution of individual criminal responsibility for the transfer of civilian population 'by the Occupying Power'. It discusses at length the involvement of the occupying power that would bring a transfer of population into the purview of the criminal prohibition, but offers no guidance on who, within the apparatus of the occupying power, could be responsible under ICC Statute Article 8(2)(b)(viii). Michael Cottier, 'Article 8 War Crimes', in Otto Triffterer (ed.), *Commentary on the Rome Statute of the International Criminal Court*, 2nd edn (Munich: C. H. Beck, Hart, Nomos, 2008) 275, 368–369.

can jeopardize the exercise of the right to self-determination of the post-transition regime in a number of ways. First, it may be an obstacle to the recuperation (or development) of the new regime's national identity. The larger the settler population and the greater its political or economic weight, the more likely is the indigenous population of the post-transition regime to feel that its own identity is under threat. Such concerns cannot be dismissed as abstract when they are a reaction to actual detriment already caused by the illegal regime to the lawful regime's national identity.

Another aspect of self-determination is the political identity and integrity of the post-transition regime. This may be challenged if the withdrawn, illegal regime uses the presence of its diaspora to exert political pressure and intervene in the affairs of the post-transition regime. Such intervention may be military, as the Turkish military intervention in Cyprus in 1974 demonstrates, yet non-military pressure and intervention can be even more pervasive than military pressure, because they are less overt and there are fewer legal and other inhibitions resorting to them.

Protection of national security

A specific national security concern is that the presence of the settlers would amount, under certain circumstances, to presence of foreign military forces on the post-transition regime's territory. In time of conflict, this presence may act against the interests of the post-transition regime and in support of the previously illegal regime. There is no dispute that a state need not allow foreign troops on its territory. As the ECtHR said:

> the withdrawal of the armed forces of one independent State from the territory of another, following the dissolution of the state to which they both formerly belonged, constitutes, from the point of view of the Convention, a legitimate means of dealing with the various political, social and economic problems arising from that dissolution.[75]

The question is, however, how far beyond active military personnel this ground can expand without expulsion constituting excessive interference with the right to private life. One aspect of this question concerns reserve personnel. Ordinarily, a person's previous military training does not by itself justify a presumption of danger which trumps individual rights.

[75] ECtHR, *Slivenko* v. *Latvia*, [117]; HCNM 1993 Letter to Latvia.

Yet depending on other factors, such as the link with the state of origin, former military personnel and reservists might facilitate military intervention by the withdrawn illegal regime in time of conflict or in expectation of conflict.[76]

The other aspect of this issue concerns family members of military personnel. This aspect came before the ECtHR in 2003 in *Slivenko* v. *Latvia*. The question was whether treatment of retired military personnel and their families similar to the treatment of military personnel on active duty would constitute a disproportionate interference with their private lives. The first applicant, Tatjana Slivenko, was a permanent Latvian resident of Russian origin. She had moved to Latvia when she was one month old, when her father was an actively serving officer in the Soviet army. She later married Nikolay Slivenko, who was also a serving Soviet military officer stationed in Latvia. Their daughter Karina, the second applicant, was born in Riga. In 1994 Latvia and Russia reached agreement on compulsory departure from Latvia of military personnel on active duty, and on a right to remain in Latvia for retired military personnel.[77] Accordingly, Nikolay Slivenko was required to leave Latvia, while Tatjana Slivenko's parents were allowed to remain. Tatjana and Karina Slivenko were also required to leave, since they fell within the Latvian domestic law category of 'family members who had arrived in Latvia as a result of accompanying a military person', who were also expellable.

The applicants claimed that their removal from Latvia would violate their right under ECHR Article 8. They claimed that their presence in Latvia did not result from a family connection with a serving military person who was required to leave, Tatjana having arrived in Latvia long before she met her husband. The Latvian government maintained that its policy pursued the legitimate aims of protecting national security and preventing disorder and crime. It claimed that under the Latvian–Russian Treaty, family members of active military personnel could be required to leave regardless of the circumstances of their arrival in Latvia.

It was evident to the ECtHR that the continued presence of active servicemen of a foreign army, with their families, may be seen as incompatible with the sovereignty of an independent state and as a threat to national security.[78] The ECtHR therefore accepted that the Latvian–Russian treaty sought to protect legitimate interests with respect to military personnel. The court ruled that expulsion of family members of active servicemen

[76] E.g. Estonia's position in HRC; *Borzov* v. *Estonia*, [4.10].

[77] Latvian–Russian Troop Withdrawal Treaty.

[78] ECtHR, *Slivenko* v. *Latvia*, [77].

under the Treaty, regardless of the circumstances of their arrival in Latvia, would normally not be a disproportionate interference, having regard to the conditions of service of military officers who occasionally transfer from one place to another. The Latvian–Russian Treaty even respected the family life of the persons concerned by obligating Russia to accept the whole family unit within its territory, irrespective of the origin or nationality of individual family members. However, the applicants' expulsion was sought on the basis of the implementing Latvian law, the provisions of which were different from those of the treaty. Domestic Latvian law allowed expulsion based not on a familial relationship with active military persons, but on *arrival in connection with* the service of a military person, regardless of whether that person had since retired. This led the court to consider the status of retired personnel and their family members.[79] The court noted that national security does not justify expulsion of retired military officers and their families to the same extent that it justifies expulsion of active military officers. Greater weight must be attached to the legitimate private interests of retirees and their family members.[80] In the eyes of the court, the expulsion of family members of a retired officer who was himself entitled to remain in Latvia, on the basis of an unsubstantiated presumption of danger to national security because they were also family members of an active serviceman, was a disproportionate interference with the right to private life of those family members. It therefore ruled that expulsion of the applicants would violate ECHR Article 8.

The dissenting minority saw no reason to distinguish between military personnel and their families, or between active and retired personnel. They argued that the purpose of the Latvian–Russian Treaty was to repatriate the 'totality of a foreign army'. Requiring that family members present an actual danger to territorial security as a condition for their expulsion would undermine the effectiveness of the treaty in repatriating 'the totality' of the foreign army.[81] The minority was therefore willing to sanction the expulsion of the applicants. This position is difficult to accept. First, it is questionable why the 'totality' of an army necessarily includes retirees and their families. Second, Latvian law did not allow expulsion

[79] It is not clear to what extent the Court took into consideration the fact that the family had not arrived in Latvia as a result of the active serviceman's service.

[80] ECtHR, *Slivenko* v. *Latvia*, [118].

[81] ECtHR, *Slivenko* v. *Latvia*, joint dissenting opinion of Judges Wildhaber, Ress, Sir Nicolas Bratza, Cabral Barreto, Greve and Maruste, [7].

based merely on a familial relationship with active military persons but required arrival in connection with a military person. The minority was nonetheless willing to go well beyond Latvian law and accept expulsion based on a familial relationship with retired military persons who were themselves entitled to remain in Latvia.

The treatment of family members of foreign troops – active or retired – as inextricably linked to the military may be related to the dissenting judges' perspective on the political context in which the removal of troops was taking place. Unlike the majority,[82] the dissenting judges took account of 'the specific historical context and purpose for which the treaty was signed, namely the elimination of the consequences of the Soviet rule of Latvia'.[83] If expulsion is considered in this wider context, namely the reversal of the illegal regime, then the difference between retired and active military personnel is less significant, given that both groups had taken part in the consolidation of the illegal regime.[84] An argument along these lines was made expressly by Judge Maruste in a dissenting opinion and is considered next.

Redress for historical injustice

In *Slivenko*, Judge Maruste opined that 'the restoration of the independence of the Baltic States on the basis of legal continuity and the withdrawal of the Soviet/Russian troops has to be regarded as redress for an historical injustice', and that 'the withdrawal of the armed forces of one independent State from the territory of another constitutes an appropriate way of dealing with the various political, social and economic problems arising from that historical injustice'.[85] On that basis he accepted the legitimacy of expulsion of family members of military personnel from Latvia.

'Redress of historical injustice' might be regarded as a matter of 'protection of the rights and freedoms of others'. It is true that the presence of the settler community facilitated large-scale deprivation of the indigenous communities, through political alienation, economic marginalization and so on. Such deprivation may even have constituted a violation

82 ECtHR, *Slivenko* v. *Latvia*, majority opinion, [111].

83 ECtHR, *Slivenko* v. *Latvia*, joint dissenting opinion of Judges Wildhaber, Ress, Sir Nicolas Bratza, Cabral Barreto, Greve and Maruste, [4].

84 Civilian family members should still be treated differently, unless they were directly involved in the maintenance of the illegal regime.

85 ECtHR, *Slivenko* v. *Latvia*, separate dissenting opinion of Judge Maruste. Compare with the majority view, [117], which presents the Treaty as necessary for addressing the consequences of dissolution rather than for redressing a historical injustice.

of the obligation to respect the right of peoples to self-determination. Yet removal of an entire group on the ground of historical injustice caused by the consequences of political manoeuvring blurs the distinction between individual and state responsibility. Where individuals are responsible for specific acts of injustice, their exclusion from the state is justifiable, falling easily within 'prevention of disorder and crime' or 'national security'.[86] But violation of the right to self-determination as such through residence in the territory is not a matter of individual responsibility.[87] Unlike 'protection of rights and freedoms of others' through preventive measures which are forward-looking and envisage potential harm, expulsion as redress of historical injustice is a punitive measure. In circumstances where it has no conceivable role of prevention or deterrence, it must be justified on the ground of personal fault. Otherwise it would be an arbitrary making of the individual a scapegoat for the illegal regime's conduct.

Protection of limited resources

The presence of settlers may have immediate, tangible repercussions for the local population in the enjoyment of resources that are limited. The post-transition regime may wish to remove settlers in the interest of the 'economic wellbeing of the country', e.g. when they are perceived as dominating economic development at the expense of the indigenous population. Their presence may also have an adverse effect on 'the rights and freedoms of others'. A particularly acute problem is that of immovable property, since illegal regimes often engage in the transfer of such property from the local population to its own settlers. In the case of Cyprus, this was a major cause for the rejection of the Annan Plan by Greek Cypriots. In theory, the right to property and the right to residence are not inherently linked, and can formally be regulated independently of each other. In practice, the two are intimately linked: without property, a person has fewer means of establishing residence; without residence, a person has little access to property.[88]

[86] HCNM 1993 Letter to Latvia.

[87] Unless it also constitutes a specific international crime, an issue outside the scope of the present discussion.

[88] UN Sub-commission on the Promotion and Protection of Human Rights of the UN Commission on Human Rights, UN Doc E/CN.4/Sub.2/2002/17, paragraph 13; Eric Rosand, 'The Right to Return under International Law Following Mass Dislocation: The Bosnia Precedent?' (1997–1998) 19 *Michigan Journal of International Law* 1091.

6.2.3 Conclusions

Many of the concerns of the post-transition regime arise from the presence in the territory of a large settler population, although no risk emanates from any specific individual. There is something troubling about the notion that the scope of a person's individual right depends on whether his or her status is shared by other individuals for whom that person is not legally responsible and on the political circumstances in which that status arises. In other words, it is difficult to apply the criteria relating to individual rights when at issue is the resolution of a political conflict involving masses of individuals.

Clearly, few human rights are absolute, and in most cases the right of an individual may be balanced against the interests of the community. Particularly with respect to situations of mass movement, it has been suggested that not only are individual rights subject to limitations, but that international human rights law should not be fully applicable. For example, when the prohibition on *refoulement* was incorporated in the Refugee Convention of 1951, it was suggested by some delegations that it should not apply in situations of mass influx. Some scholars argue that ICCPR Article 12(4) is intended to apply only to individuals asserting an individual right, and that there was no intention to address claims resulting from mass displacement following political transfers of population.[89] A more general argument is that human rights discourse is not the appropriate tool for migration issues. In order to discharge their special duties of security, welfare, self-determination and community towards their own citizens and residents, states must have greater control over who comes within these categories. Accordingly, regulation of entry of foreigners into the country should be made not through human rights discourse but through policy considerations.[90] All these arguments posit not that the right in question may be interfered with, but that in certain circumstances it does not exist at all.

There are various reasons to reject the relevance of these arguments with respect to the permissibility of expelling settlers under an illegal regime. First, there should be a legal distinction between not allowing

[89] Jagerskiold, 'The Freedom of Movement', 180, Hannum, *The Right to Leave and Return*. 59–60, but see Guy Goodwin-Gill and Jane McAdam, *The Refugee in International Law* (Oxford: Oxford University Press, 2007), 206–208.

[90] Ruth Gavison, 'Immigration and the Human Rights Discourse: The Universality of Human Rights and the Relevance of States and of Numbers' (2010) 43 *Israel Law Review* 7.

persons into the country – refugees, returnees or other migrants – and forcing them out. As pointed out earlier, as a matter of *lex lata* there is an express prohibition under international law on collective expulsion. Second, for the most part, the problem of settlers does not directly raise questions of resource allocation. It is not a quantitative issue but a qualitative one: the argument is that the settler community *only as a community* presents a threat to the identity, national security and so on of the post-transition regime. This does not mean that the threat may not be taken into account. But in balancing it against the rights of the individual, it must not be overstated.

6.3 Practice

6.3.1 Rhodesia

Settlers under the Rhodesian regime

In 1965, the population of Rhodesia comprised about five million people, 4 per cent (210,000) of whom were White.[91] UDI was followed by a brief rise of emigration of Whites, Asians and Coloureds, arising from insecurity about the political future of the country. Immigration, on the other hand, increased during the late 1960s and early 1970s. This was partly the result of a governmental immigration campaign which began in 1964 with the goal of attracting a million White settlers to the country, by offering them considerable financial and social-integration incentives. In addition, as African states gradually achieved independence, Rhodesia became the destination for many Whites who sought to preserve a colonial lifestyle. This continued in the late 1970s, by which time Rhodesia's deteriorating political and economic situation[92] was discouraging immigration and emigration was again on the rise.[93]

Overall, from 1966 to 1980, the net population of non-Blacks grew only marginally, by less than 5 per cent. Moreover, because the growth rate of

[91] Barry M. Schutz, 'European Population Patterns, Cultural Persistence, and Political Change in Rhodesia' (1973) 7 *Canadian Journal of African Studies/Revue canadienne des études africaines* 3, 21.

[92] Lovemore M. Zinyama, 'International Migrations to and from Zimbabwe and the Influence of Political Changes on Population Movements, 1965–1987' (1990) 24 *International Migration Review* 748, 751–752; Glenn V. Stephenson, 'The Impact of International Economic Sanctions on the Internal Viability of Rhodesia' (1975) 65 *Geographical Review* 377, 385.

[93] Schutz, 'European Population Patterns', 21–22.

the Black population increased, the relative size of the non-Black population consistently grew smaller.[94] Yet the composition of the non-Black population changed dramatically: by 1980, about half of it comprised post-UDI settlers.[95]

Transition

During the Lancaster House negotiations on the withdrawal of the Smith regime and the establishment of Zimbabwe, the Popular Front (PF), representing the Black population of Rhodesia, objected to the validation of citizenships granted since 1965. The PF assumed – with good basis, given the motives for immigration noted above – that post-UDI settlers were for the most part supporters of the illegal regime, and therefore constituted a security risk for Zimbabwe.[96] The PF was particularly concerned that validating such citizenships would create a large population of dual nationals of both Zimbabwe and South Africa, which by 1980 had become an isolated island of White minority dominance over a Black majority, and that this dual nationality would result in excessive South African involvement in Zimbabwe under the guise of protection of its nationals.[97] As a compromise, the PF suggested that potential dual nationals would be required to opt for either Zimbabwean or their other nationality within one year of independence.

These proposals were not adopted in the Lancaster House Agreement. In line with a general validation of pre-1980 law,[98] the Independence Constitution confirmed the validity of pre-transition Rhodesian citizenship, and provided that persons holding it immediately prior to the date on which Zimbabwe became independent would automatically become Zimbabwean citizens. The constitution did not distinguish the date on which that citizenship had been acquired. Moreover, persons not holding Rhodesian citizenship but entitled to it under pre-transition law would have an unqualified right to claim Zimbabwean citizenship for a period

94 Schutz, 'European Population Patterns', 20.

95 In the 1969 census their total number was only 252,414. The net immigration of about 11,000 non-Blacks consisted of some 145,000 immigrants and 134,000 emigrants. Based on data provided in Zinyama, 'International Migrations to and from Zimbabwe', 751–752.

96 Schutz, 'European Population Patterns', 21–22.

97 Adolphe Lawson, *Les accords de Lancaster House en 1979: L'aboutissement de deux décennies de débats sur les conditions de l'indépendance du Zimbabwe* (Uppsala: Uppsala University, 1988), 145.

98 Southern Rhodesia, Constitution (Interim Provisions), Ordinance 1979 Section 4.

of five years following independence.[99] Descendants of Zimbabwean citizens were also entitled to Zimbabwean citizenship, regardless of the basis on which their parents had acquired that citizenship.[100]

The Zimbabwean citizenship of Whites, including post-1965 settlers, was thereby guaranteed. However, the Mugabe government made an unarticulated bargain with the remaining Whites: they could remain and continue to lead the 'colonial' lifestyle to which they had been accustomed. Their children, however, were discouraged from staying. This bargain was signalled by many government actions and policies that created economic disincentives for Whites to stay in Zimbabwe. For example, foreign companies, when selling their assets in Zimbabwe, could only remit their funds abroad if the purchasers were Black individuals, or co-operatives, or the government. Measures of this type ensured that, gradually, the economy would be Africanized while the White population dwindled.[101] This matter was surely more significant in terms of decolonization of Zimbabwe than in any other context, and is comparable to the practice of other post-colonial states; it was not related, in any direct way, to the Smith regime. The underlying sentiments, however, were relevant. Zimbabwe's policy led to the departure of most of the population whose presence lay at the root of the illegal situation that preceded Zimbabwe's independence.

6.3.2 The Baltic states

Settlers under the Soviet regime

Soon after the annexation of the Baltic states, the Soviet government adopted a policy of Russification of the Baltic states in order to give permanence to Soviet rule.[102] This policy was particularly prominent in

99 Zimbabwe, Independence Constitution, B1.

100 Zimbabwe, Independence Constitution, B3. At the same time, the agreement empowered parliament to make provisions for taking away the Zimbabwean citizenship of a person who had acquired it other than by birth or descent. Theoretically this left the door open to deny citizenship of post-UDI settlers. Zimbabwe, Independence Constitution, B6(B).

101 Jeffrey Herbst, *State Politics in Zimbabwe* (Berkeley: University of California Press, 1990), 222.

102 Lauri Mälksoo, *Illegal Annexation and State Continuity: The Case of the Incorporation of the Baltic States by the USSR* (Leiden: Martinus Nijhoff, 2003), 216–221; Dovilé Budryté, 'Today's Politics and Yesterday's Embitterments: Ethnic Restructuring and Its Aftermath in the Baltic States', in Rainer Münz and Rainer Ohliger (eds.), *Diasporas and Ethnic Migrants: Germany, Israel and Post-Soviet Successor States in Comparative Perspective* (London: Frank Cass Publishers, 2003), 207–214. The term 'Russification' indicates the introduction of a russophone population. Ethnically this population not only comprises Russians but also is characterized by being non-Baltic. For the purpose of

Estonia and Latvia. Large waves of immigration took place between 1945 and 1950, and between 1961 and 1970.[103] Many russophones were tempted to migrate to the Baltic states because of the region's better socioeconomic conditions and perceived 'Europeanness'. Significant numbers of the present russophone residents of the three states had been posted there while on military duty and then remained in place upon retirement, particularly in Latvia, where the Soviet army's Baltic region headquarters were located.[104] By the late 1980s, the russophone minority in Estonia and Latvia was much larger than any migrant group in any European country. In Estonia, the indigenous population declined from over 88 per cent in 1934 to 61.5 per cent in 1989,[105] while that of russophones grew from 8 per cent to 35 per cent. In Latvia, the indigenous population declined from 77 per cent to 52 per cent during the same period, while the russophone population grew from 12 per cent to 42 per cent.[106] Only in Lithuania did the share of the indigenous population remain almost constant, at 88 per cent. Inhabitants of the three states were considered nationals of the Soviet Union and residents of the respective Soviet republic.

Transition

At the time of reversion to independence, the status of Soviet-era russophone settlers was by far the most pressing and contentious issue in the Baltic states, particularly in Estonia and Latvia. The Baltic independence movements argued that the mass immigration of settlers had violated the prohibition on the transfer of civilian population to occupied territory. The elected transitional congresses of Estonia and Latvia[107]

this article its designation as russophone is sufficient to indicate its non-Baltic character and the fact that its dominant language is Russian.

103 CERD, Reports Submitted by States Parties under Article 9 of the Convention, Fourth Periodic Reports of States Parties Due in 1998, Addendum, Estonia (5 July 1999), UN Doc CERD/C/329/Add.2, paragraph 41.

104 Ineta Ziemele, *State Continuity and Nationality: The Baltic States and Russia* (Martinus Nijhoff, 2005), 364.

105 CERD, Reports Submitted by States Parties under Article 9 of the Convention, Fourth Periodic Reports of States Parties Due in 1998, Addendum, Estonia (5 July 1999), UN Doc CERD/C/329/Add.2, paragraph 38.

106 PACE, Doc 7169 (6 October 1994), Annex VII; James Hughes, 'Exit in Deeply Divided Societies: Regimes of Discrimination in Estonia and Latvia and the Potential for Russophone Migration' (2005) 43 *Journal of Common Market Studies* 739, 743–744.

107 Established by elections organized in 1990 by the Citizens Committees (restorationist grassroots organizations led by former anti-Soviet dissidents). Vello Pettai and Klara Hallik, 'Understanding Processes of Ethnic Control: Segmentation, Dependency and Co-optation in Post-communist Estonia' (2002) 8 *Nations and Nationalism* 505, 509.

considered Soviet-era settlers 'as at worst colonial occupiers, and at best immigrants'.[108] The fear that the settler community would stand in the way of asserting the new regime's national identity was explicitly noted in an Estonian congress resolution:

> Subsequent to its annexation of the Republic of Estonia, the Soviet Union organized extensive immigration by its citizens into Estonia. As a result of this, non-citizens form over one-third of the population of Estonia, which is now threatening the preservation of the native population of Estonia and the security and unity of the entire Estonian nation.[109]

Radical nationalists in Estonia emphasized the need to 'guarantee the existence of the Estonian nation and culture in the future' by excluding russophones from citizenry.[110] Russophones and even ethnic Estonians who held moderate positions were labelled 'internal enemies' who were attempting to 'help the external enemy, strengthening their conquest and their achievements here'. Further concern was expressed that if russophone settlers were to become citizens, new waves of immigration would follow, which would eventually make russophones the majority of the population.[111]

Similar sentiments were voiced in Latvia. Gvido Zemrido, the chief justice of the Latvian Supreme Court, said in 1993, 'It is clear that Latvians want to regain their national identity and that they are trying to preserve that identity against what they consider foreign intruders.'[112] The National Independence Movement, one of the influential nationalist parties, believed that independent Latvia would be threatened with extinction given the russophones' higher birth rate.[113]

[108] Helsinki Watch, 'New Citizenship Laws in the Republics of the Former USSR' (1992) 1–2, quoted in Henckaerts, *Mass Expulsion*, 93.

[109] Quoted in Lowell W. Barrington, 'The Making of Citizenship Policy in the Baltic States' (1999) 13 *Georgetown Immigration Law Journal* 159, 188, quoting Congress of Estonia Position on the Immigrants from the Former USSR Residing in the Republic of Estonia (1992).

[110] Andrus Ristkok (politician, in 2006 awarded presidential state decoration in recognition of his activities in the restoration and strengthening of the Estonian State), quoted in Peet Kask, 'National Radicalization in Estonia: Legislation on Citizenship and Related Issues' (1994) 22 *Nationalities Papers* 379, 382.

[111] Kask, 'National Radicalization in Estonia', 387–388; Andris Spruds, 'Minority Issues in the Baltic States in the Context of the NATO Enlargement' (2001), NATO Individual Research Fellowship, Final Report 9.

[112] Quoted in Barrington, 'The Making of Citizenship Policy in the Baltic States', 190.

[113] Spruds, 'Minority Issues in the Baltic States', 7.

There was also considerable concern in the Baltic states that the Russian Federation would use the presence of its diaspora as leverage in bilateral relations. This concern proved justified when Russia's support for ethnic Russians played significantly into its negotiations with the three states on withdrawal of troops, economic measures and more. The Russian Compatriot Policy, developed in 1992 and since reaffirmed by the Russian Foreign Policy Concept, perceived the territory of the former USSR as a region of special interest and mandates for Russia. These include the protection of the interests of ethnic Russians living abroad. This policy seeks to minimize the naturalization and integration of russophone non-nationals into the societies of the Baltic states, and reinforces Russia's influence in the Baltic states.[114] Russia went so far as to indicate in its 1993 Military Doctrine that it reserved the right to use military force if the rights of Russian citizens in other countries were violated.[115]

In both Estonia and Latvia, public opinion contained an element of seeking revenge on the settler communities. Calls were made for 'a counterattack against the colonists' by a strong policy of discouraging settlers from remaining in the restored states.[116] Reversion to the *status quo ante* with respect to nationality was perceived as a means of removing the russophone population from the state.

The CSCE High Commissioner for National Minorities (HCNM)[117] acknowledged Latvia's concern for its national character: 'I fully understand and respect the determination of your Government to maintain and strengthen the Latvian identity after 50 years of Soviet occupation

[114] Kristine Krūma, 'Checks and Balances in Latvian Nationality Policies: National Agendas and International Frameworks', in Rainer Bauböck, Bernhard Perchinig and Wiebke Sievers (eds.), *Citizenship Policies in the New Europe*, expanded and updated edn (Amsterdam: Amsterdam University Press, 2010), 80–81.

[115] Ceslovas Stankevicius, 'Enhancing Security of Lithuania and Other Baltic States in 1992–94 and Future Guidelines' (1996), Final Report of Individual Democratic Institutions Research Fellowships 1994–6, www.nato.int/acad/fellow/94-96/stankevi/home.htm, Chapter 6, paragraphs 57–60; Spruds, 'Minority Issues in the Baltic states', 22, 26–27.

[116] Kask, 'National Radicalization in Estonia', 386–387; Hughes, 'Exit in Deeply Divided Societies', 748; Budrytė, 'Ethnic Restructuring in the Baltic States', 214–216; Priit Järve, 'Estonian Citizenship: Between Ethnic Preferences and Democratic Obligations', in Rainer Bauböck, Bernhard Perchinig and Wiebke Sievers (eds.), *Citizenship Policies in the New Europe*, expanded and updated edn (Amsterdam: Amsterdam University Press, 2010), 53–54.

[117] According to Zurjari-Ossipova, the establishment of the HCNM post was a Russian initiative. Olga Zurjari-Ossipova, 'Human Rights as the Political–Juridical Issues of the Estonian–Russian Inter-state Relations', 18 NATO Research Fellowships Programme 1995–7 (June 1997), www.nato.int/acad/fellow/95-97/zurjari.pdf.

which greatly endangered the maintenance of that identity.'[118] Although Latvia's goal of preserving its national identity and political independence was perceived as legitimate, it did not justify the expulsion of settlers other than those who personally and directly jeopardized the achievement of that goal.[119] Commenting on the Latvian policy with regard to the russophone community, the HCNM wrote to the Latvian authorities:[120]

As I pointed out in my recommendation of 7 April 1993, your Government has of course the right to remove from Latvia territory non-citizens whose continuous presence could be damaging to its vital interest, such as persons who have been found in proper judicial procedures to have committed grave crimes. But on the other hand, massive expulsion of non-Latvian residents would be contrary to generally accepted international humanitarian principles even more so because the overwhelming majority of the non-Latvians living in your country have not been actively engaged in oppressive practices during the years of the Soviet occupation of Latvia. I am glad that your Government is not considering this option.

The HCNM advocated a strategy that would defuse the danger presented by the settler population to the restored states' attempt to re-establish their national identity. He encouraged Estonia and Latvia to provide the russophone population with a genuine opportunity to integrate within the state, formally by acquiring citizenship, and substantively through cultural and educational means. The HCNM considered that integration would increase the chances that the russophone minority would embrace Estonian or Latvian identity rather than act to modify it or prevent its consolidation.[121] This, he argued, would provide a convincing proof of their willingness to integrate without having to sacrifice their cultural or linguistic identity,[122] and 'would certainly not be incompatible with the wish of the Estonians to ensure and strengthen their political, cultural and linguistic identity'.[123]

118 HCNM 1994 Communication, 2.

119 Subsequent legislation in all three Baltic states denies residence (let alone nationality) to persons involved in crimes against the state, crimes against humanity or war crimes. Estonia, Citizenship Act 1995, Article 21(1)(3); Estonia, Aliens Act, Article 12(4)(3), (12), (13); Latvia, 1994 Citizenship Law, Article 11(1); Lithuania, Law on Citizenship Articles 13(1), (2); Lithuania, Law on the Legal Status of Aliens, Article 35.1(1)(8).

120 HCNM 1994 Communication, 3.

121 HCNM 1993 Letter to Latvia; HCNM 1993 Letter to Estonia.

122 HCNM 1993 Letter to Latvia, 8–9.

123 HCNM 1993 Letter to Estonia, 3; HCNM 1994 Communication, 3.

Nationality – reversion to the status quo ante

The formal nationality policy adopted by the Baltic states reflected their formal legal position of continuity with the pre-1940 states, and constituted a reversion to the *status quo ante*: all three states reinstated their pre-1940 legislation. Consequently, original nationality was made available only to pre-1940 citizens and their descendants.[124]

Since the legislation was not ethnically defined, there was not an absolute correlation between ethnicity and eligibility for original nationality. All pre-1940 nationals of the Baltic states were entitled to reacquire their nationality, regardless of their ethnicity. Conversely, the qualification for reversion to the pre-1940 situation also affected persons of Baltic descent.[125] The exclusion of russophones from nationality was therefore claimed to be only an incidental consequence of the legitimate reinstatement of earlier law rather than an ethnically related measure.[126]

Lithuanian policy on the grant of original nationality differed from that of Estonia or Latvia. The small russophone population, of less than 12 per cent, was not perceived as a serious threat. Accordingly, the Lithuanian citizenship legislation is much more inclusive than that of Estonia or Latvia. Under the 1989 Law on Citizenship, persons residing permanently in Lithuania on the date of enactment of the law but not regarded as

[124] Estonia, Resolution of the Supreme Council of the Republic of Estonia 'On Implementation of Citizenship Act' (RT 1992, 7, 109); Latvia: on 15 October 1991 the Supreme Council of the Latvian SSR adopted the Resolution on the Renewal of Republic of Latvia's Nationals' Rights and Fundamental Principles of Naturalization. The resolution declared the invalidity of the 'USSR Decree on the Order in Which the Lithuania, Latvia and Estonia SSR Nationals are Granted USSR Citizenship' of 7 September 1940, and restored the rights of Latvian nationals. Under the resolution, Latvian nationality was reserved to nationals on 17 June 1940 and their descendants, as well as to persons who had been permanent residents in Latvia on that date. Ziemele, *State Continuity and Nationality*, 155; Latvia, 1994 Citizenship Law, Article 2(1); Lithuania, 1991 Law on Citizenship, Article 1(1).

[125] E.g. former nationals of Lithuania not resident in Lithuania or who had acquired other nationality. Lithuania, 1991 Law on Citizenship, Article 1(3). A post-transition regime wishing to reverse the situation is doubtless entitled to offer nationality and residence status to persons who had previously been denied it. While it is generally accepted that a state may not *impose* its nationality on persons not resident in its territory, the question here is whether the post-transition regime may *restore* status to non-residents without their personal consent.

[126] Although legally there was no singling out of the settler population, there is no doubt that the political motivation for the legislation was ethnically oriented. Vello Andres Pettai, 'The Construction of State Identity and Its Legacies: Legal Restorationism in Estonia' (2007) 3 *Ab Imperio* 1; Kask, 'National Radicalization in Estonia', 379.

original citizens on the basis of pre-1940 nationality (i.e. post-1940 settlers and their descendants) were given two years to opt for Lithuanian citizenship.[127] The only condition for eligibility was a permanent place of lawful employment, or a constant legal source of support.[128] By 1991, this offer of quasi-original nationality enabled 90 per cent of the settlers to have acquired Lithuanian nationality,[129] making the residence and naturalization of non-nationals a minor issue.

Residence

The significance of continuity of status in providing stability and security did not escape policy makers. But policy makers did not necessarily aim to provide stability and security. For example, in Estonia, all non-nationals, including pre-1990 long-term residents, were required to apply for a residence permit within two years.[130] In 1993 legislation was tabled which rejected the possibility that Soviet-era residence 'registration' could be automatically exchanged for a new Estonian residence permit; instead, settlers would have been required to apply for new permits. One of the drafters expressed it most frankly: 'By means of the present law we have to create a situation where the colonists feel the earth shaking under their feet'.[131] In Latvia, legislation on residence remained for a long time inconsistent and unclear, leading to arbitrary executive decisions, including of expulsion.[132] Ziemele argues that such executive action resulted from lack of detailed analysis of the situation of different groups of residence and lack of clear political and legal guidance, rather than from a unified government view that all Soviet-era settlers should be expelled or that their residence should be challenged en masse.[133] But the inability to formulate clear policy was itself the result of heated political debate on the future identity of Latvia. These policy choices (or lack thereof) were greatly criticized by the European institutions on grounds of both

[127] Lithuania, 1989 Law on Citizenship, Article 1(3). The deadline was 4 November 1991.

[128] W. Rogers Brubaker, 'Citizenship Struggles in Soviet Successor States' (1992) 26 *International Migration Review* 269, 280; Lithuania, *Constitutional Court Case 7/94*.

[129] Wim van Meurs, 'Social Citizenship and Non-immigration: The Immobility of the Russian Diaspora in the Baltics', in Rainer Münz and Rainer Ohliger (eds.), *Diaspora and Ethnic Migrants: Germany, Israel and Post-Soviet Successor States in Comparative Perspective* (London: Frank Cass Publishers, 2003), 192.

[130] Estonia, 1993 Aliens Act. The deadline was later extended.

[131] Kask, 'National Radicalization in Estonia', 386.

[132] Ziemele, *State Continuity and Nationality*, 160–162.

[133] Ziemele, *State Continuity and Nationality*, 164.

international human rights law and policy.[134] In Estonia the law was subsequently amended so that residence granted by the Soviet authorities was automatically given validity. By 1996 practically all settlers could register for residence permits.[135] In Latvia, also, moderate forces who advocated a more liberal policy succeeded in toning down the debate, which gradually coalesced around a consensus that the expulsion of the settler population was politically impossible.[136] Legislation of 1995[137] finally determined the right to permanent residence of former USSR nationals who were resident and registered in Latvia before 1992.[138] Emigration ebbed in the mid-1990s,[139] although Latvia is still criticized for not sufficiently integrating non-national russophone residents into Latvian society.[140]

Naturalization

In Lithuania, after the expiry of the opting-in period, the Citizenship Law was modified so that Soviet-era settlers could naturalize under the same terms as other foreigners. This included a ten-year residence requirement, excluding residence under the Soviet regime.[141] Since by then most of the settlers had already acquired Lithuanian nationality, this exclusion was

134 CSCE 1994 Communication, 3.

135 PACE Doc 7715 (20 December 1996), explanatory note, paragraph 16: 'It can be expected of the aliens currently living in Estonia that they register themselves with the state, instead of simply not acting at all. These people have only themselves to blame, if they are open to deportation now.'

136 Helen M. Morris, 'EU Enlargement and Latvian Citizenship Policy' (2003) *Journal on Ethnopolitics and Minority Issues in Europe* 3, 3–4; Hughes, 'Exit in Deeply Divided Societies', 747; Mälksoo, *Illegal Annexation and State Continuity*, 223–224.

137 Latvia, 1995 Law on the Status of Those Former USSR Citizens Who Do Not Have the Citizenship of Latvia or That of Any Other State.

138 Ziemele, *State Continuity and Nationality*, 162. Inconsistencies nonetheless remain because the Soviet system provided for various types of registration.

139 Budrytė, 'Ethnic Restructuring in the Baltic States', 216.

140 PACE Doc 11094 (8 November 2006); CERD, Considerations of Reports Submitted by States Parties under Article 9 of the Convention, Concluding Observations of the CERD, Latvia (10 December 2003), UN Doc CERD/C/63/CO/7, paragraphs 12, 13. For example, non-nationals still cannot hold office in public administration and the court system; they may not acquire ownership of land in borderland zones and in protective zones for public water bodies; and they may not work as lawyers, private detectives or armed guards. Latvian Centre for Human Rights and Ethnic Studies, 'Human Rights in Latvia in 2004' (Riga, 2005), 23; HRC, Latvia Second Period Report (29 November 2002), UN Doc CCPR/C/LVA/2002/2, paragraph 15.

141 Lithuania, 1991 Law on Citizenship, Article 12.

a moot issue. By the year 2000, 99 per cent of the residents of Lithuania held Lithuanian citizenship.[142]

Estonia and Latvia were more resistant to granting nationality to settlers. As residence of settlers became an accepted reality, the debate shifted to whether settlers would be entitled to nationality and under what conditions. The requirements for naturalization in both states included long-term residence and knowledge of the national language, of the constitution and of national history; the taking of a loyalty oath to the state; a legitimate source of income; and payment of an application fee.[143] In both states, the earliest date of residence qualifying for naturalization was the date of restoration of independence.[144] In other words, Soviet-era settlers could not benefit from their residence in the territory during the period of purported annexation in order to satisfy the requirements for naturalization. The greatest obstacle for Soviet-era settlers in naturalization in Estonia and Latvia was not, however, the requirement of residence, but their poor command of the local language. In Latvia, standards required with regard to knowledge of the constitution and of history were excessively high,[145] and together with an originally exorbitant fee (a month's wages) discouraged applications and resulted in a large population of non-nationals, who were primarily russophone settlers and their families. This strategy was vehemently rejected by the European institutions as disproportionately harmful to the settlers. These institutions exerted heavy pressure on both states to enable the settler minority to naturalize and to minimize the differences with regard to political

[142] Statistical Office of Estonia, Central Statistical Bureau of Latvia and Statistics Lithuania, '2000 Round of Population and Housing Censuses in Estonia, Latvia and Lithuania' (Vilnius, 2003), 33.

[143] Estonia, 1995 Citizenship Act, Article 6; Latvia, 1994 Law on Citizenship, Article 12. Naturalization became a real option in Latvia only in 1994, when the Law on Citizenship was promulgated. Ziemele, *State Continuity and Nationality*, 150. Application for naturalization was possible from 1998 through 'naturalization windows', reserving certain periods of time for persons of different ages. Following international criticism, these 'windows' were abolished in 1999. See e.g. the letter of the Minister of Foreign Affairs of the Republic of Latvia to OSCE High Commissioner on National Minorities, dated 24 December 1996 (7 January 1997), OSCE Doc REF.HC/2/97, www.osce.org/documents/hcnm/1997/01/2731_en.pdf.

[144] Estonia, 30 March 1990, the date of the Resolution of the Supreme Soviet of the Estonian SSR 'On the State Status of Estonia'; Latvia, 4 May 1990, the date of Latvia's Declaration of Restoration of Independence, Latvia, Citizenship Law, Article 12(1)1).

[145] For examples of ludicrous questions see HCNM letter dated 23 May 1997 to the minister for foreign affairs of the Republic of Latvia and the letter of reply dated 11 September 1997 (11 September 1997), OSCE Doc HCNM.GAL/1/97.

and economic rights between nationals and non-national permanent residents. Frustration over state policy led in 1998 to demonstrations and violence in Riga. Russia threatened to place sanctions on Latvia.[146] Estonia's and Latvia's aspirations to join the EU and NATO led them to gradually relax the requirements for naturalization.[147] This allowed greater access for settlers to nationality. There have since been waves of requests for naturalization, with surges in 1999 and 2004, shortly before the entry of Latvia into the EU.

Programmes were also undertaken to integrate non-Baltic nationals into state and society.[148] Research in the 1990s revealed that contrary to the perception that dominated Estonian and Latvian political discourse, russophone nationals of the Baltic states were gradually distancing themselves from the Russian core group.[149]

In mid-2008, the number of non-nationals resident in Latvia was still close to 420,000,[150] making up about 18 per cent of the entire population. Over 90 per cent of those persons were russophones.[151] Estonia's naturalization legislation is still criticized for being overly exclusive,[152] as 8 per cent of the resident population have remained with no nationality at all.[153]

Special arrangements for military personnel

The Baltic states were home to large numbers of retired military personnel and their family members. In 1995, retired servicemen in Estonia

[146] Aivars Stranga, 'The End Product, a Crisis in Latvian–Russian Relations (March–August 1998)', NATO Research Fellowships Programme 1996–8, www.nato.int/acad/fellow/96–98/stranga.pdf.

[147] For an account of these organizations' involvement until 1999 see Barrington, 'The Making of Citizenship Policy in the Baltic States', 191–197.

[148] On Estonia's policy see Pettai and Hallik, 'Ethnic Control', 520.

[149] Jekaterina Dorodnova, 'The Russian-Speaking Identity under the Latvian Language Policy', in Rainer Münz and Rainer Ohliger (eds.), *Diasporas and Ethnic Migrants: Germany, Israel and Post-Soviet Successor States in Comparative Perspective* (London: Frank Cass Publishers, 2003), 223, 226.

[150] Latvia Ministry of Foreign Affairs, www.am.gov.lv/en/policy/4641/4642/4651/.

[151] PACE, 'Rights of National Minorities in Latvia' (8 November 2006), Doc 11094, Explanatory Memorandum, paragraph 13, http://assembly.coe.int/Documents/WorkingDocs/Doc06/EDOC11094.pdf.

[152] CERD, Considerations of Reports Submitted by States Parties under Article 9 of the Convention, Concluding Observations of the CERD, Estonia (19 October 2006), UN Doc CERD/C/EST/CO/7, paragraph 15.

[153] Järve, 'Estonian Citizenship', 60; Estonia Citizenship and Migration Board 2006 Yearbook, 13.

numbered 10,500, with their families totalling 40,000;[154] in Latvia there were some 22,000 retired military personnel, with their families numbering 87,000; retired military personnel in Lithuania numbered almost 10,000, with their families numbering 30,000.

In all three Baltic states, military personnel, both active and retired, are generally excluded from acquiring nationality through naturalization.[155] This general scheme was confirmed by the Human Rights Committee as justified on grounds of national security.[156] Active servicemen are not even entitled to temporary residence.[157]

Both Estonia and Latvia undertook to guarantee residence for retired servicemen and their family members under treaties with the Russian Federation.[158] In contrast, in Lithuania, which otherwise had the most liberal policy of naturalizing russophones, the presence in Lithuania of retired servicemen was deemed illegal, and their employment in the military not a lawful source of income.[159] Lithuania therefore refused to commit itself to granting residence even to retired military personnel.[160] Family members who arrived in connection with the service of military personnel could also be prevented from remaining in Lithuania.

154 Stankevicius, 'Enhancing Security of Lithuania and Other Baltic States', Chapter 6.

155 Estonia, 1995 Citizenship Act, Article 21(1)(6), (2) (with the exception of retirees who have been married for five years to an Estonian national by birth). The constitutionality of Article 21(1) was unsuccessfully challenged in Estonian courts; Latvia, 1994 Law on Citizenship Article 11(3), (4), (5), (6) (with the exception of those who had been permanent residents prior to conscription). Lithuania, 1991 Citizenship Law, Article 12(3).

156 HRC, *Borzov* v. *Estonia*.

157 Estonia, 1993 Aliens Act, Article 12(4)(6). The same applies to reserve forces – Article 12(4)(7). Latvia, 1992 Aliens and Stateless Persons (Entry and Residence), Article 23^1(2), (3). Active servicemen are persons who retired from active military service after 28 June 1992. Their families are also excluded from residence (unless they had been permanent residents when taking up service or are family members of Latvian nationals) if, irrespective of the date of their arrival, they arrived in Latvia in connection with that service. 1995 Law on the Status of those Former USSR Citizens Who Do Not Have the Citizenship of Latvia or That of Any Other State Article 1(3).

158 Agreement between the Republic of Estonia and the Russian Federation on Social Guarantees for Pensioners of the Armed Forces of the Russian Federation in the Territory of the Republic of Estonia, RT II 1995, 46, 203, cited in Vadim Poleshchuk, 'Non-citizens in Estonia' (Legal Information Centre for Human Rights, 2004), 11. Estonian domestic law secures residential status also for family members of retired servicemen, if they do not constitute a threat to national security. CERD, Estonia Sixth and Seventh Periods Combined Report (1 April 2005), UN Doc CERD/C/46/Add.1, paragraph 91; Latvian–Russian Retired Military Personnel Social Protection Agreement; and Latvia, 1992 Aliens and Stateless Persons (Entry and Residence), Article 23^1(2),(3).

159 Lithuania, *Constitutional Court Case 7/94*.

160 Stankevicius, 'Enhancing Security of Lithuania and Other Baltic States', Chapter 6.

6.3.3 *The TBVC*

Settlers in the TBVC

A large number of persons became citizens of the TBVC who had not been South African citizens previously. These naturalized TBVC nationals fell within two main categories. A small group comprised criminals and mafia members from around the world, who profited from the lack of international relations and co-operation with the TBVC to evade the law.[161] They often acquired TBVC nationality through illegal payment to the TBVC's despot leaders. The other, much larger group, comprised people from various African states who wanted to immigrate to South Africa. They preferred to naturalize in the TBVC since this was more easily done there than in South Africa, and because the rural TBVC were more similar to their states of origin than urban South Africa.[162]

Transition

The validity of TBVC citizenship first arose in the lead up to the elections. It was generally agreed that all South Africans, including those in the TBVC, would participate in the elections. However, there was some insistence that individuals who had become citizens of the TBVC through naturalization (and had never been South African citizens), particularly those who had taken advantage of the outlaw status of the TBVC, would be excluded from participation. This small population would have had no visible effect on the election results. The insistence on its non-participation reflected the strong sentiment of reclaiming ownership of the polity, and some animosity towards symbols of the unlawful regime.[163] Eventually it was decided to give legal effect to pre-transition grants of status.[164] First, the 1993 Restoration and Extension of South African Citizenship Act adopted the principle that post-'independence' naturalized nationals of the TBVC would have to apply for South African nationality by naturalization. This provision was criticized as discriminatory because it applied to former

[161] E.g. South Africa, *Geuking* v. *President of the Republic of South Africa and Others*, 2003(3) SA 34 (CC), [3].

[162] Interview by the author with Dr Jonathan Klaaren, University of Witwatersrand, Johannesburg, 5 April 2004.

[163] Interview by the author with Mr Zam Titus, special adviser to the minister of provincial and local government and formerly director-general of the Ministry of Constitutional Development, administrator-general of Ciskei, participant in the MPNF, Pretoria, 7 April 2004.

[164] Interview by the author with Dr Jonathan Klaaren, University of Witwatersrand, Johannesburg, 5 April 2004.

TBVC nationals and not to other nationals of South Africa.[165] Accordingly, the 1995 Citizenship Act made the acquisition of South African citizenship by these persons automatic.[166] At the same time, the Act permitted the minister of home affairs to deprive a person of South African nationality if his or her certificate of naturalization had been obtained by fraudulent means.[167] This paved the way for a distinction between good-faith settlers and criminals fleeing the law. There is no publicly available information on use of this provision with respect to former TBVC nationals.[168]

6.3.4 *Timor-Leste*

Settlers under the Indonesian administration

It is estimated that in 1974 Timor-Leste's population numbered around 650,000.[169] Non-governmental sources claim a fall of over 20 per cent in the indigenous population by 1980, principally because of mass killings by Indonesia, and as a result of famine and the departure of refugees.[170] In addition, during Indonesia's rule, Timor-Leste was a migration destination under the Indonesian 'transmigration' policy (aimed at dispersing populations from dense and poor areas to outlying islands of the archipelago),[171] as well as a destination for voluntary Indonesian

165 Restoration and Extension of South African Citizenship Act, Article 4. Jonathan Klaaren, 'Post-apartheid Citizenship in South Africa', in T. Alexander Aleinikoff and Douglas Klusmeyer (eds.), *From Migrants to Citizens Membership in a Changing World* (Washington, DC: Carnegie Endowment for International Peace, 2000), 228, 234–235.

166 South Africa, Citizenship Act, Article 4(1)(iii). The Act was amended by the Citizenship Act Amendment Act of 1997, deleting this subparagraph, to rectify the fact that the 1995 wording did not grant South African citizenship as of right to persons who were citizens of the former TBVC states by registration. See South African Citizenship Act Amendment Bill of 1997, Article 8.

167 South Africa, Citizenship Act, Article 8(1)(a).

168 Since many post-independence TBVC nationals were fleeing criminals, the matter might have arisen in the context of extradition procedures. However, since South African law does not prohibit extradition of South African nationals, the nationality of such persons was not particularly relevant for such procedures. Neville Botha, 'Extradition again before the Constitutional Court' (2003) 28 *South African Yearbook of International Law* 318, 319.

169 Ben Kiernan, 'The Demography of Genocide in Southeast Asia: The Death Tolls in Cambodia, 1975–79, and East Timor, 1975–80' (2003) 35 *Critical Asia Studies* 585, 590.

170 Kiernan, 'The Demography of Genocide', 169, 594; Graeme Hugo, 'Forced Migration in Indonesia: Historical Perspectives' (2006) 15 *Asian and Pacific Migration Journal* 53.

171 Mark J. Miller, 'Demography and Security (MIT Center for International Studies, December 11–12, 1998)' (1999) 33 *International Migration Review* 193, 195.

migrants, attracted for the most part by economic incentives offered by Indonesia to settlers in Timor-Leste.

Although Indonesia conducted a number of censuses, exact data on the demographic composition of Timor-Leste are hard to obtain. This is due to suspected excess counts and undercounts, as well as to lack of information on internal migration. Low counts provided by the Indonesian government suggest that Timor-Leste was a migration destination for a little over 10,000 persons,[172] and that overall only about 6 per cent of Timor-Leste's population was previously resident in another province. However, this data only accounts for first-generation migrants, as government censuses count subsequent generations of Indonesian internal migrants as native Timorese despite their non-Timorese ethnicity. Estimates by non-governmental sources suggest that by 1997 there were between 160,000 and 180,000 non-Timorese inhabitants in Timor-Leste in the 15–60 age group,[173] constituting 20 per cent of the population.

Indonesian settlers in Timor-Leste were a favoured political and commercial elite.[174] The continued presence of these settlers might therefore have given independent Timor-Leste cause for concern. However, following the 1999 referendum and in the midst of the ensuing violence, Indonesia conducted a massive pre-planned evacuation. About 250,000 persons were evacuated (70,000 military personnel and other non-Timorese, and 180,000 Timorese). It has been suggested that the evacuation and forcible displacement had two purposes. First, it served as the basis for later challenges to the credibility of the vote and for demands for the partition of Timor-Leste. Second, the creation of a huge refugee population just across the border was intended to create opportunities for undermining the new regime in Timor-Leste.[175]

[172] Graeme Hugo, 'Pengungsi – Indonesia's Internally Displaced Persons' (2002) 11 *Asian and Pacific Migration Journal* 297. This is less than one percent of all official transmigrants in the period 1968–2000: Riwanto Tirtosudarmo, 'Mobility and Human Development in Indonesia', Human Development Reports Research Paper 2009/19 (UNDP, June 2009), Table 2.2, http://hdr.undp.org/en/reports/global/hdr2009/papers/HDRP_2009_19.pdf, 8.

[173] Kiernan, 'The Demography of Genocide', 597. A different estimate is that of 5,000 transmigrant families. Miller, 'Demography and Security', 195.

[174] Stephen Sherlock, 'Political Economy of the East Timor Conflict' (1996) 36 *Asian Survey* 835, 837–838; UNDP, 'East Timor: Building Blocks for a Nation' (2000), 22–23.

[175] Geoffrey Robinson, 'People Power: A Comparative History of Forced Displacement in East Timor', in Eva-Lotta E. Hedman (ed.), *Conflict, Violence and Displacement in Indonesia* (Ithaca, NY: Cornell South East Asia Program, 2008), 87, 110–113.

By 2002, when Timor-Leste's Law on Nationality came into effect, the residence and nationality of Indonesian-era settlers was of little practical significance, although there have been isolated incidents of disputes concerning the expulsion of non-indigenous Timorese.[176] The matter may re-emerge as the regulation of land rights progresses, since Timorese law excludes non-nationals from ownership of real property, thereby rendering nationality an important economic asset.[177]

Transition

Nationality

Timor-Leste's 2002 Law on Nationality determines the country's original nationals without any reference to previous nationality, neither under Portuguese nor under Indonesian law. An original national of Timor-Leste is a person born in the national territory to a parent born in Timor-Leste, or to a foreign parent and who, being over seventeen years old, opts to become a Timorese national of his or her own accord.[178] It thus largely limits nationality to ethnic Timorese, but there is nothing in the legislation singling out Indonesian settlers. Moreover, Timorese-born individuals may acquire nationality by declaration, thereby allowing Indonesians and other second-generation immigrants to become nationals.

Residence

Article 131(1) of the Immigration and Asylum Act (2003) clarifies that Indonesian-era settlers cannot rely on residential status granted by Indonesia, but must obtain permission to reside in Timor-Leste from the new Timorese government:

> Foreigners who entered the country after December 7, 1975, and who are conducting activities in the national territory for which under the present provisions it is mandatory to be a resident or holder of a proper visa, must, within 90 days from the entry into force of this Act, request a visa that will allow them to stay or to practice a professional activity.

[176] US Department of State, 2005 Country Reports on Human Rights Practices, East Timor, Section 2(c).

[177] Timor-Leste Constitution Article 54. It is not clear whether this reservation operates prospectively or applies also to existing ownership.

[178] Timor-Leste, Law on Nationality, Article 8(1)(a), (c). Article 8(1)(b) grants original nationality to a person born in Timor-Leste to incognito parents, stateless parents or parents of unknown citizenship. These provisions more or less duplicate Timor-Leste's constitution, Article 3.

Unlike the status of post-independence immigrants, the residence of settlers under Indonesian rule is regulated by the instruction of the minister of the interior, rather than by the standard immigration authorities.[179] Indonesian-era settlers are therefore subject to stricter control in acquiring permanent status in Timor-Leste.

Naturalization

The Law on Nationality provides for discretionary naturalization on the basis of long-term residence for a person who has been a 'usual and regular resident of Timor-Leste for at least ten years prior to 7 December 1975 or after 20 May 2002' and able to speak one of the official languages of Timor-Leste (Portuguese and Tetum).[180] Settlers under Indonesian rule may thus acquire nationality on the same footing as other foreigners, but, as in the Baltic states, the period of purported annexation would not be counted towards the requisite period of lawful residence. The law emphasizes that a 'foreign citizen who has settled in Timor-Leste as a result of transmigration policy or foreign military occupation shall not be considered as a usual or regular resident'.[181] Moreover, since under the Indonesian administration the use of both Portuguese and Tetum was suppressed by the dominant Indonesian, the majority of settlers from that period are unlikely to be fluent in either of the two official languages.

6.3.5 *The TRNC*

Settlers in the TRNC

The population of the island of Cyprus, altogether over a million persons today,[182] comprises approximately 80 per cent Christian Greek Cypriots and 20 per cent Muslim Turkish Cypriots. In 1974 Turkish Cypriots numbered about 118,000.[183] Since then the composition of this population, residing mostly in the territory now under TRNC rule, has changed

179 Timor-Leste, Immigration and Asylum Act, Article 131(2).

180 Timor-Leste, Law on Nationality, Article 12(1)(b), (c).

181 Timor-Leste, Law on Nationality, Article 12(2).

182 The government of Cyprus estimates the population of government-controlled areas at 867,600. Cyprus Demographic Report 2006, 11. Estimates on the population of the TRNC vary as discussed below.

183 Department of Statistics and Research of the Republic of Cyprus, quoted in the Cuco Report, paragraph 35.

dramatically. On the one hand, Turkish Cypriots arrived from the south,[184] on the other, massive emigration of Turkish Cypriots took place in later years.[185] But the most significant demographic change, and on which this chapter focuses, was the settlement in the TRNC of mainland Turks, with the encouragement of both Turkey and the TRNC. Large waves of settlers arrived in 1975 and 1977. These were estimated to make up more than 10 per cent of the population in the territory at the time.[186] Another wave of mainland Turks arrived in the early 2000s as construction workers, following a building boom in the TRNC.

The demographic composition of the TRNC is difficult to establish. Censuses carried out by the TRNC are rejected by the government of Cyprus as unreliable and intentionally misleading with regard to the number of Turkish settlers. The population categories used by the opposing sides are defined differently, frustrating any attempt at comparing data.[187] Estimates of the number of settlers therefore vary enormously: from a Turkish government estimate of 31,000 settlers in 2003–2004,[188] to a 2006 government of the Republic of Cyprus estimate of 150,000–160,000.[189] A 2006 TRNC census, on which the Cypriot estimate is based, quotes the total number of immigrants since the 1970s at a little over 67,000.[190] In 2003 the Council of Europe noted that mainland Turkish settlers have outnumbered indigenous Turkish Cypriots.[191]

Turkish settlers fall into two main categories. A small minority holding significant political clout comprises professionals, businessmen, retired

[184] UN and ICRC estimates of 43,000, quoted in the Laakso Report, paragraph 18. The TRNC reports 65,000 displaced Turkish Cypriots.

[185] UK House of Commons, 2004–2005 Report, paragraph 201, based on the Laakso Report, Appendix 5.

[186] Cuco Report, paragraph 89.

[187] UK House of Commons, Written Evidence. The Council of Europe has initiated its own studies on the population of the TRN, e.g. Cuco Report. Claire Palley, *An International Relations Debacle: The UN Secretary-General's Mission of Good Offices in Cyprus 1999–2004* (Oxford: Hart, 2005), 67, argues that the TRNC Government objected to these initiatives because it was reluctant to expose the large number of Turkish settlers.

[188] Laakso Report, paragraph 24.

[189] Government of Cyprus PIO, 'Analysis of the '2006 Population Census' in the Occupied Area of Cyprus and Aide Memoire.

[190] TRNC, Final Results of TRNC General Population and Housing Unit Census, Additional Tables, http://nufussayimi.devplan.org/Kesin-sonuc-index_en.html.

[191] Laakso Report, paragraphs 24–27. Additional data is available in the UK House of Commons, 2004–2005 Report. In 2007 the UK House of Commons quoted the figure of 200,000 permanent residents, of which only about 50,000 are permanent Turkish settlers and another 100,000 are short-term residents, mostly Turkish. UK House of Commons, 2006–2007 Report, paragraph 104.

military officers and former students.[192] They live mainly in mixed neighbourhoods in urban areas and are often married to Turkish Cypriots.[193] The vast majority of settlers are peasants and shepherds who arrived between 1975 and 1977 from poor regions in Turkey. These farmers were invited to emigrate by radio and by announcements by heads of villages made in Turkish village coffee shops. Rural Turks have low professional skills and their customs and traditions differ in a significant way from those in Cyprus.[194] The government of the Republic of Cyprus claims (with the endorsement of the Council of Europe) that these differences are the main reason for the tensions and dissatisfaction of the indigenous Turkish Cypriot population, who tend to view the settlers as a foreign element.[195] Although their immigration to the TRNC was facilitated by the Turkish and TRNC governments for political reasons, the settlers themselves were not politically motivated in coming, and a substantial number of them may even have had little idea of where Cyprus was located before their arrival. They do not form a monolithic group and they do not all support a nationalist agenda.[196]

Until 2004 TRNC legislation was very permissive with regard to acquisition of TRNC nationality. TFSC legislation had made naturalization available by request, particularly to members of the Turkish armed forces who had served in Cyprus, and their families.[197] In 1981 complementary provisions extended nationality to persons permanently resident in the territory for at least one year, those who made or could make an important contribution to the economy or the social and cultural life of the TFSC, and

[192] Cuco Report, paragraph 90; Mete Hatay, 'Beyond Numbers: An Inquiry into the Political Integration of the Turkish "Settlers" in Northern Cyprus', PRIO Report 4 (Nicosia, 2005), 11–13.

[193] UK House of Commons, 2004–2005 Report, paragraph 54. In 1992, the Cuco Report quoted a figure of 1,500 intermarriages notified between 1974 and 1990 to the Turkish consulate in the TRNC. Cuco Report, paragraph 82. Hatay, 'Beyond Numbers', 11, quotes the number of Peace Force veterans married to Turkish Cypriots at around 800.

[194] Hatay, 'Beyond Numbers', 49–50; UK House of Commons, 2006–2007 Report, paragraph 77.

[195] Laakso Report, paragraphs 40–43; PACE Recommendation 1197 (1992), paragraph 7; Leonard W. Doob, 'Cypriot Patriotism and Nationalism' (1986) 30 *Journal of Conflict Resolution* 383, 394.

[196] For an analysis of Turkish settlers' politics see Hatay, 'Beyond Numbers', 7; Othon Anastasakis, Gilles Bertrand and Kalypso Nicolaïdis, 'Getting to Yes: Suggestions for Embellishment of the Annan Plan for Cyprus', South East European Studies Programme (SEESP) European Studies Centre, St Anthony's College, University of Oxford, February 2004, 4.

[197] Law No. 3/1975. On the practical consequences of this law see Hatay, 'Beyond Numbers', 11.

those who have rendered services to the security forces.[198] The 1985 constitution of the TRNC provides that original nationals of the TRNC include original nationals of the Republic of Cyprus ordinarily resident in the TRNC when it declared independence, and nationals of the TFSC.[199] TRNC legislation of 1993 confers original TRNC nationality on persons born to a TRNC parent. TRNC nationality is also available to spouses of TRNC citizens. In addition, the law provides for discretionary naturalization for foreigners of various categories. Ordinarily, naturalization is contingent upon a five-year residence in the TRNC. However, individuals of certain categories are exempt from this requirement. These include veterans of the Turkish Resistance Organization and of the 1974 Peace Operation, and their families.[200] Finally, according to the government of the Republic of Cyprus, on 12 October 2004 a protocol was signed between Turkey and the TRNC to regularize the presence of the construction workers arriving in the 2000s, adding some 40,000 new residents – and potential nationals – to the TRNC.[201] Since 2004, the granting of TRNC nationality has become more selective,[202] and mass grants, which had apparently been a common occurrence, dwindled.

Greek Cypriots argue that Turkish settlers are culturally different from Turkish Cypriots; it is feared that they will change the character of Cyprus, and effectively transform the northern part of the island into a province of Turkey.[203] This concern is heightened by the fact that Turkish settlers may already be a majority on the electoral rolls of the TRNC, which under the Annan Plan is the future Turkish Cypriot constituent state of the UCR. Greek Cypriots are concerned that settlers could control the Turkish Cypriot constituent and consequently share in the federal system, as representatives of the Turkish Cypriot constituent state.[204]

198 Laakso Report, 37–38.

199 TRNC Constitution Article 67(1).

200 Law 52/1993 of 27 May 1993, Articles 4(1), 7, 8(1)(B), 9(1)(D), 9(1)(E). The Turkish Resistance Organization (TMT) was a pre-independence, Turkish-Cypriot pro-partition paramilitary force.

201 The mass arrival of construction workers was partly linked to the release of bonds related to Greek Cypriot abandoned property that until then had prevented building improvements.

202 UK House of Commons, 2006–2007 Report, paragraph 106.

203 Loukis G. Loucaides, 'Expulsion of Settlers from Occupied Territories: The Case of Turkish Settlers in Cyprus', in Loukis G. Loucaides, *Essays on the Developing Law of Human Rights* (Dordrecht: Martinus Nijhoff, 1995) 108, 129; Palley, *International Relations Debacle*, 227; Doob, 'Cypriot Patriotism', 394.

204 Observations made by the Ministry of Foreign Affairs of Cyprus, annexed to European Commission against Racism and Intolerance (ECRI), Third Report on Cyprus (adopted 16 December 2005), 42 footnote 43.

The presence of the Turkish settlers in Cyprus is also regarded as a means by which Turkey will have direct influence over the whole of the UCR, since most Turkish settlers are highly susceptible to Turkish influence.[205] This concern was reinforced by Turkey's characterization of the settlers as 'security' for Turkey, giving rise to the fear that in the case of intercommunal clashes, Turkey would jump at the opportunity to intervene in the Greek Cypriot constituent state of the UCR.[206] Moreover, Greek Cypriots argue that since many Turkish settlers are military reservists who have immigrated after completing compulsory military service,[207] even if the UCR is demilitarized, Turkey would have a ready army waiting, merely requiring air drops of equipment and some target practice.[208] For these reasons, Greek Cypriots maintain that Turkey's rights under the Treaty of Guarantee, which was its pretext for military action in 1974, should be clearly restricted.[209] Nonetheless, the final version of the plan not only maintains the Treaty of Guarantee but expands it to cover, in addition to the independence, territorial integrity, security and constitutional order of the UCR, also the territorial integrity, security and constitutional order of each of the constituent states.[210]

Transition under the Annan Plan

Nationality

As noted in Chapter 5 above, an observation to Main Article 12 of the Annan Plan excludes nationality and immigration from the general validation of past acts of the TRNC, and provides:

> Matters of citizenship, immigration, and properties affected by events since 1963 are dealt with in a comprehensive way by this Agreement; any validity of acts prior to entry into force of this Agreement regarding these matters shall thus end unless they are in conformity with the relevant provisions of this Agreement.

205 Cuco Report, paragraph 93; Palley, *International Relations Debacle*, 234.

206 Palley, *International Relations Debacle*, 223, 227.

207 The majority, according to Greek Cypriots: Palley, *International Relations Debacle*, 71. Professional Turkish military personnel for the most part left the TRNC in the 1980s.

208 Observations made by the Ministry of Foreign Affairs of Cyprus, annexed to European Commission against Racism and Intolerance (ECRI), Third Report on Cyprus (adopted 16 December 2005), 43 footnote 44.

209 For a description of the negotiations see Palley, *International Relations Debacle*, 147–153.

210 Annan Plan, Treaty between Cyprus, Greece, Turkey and the United Kingdom Related to the New State of Affairs in Cyprus, Annex III: Additional Protocol to the Treaty of Guarantee, Article 1.

Accordingly, original nationals of the UCR would only be persons who had Cypriot citizenship in 1963 and their descendants.[211] Persons who obtained nationality from the TRNC (or its precursor, the TFSC) – that is, mainly settlers from mainland Turkey – would not be entitled to original nationality in the UCR. Although post-1963 settlers include not only mainland Turks,[212] the political debate focuses on the future of Turkish settlers.

The government of the Republic of Cyprus argues that under the law of occupation Turkey is obligated to remove its nationals from the TRNC.[213] Nonetheless, it has conceded that the consequences for individual settlers of long standing should be examined in a humane fashion.[214] Accordingly, from the outset of the negotiations on the Annan Plan, it accepted that in addition to pre-1963 nationals and their descendants, concessions would be made towards long-term residents with respect to nationality and residence. In August 2002, Rauf Denktaş, then leader of the TRNC, declared that there were only about 30,000 Turkish settlers and that persons who had gained nationality of the TRNC should be accommodated. The then president of the Republic of Cyprus, Clerides, agreed that subject to these being the correct numbers, he would accept the principle that whoever was a 'national' of either side would become a national of the UCR.[215] From that time until the final drafting of the Annan Plan, the numbers and categories of persons entitled to original nationality have undergone various changes. The final version of the Annan Plan contains the following provision on original citizenship:

Article 3 – Cypriot citizenship upon entry into force of the Foundation Agreement

Upon entry into force of the Foundation Agreement, the following persons shall be considered citizens of the United Cyprus Republic:

[211] Annan Plan, Draft Federal Law on Citizenship of the United Cyprus Republic; Annan Plan, Foundation Agreement, Annex III, Attachment IV. 1963 is a significant date not in the context of nationality in the TRNC, but in that of property; see Chapter 7 below. Nationality and property are mentioned together in the exception to validation of acts of the TRNC.

[212] According to the TRNC 2006 census, there are over 8,000 non-TRNC and non-Turkish nationals residing in the TRNC. Final Results of TRNC General Population and Housing Unit Census, Additional Tables, http://nufussayimi.devplan.org/Kesin-sonuc-index_en.html.

[213] Geneva Convention IV Article 49(6); ICC Statute Article 8.

[214] Observations made by the Ministry of Foreign Affairs of Cyprus, annexed to European Commission against Racism and Intolerance (ECRI), Third Report on Cyprus (adopted 16 December 2005), 44.

[215] Palley, *International Relations Debacle*, Chapter 17.

a. Any person who held Cypriot citizenship in 1963 and his or her descendants and the spouses of such citizens ...
b. Any person whose name figures on a list handed over to the Secretary-General of the United Nations by each side no later than 25 March 2003. Each side's list may number no more than 45,000 persons, inclusive of spouses and children, unless there are specific reasons preventing such spouses and children from being considered Cypriot citizens. The list shall contain the name of each person and the basis for their inclusion on the list, as well as, where relevant, the date of their entry into Cyprus. Applicants shall be included on the list based on the following criteria and in the following order of priority:
   i) persons 18 years of age or older who enjoyed permanent residence in Cyprus for at least seven years before reaching the age of 18 and for at least one year during the last five years and their minor children who enjoy permanent residence in Cyprus;
   ii) other persons who have enjoyed permanent residence in Cyprus for more than seven consecutive years, based on the length of their stay.[216]

When the negotiations resumed in 2008, Cyprus's President Christofias announced unilaterally that the 45,000 quota would be increased to 50,000.[217]

Naturalization and residence

Under the Annan Plan, persons outside the quota may acquire UCR nationality by naturalization. The requisites for naturalization include nine years of consecutive residence in the UCR. Up to five years of residence under the TRNC may be counted towards naturalization.[218] In this the Annan Plan differs from the arrangements in the Baltic states and Timor-Leste, where residence under the illegal regime could not be counted at all towards naturalization. For a transitional period of nineteen years or until Turkey's accession to the European Union, whichever is earlier, Cyprus may limit the right of Turkish nationals to reside in Cyprus if their

216 Annan Plan, Draft Federal Law on Citizenship of the United Cyprus Republic, Article 3. Part F of the Annan Plan (entitled 'Measures to Be Taken during April 2004') includes the following item: 'Hand over by 10 April 2004 to the Secretary-General the list numbering no more than 45,000 persons as specified in the proposed Federal Law on Citizenship of the United Cyprus Republic (failing which the Citizenship Board shall, after entry into force of the Foundation Agreement, prepare the list in accordance with that law).'

217 'Christofias Firm on Settlers', *Cyprus Weekly*, 29 August–5 September 2008, www.cyprusemb.se/dbase/cypemb/svenska/ref1162.asp.

218 Annan Plan, Draft Federal Law on Citizenship, Article 5.

number reaches 5 per cent of the number of resident Cypriot citizens holding Turkish Cypriot internal constituent state citizenship status.[219] The Annan Plan therefore provides for either acquisition of original nationality or removal from the territory, with an exception for persons entitled to remain with the prospect of eventual naturalization. Permanent residence without an option of naturalization and with restrictions on civil rights was perceived as unacceptable.

Anticipated impact of the Annan Plan

Conclusions on the implications of the plan remain vastly disparate. The uncertainty stems not only from uncertainty as to the actual number of settlers in the various categories, but also from different readings of the Annan Plan. Palley reports that the UN team created different expectations in each of the parties, for example with respect to whether spouses of Turkish Cypriots would be entitled to nationality outside the quota.[220] Different expectations also exist with regard to thousands of students and academic staff. The ambiguity of the situation is apparent in the difference between the July 2003 statement of the Secretary-General's Special Adviser's own legal adviser that 'the Plan does not foresee that anybody will be forced to leave',[221] and the Secretary-General's 2004 statement that 'about half' of the settlers would have to leave the island.[222] The government of the Republic of Cyprus warns that under the 2004 version of the plan, 111,000 Turkish settlers were entitled to either UCR nationality or residence.[223] These ambiguities suggest that the removal of Turkish settlers might not be as dramatic as the Annan Plan appears to suggest.

219 Foundation Agreement, Main Article 3(5).

220 Palley, *International Relations Debacle*, 67–71; Annan Plan, Draft Federal Law on Citizenship of the United Cyprus Republic, Article 6. See also Statement by the Secretary-General's Special Adviser on Cyprus, Alvaro de Soto, at the Joint Meeting of the Foreign Affairs Committee and the Delegation of the European Parliamentary Committee with the Republic of Cyprus, Brussels, 14 April 2004.

221 Didier Pfirter, Statement at The Annan Plan: Myths and Realities conference at Bögaziçi University in Istanbul on 17 July 2003, quoted in Comments by the Government of Cyprus on the Report of the Secretary General on His Mission of Good Offices in Cyprus (28 May 2004), UN Doc S/2004/437, paragraph 41; UK House of Commons Foreign Affairs Committee, Cyprus – Second Report Volume II, Oral and Written Evidence HC113-II Incorporating HC 1172 i–iv, Session 2003–2004 (22 February 2005), 85.

222 Report of the Secretary-General on His Mission of Good Offices in Cyprus (28 May 2004), UN Doc S/2004/437, paragraph 60. The UK Foreign Affairs Committee pointed out that about 42,000 Turkish settlers who are not married to Turkish Cypriots would have to leave. UK House of Commons, 2006–2007 Report, paragraph 105.

223 UK House of Commons, 2004–2005 Report, paragraph 59.

Indeed, the Turkish Cypriot side prepared a list of candidates for immediate naturalization, which reportedly contained no more than 41,000 names.[224] However, this limited list may be based on the assumption that various categories, such as spouses, are entitled to original citizenship outside the quota.

The quota provision allows preferential treatment to certain settlers with respect to residence and eventual naturalization. Preferential treatment is permitted under international law, if it does not discriminate against any ethnic or national group.[225] Inclusion on the list was never limited by any ethnic or national criteria, but according to the reports it contains names of Turks only.[226] Given that they constitute the overwhelming majority of settlers, the exclusion of other foreigners does not appear discriminatory. Furthermore, it is not clear whether current non-Turkish residents of the TRNC claim to hold its nationality or only residence.

6.4 Conclusions

This chapter examined the law applicable to settlers brought by the illegal regime into the territory, addressing both the validity of status granted by the illegal regime, and the consequences of a prolonged residence in the territory in terms of international human rights law. Against this background, this chapter considered the policy of post-transition regimes with respect to settlers present in their territories, paying particular attention to whether the post-transition regimes attempted to remove the settlers from their territories, and the extent to which these attempts were successful.

It should be clear that where settlers were permitted to remain, this did not necessarily follow from a perception that expulsion was prohibited. Not all post-transition regimes were inclined to remove settlers from their territory, and where they did, this inclination was not necessarily linked with the illegality of the previous regime. In this context, there is a clear differentiation between the Baltic states, Timor-Leste and Cyprus on the one hand, and the southern African cases on the other hand.

224 Interview by the author with Dr Kudret Özersay, Eastern Mediterranean University, Lefkoşa, 27–28 February 2008.

225 CERD, Article 1(4).

226 Interview by the author with Dr Kudret Özersay, Eastern Mediterranean University, Lefkoşa, 27–28 February 2008.

In the Baltic states and Cyprus, resolving the settler problem was (and in Cyprus, still is) a pivotal political issue. In the Baltic states, although a satisfactory resolution of the settler problem was not a requisite for the formal reversion to independence, it was perceived as a requisite for the political success of the reversion. In Cyprus, resolution of the settler problem is a key issue in the negotiations between the parties. In both cases, the concern of the post-transition regime over the presence of settlers was directly linked to the continuing existence of the kin-state with which the illegal regime was or is associated, and to the perceived threat from that state to the post-transition regime. The settlers were or are regarded as proxies or agents of that state. This concern of the post-transition regime has found expression in the transitional arrangements, in a manner which directly links the status of settlers to the illegality of the previous regime. The same challenge to the post-transition regime, namely of a large settler population affiliated with a kin-state with which the illegal regime was associated, might also have arisen in Timor-Leste, if the settlers had not left of their own accord. Interestingly, even though the settlers have left, the transitional arrangements in Timor-Leste also give expression to the illegality of settlement under the illegal regime.

In the southern African states, settlement patterns, such as there were, were entirely different. In Namibia, for example, there was no numerically significant settler population. In the TBVC, only a small number of persons had acquired TBVC nationality, and they were not associated with the policy of the illegal regime. In Zimbabwe, settlers under the Smith regime made up about half of the White population, but they were not perceived as distinct, in any way, from the veteran White minority in the territory. In all three instances, the status of individuals was regarded as a purely domestic, post-colonial issue. Even in Namibia, where the illegal regime was foreign to the territory, there was little concern that the presence of settlers would preserve the power base of the illegal regime. This relaxed attitude can be explained by the fact that the transition to democracy of South Africa largely eliminated concerns that it would exert pressure on Namibia, particularly as it was South Africa's gradual transformation which facilitated Namibia's path to independence in the first place. There was therefore no danger of the settlers being used as pawns in a grand design by an usurper regime.

The composition of the population was, of course, an important element in the policy of the post-transition regime also in southern Africa. But the conflict was perceived not as between the indigenous population and foreign settlers, but between Blacks and Whites, with both populations being regarded as local. The settler problem was inconsequential in comparison with the daunting challenges of decolonization and democratization faced by the southern African states. These challenges raised issues that went further back in time and were deeper in substance than the illegality of the immediately preceding regimes. Removing settlers, such as there were, might have reduced the size of the White population but it would not have relieved the burdens of resocialization, which required enormous investments. In other words, settlers as such constituted a relatively minor threat to the development of the new state's identity.

Where the settler population was regarded as an obstacle to national interests, i.e. in the Baltic states and Cyprus (as well as in Timor-Leste), the attempt to resolve the settler problem was clearly carried out by reference to the illegality of the previous regime and to the consequent invalidity of any status granted by it. In the Baltic states, this was carried out by reversion to pre-1940 nationality grants; under the Annan Plan, reversion in the three areas of law singled out (citizenship, immigration and property) goes back to 1963; Timor-Leste adopted a clean-slate policy, thereby removing the need to address continuity of purported nationality of settlers. But even with respect to naturalization based on long-term residence in the territory, residence during the period of Indonesian administration does not qualify as lawful for the purpose of naturalization. In short, in all three cases there was an attempt to reverse the consequences of the illegal regime's policy, relying heavily on the illegality of that regime.

A separate question is the extent to which the attempts at removal of the settlers through the pursuit of the consequences of illegality were successful. In the Baltic states, settlers were by and large permitted to remain in the territory as residents and eventually to naturalize. In Timor-Leste, the legislation which totally excludes Indonesian settlers from acquiring any status in the country was never put to the test. In Cyprus under the Annan Plan, removal is the default arrangement, with exceptions for a quota of persons becoming immediate nationals, and a limited quota of future nationals through naturalization. Its implications, had the plan been adopted, are disputed, but it is clear that removal of settlers would have been far from comprehensive.

Both in the Baltic states and in Cyprus under the Annan Plan, the category of foreign nationals who are permanent residents was largely avoided. This is not surprising given the European trend, which by 2007 was incorporated in Directive 2003/109, of eliminating the existence a second-class population of permanent residents, by assimilating long-term residents to nationals. However, in each case this was achieved in a different way. In the Baltic states, residence and naturalization requisites have been liberalized to enable most permanent residents to remain in the country and eventually naturalize. In contrast, the Annan Plan avoids a large permanent resident population by stipulating either limited immediate naturalization or departure from the island altogether. One explanation for this difference might be that the Cyprus case lends itself, more than that of the Baltic states, to legal arrangements which formally uphold the consequences of illegality, regardless of the extent to which these consequences actually materialize. The Cypriot conflict has from the outset and consistently been addressed in a legal framework. The illegality of the TRNC has been declared by the Security Council, given effect by states through the policy of non-recognition, and upheld by international judicial institutions such as the ECJ. Even the judgments of the ECtHR, which is mandated with human rights questions rather than with inter-state ones, have proceeded, until the mid-2000s, on the basis of the nullity of the TRNC's actions. As a result, the formal framework for resolving the conflict relies heavily on the invalidity of the acts of the TRNC. This approach is in stark contrast with the resignation, in the Cold War era, of the international community – legally as well as politically – to the annexation of the Baltic states by the Soviet Union. This does not mean, however, that in practice Turkish settlers would be easily removed from Cyprus. Moreover, the steadfast adherence to the consequences of invalidity may be weakening in view of the shift in ECtHR jurisprudence towards recognition of TRNC acts as valid for the purposes of the ECtHR.

In both the Baltic states and Cyprus, the bar to removal of settlers does not lie in the grant of status by the illegal regimes. As the doctrinal analysis shows, the post-transition regime is not obligated to recognize the validity of formal status granted by the illegal regime. This status is invalid *ab initio* under international law, and even if it merits partial or ad hoc recognition under the *Namibia* exception, the general law of state succession does not enable it to transcend the change of regime. Rather, the obstacles to removal of settlers lie in international human rights law, which gives effect to factual developments and places certain limitations on the power of a state to expel individuals, with limited regard to the illegal origins of the factual situation. Accordingly, even in Cyprus, large-scale expulsion does not seem to be legally possible, although the Greek Cypriot community might still entertain hopes in this direction. In both the Baltic states and Cyprus, international law protects the right of settlers to remain in the territory. This is not to say that there are no differences between the two instances, with respect both to the interests of the post-transition regime and to the extent of interference with individuals' rights, but those do not necessarily yield entirely different equilibria. For example, the formal status of Turkey under the Annan Plan as guarantor of the UCR gives rise to apprehension that the presence of Turkish settlers might trigger and exacerbate the military and other involvement of Turkey in Cyprus. Yet the danger of Turkish military involvement in Cyprus is not qualitatively greater than the risk of the Russian Federation intervening – as it has declared its willingness to do in some circumstances – to protect ethnic Russian communities. The russophone settler communities are a generation older than the Turkish settler community, but settlers in both places are likely to be attached to their place of residence to the exclusion of any other. Some difference may lie in the fact that unlike mainland Turks, who were not formally forced to move to the TRNC, many of the russophone settlers had little, if any, choice in relocating to the Baltic states. In fact, the russophone settlers have to a large extent been regarded as blameless pawns in a political game. In addition, expulsion of the many russophone settlers would have been impossible, since, following the breakdown of the Soviet Union, many russophone settlers found themselves stateless. Against this background, it is possible to appreciate the pressure on, and the efforts in, the Baltic states to integrate the russophone community into the titular society. There was much less pressure on the government of the Republic of Cyprus to accommodate Turkish settlers under the UCR.

It may be said that the russophone community was regarded by the international community more as an ethnic minority than as a foreign element. In Cyprus, inter-communal relations are expected to take a different shape. On the one hand, immediate integration of mainland Turks within the Turkish Cypriot constituent state is likely to be simple, given the cultural and linguistic similarities. Distinguishing settlers from local Turkish Cypriots is likely to become increasingly difficult with time. On the other hand, this integration does not remove what the Greek Cypriots regard as a threat, namely the increase of the relative size of the Turk-affiliated population (whether indigenous Turkish Cypriots or former settlers) of the island, to the detriment of Greek Cypriot dominance.

It seems, therefore, that the difference in level and type of support that the settler populations received from the international community derives from political siding. Indeed, the political forces operating in the resolution of the two conflicts are very different. The refusal to entertain the possibility of expulsion of the russophone settlers from the Baltic states is linked to the reluctance of the international community, represented primarily by western European states, to enter into conflict with the Russian Federation, which retained significant political and military power even after the dissolution of the USSR. In the euphoria of the demise of Soviet rule, it may have seemed unfair to castigate individuals for the misdeeds of a dead empire, of which they themselves were often victims. With respect to the Cyprus conflict, the same states more readily aligned with the prospective post-transition regime, a soon-to-be member of the EU, than with Turkey, the kin-state of the settlers. Indeed, the continued presence of Turkish settlers in Cyprus may worry certain international actors no less than it worries the government of Cyprus, since such presence has a direct effect on the EU, which is less than enthusiastic about incorporating Muslim elements.[227]

Interestingly, the fact that transition in the Baltic states was unilateral while in Cyprus it is expected to be consensual does not appear to have been a significant factor in the formal approach. One might have expected a normative arrangement adopted in a consensual transition (Cyprus) to be less confrontational than one adopted unilaterally (Baltic states). Indeed, the legislation in the Baltic states was, at the outset, very unaccommodating towards the settlers, and only following heavy pressure by the international community, which did not wish to see a new wave of mass population movements, was it made more inclusive. However, it is the approach of the Annan Plan, which one might have expected to be the more compromissory, that is very legalistic, in that it is based, at least formally, on exclusion of the settlers who do not become original nationals of the UCR.

In conclusion, although the implantation of settlers is one of the most visible and objectionable practices of illegal regimes,[228] it is not an easily reversible one. Once the settler community is established in the territory,

[227] Shireen T Hunter, 'Europe's Relationship with the Muslim World: Emerging Patterns of Conflict and Cooperation', in Ola Tunander, Pavel Baev and Victoria Ingrid Einagel (eds.), *Geopolitics in Post-Wall Europe: Security, Territory and Identity* (Oslo: International Peace Research Institute, 1997), 120; Netherlands Scientific Council for Government Policy (WRR), *The European Union, Turkey and Islam* (Amsterdam: Amsterdam University Press, 2004).

[228] Compare with UNSC Resolution 896 (31 January 1994) on the situation in Georgia (demographic change in Abkhazia), paragraph 12; UNGA Resolution 59/124 (10 December 2004) on Jerusalem (property and population) preambular paragraph 15; UNSC Resolution 1582 (28 January 2005) on the situation in Georgia (demographic change in Abkhazia), paragraph 17.

international human rights law places various obstacles on its removal, insofar as that removal is pursued on the basis of the illegality of the previous regime rather than on the personal conduct of individual settlers. Accordingly, even where there was a strong political will, post-transition regimes have had difficulties reverting to the *status quo ante* with respect to the population in their territory.

7 The effect of transition on land titles

7.1 Introduction

People are attached to land in a variety of ways: spiritual, economic, political. Land provides the individual with a shelter, a home, a source of subsistence and security. It is also a public good, forming an indispensable component of culture and life. Land is therefore a powerful tool in pursuing political goals. Hardly an international conflict exists which does not have a territorial dimension.

Illegal regimes characteristically change land ownership patterns in the territory under their control. This change serves both to undermine existing power structures that may challenge the regime, and to strengthen power structures that benefit it, such as its military forces, its civilian settler population and local sycophants. Land holds political promise also for post-transition regimes. Large-scale adjustments of land rights have therefore been a prominent feature of many post-conflict situations.

Illegal regimes are not unique in manipulating land rights to pursue political goals. Involvement in land distribution is particularly characteristic of governments driven by ideologies that are inconsonant with liberal perceptions of the right to property, such as colonialism, racism and communism; but which are not, or originally were not, illegal themselves. In southern Africa, deprivation of inhabitants of their land long preceded the illegal regimes. Similarly, the denial of private ownership under communist rule was not reserved to the Baltic states, but extended throughout the east European bloc. Consequently, the post-transition regimes' land policies may be motivated not only by the illegality of the previous regime, but by the unacceptability of previous land policies on their merits, irrespective of the status of the regime.[1]

Nonetheless, the fact that certain land policies were also unacceptable in light of international human rights law does not render the illegality of the regime irrelevant. The redress mechanism for violation of the human right to property differs from the mechanism for redress based on the illegality of the regime in a number of aspects. First, under international law, violations of human rights are invocable by individuals while other violations of international law are not. In addition, claims of violation of human rights have to be examined on a case-by-case basis (although there could be numerous claims relating to mass violations). The onus is on the individual to show that a recognized human right is at issue, and that a specific act constituted a violation of that right. In contrast, under the law applicable to illegal regimes, the point of departure is that all acts of the regime, including the taking of property, are invalid, and the onus is on the regime to show that specific acts (even if numerous) merit recognition on an exceptional basis. As for the substantive differences between a violation of a human right and an act of an illegal regime, since the acts of an illegal regime are invalid *ab initio*, subsequent grantees of land taken by the illegal regime acquire no right because the grantor had none to give. The dispossessed owner is deprived in this case not of ownership but of use.[2] In contrast, under international human rights law, the illegality of the taking of a property does not necessarily prevent it from having legal effect.

In order to identify the extent to which the measures taken by an illegal regime are reversible, it is necessary first to establish the legal legacy which the post-transition regime faces upon its assumption of power. The doctrinal analysis in this chapter examines the validity of land changes involving the illegal regime and considers whether any such validity can survive the transition to the lawful regime. It then examines the extent to which international human rights law requires the post-transition regime to give effect to changes that had taken place under the illegal regime, regardless of their formal status, and suggests factors that affect the manner in which competing interests should be balanced against each other. The practice review examines the changes introduced by the

[1] One might even surmise that where the land policy of an illegal regime is in itself unobjectionable, the illegality of the regime as a whole would have little if any consequence for the policy of the post-transition regime.

[2] ECtHR, *Loizidou* v. *Turkey (Merits)*.

illegal regimes to land allocations, the stances taken by the post-transition regimes as to maintenance or existing allocations or reversion to the *status quo ante*, and the extent of reversion to the *status quo ante* where such was sought.

7.2 Doctrine

7.2.1 Types of changes to rights in land under the illegal regime

The involvement of a government in land transfers can assume many forms. The principal ones are registration of transactions carried out between individuals, expropriation for public purposes and expropriation with a subsequent grant to private entities.

Registration of voluntary private transactions

Registration of voluntary transactions carried out in good faith in the ordinary course of everyday life is a technical governmental function that is essential for the financial security of the individuals involved, and consequently for the economic wellbeing of the population as a whole.

Although the *Namibia Advisory Opinion* does not specifically mention the registration of private transactions in land as falling within the exception to non-recognition, this notion is not new. In *Texas* v. *White* the US Supreme Court noted that 'acts necessary to peace and good order among citizens, such for example as acts . . . *regulating the conveyance and transfer of property, real and personal* . . . must be regarded in general as valid when proceeding from an actual, though unlawful government'.[3] In *Loizidou* v. *Turkey*, Judge Jambrek noted that the registration of transactions had been given effect in the past, regardless of the validity of certain regimes.[4] Transactions between private individuals in which the involvement of the regime is limited to registration should therefore be given legal effect under the *Namibia* exception.

Expropriation for public purposes

When the expropriation is carried out for the benefit of the population – that is, in the public or general interest[5] – its legal effect may be recognized under the *Namibia* exception, subject to the reservation raised

[3] *Texas* v. *White*, 733, emphasis added. See also *Horn* v. *Lockhart*, 580.

[4] *Loizidou* v. *Turkey (Merits)*, dissenting opinion (but not necessarily on this point) of Judge Jambrek, [5].

[5] ECHR Protocol No 1, Article 1.

in Chapter 3 above, namely that care should be taken to ensure that the illegal regime does not abuse its authority to discharge its human rights obligations in order to achieve illegal goals. The illegal regime may need property in order to address the needs of the general public as a whole, such as public facilities (hospital and schools) and infrastructure for utilities (such as water and electricity). It may also need property in order to address the needs of individuals, when the community has an interest in their wellbeing. In *Loizidou* (1996), the Turkish government argued that the taking of Greek Cypriot property was necessary in order to house Turkish Cypriot refugees fleeing from the south of the island.[6] The assumption behind the permissibility of expropriation as a matter of principle is that a government may set its economic and social priorities, and in some cases may legitimately conclude that it is justifiable to cause detriment to a single individual for the benefit of the community. This assumption is justified when the state is perceived as acting for the benefit of the population at large. Under the ECHR, for example, the leeway given to governments with respect to expropriation is quite extensive, permitting them to take property not only when 'necessary in a democratic society' but also when it is 'in the public interest'.[7] In the case of non-sovereign regimes this assumption may be misplaced. Specifically with respect to illegal regimes, a conflict of interests between the governing authority and the population is even inherent in the illegality of the regime. The scope of discretion allowed to illegal regimes should therefore be narrowly circumscribed. Expropriation may be given effect on the ground that it is necessary to discharge human rights obligations only on a very exceptional basis, for example where the need involved is apparent and indisputable, and, of course, when the expropriation is carried out in compliance with other requirements, such as proportionality and the payment of compensation.[8]

Expropriation for non-public purposes

The overwhelming majority of land expropriation by illegal regimes has been for non-public purposes. In some cases, land was not only taken

[6] ECtHR, *Loizidou* v. *Turkey (Merits)*, [35], [64].

[7] *James and Others* v. *the United Kingdom*, [41], [46].

[8] In *Loizidou* v. *Turkey (Merits)*, the majority opinion laconically dismissed the Turkish 'passing reference to the doctrine of necessity', namely the need to rehouse displaced persons. It considered that the harm caused by the purported expropriation was disproportionate to the need that it allegedly served. *Loizidou* v. *Turkey (Merits)*, [64].

from individuals, but also later granted to others, characteristically settlers brought in by the illegal regime and other cronies. In many cases the terms under which third parties were granted the land were favorable to them in comparison with open-market acquisitions, and they were often aware of the provenance of the grants. This does not mean that these grants should be excluded from the operation of the *Namibia* exception. Although the grants contributed to the entrenchment of the illegal regime, the protection of the population from detrimental consequences might justify giving them legal effect. Additional factors should also be examined, such as whether the receipt of the grant was voluntary.[9] In the Baltic states, Timor-Leste and the TRNC, for example, no alternative property was realistically available to grantees that was untainted by prior expropriation. Receipt of property from the illegal regime could therefore hardly be regarded as a voluntary choice to collude with the regime. The situation is different with respect to investors who voluntarily subject themselves to the illegal regime,[10] particularly where they have the means of ascertaining the legal status of the property,[11] or where such means are not available but the investors nonetheless pursue the transaction. The inconvenience caused to them through upholding the illegality of the illegal regime's acts does not outweigh the interests of the inhabitants deprived of the property. Needless to say, determining whether a specific individual could not realistically be expected to have acquired other land, or was an opportunist beneficiary of illegal action, may be difficult.

Where an expropriation is followed by a grant to another individual, that grant itself might merit validity under the *Namibia* exception. In that case, not only does the factual situation change, but also the legal one: ownership passes from the dispossessed owner to the subsequent grantee. If the grant does not merit exceptional recognition, the expropriation and the subsequent grant are invalid.

7.2.2 The effect of transition on land rights granted by the illegal regime

The post-transition regime may face two types of alleged land rights created during the existence of the illegal regime. One set of changes are those which are invalid due to the illegality of the regime and do not merit exceptional recognition. The post-transition regime is not bound to give any effect to such alleged rights by virtue of their purported formal status. The other set of changes are those that are valid under the

[9] UK House of Commons, '2004–2005 Report', [200]. [10] US, *Lamar* v. *Micou*.
[11] See discussion of *Orams and Orams* v. *Apostolides (Appeal)*, below.

Namibia exception. They include private transactions where the regime is involved only procedurally, land changes legitimately carried out in the public interest, and grants by the regime to individuals that should be given effect in order to avoid detriment to the individuals involved. Since these changes are deemed valid even under the law governing illegal regimes, their continuity may be examined against the law of state succession.[12]

There is a remarkable consensus that in ordinary cases of state succession, a change of sovereignty does not affect acquired rights of individuals,[13] although the type of rights that are capable of being 'acquired' has for a long time remained controversial.[14] Least disputed are rights obtained between individuals.[15] As regards legal relations to which the state is party, particularly as grantor, doctrinal debates originally focused on whether such relations should be regarded as private-law transactions which create acquired rights, or as public-law transactions.[16] Another often-cited distinction was made in the past between property rights, which may be acquired, and contractual rights, which may not.[17] International and state practice has been more generous in

12 The international instruments on the law of state succession (some of which codify customary international law) all provide that they are limited to state succession occurring in conformity with international law (VCST Article 6; VCSPAD Article 3; ILC, *Draft Articles on Nationality of Natural Persons in Relation to State Succession*, Article 3, and commentary to Article 3, paragraph 2). Equally, then, they cannot apply to situations of emergence from illegal annexation (or other territorial situations created in violation of international law). They can be applied by analogy.

13 Arthur B. Keith, *The Theory of State Succession, with Special Reference to English and Colonial Law* (London: Waterlow and Sons, 1907), 78; Francis B. Sayre, 'Change of Sovereignty and Private Ownership of Land' (1918) 12 *American Journal of International Law* 475, 477; in 1957 Lord Arnold D. McNair, in 'The General Principles of Law Recognized by Civilized Nations' (1957) 22 *British Yearbook of International Law* 1, 16, listed the doctrine as a general principle of law for the purpose of ICJ Statute Article 38(b); J. L. Brierly, *The Law of Nations: An Introduction to the International Law of Peace*, 6th edn (Oxford: Clarendon Press, 1963), 157; Daniel P. O'Connell, *State Succession in Municipal Law and International Law* (London: Stevens and Sons, 1967), Volume I, 78, 99; L. Benjamin Ederington, 'Property as a Natural Institution: The Separation of Property from Sovereignty in International Law' (1997–1998) 13 *American University International Law Review* 263, 298.

14 Quincy Wright, 'The End of a Period of Transition' (1937) 31 *American Journal of International Law* 604, 609–610.

15 Georges Kaeckenbeeck, 'The Protection of Vested Rights in International Law' (1936) 17 *British Yearbook of International Law* 1, 8–9, quoting *US* v. *Perchman* 7 Peter 51.

16 Kaeckenbeeck, 'Vested Rights in International Law', 12.

17 Wright, 'The End of a Period of Transition', 610. One rationale for recognizing only the former as acquired rights was that such rights remain unaffected by the disappearance of the state which created them, while a contractual right is susceptible to changes when a party disappears. Baty Thos, 'Division of States: Its Effect on Obligations'

acknowledging rights as acquired,[18] and as early as 1923 the PCIJ stated that even those who contest the existence in international law of a general principle of state succession 'do not go so far as to maintain that private rights including those acquired from the state as the owner of the property are invalid as against a successor in sovereignty'.[19] With the development of a right to property under international law, and the growing governmental involvement in economic activity, the doctrine appears to have become definitive and widely applicable, including with respect to grants of land by the state.[20]

The doctrine of acquired rights is not entirely unqualified. One exception put forward to its application regards grants *flagrante bello*, i.e. in aid of war against the sovereign. This qualification may be eminently relevant to grants of land by the illegal regime to third parties, even when those parties acted in good faith, since that good faith does not detract from the aim of the illegal regime to entrench its authority against the previous or future lawful regime. This qualification was enunciated by the British government following the annexation of the Boer Republics in 1900. Although the British position was not entirely consistent with regard to whether the doctrine of acquired rights was binding as a matter of law or merely of ethics, it maintained that concessions acquired during the war or in contemplation of it were not binding upon the new sovereign.[21] A similar doctrine developed in the US with respect to 'odious concessions'.[22]

(1923) 9 *Transactions of the Grotius Society* 119, 125–126. This rationale was offered in the context of inter-state relations, but seems equally applicable to state–individual relations.

[18] Francis B. Sayre, 'Change of Sovereignty and Concessions' (1918) 12 *American Journal of International Law* 705.

[19] *German Settlers in Poland (Advisory Opinion)*, 36. This statement embodies in the eyes of the PCIJ the situation relating to 'private rights', not only rights in property.

[20] For a recent explicit expression of this principle see UNMIK Regulation No. 2000/60 on Residential Property Claims and the Rules of Procedure and Evidence of the Housing and Property Directorate and the Housing and Property Claims Commission (31 October 2000), Section 2.1 ('Any property right which was validly acquired according to the law applicable at the time of its acquisition remains valid notwithstanding the change in the applicable law in Kosovo, except where the present regulation provides otherwise'). The entry of UNMIK into Kosovo is not strictly a case of state succession.

[21] Compare the British Law Officers' opinion with the Report of the Transvaal Concessions Commission. Daniel P. O'Connell, 'Economic Concessions in the Law of State Succession' (1950) 27 *British Yearbook of International Law* 93, 106–107.

[22] Sayre, 'Change of Sovereignty and Private Ownership of Land', 494; Sayre, 'Change of Sovereignty and Concessions', 727.

The *flagrante bello* exception resembles the notion of odious debt,[23] according to which war debts and regime debts may be repudiated by the successor state if they were hostile to the needs and interests of the obligated state, if the obligation had been incurred without the consent of the governed[24] or if the beneficiaries must have been aware that their loans would be used to oppress the population of that state.[25] The permissibility of repudiation of an odious debt is controversial. But even if it is acknowledged, no analogy should be drawn from it to succession to property granted *flagrante bello*. Loan and debt are contractual issues (*in personam*), to which the identity of the parties and their conduct may be eminently relevant. Non-recovery of a debt is a risk inherent to any loan transaction. Engagement in a loan transaction to a state is therefore a speculative enterprise, regardless of the subject matter of the transaction. The susceptibility of loan transactions to repudiations upon state succession because of odiousness reflects this inherent insecurity. In contrast, property rights provide particularly strong protection as they operate *erga omnes*. Once perfected, they should not be vulnerable to repudiation. Another difference between the two types of rights is that a debtor state which is unable to recover an odious debt may have recourse to other remedies under international law against the debtor. In contrast, individuals deprived of 'odious property' rights are unlikely to have any means of recovering their losses under international law. The exception to the doctrine of acquired rights when the grants are made *flagrante bello* should therefore be interpreted narrowly, with the legitimate expectations of the individual carrying great weight against repudiation. Only if the individual is directly responsible for conduct in bad faith or for collusion with the regime is there a justification for repudiating the grant.

The PCIJ has also rejected the notion that the political circumstances in which a grant was made may affect its survival of succession. It emphasized that a political motive for the granting of rights is not by itself a bar to the application of the acquired-rights doctrine, and cannot affect the private rights acquired under the law applicable at the time

[23] Hans J. Cahn, 'The Responsibility of the Successor State for War Debts' (1950) 44 *American Journal of International Law* 477, 484.

[24] Sayre, 'Change of Sovereignty and Concessions', 712–717.

[25] Tai-Heng Cheng, 'Renegotiating the Doctrine of Odious Debt' (2007) 70 *Duke Law and Contemporary Problems* 7, 13. The concept of 'regime debt' reflects the expansion of the right to self-determination as a concept related also to the internal function of a state.

of acquisition.[26] In conclusion, under the law of state succession, transactions and grants that are valid under the *Namibia* exception survive transition. As an exception, when at issue is the acceptance of a grant *flagrante bello*, in bad faith and in collusion with the illegal regime, there is no reason to afford it protection.

7.2.3 Limitations on restoration of land based on international human rights law

The application of the acquired-rights doctrine does not render land or other grants entirely immune to any change.[27] It merely confirms their existence as a point of departure for the post-transition regime. It is for the post-transition regime to decide on whether to restore land to its original owners or to maintain the prevailing situation. Probably the greatest difficulty in providing justice to individuals injured by the illegal regime is the risk of doing so at the expense of other individuals.[28] Maintenance of the situation would interfere with the right of dispossessed owners to property. Reversion to the *status quo ante* might interfere with the rights of current occupants to property, privacy and home and adequate housing.[29] The present section examines the significance of these rights in the context of restoration of property expropriated by an illegal regime, and factors governing the balance between competing interests.

The right to property

The right to property is protected by various regional instruments,[30] but the universal instruments guarantee only equality with respect to rights in property, not the right to property itself.[31] There is wide disagreement among states as to the content and scope of the right, weighing against the conclusion that this is a principle of customary law.[32] Generally speaking, the right to property comprises the rights to physical possession, peaceful

26 *German Settlers in Poland (Advisory Opinion)*, 36.

27 *German Settlers in Poland (Advisory Opinion)*, 36, noting that this is a separate question.

28 ECtHR, *Demopoulos and Others* v. *Turkey*, [117].

29 The term 'current occupants' indicates persons in actual occupancy of the property at the time of transition. It is neutral with regard to the proprietary rights of these persons, a matter addressed below.

30 ECHR Protocol 1; ACHR Article 21; 'Banjul Charter' Article 14. See also UDHR Article 17; generally see C. Krause, 'The Right to Property', in A. Eide *et al.* (eds.), *Economic, Social and Cultural Rights*, 2nd edn (Dordrecht: Martinus Nijhoff, 2001).

31 ICCPR Article 26; CERD Article 5(d)(v); CEDAW Articles 15(2) and 16(1)(h).

32 *Restatement of the Foreign Relations Law of the United States, Third*, Restatements of the Law Series (Washington, DC: American Law Institute, 1987), Volume II, 165 [702].

enjoyment, transfer and disposal of the property. The present analysis utilizes the standard adopted by ECHR Protocol 1, which sets the most stringent conditions for interfering with a person's property, and thus offers the greatest protection to grantees under the illegal regime, against expropriation by the post-transition regime.

Owners of property are not immune to interference with their right to property. Under ECHR Protocol 1, the right to property is not absolute, but may be limited 'in the public interest' and 'subject to the conditions provided for by law'. Limitations may take the form of expropriation or legislative controls over the use of property. They must be carried out in accordance with the principle of lawfulness and proportionality, by striking a fair balance between the general interests of the community and the protection of the right of property.[33] The national authorities enjoy a margin of appreciation in determining what constitutes a 'public interest'.[34]

An abstract legal stance advocating reversion to the legal *status quo ante* in light of the illegality of the previous regime is unlikely to justify interference with individuals' right to property. The public interest must be forward-looking. The ECtHR has on a number of occasions acknowledged the public interest in redress of infringements on property rights that occurred under a communist regime, even if the current owners have acquired their own rights in good faith. The legality of the communist regimes was not at issue before the ECtHR, but only the legality of specific acts of their governments. The court accepted that the systemic violation of human rights allowed the state to resolve the problem through a global policy of restoration (as long as it enabled individual re-examination of exceptional cases).[35] The same principle should apply to non-communist regimes if they are known to have engaged in systematic violations of human rights.

Another aim in the public interest is the realization of fundamental changes to a country's system, such as the transition from a totalitarian regime to a democratic form of government, and the reform of the state's political, legal and economic structure.[36] Illegal regimes are not by definition totalitarian and their termination does not necessarily require

[33] ECtHR, *Mellacher and Others* v. *Austria*, [42], [48].

[34] ECtHR, *Brumărescu* v. *Romania*, [78]; *Zvolský and Zvolská* v. *the Czech Republic* [67].

[35] *Zvolský and Zvolská* v. *the Czech Republic*, [68], [72]; *Wittek* v. *Germany*, [51]; but see *Străin and Others* v. *Romania*, [50].

[36] ECtHR, *Broniowski* v. *Poland*, [149].

political, legal and economic revisions. In practice, however, the maintenance of power more often than not involves various restrictions on the population; consequently, transition from an illegal regime involves, by nature, even if not by definition, a reform of law and economy.[37] Reversion of some of the illegal regime's acts to the *status quo ante* in spheres such as housing, which plays a central role in the welfare and economic policies of modern societies, may therefore be in the general interest.

In conclusion, the right to property does not a priori prevent a post-transition regime from expropriating land validly transferred under the *Namibia* exception. However, this would be an interference with the current owner's right to property. For the expropriation to be lawful it must comply with the requirement of legality and proportionality. The assessment of proportionality can only be made on a case-by-case basis. Particular factors that affect the evaluation whether the interference is proportionate to its purpose that are related to the process of transition from an illegal regime are considered further below.

The rights to privacy and home

ICCPR Article 17 provides that no one shall be subjected to 'arbitrary or unlawful interference with . . . his home'. ECHR Article 8 guarantees everyone 'the right to respect for . . . his home', subject to limitations under the law and necessary in a democratic society in the interests of, inter alia, the economic wellbeing of the country and the protection of the rights and freedoms of others. Again, as the ECHR sets the more stringent standard by limiting the permissibility of interference with the home to specific, substantive grounds, it will serve to examine whether the protection of current occupants' right to privacy of the home goes so far as to prevent the post-transition regime from returning to the *status quo ante* by restoration of the property to its original owners.

A home is defined not by legal title but by the nature of its use.[38] The concept of 'home' is not limited to premises which are lawfully occupied or which have been lawfully established. Whether or not a particular habitation constitutes a 'home' depends on the factual circumstances,

[37] Of the illegal regimes studied in this book, the TRNC is the only one which has not adopted an ideology which is in substance considered illegitimate, such as non-democratic, racist, etc. However, an overhaul of the legal system may still be required in order to adapt TRNC law to EU law.

[38] Manfred Nowak, *U.N. Covenant on Civil and Political Rights: CCPR Commentary*, 2nd edn (Kehl: N. P. Engel, 2005), 399 marginal 42; ECtHR, *Blečić* v. *Croatia*, [52]; ECtHR, *Demopoulos and Others* v. *Turkey*, [136].

namely the existence of sufficient and continuous links with a specific place.[39] Eviction is a most extreme form of interference with the right to respect for the home.[40] Protection from interference with the home and its privacy may therefore prevent the eviction of current occupants, allowing them to continue residing in a property even if they are not its owners.

The same grounds that may justify interference with the right to property of current occupants, namely redress of violations of human rights and the economic wellbeing of the country, are also valid with respect to interference with their right to privacy of the home.[41] However, the state's margin of appreciation with respect to the right to privacy tends to be narrower than with respect to the right to property. First, the right to privacy is of central importance to the individual's identity, self-determination, physical and moral integrity, maintenance of relationships with others and secure place in the community.[42] Second, upholding the right of current occupants to privacy is less detrimental to dispossessed owners than upholding the right of current occupants to property. In the former case, the owners are not deprived of the property entirely but only of its use. In light of these differences, even when property is restored to dispossessed owners, current occupants may not always be evicted. The dispossessed owners would receive ownership of the property, encumbered by tenants.

The right to adequate housing

ICESCR Article 11 recognizes 'the right of everyone to an adequate standard of living for himself and his family, including adequate food,

[39] *Prokopovich* v. *Russia*, Application No 58255/00, Judgment of 18 November 2004, ECHR 2004-XI (extracts), [36], citing *Buckley* v. *the United Kingdom*, Judgment of 25 September 1996, ECHR 1996-IV, [52]–[54], and Commission's report of 11 January 1995, [63]; *Gillow* v. *the United Kingdom*, Application No 9063/80, Judgment of 24 November 1986, Series A No. 109, [46]; *Wiggins* v. *the United Kingdom*, Application No 7456/76, Commission decision of 8 February 1978, Decisions and Reports (DR) 13, 40.

[40] ECtHR, *Larkos* v. *Cyprus*; ECtHR, *Chapman* v. *the United Kingdom*, Application No 27238/95, Grand Chamber Judgment of 18 January 2001, ECHR 2001-I; ECtHR, *Connors* v. *the United Kingdom*, Application No 66746/01, Judgment of 27 May 2004, unpublished; ECtHR, *Prokopovich* v. *Russia*, Application No 58255/00, Judgment of 18 November 2004, ECHR 2004-XI (extracts); *Cosic* v. *Croatia*, Application No 28261/06, Judgment of 15 January 2009, unpublished, [22].

[41] ECHR Article 8, ICCPR Article 17.

[42] *Connors* v. *the United Kingdom*, Application No 66746/01, Judgment of 27 May 2004, unpublished, [82].

clothing and housing'.[43] For housing to be considered 'adequate', several basic criteria must be fulfilled: security of tenure, habitability, affordability, accessibility, availability of materials, location and cultural adequacy.[44]

Prima facie, the right to adequate housing enjoys only weak protection, since it entails a discretionary allocation of resources by the state. Under ICESCR Article 2(1) a state is only obligated to take steps 'to the maximum of its available resources, with a view to achieving progressively the full realization of the rights recognized' in the covenant. The concept of 'progressive realization' reflects recognition of the fact that full realization of all economic, social and cultural rights is generally not possible within a short period of time. Accordingly, only a minimum core obligation is incumbent upon every state to ensure the satisfaction of minimum essential levels of each of the rights.[45] Any assessment whether a state has discharged the core obligation must also take account of resource constraints applying within it. In the case of poor, developing states, demonstrating lack of resources may prove all too easy.[46]

However, the core obligation towards current occupants of property marked for restoration does not entail positive expenditures. It implies first and foremost a prohibition on forced eviction, which is a negative obligation and which therefore has immediate effect, regardless of the development stage of the state.[47] Moreover, Article 11 does not prevent eviction altogether, but only places limitations on the manner in which eviction may be carried out, namely it must not be forced or without the

[43] See also 1996 Revised European Social Charter, Part I, Item 31, and Part II, Article 31. Estonia has been party to the Social Charter since 1 November 2000 but has not declared itself bound by the right to housing in Item 31. See also UDHR Article 25; CERD Article 5; CEDAW Article 14(2); CRC Article 27(3). Generally see Scott Leckie, 'The Right to Adequate Housing', in A. Eide *et al.* (eds.), *Economic, Social and Cultural Rights*, 2nd edn (Dordrecht: Martinus Nijhoff, 2001).

[44] CESCR, General Comment 4, in 'Compilation of General Comments' (27 May 2008), UN Doc HRI/GEN/1/Rev.9 Volume I, paragraph 8.

[45] CESCR General Comment 3, in 'Compilation of General Comments' (27 May 2008), UN Doc HRI/GEN/1/Rev.9 Volume I, paragraph 10.

[46] E.g. Timor-Leste's 2007 GDP per capita estimate is $392. In 2001, 40 per cent of the population was below the poverty line, and 74 per cent of households had no access to electricity; in 2004, 42 per cent of households had no access to drinking water. International Monetary Fund, 'Democratic Republic of Timor-Leste: Selected Issues and Statistical appendices' Country Report No. 08/203 (June 2008).

[47] CESCR, General Comment 4, in 'Compilation of General Comments' (27 May 2008), UN Doc HRI/GEN/1/Rev.9 Volume I, paragraph 10.

protection of appropriate legal and other safeguards.[48] Evictions must be carried out in conformity with general principles of reasonableness and proportionality.[49] Indeed, despite the general difficulty associated with ICESCR Article 11 in establishing a failure to comply with minimum standards, the Committee on Economic, Social and Cultural Rights has in the past found states to be in violation of Article 11(1), in view of the extent and manner of evictions that they had carried out.[50]

In conclusion, the right to adequate housing does not obstruct restoration of property, but it may temporarily limit the freedom of use of returning owners, as would the right of current occupants to privacy of the home. The ECtHR has acknowledged that states enjoy a margin of appreciation in taking measures to ensure protection of tenants in a poor financial situation against eviction, specifically with regard to economies in transition following the collapse of the communist regime bloc.[51]

Balancing competing interests

Human rights obligations of states do not give either original owners or current occupants absolute primacy in case of conflict, instead requiring that the interests be balanced against each other with neither one being entirely discarded for the sake of the other. The decision whether to prefer original owners or current occupants is, ultimately, a political choice.

In the immediate term, reversion to the *status quo ante* may be significantly more detrimental to current occupants who are relying on the existing situation than to dispossessed owners who through the years

[48] CESCR, General Comment 7, in 'Compilation of General Comments' (27 May 2008), UN Doc HRI/GEN/1/Rev.9 Volume I, paragraph 4.

[49] CESCR, General Comment 7, in 'Compilation of General Comments' (27 May 2008), UN Doc HRI/GEN/1/Rev.9 Volume I, paragraph 15. Forced evictions are prohibited or restricted under other instruments, both binding and guiding, although they are not defined there. E.g. Commission on Human Rights, Resolution 1993/77, paragraph 1; Report of the UN Conference on Environment and Development, Rio de Janeiro, 3–14 June 1992, UN Doc A/CONF.151/26/Rev.1 Volume I, Annex II, Agenda 21, Chapter 7.9 (b); 'Report of the United Nations Conference on Human Settlements (Habitat II)', Istanbul 3–14 June 1996 (7 August 1996), UN Doc A/CONF.165/14, Annex II, paragraph 40(n).

[50] See with regard to the Dominican Republic and Panama: Forced Evictions: Analytical Report Compiled by the Secretary-General Pursuant to Commission Resolution 1993/77 (7 December 1993), UN Doc E/CN.4/1994/20, paragraph 104; UN Doc E/1991/23-E/C.12/1990/8 paragraph 249; UN Doc E/1992/23-E/C.12/1991/4, paragraph 135(c).

[51] ECtHR, *Hutten-Czapska* v. *Poland*, 628 [178], [223]; ECtHR, *Schirmer* v. *Poland*, [38]. To date the ECtHR has not considered other post-conflict situations. But the same considerations would appear to be applicable *mutatis mutandis* to transition from non-communist regimes, including illegal regimes.

have managed to find alternative means of accommodation and subsistence. By upsetting an existing order, regardless of its original legitimacy, reversion to the *status quo ante* invites new hardship. Conflicts between original owners and current occupants may therefore be resolved in a variety of manners: by granting possession to the owner and evicting the occupant; by allowing the occupant to remain in the property under a controlled tenancy from the original owner; by allowing the occupant preferential rights in acquiring the property from the original owner; or, in the most extreme case, by granting ownership to the current occupant and compensating the original owner. The assessment of proportionality must be made with respect to the specific legislation and with respect to its application in the circumstances of each individual.[52] No universal formula can be offered. Nonetheless, certain considerations characteristically arise in transition from illegal regimes. The present section examines two of them.

Residence of the parties

Throughout the twentieth century, property rights in situations of mass displacement have been regarded as dependent on residence. International agreements that foresaw or regulated resettlement of populations overwhelmingly provided for compensation for land for persons leaving the country rather than retention of ownership.[53] The linkage of property

[52] ECtHR, *Zvolský and Zvolská* v. *the Czech Republic*, [72].

[53] E.g. the Convention between Greece and Bulgaria Respecting Reciprocal Emigration (signed 27 November 1919), 1 LNTS 68; Financial Agreement between Bulgaria and Greece (signed 9 December 1927), 87 LNTS. 201; Convention Concerning the Exchange of Greek and Turkish Populations (signed 30 January 1923), 32 LNTS 77; Agreement between Greece and Turkey to Facilitate the Application of Certain Provisions of the Treaty of Lausanne and of Declaration No IX annexed to that Treaty (signed 1 December 1926), 68 LNTS 13; Convention of Ankara (signed 10 June 1930), reproduced in Stephen P. Ladas, *The Exchange of Minorities: Bulgaria, Greece and Turkey* (New York: The Macmillan Co., 1932), 817; Agreement between the Government of the Kingdom of Greece and the Government of the Romanian People's Republic Concerning the Settlement of Economic Questions Pending between the Two Countries Since 1939 (signed 25 August 1956, entered into force 14 February 1958) 299 UNTS 231; Agreement between the Polish People's Republic and the Czechoslovak Republic Concerning the Settlement of Outstanding Property Matters (signed 29 March 1958, entered into force 9 January 1959) 340 UNTS 199; Agreement between the Republic of Italy and the Federal People's Republic of Yugoslavia for the Final Settlement of All Reciprocal Economic and Financial Obligations Arising out of the Treaty of Peace and Subsequent Agreements (signed 18 December 1954, entered into force 10 February 1956) 284 UNTS 239, Articles 2, 5; Treaty between the Italian Republic and Federal People's Republic of Yugoslavia on the Delimitation of the Boundary Line for the Part Not Indicated as Such in the Peace Treaty of 10 February 1947 (with annexes and final act) (signed 10 November 1975,

with residence converged with indifference towards whether refugees and displaced persons should be encouraged to return to their countries or to resettle elsewhere.

With the strengthening of international human rights law, the international regulation of situations of mass displacement is changing shape. These changes are reflected, for example, in the Principles on Housing and Property Restitution for Refugees and Displaced Persons (the Pinheiro Principles), adopted by the Sub-commission on the Promotion and Protection of Human Rights of the UN Commission on Human Rights. According to the principles, states should prioritize the right to restoration over compensation, with prejudice neither to the actual return nor to the non-return of refugees and displaced persons entitled to housing, land and property restoration.[54] Other instruments that concern individual or mass displacement following territorial changes contain similar provisions guaranteeing the right to property.[55] In addition, post-conflict arrangements increasingly give precedence to the right of internally displaced persons and refugees to resettle in the place of their former habitual residence over resettlement elsewhere.[56] The Pinheiro Principles

entered into force 3 April 1977) 1466 UNTS 72 Article 4; Agreement between the Republic of Italy and the Federative Socialist Republic of Yugoslavia for the Definitive Settlement of All the Mutual Obligations Deriving from Article 4 of the Treaty Signed at Osimo on 10 November 1975 (signed 18 February 1983, entered into force 15 February 1989 in Burns H. Weston, Richard B. Lillich and David J. Bederman, *International Claims: Their Settlement by Lump Sum Agreements, 1975–1999* (Ardesley: Transnational, 1999), 287; Agreement between Italy and Tunisia Relative to Indemnification and to Economic and Financial Cooperation (signed 29 August 1967, entered into force 29 August 1967), Article 3, in Richard B. Lillich and Burns H. Weston, *International Claims: Their Settlement by Lump Sum Agreements* (Charlottesville: University Press of Virginia, 1975), Part 2, 346; Agreement between the Federal Republic of Germany and the Empire of Ethiopia Concerning the Compensation of German Property in Ethiopia (signed 21 April 1965, entered into force 21 October 1965) in Lillich and Weston, *International Claims*, Part 2, 287. Agreement between the Government of the United Kingdom of Great Britain and Northern Ireland concerning Financial and Commercial Relations and British Property in Egypt (signed and entered into force 28 February 1959), 343 UNTS 159 Article 3. For India and Pakistan see Muhammad Ali Chaudhri, *The Emergence of Pakistan* (New York: Columbia University Press, 1967), 268–270.

54 Pinheiro Principles 2.2, 21.1. In the principles, the term 'restitution' is used in the sense of 'restoration', i.e. return of the property in kind.

55 European Commission for Democracy through Law, Declaration on the Consequences of State Succession for the Nationality of Natural Persons, adopted at its 28th Plenary Meeting, Venice, 13–14 September 1996, and Explanatory Report Doc CDL-NAT (1996) 007e-rev-restr section 16.

56 1995 Bosnia Herzegovina Framework Agreement, Annex 7. For details of the property dispute resolution mechanism, see L. von Carlowitz, 'Settling Property Issues in Complex Peace Operations: The CRPC in Bosnia and Herzegovina and the HPD/CC in Kosovo' (2004) 17 *Leiden Journal of International Law* 599. On the difficulties in

guarantee all refugees and displaced persons 'the right to voluntarily return to their former homes, lands or places of habitual residence, in safety and dignity'.[57] These two factors – the stand-alone right to restoration of property and the encouragement of physical return – converge to strengthen the role of restoration in post-conflict resolution.

The Pinheiro Principles were designed for situations of displacement which have led to arbitrary or unlawful deprivation. The commentary attached to the principles invites their application to all situations of displacement, regardless of the circumstances by which displacement originally occurred.[58] Yet dispossession under illegal regimes does not always involve displacement as the primary cause for dispossession (e.g. in the Baltic states). The principles are therefore not directly applicable to transition from an illegal regime, but can be applied by analogy. If dispossessed owners are entitled to restoration of property when they have been displaced, a fortiori they are entitled to it when they have remained *sur place*. This analogy is particularly important for ensuring non-discrimination in cases where dispossession took place with regard to both displaced persons and those that remained in place. In the Baltic states, for example, large parts of the population but not all of it were forcibly removed from their homes. Later, all property, of absentees and persons present alike, was nationalized. To distinguish between the two groups insofar as the right to restoration is concerned could be discriminatory, although admittedly restoration is particularly important to displaced persons because it is the vehicle that enables their return.

The principle that restoration is not inherently dependent on residence in the territory is gradually permeating into practice. In the HRC the question arose whether a law that required re-establishing permanent residence in the state as a requisite for eligibility for restoration or compensation was discriminatory. In the HRC's view, unless the original entitlement to property was predicated on citizenship or residence,

implementing these provisions because of the reluctance to return, see Timothy W. Waters, 'The Naked Land: The Dayton Accords, Property Disputes, and Bosnia's Real Constitution' (1999) 40 *Harvard International Law Journal* 517; Marcus Cox, 'The Dayton Agreement in Bosnia and Herzegovina: A Study of Implementation Strategies' (1998) 69 *British Yearbook of International Law* 210, 238–239.

57 Pinheiro Principle 10.1.

58 Pinheiro Principles 1.1, 1.2; Sub-commission on the Promotion and Protection of Human Rights of the UN Commission on Human Rights, Final Report of the Special Rapporteur, Paulo Sérgio Pinheiro, Addendum, Explanatory Notes on the Principles on Housing and Property Restitution for Refugees and Displaced Persons, UN Doc E/CN.4/Sub.2/2005/22/Add.1 (11 July 2005), paragraph 3.

predicating restoration on citizenship or residence would discriminate among victims of the original dispossession and be unreasonable.[59] The HRC did not discuss whether a return to the territory was itself a legitimate requirement, since the ICCPR does not protect the right to property per se. This decision concerned a situation where there was no immediate conflict of interests with other individuals, and the dispossessed owners were deprived, because of their foreign residence, of both restoration and compensation.

Where a conflict does exist between the interests of dispossessed owners and those of current occupants of the property, priority in possession might be legitimately given to the party intending to occupy the property. Since intention is an impractical criterion for determining precedence in rights, entitlement to reside in the territory of the post-transition regime can serve as a proxy for intention. This might be a relevant factor in a conflict between a dispossessed owner and a current occupant who is a settler. If settlers are not allowed to remain in the territory, there is justification in entitling them only to compensation rather than to ownership. This ties the resolution of property disputes to the question of settlers' right to remain in the territory, considered in Chapter 6 above. Needless to say, if settlers leave the territory, whether voluntarily or otherwise, the rights to privacy of the home and to an adequate standard of living become moot and no conflict arises on these issues between settlers and the dispossessed owners.

If, on the other hand, both parties remain in the territory, other criteria are required for balancing competing interests. The superiority noted above of the right to privacy over the right to property and the non-flexibility of the core right to adequate housing are likely to lead to their prima-facie primacy over the right to property, in which case current occupants may well have a right to remain in the property. The specific circumstances will determine the outcome in each case.

Good faith of current owners and occupants

The conduct through which the current owners or occupants acquired the property may play a role in the balancing between competing interests. It is important to recall that insofar as the right of settlers as current owners of property is recognized, it is based on their having acted in good faith in arriving in the territory and in acquiring the property in the first

59 HRC, *Simunek, Hastings, Tuzilova and Prochazka* v. *the Czech Republic*, [11.6]; *Adam* v. *the Czech Republic*, [12.5].

place, thereby placing them within the purview of the *Namibia* exception. Once this is acknowledged, the illegality of their original presence in the territory under international law should not be held against them. The rights to privacy and adequate housing, which are protected irrespective of the right to property under the *Namibia* exception, are not dependent directly on the legality of the conduct that led to the occupation of the property. This was addressed specifically in the context of the TRNC by Judge Schermers who opined, in a separate opinion in *Cyprus* v. *Turkey* (1978):

> As Article 8 guarantees the right to respect for his home to everyone, the rights of the new occupant should be taken into account, *even if the occupation was originally established on an invalid title*. After a long period of time restoration of the *status quo ante* will become a violation of Article 8 with respect to the new occupant. It is difficult to establish how long this period is to be, because in fact it is a gradual process . . . children will be born in the house who have no other place which they could consider as their home . . . I cannot accept as the only possible remedy that Turkey should be obliged to break up the homes of all present occupants in order to allow the original occupants to return.[60]

Three decades later, the ECtHR repeated the same principle in a majority opinion.[61] The same holds true with respect to the right to adequate housing (which ordinarily arises precisely when occupation of the property is in contravention of the law). Nevertheless, the legitimacy of the original act of occupying the property is a relevant factor in assessing proportionality between the burden which an interference causes to the individual and the goal pursued by that interference.

7.3 Practice

7.3.1 Rhodesia

Land administration prior to 1980

Land rights have been a central tool of White domination in Rhodesia since the arrival of the White settlers. In 1892, under the newly established protectorate of the British Crown,[62] the first 'native reserves' were created. By 1901 only a little over 25 per cent of the land was allocated to Blacks,

[60] EComHR, *Cyprus* v. *Turkey (1978)*, emphasis added.

[61] ECtHR, *Demopoulos and Others* v. *Turkey*, [116].

[62] For the history of British involvement in Rhodesia/Zimbabwe see Arthur Keppel-Jones, *Rhodes and Rhodesia: The White Conquest of Zimbabwe 1884–1902* (Kingston and Montreal: McGill-Queen's University Press, 1983), 313–329.

who constituted 97 per cent of the population, while Whites held the remaining 75 per cent of the land.[63] The Land Apportionment Act of 1930 legalized the division of the country's land, and prohibited members of either racial group from owning land in areas assigned to the other. At that time almost 51 per cent of the land had been declared 'European' while only 30 per cent was reserved for the Black population. Since control over land was an essential feature of economic and political dominance by the White population, the appropriation of land became the most important grievance of the Black population.

UDI did not change the land policy in any significant way, but allowed for its continuation. In 1977 the racial classifications were even formally abolished, except for the reservation of 47 per cent of the land for Blacks. Nonetheless, few Blacks could afford to buy land from Whites, and the racial division remained largely the same. At independence, the White minority, then some 5 per cent of the population, still held 39 per cent of Zimbabwe's land. There was also considerable disparity in the quality of the land held, as 75 per cent of the land available to Blacks was in regions prone to drought and low rainfall.

Transition

The redistribution of land was a central element in the nationalist leaders' vision of Zimbabwe.[64] It was related not specifically to the illegality of the Smith regime, but to the pre-existing discrimination in land rights. However, the Lancaster House Agreement severely limited the scope of potential land reform. First, it gave legal effect to the prevailing situation, thereby perpetuating the disparity in land distribution. Second, the Independence Constitution permitted acquisition of land for public purposes (which would have facilitated land redistribution) only against prompt and adequate compensation. This meant that the government could acquire land only on a willing-seller–willing-buyer basis. An incentive for owners to give consent was that compensation for acquisition was remittable outside Zimbabwe free of charge.[65] The constitution

63 COHRE, 'Land, Housing and Property Rights in Zimbabwe', 9.

64 The ZANU–PF 1980 election manifesto stated, 'It is not only anti people but criminal for any government to ignore the acute land hunger in the country, especially when it is realized that 83 per cent of our population live in the rural areas and depend on agriculture for their livelihood'. Cited in Jeffrey Herbst, 'The Dilemmas of Land Policy in Zimbabwe', in Simon Baynham (ed.), *Zimbabwe in Transition* (Stockholm: Almqvist and Wiksell International, 1992), 131.

65 Zimbabwe Independence Constitution, Part C (Declaration of Rights), Section V.

entrenched this protection of existing ownership by providing that for a period of ten years the protective provisions would be amendable only by the unanimous vote of the House of Assembly and a two-thirds majority of the members of the Senate.[66] This guaranteed a veto power to the White population, which held twenty of the hundred seats in the House of Assembly.[67] This separate representation of the White minority was itself guaranteed for seven years.[68] These provisions were an essential part of the compromise that enabled the resolution of the Rhodesian dispute. Thus preservation of the colonial and illegal regimes' legacies was the price paid for bringing these regimes to an end.

Upon gaining power, the Zimbabwean government initiated an ambitious program to resettle 20 per cent of the nation's peasants by purchasing 57 per cent of all White agricultural lands. Bureaucratic problems, financial constraints and other difficulties led to a gradual adjustment of the original, unrealistic goals.[69] In December 1990, as soon as the Lancaster House Agreement's restrictions expired, the Zimbabwean parliament adopted measures that allowed the government to seize farmland compulsorily and pay 'fair' compensation under a valuation that was non-appealable.[70] These measures were ostensibly aimed at meeting long-postponed resettlement goals,[71] yet such redistribution as did occur was marred by cronyism, corruption and incompetence. In the year 2000 the government launched a massive, extra-legal programme of land redistribution, spearheaded by ZANU–PF's paramilitary wing, who began occupying White-owned farms around the country and distributing them to peasants or party supporters. Among the justifications publicly cited for the government's aggressive policy was that it was the legitimate continuation of the battle for land, this time claiming to be specifically aimed at the legacy of the Smith regime.[72] In reality, this policy was advanced as

66 Zimbabwe Independence Constitution, Part E (Parliament), Section 30.

67 Zimbabwe Independence Constitution, Part E (Parliament), Section 10.

68 At the end of seven years, less stringent conditions were required for a change: Zimbabwe Independence Constitution, Part E (Parliament), Sections 28, 29.

69 Herbst, 'The Dilemmas of Land Policy in Zimbabwe', 132–133.

70 1990 Constitution of Zimbabwe Amendment Act; Land Acquisition Act, Acts 3/1992, 15/2000, 14/2001, 6/2002, 22/2001, 6/2002, 10/2002, 1/2004.

71 Herbst, 'The Dilemmas of Land Policy in Zimbabwe', 141.

72 It was dubbed the Third Chimurenga ('revolutionary struggle' in Shona), following the Second Chimurenga, namely the guerrilla war of the 1970s. See e.g. Francis Chitsike, 'A Critical Analysis of the Land Reform Programme in Zimbabwe', paper presented at the 2nd FIG Regional Conference, Marrakech, Morocco, 2–5 December 2003, www.fig.net/pub/morocco/proceedings/TS4/TS4_4_chitsike.pdf.

an attempt to strengthen Mugabe and ZANU–PF's government, which was facing escalating unpopularity. Even on the rhetorical level this argument did not garner support.[73]

7.3.2 Namibia

Land administration prior to 1990

The racial element in the allocation of land in Namibia dates back to the German colonial period. Acquisition of land was achieved through large-scale relocations of the indigenous population to ethnic reserves, unequal trade, and massacre of significant sections of the Herero and Nama populations. The alienation of people from their land continued under the South African mandate in a number of forms, always on an ethnic basis.[74]

The Odendaal Commission, which recommended in 1962 that a policy of ethnic homelands similar to that of South Africa be pursued in Namibia, allocated about 40 per cent of the territory, in ten homelands, to the 87 per cent non-White population.[75] The commission's plan was implemented in the late 1960s and the 1970s, after the revocation of the mandate in 1966, yet more had been done prior to 1966 to deprive the non-White population of its land than later. Some of the draconian measures which restricted land ownership in Namibia were even lifted in the 1970s and 1980s, such as the prohibitions on non-Whites' living in, buying, owning or renting a house in any area previously reserved for Whites. These relaxations of the rules had little practical effect, because they were made within the land-ownership structure as recommended by the Odendaal Commission, which did not make land accessible to small farmers.[76] Thus, as in Rhodesia, few non-Whites could afford to buy property or reside in White areas, and disparities in land ownership prevailed.[77] For example, at independence the Ovambo, who constituted about half of the country's

[73] William H. Shaw, 'They Stole Our Land: Debating the Expropriation of White Farms in Zimbabwe' (2003) 41 *Journal of Modern African Studies* 75, 76.

[74] For a detailed description of measures and legislation of land dispossession, see Wolfgang Werner, 'A Brief History of Land Dispossession in Namibia' (1993) 19 *Journal of Southern African Studies*, special issue: Namibia: Africa's Youngest Nation, 135.

[75] The Odendaal plan was implemented on the basis of the Development of the Self-Government for Native Nations in South West Africa Act 1968 and the South West Africa Affairs Act 1969.

[76] Werner, 'A Brief History of Land Dispossession in Namibia', 146.

[77] Laurel B. Francis, *State Succession to Rights and Obligations for Namibia* (Lusaka: UNIN, undated), 89.

population, lived on land which covered only 7 per cent of Namibia's territory.[78]

Transition

Constitutional Principle B5, agreed in 1982 by South Africa and SWAPO under the auspices of the Western Contact Group, contained a declaration of fundamental rights that included the right 'to protection from arbitrary deprivation of private property or deprivation of private property without just compensation'.[79] This was interpreted as precluding nationalization or confiscation of White-owned lands, regardless of whether they had been acquired lawfully or not.

As long as the constitutional principle remained non-binding, two major issues dominated the debate over future land administration. The first was the expectation of a mass exodus of Whites from independent Namibia, which led to a redistribution of abandoned land.[80] This expectation proved unfounded. The White population for the most part remained in Namibia, and even continued to dominate the civil service, thereby maintaining considerable administrative and decision-making power.[81] The debate over land administration was also conducted in the shadow of the commitment of SWAPO (and other parties) to land reform, inspired not only by rejection of racial discrimination, but also by a socialist economic vision 'to redress the imbalance created by the colonial policies of land allocation on [a] racial basis' through transfer of land from the affluent few to the landless majority.[82] Yet the collapse of the communist bloc weakened the ideological force motivating SWAPO, while the economic dependence on agricultural production meant that any institutional changes were a risky enterprise.[83] Moreover, SWAPO was committed to reconciliation. This meant appeasing the White population by not challenging its privileges, and SWAPO gave repeated reassurances that it would not engage in wholesale nationalization of land. The debates of the

[78] Virginia Curtin Knight, 'Namibia's Transition to Independence' (1989) 88 *Current History* 225, 227.

[79] UN Doc S/15287 (12 July 1982), Annex, Section B.

[80] UNIN, *Economic Development Strategies for Independent Namibia*, based on the work of Harbans S. Aulakh and Wilfred Wasombang, Namibia Studies Series No. 9 (ed. N. K. Duggal) (Lusaka: UNIN, 1985), 27.

[81] Linda Freeman, 'The Contradictions of Independence: Namibia in Transition' (1991) 46 *International Journal (Canadian Institute of International Affairs)* 687, 706.

[82] SWAPO Directorate of Elections, 'Towards an Independent and Democratic Namibia: SWAPO's Policy Positions' (July 1989) 9.

[83] UNIN, *Economic Development Strategies for Independent Namibia*, 27.

Constituent Assembly eventually allayed any fear of new economic policies. In its first meeting, the Assembly resolved unanimously to adopt the 1982 Constitutional Principles as a 'framework to draw up a constitution for South West Africa/Namibia'.[84] The Namibian Constitution incorporated the content of Constitutional Principle B5,[85] rendering the right to property, as guaranteed under it, immune to repeal or amendment.[86] This confirmed the continuity of the land rights that preceded independence.[87]

As an exception to the maintenance of the land regime and to the protection of acquired rights, in one exceptional instance the Namibian parliament repudiated a land grant. Following the Namibian government's probe into the Cultura 2000 transaction, which was suspected of being pre-emptive action to benefit Whites prior to majority rule[88] and of being an attempt to frustrate the results of the first free elections,[89] the Namibian parliament enacted, in December 1991, the State Repudiation (Cultura 2000) Act 1991. The Act first repudiated any sale, donation, lease, loan or other financial assistance rendered under the South African administration to Cultura 2000. It then provided that monies paid became repayable to the government of Namibia, and that any property transferred to Cultura 2000 was vested in the government. Cultura 2000 appealed against the Act. The Namibian Supreme Court emphasized that the repudiation provision (as distinct from the provision on nullity of the transactions and restitution),[90] did not purport to deny the factual changes which had been

84 Marinus Wiechers, 'Namibia: The 1982 Constitutional Principles and Their Legal Significance' (1989–1990) 15 *South African Yearbook of International Law* 1, 13.

85 Constitution of Namibia, Article 16. 86 Constitution of Namibia, Article 131.

87 On the Namibian land issue, see Sidney L. Harris, 'The Constitution of Namibia and the "Rights and Freedoms" Guaranteed Communal Land Holders: Resolving the Inconsistency between Article 16, Article 100, and Schedule 5' (1996) 12 *South African Journal on Human Rights* 467; Werner, 'A Brief History of Land Dispossession in Namibia'; Bertus De Villiers, 'Land Reform: Issues and Challenges, a Comparative Overview of Experiences in Zimbabwe, Namibia, South Africa and Australia' (Konrad Adenauer Foundation Occasional Papers, Johannesburg, 2003); Wolfgang Werner, 'Land Reform in Namibia: The First Seven Years', NEPRU Working Paper No. 61 (Windhoek: NEPRU, 1997); Melber Henning, 'Contested Territory: Land in Southern Africa. The Case of Namibia' (2002) 50 *Namibia Scientific Society (Windhoek) Journal* 77; Justine Hunter (ed.), *Who Should Own the Land? Analyses and Views on Land Reform and the Land Question in Namibia and Southern Africa* (Windhoek: Konrad-Adenauer-Stiftung Namibia Institute for Democracy, 2004).

88 Lionel Cliffe *et al.*, *The Transition to Independence in Namibia* (Boulder, CO: Lynne Rienner, 1994), 228–229.

89 *Government of the Republic of Namibia* v. *Cultura 2000*, 178.

90 State Repudiation (Cultura 2000) Act, Section 2(1).

made by the South African administration prior to the independence of Namibia; it merely reverses a legal fiction as to attribution of the act to the Namibian government.[91] As a consequence of the repudiation, the grant of land (and monies) by the South African administration reverted to being an act of that regime alone. The question could have arisen as to the validity of the grant under that regime, given that the individuals concerned were acting in collusion with the administration in an attempt to perpetuate it. However, the Namibian Supreme Court did not examine this question. A compromise was eventually reached on disposal of the land by Cultura 2000.[92] The validity of the South African grant, and the applicability of the doctrine of acquired rights to land granted in furtherance of the illegal regime as a matter of general law, remained unexplored.

7.3.3 The Baltic states

Soviet measures

During the 1940s, property in the Baltic states was confiscated and nationalized on a massive scale with no compensation offered. All land was declared state property; all private houses over a certain size were nationalized.[93] Some of them were used as accommodation for incoming Soviet military forces, security and party cadres. Some of the expropriated land was distributed to small farmers with a symbolic document granting them 'perpetual usage of the land'. After the war, systematic collectivization of villages and farms began, eventually amalgamating them into large state farms.[94]

Under the Soviet system, the state was the owner of all land. Enterprises and individuals in some cases could build, buy and sell houses as well as apartments in housing co-operatives, but were legally entitled only to the building without the land. The majority of properties, including most of the dwellings nationalized in the 1940s, were in public ownership

91 *Government of the Republic of Namibia* v. *Cultura 2000*, 187. See further on this case in Chapter 5 above.

92 Interview by the author with Adv. Peter Koep, formerly head of NPP 435 Action Group, Windhoek, 23 February 2004.

93 In Estonia, 220 or 170 square metres; in Latvia, 220 or 130 square metres; and in Lithuania, 150 square metres. World Bank, 'Estonia (1993)', 218; World Bank, 'Latvia (1993)', 155; World Bank, 'Lithuania (1993)', 221.

94 Arvo Kuddo, 'Aspects of the Restitution of Property and Land in Estonia', in Ray Abrahams (ed.), *After Socialism: Land Reform and Social Change in Eastern Europe* (Providence: Berghahn, 1996), 160–162; Peeter Maandi, 'The Silent Articulation of Private Land Rights in Soviet Estonia: A Geographical Perspective' (2009) 40 *Geoforum* 454, 458.

and subordinated to the rights of tenants.[95] Those equalled or exceeded in many ways the rights conventionally associated with ownership in capitalist systems.[96]

Changes in property patterns occurred under the Soviet regime not only because of legal reform but also because of population movements. Large numbers of nationals of the Baltic states, especially the socioeconomic elite, either fled from the Soviet regime or were killed or deported by it. Their properties, often in prestigious areas, were abandoned. Many of the settlers brought in by the Soviet regime were allocated apartments in these properties. Other Soviet settlers were housed in Soviet-built accommodation.[97] Rents, determined by living space regardless of location and amenities, remained fixed from 1945, resulting in continually growing government subsidies for maintaining rental housing. Given the few housing options that existed, households usually did not move, and the demand for housing services remained unsatisfied.[98]

Transition

In contrast with other areas of law, with respect to real property all three Baltic states adopted express legislation declaring the illegality and invalidity of the Soviet measures.

Lithuanian legislation is explicit as to the invalidity of the Soviet measures. The Law on the Restoration of the Rights of Ownership of Citizens to the Existing Real Property emphasizes that

> after the Supreme Council – Reconstituent Seimas of the Republic of Lithuania restored the independence of the Republic of Lithuania under the 11 March 1990 Acts, the laws, imposed by the foreign state, by which the occupational powers had seized from the citizens of the Republic of Lithuania the property possessed by them, ceased to be in force;
>
> the rights of ownership acquired by the citizens of the Republic of Lithuania before the occupation are not revoked and have continuity . . .[99]

95 World Bank, 'Latvia (1993)', 152.

96 Merje Feldman, 'Justice in Space? The Restitution of Property Rights in Tallinn, Estonia (1999) 6 *Cultural Geographies* 165, 167.

97 Feldman, 'Justice in Space?', 167; Vello Andres Pettai, 'The Construction of State Identity and Its Legacies: Legal Restorationism in Estonia' (2007) 3 *Ab Imperio* 1, 13–14.

98 World Bank, 'Estonia (1993)', 218.

99 Lithuania, 1997 Law on the Restoration of the Rights of Ownership of Citizens to the Existing Real Property; see also Law on the Contracts and Property Unlawfully Possessed by the USSR Military Units and other Military Structures on the Territory of the Republic of Lithuania, Article 1.

The law is equivocal on whether the nationalization ceases to be in force only prospectively or, as implied by the 'continuity' of ownership, was invalid *ab initio*. A Lithuanian Supreme Court judgment given in 1994 suggests the latter, stating that:

> Lawful State property could not and did not appear on the basis of such arbitrary acts of occupation government, as rights may not originate on [an] unlawful basis. Therefore, property taken from people in such a way, may be considered as property which is only factually managed by the State.[100]

Estonian legislation refers to 'the continuity of rights of former owners and the interests of current land users that are protected by law'.[101] This also suggests that nationalization was invalid *ab initio*. However, the meaning of 'continuity' remains unclear, while subsequent legislation refers to new holders of property as also having 'ownership'.[102] Dispossessed owners in Estonia have objected that by referring to them as 'previous owners' to whom property is 'returned', the legislation does not sufficiently uphold their right to property.[103] Latvian legislation laconically provides that the Soviet nationalization and collectivization decrees 'are repealed' and that the properties 'shall be returned to their previous owners'.[104]

The invalidity of dispossession by the Soviet regime was not based solely on the illegality of the annexation but also on the violation of the individual's right to property[105] through collectivization and the forcible taking of property. For example, the Estonian Supreme Council recognized that changes of ownership relations by the USSR had been forcible and in violation of the right to property under international law, and declared the principle of the legal continuity of ownership. Its resolution provides:

> Recognising that the changing of ownership relations of the Republic of Estonia by the occupation authorities of the Soviet Union was forcible,
>
> Based on the principle of inviolability of property recognised in the international law . . .

100 Lithuania, Case No. 12/93, *Constitutional Court of the Republic of Lithuania Ruling on the Compliance of the Parts of Item 3 of the Law of the Republic of Lithuania 'On Appending and Amending the Law of the Republic of Lithuania "On the Procedure and Conditions of the Restoration of the Rights of Ownership to the Existing Real Property"'*.

101 Estonia, Land Reform Act, Article 2.

102 Estonia Principles of Ownership Reform Act, Article 12(3)(3).

103 Feldman, 'Justice in Space?', 170–171.

104 Latvia, Law on the Denationalisation of Building Properties in the Republic of Latvia, Articles 1, 2.

105 Constitution of Estonia, Article 32; Constitution of Latvia, Article 105; Constitution of Lithuania, Article 23.

The Supreme Council of the Republic of Estonia *resolves*:

1. To recognise the unlawfulness of the adoption and implementation of the Declaration on the Nationalisation of Banks and Large-scale Industry and the Declaration on Declaring Land the Property of the Entire Nation, adopted by the Estonian SSR Chamber of Deputies on 23 July 1940, as well as of further legal acts, which changed the ownership relations.

2. To recognise that the collectivisation in Estonia . . . was carried out forcibly, in violation of owners' rights.[106]

Unlawfully expropriated property was similarly defined by reference both to the illegal acts that effected it and to the substantive violations of human rights that were involved in the expropriation:

1) property which was nationalised pursuant to legislation which has been declared unlawful by the Republic of Estonia Supreme Council Resolution of 19 December 1990 'Concerning Restoration of Continuity of Right of Ownership' (RT 1990, 22, 280) (denationalisation);

2) property which was communised during collectivisation (decollectivisation);

3) property which was expropriated through unlawful repression or by any other method which violated the rights of the owner.[107]

Lithuanian legislation also restores the right of ownership with respect to property 'which was nationalized under the laws of the USSR (Lithuanian SSR), or which was otherwise unlawfully made public'.[108]

The Baltic states' restitution policy is among the most comprehensive in existence.[109] Its proponents argued that the restoration of property relations was a legal and moral prerequisite for the reinstatement of

106 Resolution of the Supreme Council of the Republic of Estonia of 19 December 1990 on Restoring the Continuity in the Right of Ownership. I am grateful to Mr Mart Paberit, translator, Chancellery of the Riigikogu, for having translated the resolution upon my request.

107 Estonia, Principles of Ownership Reform Act Article 3(1).

108 Lithuania, 1991 Law on the Procedure and Conditions of the Restoration of the Rights of Ownership to the Existing Real Property, Article 1.

109 For a description of Baltic legislation, see Frances H. Foster, 'Restitution of Expropriated Property: Post-Soviet Lessons for Cuba' (1996) 34 *Columbia Journal of Transnational Law* 621; Nicolás J. Gutiérrez Jr, 'Righting Old Wrongs: A Survey of Restitution Schemes for Possible Application to a Democratic Cuba' (1995) 4 *University of Miami Yearbook of International Law* 111; William Valletta, 'The Hesitant Privatization of Lithuanian Land' (1994–1995) 18 *Fordham International Law Journal* 198; Mark Blacksell and Karl Martin Born, 'Private Property Restitution: The Geographical Consequences of Official Government Policies in Central and Eastern Europe' (2002) 168 *Geographical Journal* 178; Kuddo, 'Aspects of the Restitution of Property and Land in Estonia'.

the pre-1940 states. It was an ideological and political project of erasing the marks of the Soviet regime, providing historical justice and reuniting the nation.[110] This also included inducing settlers under the Soviet regime to leave the country.[111] A related motive was to encourage nationals driven out by the Soviet regime to return with their money and professional expertise. Restoration was also perceived as a rapid, efficient means of privatization on the way to a market economy.[112] The process was therefore launched despite its expected prohibitive costs.

In Estonia, restoration is available to former owners that are capable of using the property for residence, namely residents of Estonia in 1991, as well as to persons who were citizens of Estonia on 16 June 1940 and their heirs (who are automatically regarded as Estonian nationals). Property rights are therefore tied to a right of residence in the territory of the post-transition regime. Foreign claimants must resolve their claims through mutual agreements between Estonia and their respective states.[113] Latvia's restitution legislation applies to previous owners or their heirs, regardless of their present nationality or residence.[114] Lithuania generally restricted the right to restoration to former owners or their heirs if they are both current nationals and permanent residents.[115] As an exception, the exclusion of non-residents does not apply to those who left because of the regime.[116]

In line with their extensive restoration policy, Both Estonia and Latvia have entered reservations to ECHR Protocol 1, according to which Article 1

[110] Feldman, 'Justice in Space?', 168–170.

[111] Blacksell and Born, 'Private Property Restitution', 187.

[112] Foster, 'Restitution of Expropriated Property', 626. A comparison of practice reveals that the satellite states of the USSR opted for a process of restoration and compensation, while the successor states of the USSR maintained the property regime that they had inherited, in some cases followed by a forward-looking land reform scheme. Istvan Pogany, *Righting Wrongs in Eastern Europe* (Manchester: Manchester University Press, 1997); Gutiérrez, 'Righting Old Wrongs'. It is noteworthy that the Baltic states opted for the same scheme as the satellite states, reinforcing their claim to non-succession of the USSR.

[113] Estonia, Principles of Ownership Reform Act, Articles 7, 8.

[114] Foster, 'Restitution of Expropriated Property', 630.

[115] Lithuania, Law on the Procedure and Conditions of the Restoration of the Rights of Ownership to the Existing Real Property, Article 2.

[116] Lithuania, Resolution of the Supreme Council of the Republic of Lithuania Regarding the Process of Enforcement and Application of the Law of the Republic of Lithuania on the Procedures and Conditions of the Restoration of the Ownership Rights of Existing Real Property, Article 2.

shall not apply to the laws on property reform which regulate restoration or compensation to former owners or their legal heirs of property nationalized, confiscated, requisitioned, collectivized or otherwise unlawfully expropriated during the period of Soviet annexation. Consequently, the taking of property from current owners for the purpose of restoration (or of other land reforms, outside the scope of this study) cannot be challenged at the ECtHR. Lithuania, which has the most limited restoration programme,[117] did not enter such a reservation.

Restoration in all three Baltic states is subject to general restrictions that are not related directly to current occupants, such as the exclusion of property used for public purposes.[118] Latvia initially permitted restoration of farms only to those who would use the property for agricultural purposes,[119] but later regulations dropped this limitation. Lithuanian law limits the size of returnable plots, and places significant limitations on ownership, use and transfer of residential property.[120] Such limitations were not made in Estonia and Latvia. Where restoration is impossible, either because an exception applies or because the property no longer exists in its original form, the laws in all Baltic states offer either replacement property or compensation.[121]

Despite the principled position on continuity of ownership, the right to restoration is also limited in order to protect current owners and occupants. In Estonia and Latvia, restoration is replaced by compensation where the property has been purchased by natural persons acting in good faith. A purchaser is not considered to have acted in good faith if he or she has facilitated the transfer of a building property to his or her ownership 'by participating in repressions'.[122] This qualification, which resembles the *flagrante bello* exception to the acquired-rights doctrine but transports it to the international human rights field, can be interpreted very widely. A reasonable interpretation should limit it to persons who took active part in repressions, rather than, for example, extend it to all Soviet-era

117 For a summary of Lithuanian land reform and restitution, see Valletta, 'The Hesitant Privatization of Lithuanian Land'.
118 Foster, 'Restitution of Expropriated Property', 634.
119 World Bank, 'Latvia (1993)', 93.
120 Lithuania, Law on the Procedure and Conditions of the Restoration of the Rights of Ownership to the Existing Real Property.
121 E.g. Estonia, Principles of Ownership Reform Act, Article 13; Lithuania, Law on the Procedure and Conditions of the Restoration of the Rights of Ownership to the Existing Real Property, Article 4.
122 Estonia, Principles of Ownership Reform Act, Article 12(3)(3); Latvia, Law on the Denationalisation of Building Properties in the Republic of Latvia, Article 2.

settlers who, by their very presence in Latvia, contributed to the existence of the illegal regime.

The rights of current occupants to privacy[123] and adequate housing are protected by extensive legislation, which includes the recognition of existing leases for a limited period of time[124] and rent control.[125] Where current occupants may be evicted, the state is responsible for providing them with alternative accommodation.[126] Tenants also have preferential rights in purchasing alternative accommodation.[127] Yet these guarantees have proven to be inadequate. Not only are the rights of tenants insufficiently defined,[128] but even when they are, widespread evictions of tenants, despite statutory provisions to the contrary,[129] have created new social chasms.[130] On the other hand, rules regarding the rights of original owners are also insufficiently detailed, such as their right to compensation for depreciation in value.[131]

Various problems arose in the process of restoration. In many cases, claims have been lodged not in the original location of the property, but in the current place of residence of the claimants. This resulted in a shortage of land in some regions, particularly in the vicinity of large urban centres. In addition, there was a general shortage of agricultural land for restoration – fifty years of industrialization had reduced the area of agricultural land, and under the restored states, urban allocation

[123] Constitution of Estonia, Article 33; Constitution of Latvia, Article 96; Constitution of Lithuania, Article 24.

[124] Estonia, Principles of Ownership Reform Act, Articles 12(3)(4), 12.1; Latvia, Law on the Denationalisation of Building Properties in the Republic of Latvia, Article IV.

[125] These limits were removed in Estonia in late 2004. A Supreme Court ruling on a presidential appeal confirmed the constitutionality of this step. Estonia, *Constitutional Review Case*.

[126] Estonia, Principles of Ownership Reform Act, Article 12.1(5); Lithuania, Law on the Procedure and Conditions of the Restoration of the Rights of Ownership to the Existing Real Property, Article 21.

[127] Resolution of the Supreme Council of the Republic of Lithuania Regarding the Process of Enforcement and Application of the Law of the Republic of Lithuania on the Procedures and Conditions of the Restoration of the Ownership Rights of Existing Real Property, Articles 3, 4.

[128] World Bank, 'Estonia (1993)', 219–220.

[129] Foster, 'Restitution of Expropriated Property', note 130; COHRE, 'Housing Rights in Latvia', 8.

[130] Vello Andres Pettai, 'Framing the Past as Future: The Power of Legal Restorationism in Estonia', PhD thesis, Columbia University, 2004 (on file with the author), 215–216.

[131] Foster, 'Restitution of Expropriated Property', 645–646.

increased.[132] There is no single course of dispute resolution – each case is decided separately and the circumstances differ vastly. The process is highly convoluted legally, not least because legislation has changed numerous times.[133] Priority of restoration over other land reforms,[134] and the lengthy process of resolving claims and disputes, have resulted in an indefinite postponement of the mass privatization process.[135] Lack of secure, transparent and marketable property rights has discouraged domestic and foreign investment.[136] Nevertheless, in Estonia, over 80 per cent of the land had been registered in the cadastre by 2006;[137] in Lithuania, ownership rights had been restored with respect to almost 96 per cent of the land by 2007.[138]

Reversion to the *status quo ante* has resulted in some unexpected fallout. It was initially envisaged that Soviet-era settlers would leave the Baltic states, vacating in the process properties that would be available to those who could not afford the new rents. However, contrary to expectations in some quarters, Soviet-era settlers were not expelled. This has resulted in a greater strain on native inhabitants, who face soaring housing costs and are vulnerable to displacement. Particularly in Estonia, conflicts between dispossessed owners and current occupants characteristically arose among ethnic Balts, rather than between ethnic Balts and Soviet-era settlers. In addition, the latter enjoyed preferential rights in privatization,

[132] Stephen K. Wegren (ed.), *Land Reform in the Former Soviet Union and Eastern Europe* (London: Routeledge, 1998), 72–73.

[133] E.g. in Estonia there were twenty changes to the legislation from its adoption in 1991 until 1997. Feldman, 'Justice in Space?', 169.

[134] E.g. Latvian legislation, which requires municipal authorities to reserve land for subsequent restitution cases, expressly 'prohibits the sale, reconstruction or demolition of such buildings . . . until the end of the period for filing claims'; Foster, 'Restitution of Expropriated Property', 646; Latvia, Supreme Council Resolution on the Order in Which the Republic of Latvia Laws 'On the Return of Buildings to their Legal Owners' and 'On the Denationalization of Buildings in the Republic of Latvia' Take Effect, paragraph 1; Lithuania, Law of the Lithuanian Republic on the Initial Privatization of State Property, Article 7, noted in Foster, 'Restitution of Expropriated Property', 646.

[135] Kaj Hobér, *Transforming East European Law* (Uppsala: Iustus Förlag, 1997), 233–234.

[136] Foster, 'Restitution of Expropriated Property', 647.

[137] Siim Maasikamäe, 'Land Fragmentation and the Need for the Land Consolidation in Estonia', FAO Regional Workshop on Land Consolidation and Land Development (22–24 May 2006), www.fao.org/regional/seur/events/landcons2/landcons_en.htm.

[138] Vilma Daugaliene, 'Recent Developments in land Consolidation in Lithuania', FAO Regional Workshop on EU Rural Development Programme 2007–13 and Its Application to Land Consolidation (Prague, 25–27 June 2007), www.fao.org/regional/seur/events/landcons3/docs/Lithuania.pdf.

both because Russian working collectives had priority in privatization,[139] and because Soviet-era settlers were often housed in post-war accommodation owned by the state, which was not subject to reinstatement. In contrast, over the years many native inhabitants had moved into previously privately owned property. They later became tenants of the original owners, unable to privatize their homes and vulnerable to eviction. This led to further antagonism among ethnic Baltic occupants, who felt that they had drawn the short straw in an enterprise that had been intended to guarantee their interests over those of the Soviet-era settlers.[140]

The sense of injustice felt by current occupants at the restoration policy was exacerbated by the knowledge that they were being dispossessed by returning exiles, many of them prosperous and with the comfort of continuing links to their adopted countries. The 'locals' point out that restoration effectively places the responsibility for the past crimes of the Soviet authorities on third-generation taxpayers and renters, many of whom were themselves victimized by Soviet repression. They argue that it is the Russian Federation that should compensate for past injustice, or else restoration should be downscaled. Current occupants also call for respect for those who used and maintained the buildings 'in good conscience' for half a century, without whom the property would physically not exist today, leaving nothing to be reclaimed.[141]

Both Estonia and Latvia have used the principle of reversion to the *status quo ante* with respect to property as a rhetorical tool in their relations with Russia. In January 1994 Estonia decided to entertain applications from owners of land expropriated in territories that had been assigned to Estonia under the 1920 Tartu Peace Treaty but are now under Russian jurisdiction, following changes to the boundaries of the Soviet Republics in the early 1940s.[142] Latvia too has considered accepting applications from claimants to property located in areas that had once been Latvian, but have become Russian under changes carried out by the USSR in the 1940s.[143] Both states have declared that they do not intend to challenge existing boundaries with the Russian Federation.[144] Accordingly, the prospects for actual return of such property to its original owners are doubtful. These policies appear to be designed largely to promote the Estonian and Latvian

139 Erik André Andersen, 'The Legal Status of Russians in Estonian Privatisation Legislation 1989–1995' (1997) 49 *Europe–Asia Studies* 303, 304.

140 Feldman, 'Justice in Space?', 170–173.

141 Blacksell and Born, 'Private Property Restitution', 187.

142 Foster, 'Restitution of Expropriated Property', 632.

143 Foster, 'Restitution of Expropriated Property'.

144 See Chapter 4 above.

claims to continuity with the pre-1940 states on the basis of the illegality of the Soviet regime.

7.3.4 The TBVC

Land administration prior to 1994

Dispossession of Blacks of their land in South Africa began in the seventeenth century, when White settlers acquired control over the majority of the territory through wars of conquest.[145] The territorial segregation instituted during the colonial period was firmly entrenched by the Black Land Act of 1913, which prohibited Blacks from owning or renting land outside the native reserves. Those reserves covered only 7 per cent of the total land area in South Africa.[146] They were later increased to 13 per cent of the total land area.[147]

By 1971, when the Republic of Transkei was established, the dispossession of Blacks was already well entrenched. The existence of the TBVC nonetheless facilitated the deprivation of individuals and communities of their land. First, the South African government forcibly relocated entire communities into the TBVC (with the co-operation of the TBVC governments). Compensation was formally awarded for property taken, but the land was usually grossly undervalued and long-term investments made on it were hardly taken into account. Forced sales and restrictions on freedom of commerce resulted in distortion of market prices to the detriment of the Black 'sellers'.[148] The purported independence of the TBVC was also accompanied by stripping their inhabitants of their South African nationality, which further hindered the possibility of acquisition of land in 'White South Africa'.

[145] Laurine Platzky and Cherryl Walker, *The Surplus People: Forced Removals in South Africa* (Johannesburg: Ravan Press, 1985), 70; Aninka Claassens, 'Rural Land Struggles in the Transvaal in the 1980s', in Christina Murray and Catherine O'Regan (eds.), *No Place to Rest: Forced Removals and the Law in South Africa* (Oxford: Oxford University Press, 1990), 29.

[146] Kristin Henrard, 'The Internally Displaced in South Africa: The Strategy of Forced Removals and Apartheid' (1995–1996) *Jura Falconis* 491.

[147] Development Trust and Black Land Act of 1936.

[148] Platzky and Walker, *The Surplus People*, 103; Elaine Unterhalter, *Forced Removals: The Division, Segregation and Control of South Africa* (London: International Defence and Aid Fund for Southern Africa, 1987), 64; Henrard, 'The Internally Displaced in South Africa'; Luvuyo Wotshela, 'Territorial Manipulation in Apartheid South Africa: Resettlement, Tribal Politics and the Making of the Northern Ciskei, 1975–1990' (2004) 30 *Journal of Southern African Studies* 317.

In the Bantustans (TBVC and others), as well as in 'Black areas', dispossession also took the form of betterment, the flagship of the South African rural development programme from the 1930s onwards. Under betterment, designated areas were divided into distinct land-use zones, such as residential, arable and grazing usage. In the process, people living in betterment areas were dispossessed both of a variety of land rights and of a way of life. Betterment was not conceptualized with grand apartheid in mind, but its effects suited that project. It rendered the Bantustans easier to govern and enabled them to absorb thousands of 'surplus people',[149] removed from White South Africa. It is estimated that more than three million Bantustan residents were effectively dispossessed in this manner. It was a particularly acute problem in Ciskei and Transkei, but it was not related to their purported independence.

Transition

Common wisdom says that the land question was one of the driving forces of the liberation struggle in South Africa. Even after transition to democracy, the majority of Blacks in South Africa agree that land must be returned to Blacks in South Africa regardless of the consequences for the current owners and for the political stability of the country.[150] However, the ANC had never clearly developed a policy on the matter,[151] and had no detailed proposals for a land reform when the Codesa talks began in 1991. Its rapidly formulated policy only stated that 'priority will be given to victims of forced removal who, wherever possible, should get land back taken from them by the apartheid state'.[152] Unlike in Zimbabwe and Namibia, where preservation of White rights was key to a smooth transition, in South Africa it was land *reform* that was regarded as a catalyst for the reconciliation between Blacks and Whites, and as a necessary measure to avert the possibility of a civil war. Most population groups supported restitution in its various forms.[153] Nevertheless, objections by

[149] Platzky and Walker, *The Surplus People*.

[150] Cherryl Walker, 'The Limits of Land Reform: Rethinking "the Land Question"' (2005) 31 *Journal of Southern African Studies* 805, 805–806.

[151] Ashley Westaway, 'Bare Life in the Bantustans (of the Eastern Cape): Remembering the Centennial South African Nation-State', PhD thesis, University of Fort Hare, 2008, 49–55.

[152] ANC 1992, cited by Ruth Hall, 'Land Restitution in South Africa: Rights, Development and the Restrained State' (2004) 38 *Canadian Journal of African Studies* 654, 656.

[153] Maano Ramutsindela, 'The Geographical Imprint of Land Restitution with Reference to Limpopo Province, South Africa' (2007) 98 *Tijdschrift voor Economische en Sociale Geografie* 455, 457.

the National Party resulted in the Interim Constitution addressing restitution and property in two separate articles. Article 8, entitled 'equality', provided that:

> b) Every person or community dispossessed of rights in land before the commencement of this Constitution under any law which would have been inconsistent with Subsection (2) had that subsection been in operation at the time of the dispossession [i.e. discriminatory], shall be entitled to claim restitution of such rights subject to and in accordance with Sections 121, 122 and 123.

Restitution in South Africa was accordingly not directly related to the illegality of the TBVC. The cut-off date for claims is 1913, much earlier than the creation of the TBVC.

Article 28, entitled 'property', provided that:

> (1) Every person shall have the right to acquire and hold rights in property and, to the extent that the nature of the rights permits, to dispose of such rights.
>
> (2) No deprivation of any rights in property shall be permitted otherwise than in accordance with a law.
>
> (3) Where any rights in property are expropriated pursuant to a law referred to in Subsection (2), such expropriation shall be permissible for public purposes only . . .

The term 'public purposes', which is narrower than 'public interest', did not permit expropriation aimed at transferring property to another private owner. The Interim Constitution was therefore perceived as recognizing the supremacy of existing property rights over the right to restitution.

Some commentators argue that the ANC conceded protection of existing property rights in the interests of both political stability and food security.[154] Others argue that the ANC leadership found it easy to endorse the constitutional protection of property rights because it adopted the international human rights discourse which emphasized individual rights, and had been co-opted by White capital.[155] Still others argue that the provisions of the Interim Constitution reflected not any ideological stance, but the lack of a clear mandate and the chaos that ruled the negotiations.[156]

The 1996 constitution contains the right to restitution within the article on property, providing that:

[154] Hall, 'Land Restitution in South Africa', 656.

[155] Westaway, 'Bare Life in the Bantustans', 283.

[156] Matthew Chaskalson, 'Stumbling towards Section 28: Negotiations over the Protection of Property Rights in the Interim Constitution' (1995) 11 *South African Journal on Human Rights* 222, 237–239.

> A person or community dispossessed of property after 19 June 1913 as a result of past racially discriminatory laws or practices is entitled, to the extent provided by an Act of Parliament, either to restitution of that property, or to equitable redress.[157]

The constitution permits expropriation not only for public purposes but also in the public interest, which expressly includes the nation's commitment to land reform and to reforms aimed at equitable access to all South Africa's natural resources.[158]

Restitution was only one part of a three-pronged land policy, comprising also redistribution and tenure reform. However, restitution is perceived in South Africa as the principal tool of land reform. It is constitutionally guaranteed, and, unlike redistribution, it is provided by right, rather than being discretionary. Under the 1994 Land Rights Restitution Act, the government determined that the nature of land restitution would be in the form of land restoration, grant of alternative land, payment of compensation, priority access to government and land development programmes, or alternative relief comprising a combination of measures.[159] Yet even subsequent to the 1996 constitution, which allows the state to expropriate property in order to return it to previous owners, the state has intervened in only a handful of cases, preferring to leave restitution to a 'willing-seller–willing-buyer' policy.[160] In practice, this gives clear priority to current owners.

Over a decade after the transition to democracy, the scale of restitution remains small. Betterment was only recognized as dispossession for the purposes of restitution in 2004.[161] By 2005, over 70 per cent of the claims lodged have been settled. However, only 1 per cent of commercial land has been restored to claimants. The majority of claims are settled by compensation rather than by restoration.[162]

As in the Baltic states, the effect of reversion to the *status quo ante* did not always achieve the political goal envisaged by its designers. The popular account of land dispossession invokes a history of conquest and exploitation that Black people have experienced as a unified collective,

157 1996 constitution, Article 25(7). 158 1996 constitution, Article 25(4), (6).

159 Ramutsindela, 'The Geographical Imprint of Land Restitution', 460–461.

160 Hall, 'Land Restitution in South Africa', 660.

161 Westaway, 'Bare Life in the Bantustans', 288, 298, attributes this to the domination of the policy process by disinterested actors. Until then, an estimated two million victims of betterment planning countrywide were left out of the land restitution process. Ramutsindela, 'The Geographical Imprint of Land Restitution', 458–459.

162 Hall, 'Land Restitution in South Africa', 659; Walker, 'The Limits of Land Reform', 818.

and thus supports a general claim for redress on behalf of all Black South Africans against all Whites. An acknowledgement of White investment in or identification with the land is generally absent.[163] However, in practice land patterns are much more complex and varied. In particular, the assumption that the target of land claims would be White-owned land has not always proved justified. Dispossession often involved conflict within groups and competing claims to redress, especially in provinces that are predominantly rural. These 'Black-on-Black' land claims have caused conflicts among Black communities.[164]

7.3.5 Timor-Leste

Indonesian land administration

Expropriation

The Indonesian annexation has resulted in dramatic changes to land holdings in Timor-Leste in both law and practice. First, the Indonesian invasion led to a wave of displacement in 1975, when some 70 per cent of the population fled to the mountains. Many public and abandoned properties were taken by the Indonesian military, starting in 1975. Often the abandonment itself was the result of forced relocation of the population by the military, which in 1977 began to uproot the population living near Fretilin-held areas, moving it to more easily controlled areas. Estimates for the numbers of people relocated vary from 150,000 to 300,000.[165] Many of the owners never returned to their properties, some having left Timor-Leste altogether. Indonesian military forces also prevented return to the properties, either because of the sensitivity of their strategic location or because the properties had been reallocated to pro-integration groups and other associates of the Indonesian regime.

163 Walker, 'The Limits of Land Reform', 808.

164 Ramutsindela, 'The Geographical Imprint of Land Restitution', 460–461, Walker, 'The Limits of Land Reform', 809.

165 John G. Taylor, 'East Timor: Forced Resettlement' (1999) 5 *Forced Migration Review* 31; Amnesty International, *East Timor Violations of Human Rights, Extrajudicial Executions, 'Disappearances', Torture and Political Imprisonment, 1975–1984*, 68. These figures derive from reports relying on Indonesian officials. The discrepancies may be due to different interpretations of the term 'resettlement village' in documentation. The inability to access Timor-Leste, in order to verify testimonies, limits the reliability of data in Amnesty International's reports. Assistance from Catholic Relief Services alone extended to some 240,000 persons in the resettlement villages. CAVR Final Report, Chapter 7.3, paragraph 249. The CAVR Final Report, Chapter 7.3 paragraph 64, estimates that around 300,000 persons moved into Indonesian-controlled centers in 1978 and 1979 alone.

The military taking was based on the SKEP 40 Decree, issued in 1979 by the Indonesian military commander in Timor-Leste. It brought all abandoned and formerly Portuguese government land under the control of the Indonesian army. Documentation kept by Indonesia reveals that military control under the decree was not meant to deprive owners of legal ownership. This policy was based on a number of factors. First, under Indonesian law the military had no power to grant title to land. In addition, formal transfer of title was considered unnecessary because it was clear that returning owners would be too intimidated to pursue their rights. Recipients of land allocated in pursuance of SKEP 40 who were aware of the limited effect of the decree cannot in good faith claim today to be holding title to the land on the basis of military grants.[166]

Dispossession of native Timorese of their land was also made possible through ministerial decrees of 1975 and 1976, allowing expropriation for public-purpose development with little compensation or judicial recourse.[167] In the absence of criteria for 'public purpose', in some cases this term was only a cover for corrupt transfer of title to associates of the regime.

The majority of rural land in Timor-Leste is unregistered and is governed only by customary law. Indonesian law did not recognize all forms of customary land title, and its imposition resulted in many Timorese losing their property rights. The authorities evicted the occupants of these lands without due process and with little or no compensation.[168] Many properties were later given to Indonesians who had come into Timor-Leste after 1975 and held state-provided documentation of ownership.[169] Estimates of the number of titles issued under the Indonesian administration vary from 35,000[170] to 47,000.[171] As

166 Daniel Fitzpatrick, *Land Claims in East Timor* (Australia: Asia Pacific, 2002), 116–119.

167 The 1976 decree was repealed in 1993, but confiscation by the state and transfer to developers continued unhindered until 1999. Fitzpatrick, *Land Claims in East Timor*, 124–125.

168 Fitzpatrick, *Land Claims in East Timor*, 126. The status of customary-law tenure is one of the most vexing problems in regulating land rights in Timor-Leste today. However, this problem is unrelated to the illegality of the Indonesian regime and will not be considered further here.

169 Dionisio Babo Soares, 'Challenges for the Future', in James J. Fox and Dionisio Babo Soares (eds.), *Out of the Ashes: Destruction and Reconstruction of East Timor* (Adelaide: Crawford House, 2003), 269–270.

170 Fitzpatrick, *Land Claims in East Timor*, 44.

171 Pedro Xavier de Sousa, 'East Timor Land Management – A Long Way To Go, but We Have Started', paper presented at the Expert Group Meeting on secure land tenure, 'New Legal Frameworks and Tools in Asia & Pacific' (December 2005), www.fig.net/commission7/bangkok_2005/papers/6_3_sousa.pdf.

many as a third of them are said to have been issued through corrupt processes.[172]

In the violence and destruction following the 1999 referendum, a second wave of displacement took place, in which some 75 per cent of the Timorese again fled their homes. Approximately 30 per cent of all housing stock was totally destroyed. Pro-Indonesian militia groups, apparently acting under orders from the Indonesian military, directly targeted land title offices and records. In Dili they burnt the records as well as the building housing them. Former Timorese land title officers estimated that 80 per cent of all underlying records of land in Dili were irrecoverable.[173] The Dili land titles book was taken by the Indonesian head of the land titles office, ostensibly to safeguard it and eventually return it. However, Indonesia refuses to return the book, pending completion of the Indonesia–Timor-Leste assets and liabilities negotiations.[174]

Indonesian attitude towards pre-existing titles

Indonesia viewed the control of land as critical to achieving political security in Timor-Leste and to facilitating the full integration of Timor-Leste into Indonesia. One aspect of this integration was the harmonization of Timor-Leste's land law with that of Indonesia, including by the conversion of Portuguese titles into Indonesian ones. In the cities, particularly in Dili, land registration has been vigorous by both Portugal and Indonesia, and it is there that the majority of disputes arise.[175]

According to Indonesian statistics, only about 2,700 titles were issued and registered under Portuguese administration.[176] Some of these titles may have expired through their own terms, or have been sold under Indonesian law and consequently converted into Indonesian titles. While

[172] Daniel Fitzpatrick, 'Land Issues in a Newly Independent East Timor', research paper No. 21, 2000–2001 (Department of the Parliamentary Library, Australia, 2001), 10.

[173] Fitzpatrick, *Land Claims in East Timor*, 6–8. The extent of the damage is contested by Warren Wright, on the basis of first-hand observations. Correspondence of the author with Adv. Warren Wright , 22 June 2005.

[174] Fitzpatrick, *Land Claims in East Timor*, 6–7.

[175] Laura Suzanne Meitzner Yoder, 'Custom, Codification, Collaboration: Integrating the Legacies of Land and Forest Authorities in Oecusse Enclave, East Timor', PhD thesis, Yale University, 2005, 293–304. East Timor had a Portuguese land registry and colonial policies, unfamiliar to Indonesians, Meitzner Yoder, 'Custom, Codification, Collaboration', 308, 315.

[176] Jean du Plessis and Scott Leckie, 'Housing, Property and Land Rights in East Timor: Proposals for an Effective Dispute Resolution and Claim Verification Mechanism' (UNCHS (Habitat), 31 May 2000 and 5 August 2000), 8.

it is not difficult to trace the remaining titles, following their development since 1975 raises difficult questions of fact and law.[177]

In 1991 Indonesia adopted Government Regulation 18, which made the preservation of Portuguese land rights conditional upon their conversion into rights under Indonesian law.[178] Indonesian nationals could maintain full ownership rights, but the rights of foreigners and rights other than full ownership were downgraded.[179] In some cases such rights also had to be transferred to an Indonesian national within a year, otherwise they came to an end and the land became directly controlled by the state, subject only to the general qualification that 'the rights of other parties which encumber [the land] will be respected and regulated separately'.[180] The requirement of transfer was difficult to comply with since almost all foreigners (individuals and legal entities) had left Timor-Leste in 1975. Even if they were aware of this requirement, scarcely any would have returned to comply with it. Under international and local pressure, the full implementation of the regulation was formally postponed, but the effect of this postponement is unclear.[181] In all, only 142 Portuguese titles were ever formally converted to Indonesian titles.[182]

UNTAET administration

UNTAET Regulation 1991/1 authorized UNTAET to 'administer immovable ... property of, or registered in the name of the Republic of Indonesia, or any of its subsidiary organs and agencies, which was in the territory of East Timor'. It also authorized UNTAET to administer such property 'privately owned that was abandoned after 30 August 1999, the date

[177] Fitzpatrick, 'Land Issues in a Newly Independent East Timor', 9.

[178] Indonesia, Government Regulation 18 of 1991 on Provisions on the Conversion of Land Rights in the Province of East Timor in accordance with the Basic Agrarian Law of 1960.

[179] Catherine Elderton, 'Land Issues and Independence' (paper presented at FAO/USP/RICS Foundation South Pacific Land Tenure Conflict Symposium on Transforming Land Conflict, University of the South Pacific, 10–12 April 2002), www.usp.ac.fj/fileadmin/files/faculties/islands/landmgmt/symposium/PAPER52CATH.PDF, 9.

[180] Indonesia, Government Regulation 18, Article 5(2).

[181] Meitzner Yoder, 'Custom, Codification, Collaboration', 306; Warren L. Wright, 'A Note on Land Rights in East Timor [Government Regulation No. 18 of 1991 on the Conversion of Land Rights in East Timor] and the Purported Suspension of Article 5 by Government Regulation No 34 of 1992' (2004) (No. 1) *East Timor Law Journal*, www.eastimorlawjournal.org.

[182] Fitzpatrick, *Land Claims in East Timor*, 158.

of the popular consultation, until such time as the lawful owners are determined'.[183]

UNTAET drafted a set of regulations and directives that included the establishment of a land claims commission and land register.[184] According to the draft, land disputes would have been resolved by reference to Indonesian law and international human rights principles, accommodating holders of pre-1975 titles only if their titles had been recognized by Indonesian Law.[185] The National Cabinet of East Timor, a transitional Timorese body established within UNTAET, rejected the draft,[186] revealing deep-rooted disputes over the issue.

Differences on how to tackle the problem resulted in failure to adopt any clear policy throughout the period of UNTAET's administration.[187] Consequently, UNTAET took only two major legal measures with respect to land. One was allocation of land through temporary-use agreement, in order to address pressing problems of the local population and to provide facilities to the large international contingent that arrived on the island.[188] The other measure was a freeze on transfer of rights by Indonesians. This last measure was enacted in response to a rush by Indonesian title holders to sell their land, in anticipation of the referendum and also immediately following it. To prevent the entrenchment of corrupt dispossession under Indonesian rule,[189] UNTAET declared that any contract or agreement to grant any leasehold interest in land in Timor-Leste, by a national of Indonesia not habitually resident in Timor-Leste, or by an

183 UNTAET Regulation 1991/1, Article 7.

184 Warren L. Wright, 'UNTAET Land Policy' (2004) (No. 2) *East Timor Law Journal*, www.eastimorlawjournal.org.

185 Fitzpatrick, *Land Claims in East Timor*, 209.

186 W. Wright, 'UNTAET Land Policy'.

187 Jean du Plessis, 'Slow Start on a Long Journey: Land Restitution Issues in East Timor, 1999–2001', in Scott Leckie (ed.), *Returning Home: Housing and Property Restitution Rights of Refugees and Displaced Persons* (Ardsley: Transnational, 2003), 157; for opinions on the way forward, see Pat Walsh, 'Human Rights and the Future of East Timor – Report on Joint UNTAET Human Rights Unit and East Timor Jurists Association Workshop' (Dili, 7–8 August 2000), Sections 6.3.2(3), (10), 6.1.2(10), www.etan.org/issues/9–00reprt.htm; *La'o Hamutuk Bulletin* 1(4) (31 December 2000); for a detailed discussion of UNTAET's failure to address land policy problems, see Daniel Fitzpatrick, 'Land Policy in Post-conflict Circumstances: Some Lessons from East Timor' (2001) *Journal of Humanitarian Assistance*, www.jha.ac/articles/a074.htm.

188 UNTAET Land and Property Unit, Guidelines for the Administration of Public and Abandoned Property by District Administrations, revised 15 August 2000, www.eastimorlawjournal.org/ARTICLES/2004/untaet_land_administration_policy_guidelines.html.

189 Fitzpatrick, 'Land Issues in a Newly Independent East Timor', 10.

Indonesian corporation, would have no effect.[190] The freeze effectively made Indonesian private titles a bargaining chip for Timor-Leste in subsequent negotiations with Indonesia on assets and liabilities.[191] However, the freeze did not always benefit the Timorese. It was promulgated in August 2000, but its effect was made retroactive to 25 October 1999. This meant that Timorese who had purchased or leased land from Indonesian nationals or corporations between October 1999 and August 2000 had not acquired any rights, but were unable to recover lost monies because the sellers were no longer in Timor-Leste.[192]

Timor-Leste's legislation

At independence, the issue of land claims was still unresolved and politicians were reluctant to address it, for both domestic and international political reasons. Within Timor-Leste, Fretilin advocated land justice for traditional and dispossessed groups through land reform, although Xanana Gusmão, first president of Timor-Leste, has reportedly indicated that consideration should be given to recognizing Indonesian titles obtained in good faith.[193] In contrast, UDT supported restitution of pre-1975 titles,[194] reputedly because many of its supporters, particularly former civil servants, had accumulated significant lands under Portuguese colonial rule.[195] In relations with Indonesia, land rights were

[190] UNTAET Regulation 2000/27, Preamble, Section 2.

[191] Fitzpatrick, *Land Claims in East Timor*, 100. According to the joint statement of the second meeting of the Indonesia–Timor-Leste Joint Ministerial Commission for Bilateral Cooperation, 'Both Parties expressed its [*sic*] satisfaction with the recognition of the principle of international law that private individuals and corporations should have their legal rights duly recognized', and agreed to create an appropriate institutional framework for resolving property matters. Joint Statement, Second Meeting of the Indonesia–Timor-Leste Joint Ministerial Commission for Bilateral Cooperation (Dili, 4–6 September 2003), www.mfac.gov.tp/media/mr030912e.html. The subsequent meeting did not relate at all to property issues. Joint Statement, Third Meeting of the Indonesia–Timor-Leste Joint Ministerial Commission for Bilateral Cooperation (Jakarta, 7–8 July 2005), www.indonesia-ottawa.org/information/details.php?type=speech&id=51.

[192] See also Warren L. Wright, 'Some Observations on UNTAET Regulation No 27 of 2000 on the Temporary Prohibition of Transactions in Land in East Timor by Indonesian Citizens Not Habitually Resident in East Timor and by Indonesian Corporations' (2004) (No. 3) *East Timor Law Journal*, www.eastimorlawjournal.org.

[193] Fitzpatrick, 'Land Issues in a Newly Independent East Timor', 5.

[194] Although not necessarily to the total exclusion of Indonesian titles, at least not those acquired in good faith.

[195] Fitzpatrick, 'Land Issues in a Newly Independent East Timor', 5.

perceived as a delicate bargaining chip.[196] The land and property portfolio was consequently repeatedly reassigned to different governmental departments, and the first national budget allocated no money to addressing land claims, land disputes or policy and law development.[197]

In 2003, a first legislative step was taken towards a resolution of land issues, with the promulgation of the Law on the Juridical Regime of Real Estate (Part 1 – Ownership over Real Estate) (the Real Estate Law). The preamble to the law states that the 'occupation of Timor-Leste between 1975 and 1999 was an illegal act as recognized worldwide . . . That is the reason why Indonesia was unable to succeed the Portuguese Administration in Timor-Leste'. The preamble also notes that properties have been illegitimately or illegally occupied or owned, although this seems to refer to post-1999 events rather than to the Indonesian measures.

The law declares 'non-existent' any acts of appropriation relating to real estate owned by Portugal as of 7 December 1975 that may have taken place under whatever form between 7 December 1975 and 19 May 2002.[198] This provision was apparently motivated by Fretilin's wish to reclaim Portuguese state lands that had been granted by Indonesia to Fretilin's pro-Indonesian opponents.[199] However, the rights of buyers in good faith of state land were to be safeguarded.[200] This legislation reflects, with

196 Fitzpatrick, *Land Claims in East Timor*, 112. The importance of property claims is apparent from the Joint Ministerial Statement following the first meeting of the Indonesia–Timor-Leste Joint Ministerial Commission for Bilateral Cooperation (8 October 2002), paragraph 13, www.kbri-canberra.org.au/wnew/jminist021008e.htm; Joint Ministerial Statement following the second meeting of the Indonesia–Timor-Leste Joint Ministerial Commission for Bilateral Cooperation (4–6 September 2003), paragraphs 13–14 ('13. The Government of Indonesia requested the Government of the Democratic Timor-Leste to consider extending the period provided in the property law to claim the property belonging to Indonesian citizens. 14. Taking note of the complexity of the matters pertaining to assets, both Parties agreed to consider establishing an institutional framework to further deliberate the matters aimed at finding acceptable and comprehensive solution'), www.mfac.gov.tp/media/mr030912e.html; the Joint Statement following the third meeting of the Indonesia–Timor-Leste Joint Ministerial Commission for Bilateral Cooperation (7–8 July 2005), paragraph 21 ('The Indonesian delegation took note of Timor-Leste's efforts to set up a mechanism regulating land right matters'), www.indonesia-ottawa.org/information/details.php?type=speech&id=51.

197 Elderton, 'Land Issues and Independence', 14.

198 Real Estate Law, Section 16(1), (2).

199 An example of this is the eviction of Mario Carrascalão from his home in Dili in 2003. Correspondence of the author with Adv. Warren Wright, 22 June 2005.

200 Real Estate Law, Section 16(3).

respect to state land, a reversion to the *status quo ante* with an exception to grants that are given effect under the *Namibia* exception.

The law also initiated a land claim register, which attracted the attention of mostly foreign nationals and which has not had any clear consequences.[201] Legislation has since been adopted to assist in the short-term leasing of land in the absence of land titles, and to enable much needed private-sector economic development.[202] Additional instruments have been drafted but their adoption was not pursued because of the sensitive nature of land issues.[203]

In the meantime, land disputes have been settled mostly outside the court system, through mediation performed by government officials and by trained community leaders. Only a handful of cases have been submitted to the courts and even fewer decided by them.[204] The relationship between Indonesian and Portuguese titles remains unregulated and plagued by politics.

Land conflicts were taken to a new level when another wave of violence and displacement of some 150,000 persons occurred in April 2006. This followed tensions between eastern and western Timorese, reportedly aggravated by these communities' uneven access to land and property. More than 3,000 abandoned houses had been destroyed and another 2,000

[201] Foreign individual claimants submitted 72 per cent of the claims, national individual claimants submitted 26 per cent, and companies submitted 2 per cent of the claims. De Sousa, 'East Timor Land Management – A Long Way to Go, But We Have Started', 5.

[202] Decree Law 19/2004 on the Juridical Regime of Property: Official Allocation and Leasing of Private Property of the State. Law 12/2005 on the Juridical Regime of Real Estate (Part II – Leasing between Individuals) sets the minimum conditions of the lease agreements of private property between individuals. Klaus Rohland and Sarah Cliffe, 'The East Timor Reconstruction Program: Successes, Problems and Tradeoffs', Conflict Prevention and Reconstruction Unit Working Paper No. 2 (World Bank, 2002), 20; UNDP, 'The Way Ahead', East Timor Human Development Report (2002), 68; UNDP, 'Building Blocks for a Nation' UN Common country Assessment (November 2000), 46; Daniel Cooney, 'Messy Land Disputes Hampering East Timor's Development', AP, 16 July 2000, www.globalpolicy/org/security/issues/etimor/000717/htm. It has been suggested that security for investments does not lie in the titles to land: Meitzner Yoder, 'Custom, Codification, Collaboration', 311.

[203] A draft law on land dispute mediation and a draft law on property system, transfer, registration, pre-existing rights and title restitution, International Crisis Group, 'Timor-Leste's Displacement Crisis', Asia Report No. 148 (31 March 2008), 11.

[204] JSMP, Land Law Report (Dili, 27 September 2005), 11–12. The delay within the courts is related to the insufficient number of judges, which requires giving priority to criminal cases.

damaged.[205] Only in late 2009 did the last of the displaced persons return to their homes.[206]

In July 2008 the Timorese Ministry of Justice again launched a national land register.[207] In June 2009 the Timorese government launched a public consultation process on a Draft Land Law to Establish the Special Regime for Attributing Property Rights (the Draft Land Law). If adopted, the Draft Land Law will replace the 2003 Real Estate Law and UNTAET's Regulation 1991/1.[208]

The Draft Land Law aims to regulate the hierarchy between various rights in property as well as between rights and adverse possession. It affects primarily Timorese nationals, for two reasons. First, Indonesian settlers almost without exception left Timor-Leste in 1999 and are not at present occupying any property. Thus they are excluded from the provisions relating to adverse possession. Second, according to the constitution, only nationals of Timor-Leste may own land in the country.[209] According to the Draft Land Law, property of foreigners will revert to the state, except in cases of special adverse possession by nationals. If they maintain current possession of any immovable property reverted to the state they may continue to use the property by way of lease contracts or other forms provided in the law.[210]

Generally speaking, the Draft Land Law gives priority in acquiring ownership to the most recent peaceful adverse possessor, unless the property is held by the previous right holders under Portuguese freehold

205 Ibere Lopes, 'Land and Displacement in Timor-Leste' (June 2009), 43 *Humanitarian Exchange Magazine*, www.odihpn.org/report.asp?id=3007.

206 AFP, 'East Timor Begins Closure of Last Displaced Persons Camp', Asia One News, 17 June 2009, www.asiaone.com/News/Latest%2BNews/Asia/Story/A1Story20090617-149135.html.

207 'Nationwide Land Data Collection to Start in East Timor', *East Timor Law and Justice Bulletin* (2 July 2008), http://easttimorlegal.blogspot.com/2008/07/nationwide-land-data-collection-to.html.

208 Draft Land Law circulated for public consultation (June 2009), Article 89, www.scribd.com/doc/16767881/East-Timor-Draft-Land-Law-June-2009.

209 Timor-Leste constitution, Article 54(4), Draft Land Law circulated for public consultation (June 2009), Article 21, with regard to ownership based on peaceful adverse possession, www.scribd.com/doc/16767881/East-Timor-Draft-Land-Law-June-2009.

210 Draft Land Law, third version (February 2010), Article 11, www.scribd.com/doc/27246021/East-Timor-Draft-Land-Law-Version-3. Foreigners could apply for Timorese nationality, although in view of the requisites for naturalization in Timor-Leste, this is not a likely option for former Indonesian settlers; see Chapter 6 above.

(*propriedade perfeita*) or Indonesian freehold (*hak milik*).[211] However, both the Portuguese colonial system and the Indonesian system were based on state control of land, with individuals usually being granted only secondary rights in property rather than freehold.[212] Thus early ownership is protected against adverse possession only in a minority of cases.[213]

Peaceful adverse possession entitles ownership if it began no later than 31 December 1998.[214] This excludes persons internally displaced as a result of the 1999 violence from acquiring ownership of their dwellings. The original draft provided for legalization of adverse possession which began as late as 25 April 2006. Had that critical date been maintained, the Draft Land Law would have made many conflicts between Indonesian and Portuguese titles redundant as both would have been superseded by current adverse possessors.[215]

Peaceful possession is 'that which is obtained without violence or threat'; that is, not through physical or moral coercion.[216] Persons who entered voluntarily or were resettled by the Indonesian authorities in abandoned houses would qualify as peaceful adverse possessors, even if they were aware of the circumstances in which the property was made available, as long as they were not physically or otherwise directly involved in the dispossession. Cronies of the Indonesian regime would therefore have priority over original right holders that have fled or were removed from their homes forcibly.

With respect to conflicts between rights under Indonesian and Portuguese law in the absence of an adverse possessor, the Draft Land Law clearly gives priority to holders of the most recent title, provided they are in possession of the property. This means that Indonesian titles will prevail over Portuguese ones if the most recent right holder is in actual

[211] Draft Land Law circulated for public consultation (June 2009), Article 27(1), www.scribd.com/doc/16767881/East-Timor-Draft-Land-Law-June-2009. Indonesian law, which is the subsidiary law of Timor-Leste, does not recognize long-term adverse possession as a source of title to land.

[212] Fitzpatrick, *Land Claims in East Timor*, 88–89.

[213] Draft Land Law circulated for public consultation (June 2009), Article 31(2), www.scribd.com/doc/16767881/East-Timor-Draft-Land-Law-June-2009.

[214] Draft Land Law circulated for public consultation (June 2009), Articles 21, 33, www.scribd.com/doc/16767881/East-Timor-Draft-Land-Law-June-2009.

[215] Compare Daniel Fitzpatrick, 'Brief Memorandum of Advice on a Transitional Land Law for Timor Leste' (Singapore, 2008), with the Draft Land Law as put forward for consultation.

[216] Draft Land Law circulated for public consultation (June 2009), Article 18, www.scribd.com/doc/16767881/East-Timor-Draft-Land-Law-June-2009.

possession of the property.[217] The Portuguese right holder would only be entitled to compensation. The Draft Land Law does not clarify who would prevail if the right holder is not in possession of the property, a matter of great significance when that right holder is Indonesian rather than Timorese.

Priority extends to Indonesian titles also with regard to compensation: where ownership is granted to an adverse possessor, compensation under the Draft Land Law is awarded only to the most recent previous possessor or title holder.[218] Thus the Indonesian right holder will receive compensation, while the Portuguese right holder will remain empty-handed. Furthermore, the ineligibility of foreign nationals does not extend to the right to compensation, and compensation is not dependent on good faith on the part of the grantee or on the non-odiousness of the grant. Holders of Indonesian titles, including Indonesian nationals, are therefore eligible for ownership or compensation even if their title was obtained with full knowledge of the deprivation which preceded it.

As the overwhelming majority of Indonesians left Timor-Leste in 1999, the protection of their rights as current occupants rather than owners is largely a moot one. The Immigration and Asylum Act provides that non-Timorese nationals who wish to reside in Timor-Leste must demonstrate, inter alia, means of subsistence and ensured lodging.[219] Non-nationals who remain in Timor-Leste are therefore by definition those who are not vulnerable to eviction. Accordingly, the protection from forcible eviction is relevant primarily to Timorese nationals who possess property but do not qualify for ownership.[220]

The Draft Land Law permits administrative evictions, subject to the provision of alternative residence, or after a period of eighteen months has elapsed from the recognition or award of the right of ownership.[221] The

217 Draft Land Law circulated for public consultation (June 2009), Articles 31(2), 34, www.scribd.com/doc/16767881/East-Timor-Draft-Land-Law-June-2009.

218 Draft Land Law circulated for public consultation (June 2009), Article 36, www.scribd.com/doc/16767881/East-Timor-Draft-Land-Law-June-2009.

219 Timor-Leste Immigration and Asylum Act, Article 37. Another limitation may be that permanent-residence authorization may benefit non-citizens who have been legal residents of the national territory for at least twelve consecutive years (Immigration and Asylum Act, Article 53). If the term 'legal residents' is interpreted in accordance with its meaning under the Law on Nationality, it excludes Indonesian transmigrants.

220 Timor-Leste constitution, Article 58: 'Everyone has the right to a house, both for himself or herself and for his or her family, of adequate size that meets satisfactory standards of hygiene and comfort and preserves personal intimacy and family privacy'.

221 Draft Land Law circulated for public consultation (June 2009), Articles 48–50, www.scribd.com/doc/16767881/East-Timor-Draft-Land-Law-June-2009.

protection of the inviolability of the home under the constitution is more stringent. The constitution provides that a person's home is inviolable, except in cases provided for by law as a result of criminal proceedings. Moreover, a person's home shall not be entered against his or her will, except under the written order of a competent judicial authority and in the cases and manner prescribed by law.[222] These provisions prohibit forcible administrative eviction. Eviction under the Draft Land Law, while not prohibited in principle under international law, therefore appears to be unconstitutional.

7.3.6 The TRNC

Land administration under the TFSC and TRNC

The massive dislocation of Cypriots in 1963–1964 and again in 1974 has resulted in the extensive separation of individuals of both communities from their lands. In 1974, approximately 142,000 Greek Cypriots originally from the north became refugees in the south, and many were settled in abandoned Turkish Cypriot houses or in new houses built on Turkish Cypriot land. Around 55,000 Turkish Cypriots left their own homes in the south and fled to the north, where they were settled in Greek Cypriot property. The use of property belonging to members of the other community laid the groundwork for what was to become the island's most complex and contentious issue.[223]

The Greek Cypriots estimate that in 1974, Greek Cypriot-owned land constituted 78.5 per cent of all privately owned land in the TRNC. The Turkish Cypriots estimate it at 63.8 per cent. The Turkish Cypriot estimates for Turkish Cypriot-owned private land in 1974 on both sides of the island are 33 per cent in the TRNC and 22 per cent in the south, while the Greek Cypriot estimates are 21.1 per cent in the TRNC and 13.9 per cent in the south.[224] In the event of unification, adjustments are expected to be more marked in the TRNC than in the southern part of the island, because of the significant share of Greek Cypriot-owned properties there, and because of the legislative measures adopted in the TRNC and their consequences.

222 Timor-Leste constitution, Article 37(1), (2).

223 Rebecca Bryant and Mete Hatay, 'Suing for Sovereignty: Property, Territory, and the EU's Cyprus Problem', Global Political Trends Centre Policy Brief (2009).

224 Ayla Gürel and Kudret Özersay, 'The Politics of Property in Cyprus', PRIO Report 3/2006, 3–9.

Since 1974, TFSC- and TRNC-imposed restrictions both on movement to the north[225] and on property rights have resulted in the denial to Greek Cypriot owners of property in northern Cyprus of access to their lands, as well as control, use and enjoyment of those lands.[226] Turkish Cypriot-owned properties are held in trust by the Governmental Guardian for Turkish Cypriot Property, and there has been no transfer of ownership over these properties.[227]

The TFSC and the TRNC enacted various laws changing the property regime in the territory under their control. First, they allowed Turkish Cypriot refugees from the south to surrender their property to the authorities in the north in exchange for Greek Cypriot-owned land in the northern part of the island. This was regarded as a preliminary stage in negotiating an agreement with the Greek Cypriot-controlled government on a global population and property exchange. Land allocated under the scheme was non-transferable for a period of twenty years. TRNC law also provided for housing and land for needy Turkish Cypriots.[228] Subsequent legislation extended the possibility of land allocation to Turkish Cypriots, Turkish settlers and Turkish soldiers who had served in Cyprus.[229] The precise legal and practical consequences of this legislation remain unclear. It was not fully implemented due to international pressure.[230]

225 The northern part of the island is sealed off by the Turkish Army. Concessions were made by the TRNC in 1998 regarding family visits of Greek Cypriots and Maronites in the north. ECtHR, *Cyprus* v. *Turkey (The Fourth Interstate Case)*, [31]. In April 2003 concessions were made regarding freedom of movement of the general public: TRNC Council of Ministers, Decision on Crossings from the Turkish Republic of Northern Cyprus to South Cyprus and from the South to the Turkish Republic of Northern Cyprus, Decision No. E-762–2003 (21 April 2003); Amendment to Decision No. E-762–2003 of the Council of Ministers dated 21 April 2003 Regarding Crossings from the Turkish Republic of Northern Cyprus to the South and from the South to the Turkish Republic of Northern Cyprus, Decision No. E-770–2003 (29 April 2003), www.foreignpolicy.org.tr/documents/cypruscrossing_290403_p.htm.

226 ECtHR, *Cyprus* v. *Turkey (The Fourth Interstate Case)*, [32].

227 This policy may be attributable not only to respect for the rights of the Turkish Cypriots but also to the preservation of the collective memory of displacement. Interviews by the author with Mr Mete Hatay, PRIO Cyprus Center, and Dr Yannis Papadakis, University of Nicosia, Nicosia, 30 November 2008.

228 TRNC, Law 41/1977 on Housing, Allocation of Land and Property of Equal Value Law (1977).

229 TRNC, Law 27/1982 on Settlement, Land Allocation and Equivalent Property Law (1982); EComHR, *Cyprus* v. *Turkey (1996)*, 119.

230 Statement made by Mr Zaim Necatigil (attorney-general of the TRNC) in appendix to a letter from the Permanent Representative of Turkey to the UN addressed to the Secretary-General, UN Doc A/37/793-S/15620 (23 February 1983), 5; UN Doc S/24472 (21 August 1992), paragraph 28; statement of Mr Denktaş to the UN Secretary-General in

Under Article 159 of the TRNC's 1985 constitution, property abandoned by 13 February 1975 became state property of the TRNC.[231] The constitution allows for compensation for such land, but an implementing law for compensation was first enacted only in 2003. Until 1989 the TRNC left the pre-1974 land register unaffected, and recorded the abandoned property and its allocation separately. The beneficiaries of allocations were issued possessory certificates, but not title deeds.[232] The international community was assured from time to time that Greek Cypriot ownership rights remained intact.[233] However, by June 1989 the practice had changed: the Turkish Cypriot authorities ceased to recognize ownership rights of Greek Cypriots in respect of properties in the TRNC, and title deeds were issued to occupants of abandoned Greek Cypriot properties, following which changes in ownership were recorded in the Land Register.[234] Former TRNC Prime Minister Eroğlu stated in 1993 that 10,000 title deeds had been issued under his administration (1985–4993), and a UN Report of December 1994 mentions that 17,000 additional title deeds were about to be issued.[235] A further change took place in 2002, when land allocated in 1982 had begun to become transferable. Land purchases by foreigners grew ninefold from 2001 to 2003,[236] and a property development boom began in the TRNC.

The validity of Article 159 came before the ECtHR in *Loizidou* v. *Turkey*. Titina Loizidou, a Greek Cypriot landowner who grew up in northern Cyprus and in 1972 moved to Nicosia, claimed that her right to property under ECHR Protocol 1 Article 1 had been violated, because since

1987 according to which no actual transfer of ownership had taken place, EComHR, *Cyprus* v. *Turkey (1996)*, 120–121.

231 Article 159(1) of the TRNC's 1985 Constitution stipulates:

> (b) All immovable properties, buildings and installations which were found abandoned on 13th February, 1975 when the Turkish Federated State of Cyprus was proclaimed or which were considered by law as abandoned or not being owned after the abovementioned date . . .
>
> (c) . . . shall be the property of the Turkish Republic of Northern Cyprus notwithstanding the fact that they are not so registered in the record of the Land Registry Office;

232 EComHR, *Cyprus* v. *Turkey (1996)*, 120.

233 E.g. in a statement of Mr Denktaş to the UN Secretary-General in 1987 according to which no actual transfer of ownership had taken place, EComHR, *Cyprus* v. *Turkey (1996)*, 121.

234 UN Doc S/24472 (21 August 1992), paragraph 28.

235 EComHR, *Cyprus* v. *Turkey (1996)*, 121.

236 ANKA, 'Yabancıdan KKTC'ye akın var', *Milliyet*, 23 August 2004, www.milliyet.com.tr/2004/08/23/ekonomi/aeko.html.

1974 she had been denied access to, and use of, her property. The Turkish government responded that Loizidou had lost ownership of the land in question when the TRNC constitution came into effect in 1985. Accordingly it claimed that the applicant had no right to property that could have been violated. The TRNC's position was that ECHR Protocol 1 Article 1 protected only 'those in actual enjoyment of possessions'. It claimed that this excludes Greek Cypriots who had voluntarily deserted their property in the north.[237]

In 1996 the ECtHR rejected these arguments. Relying on UN Security Council Resolutions 541(1983) and 550(1984), which declared the legal invalidity of the TRNC and called on states not to recognize it,[238] it found that Article 159 could not be recognized as valid for the purposes of the ECHR. A number of judges in dissents argued for giving effect to legislative and administrative acts of the TRNC. Judges Baka and Pettiti tied this directly to the *Namibia* exception,[239] while Judges Jambrek and Gölcüklü opined more generally that despite non-recognition of the TRNC, the effectiveness of the regime could not be disregarded.[240] The majority found that even if rehousing Turkish Cypriot refugees in the years following the Turkish intervention in the island in 1974 was a legitimate ground for limiting the applicant's right to property, the complete negation of the applicant's property rights by the total and continuous denial of access and the purported expropriation without compensation was disproportionate to its aim. In other words, the expropriation could not be given validity even under the *Namibia* exception, because it was in violation of international human rights law.[241] Accordingly, the court ruled that Loizidou remained the owner of the property, and that the denial of access to the property and control over it constituted an unlawful interference with her right

237 Statement made by Mr Zaim Necatigil (attorney-general of the TRNC) in appendix to a letter dated 22 February 1983 from the permanent representative of Turkey to the United Nations addressed to the Secretary General' (23 February 1983), UN Doc A/37/793-S/15620, 6; letter dated 22 February 1983 from Mr Nail Atalay, representative of the Turkish Federated State of Kibris, to the Secretary-General, Annex to UN Doc A/37/793-S/15620.

238 *Loizidou* v. *Turkey (Merits)*, [42].

239 *Loizidou* v. *Turkey (Merits)*. Judge Baka said that 'the interests of the community required, if not necessitated, some form of regularisation elaborated on what he considered to be the necessity for the land transfers'; dissenting opinion of Judge Baka, 2235. Judge Pettiti also opined that 'if events had made the rehousing operation inevitable, that could justify the interference'; dissenting opinion of Judge Pettiti, 2242.

240 *Loizidou* v. *Turkey (Merits)*, dissenting opinion of Judge Jambrek, [5]; *Loizidou* v. *Turkey (Merits)*, dissenting opinion of Judge Gölcüklü, [3].

241 *Loizidou* v. *Turkey (Merits)*, [42]–[44].

to property,[242] as was the absence of compensation for the interferences caused by the purported expropriation.[243] In a later judgment the ECtHR awarded Loizidou a substantial amount in compensation.[244] By the early 2000s there were thousands of cases pending before the ECtHR, essentially repeating the *Loizidou* scenario.[245]

In June 2003, the TRNC adopted a law implementing the right to compensation envisaged in the 1985 constitution (the 2003 Compensation Law).[246] The law provided for a one-year submission period of claims based on pre-July 1974 rights in abandoned property in the TRNC,[247] failing which compensation would be determined within the framework of a political agreement.[248] The law defined the entitlement to compensation as 'the total of the market value of the immovable property on 29 July 1974 together with compensation for loss of use'.[249] The compensation for 'loss of use' suggests that ownership was considered under the law to have remained intact until compensation was awarded by the commission, in line with the ECtHR's ruling that the expropriation under the TRNC Constitution did not extinguish ownership.[250] The law allowed for compensation in the form of exchange against property in the south which Turkish Cypriot refugees had renounced in favour of the TRNC, if the claimant so agrees.[251]

[242] *Loizidou* v. *Turkey (Merits)*, [64].

[243] ECtHR, *Cyprus* v. *Turkey (The Fourth Interstate Case)*, [32], [187].

[244] *Loizidou* v. *Turkey (Article 50)*. Turkey complied with the *Loizidou* judgment only in December 2003. Commission of the European Communities 2004 Regular Report on Turkey's Progress towards Accession (6 October 2004), 30, http://europa.eu.int/comm/enlargement/report_2004/pdf/rr_tr_2004_en.pdf.

[245] A few have resulted in judgments; see *Demades* v. *Turkey*; *Michaelidou Developments Ltd and Michael Tymvios* v. *Turkey*.

[246] The law was reportedly adopted in an attempt to release Turkey from the obligation to pay compensation to Loizidou, and to thwart additional complaints on violations of the right to property. Norwegian Refugee Council/Global IDP Project, 'Profile of Internal Displacement: Cyprus, Compilation of the Information Available in the Global IDP Database of the Norwegian Refugee Council (as of 3 June, 2003)', 49; Turkish Daily News Report (29 April 2003) summarized in Cyprus Press and Information Office, Turkish Cypriot Press Review (29 April 2003), www.hri.org/news/cyprus/tcpr/2003/03-04-29.tcpr.html. The Council of Ministers of the TRNC later approved the Immovable Properties Determination, Evaluation and Compensation Commission Rules, 2003, made under the Law.

[247] 2003 Compensation Law, Articles 4, 6. The Commission is not empowered to order restitution of the property.

[248] 2003 Compensation Law, Article 18.

[249] 2003 Compensation Law, Article 6(4).

[250] See also *Michaelidou and Tymvios* v. *Turkey*, dissenting opinion of Judge *ad hoc* Gölcüklü, [23].

[251] 2003 Compensation Law, Article 10.

In 2005 the ECtHR ruled in a pilot case that the 2003 Compensation Law was not an effective domestic remedy that must be exhausted before recourse is had to the court,[252] inter alia because without the possibility of restoration, it provided an incomplete system of redress.[253]

The TRNC subsequently adopted new legislation on redress for expropriation (the 2005 IPC Law).[254] This law provides that persons claiming rights to immovable or movable property might bring a claim before the IPC until 21 December 2009. In October 2009 the deadline was extended until 21 December 2011. Under the law, applicants must prove beyond a reasonable doubt that, inter alia, the immovable property was registered in their name on 20 July 1974 (or that they are the legal heirs to such property), that they had been forced to abandon it due to conditions beyond their own volition, and that according to the Land Registry records there are no other persons claiming rights to the claimed immovable property.[255] According to the law, Greek Cypriot properties can be returned to their Greek Cypriot owners after a settlement, but only after expropriation by the TRNC from new owners.[256] This formulation, unlike that of the 2003 Compensation Law, is in line with the constitutional provision, implying that Greek Cypriot ownership expired when the constitution came into force, rather than upon the decision of the IPC. The ECtHR has noted 'that the new compensation and restitution mechanism, in principle, has taken care of the requirements of the decision of the Court'.[257] By November 2009, the number of cases brought before the commission stood at 433. Of these, eighty-five had been concluded, the vast majority by means of friendly settlement. Only a handful of decisions not based on a settlement had been issued. In four cases, the IPC had ordered restoration and compensation; in two cases, an exchange of property was agreed; and in one case, the applicant agreed to restitution on resolution of the Cyprus problem. In more than seventy cases, some 361,493 square metres of

[252] On this procedure and its implementation in *Xenides-Arestis* v. *Turkey* see Costas Paraskevas, 'The Application of the "Pilot Judgment Procedure" to Post-*Loizidou* Cases' (2009) 4 *Annuaire international des droits de l'homme* 573.

[253] *Xenides-Arestis* v. *Turkey (Admissibility)*, [44]–[45], [50].

[254] 2005 IPC Law; By-law made under Sections 8 (2) (A) and 22 of the Law for the Compensation, Exchange and Restitution of Immovable Properties Which Are within the Scope of Sub-paragraph (b) of Paragraph 1 of Article 159 of the Constitution.

[255] *Demopoulos and Others* v. *Turkey*, [35].

[256] 'Changes on Property law Approved by Parliament' (20 December 2005), www.trncinfo.com/TANITMADAIRESI/ARSIV2005/ENGLISHarcive/DECEMBER/201205.htm.

[257] *Xenides-Arestis* v. *Turkey (Merits)*, [37].

property had been restored, and approximately 47 million euros awarded in compensation.[258]

The validity of the 2005 IPC Law as a local remedy which must be exhausted before recourse is had to the ECtHR was decided by the ECtHR in 2010. The plaintiff argued that requiring exhaustion of TRNC local remedies lent legitimacy to an illegal occupation. The court relied on the *Namibia* exception to reject this argument, noting that since Turkey is being held responsible for violations of human rights irrespective of the legality of its control over the TRNC, allowing it to correct the wrongs imputable to it does not amount to an indirect legitimization of an illegal regime under international law.[259] With respect to the content of the IPC Law, the court ruled that the absence of an obligation on a state to pursue a blanket policy of restoration to owners without taking into account the current use of the property in question, and the discretionary nature of the restitutionary power, raise no legal problem.[260]

Transition under the Annan Plan

If there is any single issue that constitutes the greatest obstacle to acceptance of the Annan Plan by the Greek Cypriots, it is that of real property. The two sides have diametrically opposite perceptions of how to resolve the property issue.[261] The Greek Cypriots maintain that the property issue is essentially a matter of human rights, and demand giving all refugees unrestricted rights to repossess and return to their former homes and properties, in particular irrespectively of any bizonal arrangements. The government of Cyprus also demands that reunification be based on complete freedom of movement, residence and property – in other words, on reinstatement of property.[262] The Turkish Cypriots, while accepting the principle of respect for human rights, demand restrictions on the exercise of rights to property and return by refugees insofar as is necessary to preserve and protect bizonality.[263] In their view, this entails preserving as much as possible the present pattern of settlement. Hence the Turkish

258 *Demopoulos and Others* v. *Turkey*, [40]. 259 *Demopoulos and Others* v. *Turkey*, [96].

260 *Demopoulos and Others* v. *Turkey*, [117]–[118].

261 UN Docs S/11789 (5 August 1975), S/11789/Add.1 (10 September 1975) and S/11789/Add.2 (13 September 1975).

262 Nathalie Tocci and Tamara Kovziridze, 'Cyprus', in Bruno Coppieters *et al.* (eds.), *Europeanizaiton and Conflict Resolution: Case Studies from the Euroepan Periphery* (Gent: Academia Press, 2004), 73.

263 The Turkish-Cypriot concept of 'bi-zonality' was that the constituent states would have the unfettered right to decide who could establish residency therein. UN Doc S/2003/398 (1 April 2003), paragraph 98.

Cypriots regard a 'global exchange and compensation' formula for settlement of property claims not only as a more convenient solution than processing individual claims, but also as the only viable one.[264] Their position that a population and property exchange should take place rather than return and restoration is expressly based on the Turkish experience following the First World War.[265]

The Annan Plan attempted to accommodate these divergent positions, noting that the 'claims of persons who were dispossessed of their properties . . . shall be resolved in a comprehensive manner in accordance with international law, respect for the individual rights of dispossessed owners and current users, and the principle of bi-zonality'.[266] Like nationality and residence, matters of 'properties affected by events since 1963' are excluded from the general arrangement by which acts of the TRNC are regarded as valid. They are regulated 'in a comprehensive way' by the Annan Plan, and consequently, an observation to the Foundation Agreement provides that 'any validity of acts prior to entry into force of this Agreement regarding these matters shall thus end unless they are in conformity with the relevant provisions of this Agreement'.[267]

The plan defines 'affected' properties as properties the owners of which have lost use and control since 1963 'due to intercommunal strife, military action or the unresolved division of the island', and for which compensation due to compulsory acquisition has not been accepted.[268] By implication, where the transfer of property was voluntary, it continues to have validity. In this the plan applies the *Namibia* exception, according to which routine commercial transactions between individuals should be given effect. It carries the exception through the period of transition, reflecting the doctrine of acquired rights. The onus lies with transferees or their successors in title to prove that the transfer was voluntary.[269]

Property lost involuntarily is subject to reversion to the *status quo ante* through reinstatement. With respect to areas subject to territorial adjustment, namely areas that are currently under TRNC control but would be

264 S/2003/398 (1 April 2003), paragraph 107; Gürel and Özersay, 'The Politics of Property in Cyprus', 11–27.

265 Claire Palley, *An International Relations Debacle: The UN Secretary-General's Mission of Good Offices in Cyprus 1999–2004* (Oxford: Hart, 2005), 169, footnote 16.

266 Annan Plan, Foundation Agreement, Main Article 10; UN Doc S/2003/398, paragraphs 109–111.

267 Annan Plan, Foundation Agreement, Main Article 12, Observation.

268 Annan Plan, Annex VII, Attachment 1, Article 1.

269 Annan Plan, Foundation Agreement, Annex VII, Attachment 1, Article 1, item 1 ('affected property').

under the Greek Cypriot constituent state, it simply states that 'properties shall be reinstated to dispossessed owners'.[270] It was estimated that 54 per cent of displaced Greek Cypriots would be allowed to return to their original homes and properties, and as a result, about a quarter of the Turkish Cypriot population of the north would have to be relocated.[271]

In areas not subject to territorial adjustment, the arrangements balance the right to reinstatement of dispossessed owners with the interests of current users, by including compensation as an alternative that would allow current occupants to acquire the property in which they reside or have invested.[272] While the guiding principle is still reversion to the *status quo ante* through reinstatement, specific arrangements qualify it almost beyond recognition.

Reinstatement is subject to various limitations, such as when the property is used for military or public-benefit purposes.[273] Reinstatement of property used for non-personal residence is also limited by size,[274] with full and effective compensation for the remaining property.[275] These are absolute limitations on restitution, regardless of whether there exist competing interests in the land in question.[276]

The plan, as the Secretary-General emphasized on 1 April 2003, 'largely unlinks residency rights and the issue of reinstatement of property – two aspects which have often been confused in public discussion'.[277] Thus the entitlement of individuals under the one right is, in principle, independent of the entitlement under the other. Cypriot nationals automatically acquire internal citizenship of the constituent state in which they currently reside, not that of their original place of residence.[278] Their ability to reside in their original homes if those are not in the constituent state of which they are citizens will be limited.[279] Owners of property in one constituent state can therefore find themselves living as tenants in the

270 Annan Plan, Foundation Agreement, Main Article 10(2).
271 Gürel and Özersay, 'The Politics of Property in Cyprus', 29.
272 Annan Plan, Foundation Agreement, Main Article 10(3).
273 Annan Plan, Annex VII, Articles 10, 11.
274 Annan Plan, Annex VII, Article 16, and Attachment 1, Article 1(13).
275 Foundation Agreement, Main Article 10(3)(b).
276 Another type of priority given to compensation over restitution regardless of competing interests (at least directly identifiable ones) is in the case of a dispossessed owner opting for compensation. This is not a problematic situation given that it is based on a voluntary choice.
277 UN Doc S/2003/398 (1 April 2003), paragraph 101.
278 Annan Plan, Foundation Agreement, Annex II, Attachment III, Article 1.
279 Except in specific listed villages. Annan Plan, Foundation Agreement, Annex II, Attachment III, Articles 6, 7(3).

other constituent state. Those whose property would be reinstated would be entitled to use it as a second residence for holidays or weekends, and to lease or sell it.[280] In other words, reinstatement is not contingent upon return.

One exceptional link between return and restitution concerns persons of one of the constituent states who wish to establish residence in the other constituent state.[281] Within the permissible limit to such relocation, the plan gives priority to owners of reinstated property.[282] Ownership of property thereby enhances a right of return, but not the other way round. This separation of residence from property ownership did not meet with Greek Cypriot approval.[283]

In areas not subject to territorial adjustment, current occupants can acquire ownership in certain circumstances, even as against dispossessed owners. Priority is given to current users of at least ten years who are displaced persons, and who have left property in the other constituent state that could be surrendered in exchange.[284] Priority in acquiring title is also given to makers of significant improvements to the property (subject to payment for the value of the property in its original state).[285] This provision was intended to respond to the reality that over the years displaced persons on both sides, who had been given possession of abandoned properties, had added rooms for their expanded families, or have built new homes and business premises on previously vacant land. Yet under the plan it applies to any 'owner' of improvement, and is not limited to users of the property. In addition, the cut-off date for improvements that gives priority in acquiring title has moved during the negotiations, and the intended property board was also given discretion to grant title or compensation even for later improvements, made after the cut-off date.[286]

280 Palley, *International Relations Debacle*, 168.

281 Annan Plan, Foundation Agreement, Annex II, Article 7(1).

282 Annan Plan, Foundation Agreement, Annex III, Article 7(2).

283 Palley, *International Relations Debacle*, 228–229.

284 Annan Plan, Foundation Agreement, Main Article 10(3)(d), Annex VII, Article 12(1), (2). The exchange would be possible if the value of the property under dispute does not exceed that of the surrendered property by more than 50 per cent. The ten years can be counted cumulatively for different users. This extension protects recent purchasers. Annan Plan, Annex VII, Article 13.

285 Annan Plan, Foundation Agreement, Main Article 10(3)(e), Annex VII, Article 14, Attachment 4, Article 3.

286 Eventually determined as 31 December 2002. Annex VII Article 14 combined with Attachment 1 Article 1 item 15. There are other provisions in the Annan plan which the Greek-Cypriot side regards as encouraging property development at the expense of dispossessed persons: Annex VII, Articles 7, 18, Annex VII, Attachment 4, Article 3.

The Annan Plan thereby provided an incentive for commercial investors, rather than only for current occupants, to build in the TRNC on property otherwise eligible for reinstatement to lawful owners.[287] As a result, a provision originally introduced for humanitarian purposes has become commercially exploitable.[288] Once the entire plan has been shelved, these guarantees are no longer in effect, but the same humanitarian need that led to the provisions for 'significant improvement' in the first place will likely reappear, with a new cut-off date. The question is whether it will be possible to distinguish between bona fide improvements based on humanitarian needs and those initiated at the last minute (or later) by commercial opportunism. The 2005 IPC Law also takes account of improvements to the property in giving priority to current occupants in acquiring ownership. The cut-off date is the day of the IPC's decision in a claim. This also invites rush improvements in order to obstruct restoration, either immediately or even after a claim has been lodged.

A different aspect of the good-faith requirement concerns the ability of purchasers to know the provenance of the property. The TRNC reportedly denies access to records concerning pre-1974 ownership,[289] thereby preventing potential purchasers from ascertaining the legal status of the land. On the one hand, if purchasers cannot verify the status of property, they cannot be held responsible if it transpires that the property is that of a dispossessed person.[290] On the other hand, a person who chooses to purchase property in the TRNC despite the inability to ascertain the history of the property assumes the responsibility for whatever is later revealed, and cannot claim to have acted in good faith. This holds true at least for foreigners, who have no compelling need to purchase property in the TRNC. In the course of negotiating the Annan Plan, the TRNC apparently attempted to protect investors by proposing a new definition of a bona fide purchaser, which included a person 'who acquires an interest in affected property in good faith and for value, whether or not s/he knew

[287] This was admitted by the TRNC Minister of Finance. Palley, *International Relations Debacle*, 189–190. In addition, under Annex VII, Article 18, improvements that increase the value of the property by 10 per cent or more were also compensable. Thus any improver could safely start building and expect compensation if the value of the improvement was at least 10 per cent of the value of the property.

[288] Palley, *International Relations Debacle*, 191.

[289] Simon Bahceli, 'Who's Land Is This? – Information Restricted on Pre-1974 Property Ownership in North', *Cyprus Mail*, 30 September 2004, www.cyprus-mail.com/cyprus/who-s-land-information-restricted-pre-1974-property-ownership-north.

[290] Compare with ECtHR, *Pincová and Pinc* v. *the Czech Republic*, [58].

the property to have been in the ownership of a dispossessed person'. The UN team refused to include this definition in the plan.[291]

The conditions under which third-country nationals who rely on the laws of the TRNC to purchase the property of displaced persons could qualify as bona fide buyers has become a major issue in light of the increasing construction activities in the TRNC and transactions involving Greek Cypriot properties that end up in the hands of third-country nationals. The matter has arisen in *Apostolides* v. *Orams and Orams* (2009), a case instituted in a Cypriot court by a Greek Cypriot against a British couple who had built a villa in the TRNC in what used to be his family's orchard. The defendants argued that they were bona fide buyers of the property. The Cypriot Supreme Court rejected this defence. It said that in view of the illegality of the TRNC, any bona fide buyers should be particularly vigilant and cautious by examining any ownership title in depth and upon independent legal advice. The defendants should have requested additional data from the competent authorities of the only recognized and legal state that could provide them with information as to the legal ownership of the land, namely the Republic of Cyprus. Not having taken this simple step, the defendants did not act as bona fide buyers.[292] The Cypriot courts ordered that the defendants demolish the villa and compensate the plaintiff. When the plaintiff was unable to enforce the judgment in the TRNC, he sought to have it enforced in the UK.[293]

Non-proprietary rights of current occupants are protected if they have used the property for at least ten years and if the dispossessed owner had neither built the house nor lived in it for at least ten years. They are then entitled to maintain residence in the property without acquiring title.[294] The Annan Plan also protects from eviction current occupants who are Cypriot nationals without sufficient financial means, until alternative accommodation is made available, in kind or through preferential loans.[295] The lengthy periods of delays in reinstatement (six years at the earliest in most cases,[296] indefinitely in some) might result in

[291] Cited in Palley, *International Relations Debacle*, 191.

[292] *Orams and Orams* v. *Apostolides (Appeal)*.

[293] UK, *Orams and Orams* v. *Apostolides*, [25]. The ECJ has since given a preliminary ruling that the judgment was enforceable. ECJ, *Apostolides* v. *Orams and Orams*, [4]. For a discussion of the ECJ preliminary ruling see Bryant and Hatay, 'Suing for Sovereignty', 6.

[294] Annan Plan, Annex VII, Article 16(3).

[295] Annan Plan, Foundation Agreement, Annex VII, Attachment 3, Article 2(1).

[296] Annan Plan, Annex VII, Articles 16, 17, Attachment 3, Articles 1, 2.

reinstatement remaining largely illusory.[297] Non-nationals are protected from eviction until alternative accommodation is found, for up to two years.[298] However, since this protection is contingent upon the right to remain in Cyprus, settlers might not come within its purview.

Anticipated impact of the plan

The Annan Plan offers extensive protection to current occupants of property of involuntarily dispossessed owners. It grants them both the right to remain in the property and the right to acquire proprietary rights in it. The jurisprudence of the ECtHR further narrows down the rights of dispossessed owners to restoration of their property, in its rejection of the existence of a right to a 'home' under ECHR Article 8, in respect of property in which there has never been any, or has been hardly any, occupation, or where there has been no occupation for a considerable time.[299] Accordingly, while the right of dispossessed owners to their property remains intact despite the passage of time, realization of this right may legitimately be confined to compensation rather than reinstatement.

The perceived preferential treatment of current occupants had a crucial role in the Greek Cypriot rejection of the Annan Plan in 2004.[300] When negotiations between the Greek Cypriot and Turkish Cypriot communities resumed in 2008, they firmly expressed the expectation that the interests of dispossessed owners prevail over the rights of current users.[301]

In *Demopoulos and Others* v. *Turkey* (2010), the ECtHR for the first time considered the 'general context' of the conflict in which the property claims arose, including the Annan Plan.[302] Particularly the protraction of the conflict was crucial to the court's determination that the 2005 IPC Law is an adequately effective local remedy, despite the fact that it does not guarantee reinstatement of property.[303] The court did not explicate how the plan is relevant to its ruling, but its citation of the provisions in the plan that parallel the 2005 IPC Law suggests that it uses the Annan Plan as a yardstick by which to measure the adequacy of the redress mechanism

297 Palley, *International Relations Debacle*, 193.
298 Annan Plan, Foundation Agreement, Annex VII, Attachment 3, Article 2(3).
299 ECtHR, *Demopoulos and Others* v. *Turkey*, [136].
300 Palley, *International Relations Debacle*, 193.
301 Interview by the author with Dr Kudret Özersay, Eastern Mediterranean University, Lefkoşa, 27–28 February 2008.
302 ECtHR, *Demopoulos and Others* v. *Turkey*, [4]–[16].
303 ECtHR, *Demopoulos and Others* v. *Turkey*, [83]–[86], [113].

in the 2005 IPC Law. Indeed, in some respects the priority of reinstatement over compensation is more stringently protected under the 2005 IPC Law than under the Annan Plan.[304] Thus, while formally the Annan Plan is not binding on any party, its content appears to be the baseline for informing the legitimacy of TRNC actions. Since what the ECtHR now acknowledges as valid under the *Namibia* exception will likely survive the process of transition, the Annan Plan has in effect already prejudged the future arrangements in Cyprus.

7.4 Conclusions

The cases analysed above present a range of problems and circumstances. There is little reason to expect that the balance in all post-transition regimes would be identical, given the different causes for conflict, land policies, political aims of the balancing process and financial and other constraints. Nevertheless, a number of factors appear to be relevant in shaping those policies.

The impact of any prospective change on the social, legal and institutional stability of the country must be taken into account. While prima facie this consideration militates against any change, reversion to the *status quo ante* or otherwise, in the case of transition from illegal regimes it seems to have had relatively little importance. First, in most of the post-transition regimes, legal stability was discarded in favour of an overhaul of the tenets and content of the legal system aimed at removing the scourges of previous, undemocratic regimes. In Cyprus, the only one of the cases where there is no issue of an overhaul of the legal system (although institutional changes are perceived as essential), stability with respect to the land regime is an ambiguous concept. Already now, two legal systems are operating simultaneously: the domestic law of the TRNC, under which grants by the TRNC government are valid, and the jurisprudence of the ECtHR, which has so far rejected the validity of titles based on TRNC legislation but is binding upon Turkey as well as upon the Republic of Cyprus. Under the circumstances, it is difficult to determine what is the prevailing system on the basis of which individuals can legitimately develop expectations, and which

[304] Under the 2005 IPC Law, Article 8(2)(B), current occupants may acquire the property only if its value has more than doubled since its abandonment in 1974. Cited in ECtHR, *Demopoulos and Others* v. *Turkey*, [37]. Under the Annan Plan, the priority of current occupants requires only a 10 per cent improvement.

should therefore continue to prevail. The endorsement by the ECtHR of the TRNC redress mechanism may go a long way towards bridging this gap.

Reversion to the *status quo ante* with respect to land rights, regardless of its qualifications and modification, is a financially costly and complex process. In addition to the immediate costs of administration,[305] it may have a long-term impact on the country's economy. For example, in the Baltic states and South Africa it hindered other land reforms. In the TRNC, with the recent exploitation of foreign tourism, the immediate repercussions of undoing current uses would be very costly. The situation is different in Timor-Leste, with respect to both administration and state economy. In the absence of land records, the establishment of any regime is costly.[306] Furthermore, the continuous mis-utilization of land and the waves of violence and displacement even after the withdrawal of the Indonesian regime have debilitated the economy so profoundly, and the prevailing situation is so precarious, that reversion to the *status quo ante* has no advantage over other potential land regimes.

In light of the economic significance of land regimes, one would have expected economic and other utilitarian considerations to play a central role in the land policy of the post-transition regimes. Yet practice indicates differently. The Baltic states embarked upon restoration despite its prohibitive cost. In South Africa restoration is pursued as the primary land reform measure despite the fact that redistribution and tenure reform would have a much greater effect, and are hindered by the slowness of restoration. In Timor-Leste the situation is the reverse: land issues were continuously avoided despite the vital necessity to regulate them in order to build a state economy. Clearly, the political and symbolic significance of a land regime outweighs its economic significance when it comes to policy formulation.

The political decision on reversion to the *status quo ante* may be related to the international dimensions of the conflict. First, there is an unarticulated link between private property rights and territorial claims that

[305] Kuddo, 'Aspects of the Restitution of Property and Land in Estonia', 163; Foster, 'Restitution of Expropriated Property', 642–643.

[306] Louise Martinovic, 'The Three R's of Land Policy in East Timor: Recognition, Restitution, Reform' (Research Unit Faculty of Law, the Australian National University, 2001), 29.

emerges in the context of an illegal regime. Accordingly, where the boundaries (as well as existence) of future political entities are controversial, land disputes have to be taken in a wider context. There is, of course, a difference between a territorial claim of a political entity on the international level, and a private-property claim of an individual. However, private property carries political weight. The aggregation of Turkish Cypriot claims to land in the TRNC, for example, does not in itself establish a right of the TRNC to territory under international law. In practice, however, Greek Cypriot property has gradually become part of the social and economic fabric of the north,[307] leading to potential legalization (in a future settlement, and already in practice under ECtHR jurisprudence) of the existing situation by allowing occupants to acquire ownership, and by limitations on the right of internally displaced Cypriots to return to their homes. This in turn allows the consolidation of separate territorial entities within Cyprus (the constituent states). In *Demopoulos and Others* v. *Turkey* the ECtHR objected to the use of individual property rights as a vehicle for the vindication of norms applying between states.[308] However, by refusing reliance on the rights of dispossessed owners to reverse the consolidation of separate territorial units, it effectively advanced reliance on the individual property and other interests of current occupants to advance that consolidation. Either way, individual interests serve as a vehicle for political goals.

Another important political element in land policy may be the link between demography and land rights.[309] In some cases it was assumed that adjustment of land rights would either induce or facilitate departure of settlers or other persons associated with the illegal regime. In the Baltic states this was most apparent, as restoration was aimed at encouraging the departure of Soviet-era settlers. In Timor-Leste ownership of real estate is reserved to Timorese nationals. In Cyprus, the failure of the Annan Plan to link the right to property with Cypriot nationality was one of the factors in the objections of the Republic of Cyprus to the Annan Plan.[310] Even in Zimbabwe, the incentive for owners to sell their property was the lucrative terms of remittance; this indicates the government's assumption

[307] Ayla Gürel, 'Population and Property Issues in Divided Cyprus' (2008) (on file with the author), 4.
[308] ECtHR, *Demopoulos and Others* v. *Turkey*, [115].
[309] Compare with UNGA Resolution 59/124 (10 December 2004).
[310] Palley, *International Relations Debacle*, 227–230.

that individuals' choices on property coincide with their preferences with regard to residence and emigration.

Another explanation for the practice of the post-transition regimes of formally reverting to the *status quo ante* is the direct effect of land regimes on individuals. Unlike other issues examined in this book, any policy adopted with respect to land rights has a direct, immediate and visible effect on individuals within the post-transition regime's population. Where the illegal regime systematically violated the human rights of these individuals, as was usually the case with respect to most of the illegal regimes examined, the choice between reversion to the *status quo ante* and maintenance of the situation seems predetermined: unless the post-transition regime reverted to the *status quo ante*, it would be collaborating with the illegal regime or its legacy. When the matter is examined from this perspective, the question is not why the post-transition regimes opted for reversion to the *status quo ante* in the Baltic states, South Africa or the TRNC, but why they did not revert to the *status quo ante* in Zimbabwe, Namibia and Timor-Leste.

With respect to Rhodesia and Namibia the answer lies in the process which led to transition. In both cases, the White population was co-opted into the transition by, inter alia, the guarantee of its property rights. Hostile action by the governments to strip that population of its rights would have prevented the deal that permitted transition. With respect to Timor-Leste, three factors weigh against reversion to the pre-Indonesian regime. First, by the time a new land regime was contemplated, two waves of displacement had already occurred. Reversion to the Portuguese regime would mean undoing not one set of changes but three. In addition, by 2010 hostility towards Indonesia is less of a driving force than is frustration with domestic disorder and unrest. Third, reversion to the Portuguese land regime holds little promise for the Timorese. This land regime was itself tainted by the flaws of colonialism and corruption; close to forty years after its demise, there is no reason to resurrect it artificially for reasons of principle.

Even when the post-transition regime opts for reversion to the *status quo ante* with respect to land, its ability to do so is severely curtailed by international human rights law. Opposite the political goals and the individual right to property which reversion to the *status quo ante* serves, stand the rights of long-term current occupants. Whether those are proprietary rights or not, they often prevent the dispossessed owners from recuperating their property in kind. One might query whether dispossessed owners are better served by restoration of property encumbered by tenants than they would be by compensation for the value of the property. Considered together with its prohibitive cost, reversion to the *status quo ante* thus has little to recommend itself, other than its power in making a strong political statement, both domestically and internationally. The strength of this political statement is considered further in Chapter 8.

8 Conclusions: Non-recognition and transition

This book concerns the tension between the illegality of a territorial regime (reflected in the principle *ex injuria jus non oritur* and upheld by the obligation of non-recognition), and its effectiveness (reflected in the principle *ex factis jus oritur*). It examines the manner in which this tension informs the policy of post-transition regimes, namely the extent to which post-transition regimes attempt to reverse the factual situation created by preceding illegal regimes, and the extent to which they succeed, in light of the legal and political constraints in which they operate.

Under international law, acts that are in contravention of a peremptory norm are invalid *ab initio*. When a territorial regime is created in violation of such norms, its illegality and the invalidity of its acts are upheld by the obligation of non-recognition. The goal of this obligation is to ensure that the illegal regime cannot consolidate itself in the territory. This is intended to induce that regime to withdraw, thereby bringing the violation of the peremptory norm to an end.

However, in reality the power of non-recognition is limited, and illegal regimes have managed to exist for lengthy periods of time. At times the weakness of non-recognition lay in its non-uniform application, for example in the cases of the Soviet annexation of the Baltic states and the Indonesian annexation of Timor-Leste. In other cases, the illegal regime was strong enough to withstand isolation. Such was the case of Rhodesia. In many cases, the fact that an illegal regime consists of annexation by a recognized state enabled the marginalization of the illegality and the assimilation of the illegal conduct into the conduct of the sovereign state. In all these situations, a gap emerges between the effectiveness of the illegal regime's conduct and its invalidity under international law. It is this gap that the post-transition regime must bridge when it comes into power.

The illegality of a previous regime does not automatically lead to the invalidity of all its acts and their consequences. For one thing, the scope of the obligation of non-recognition is debatable, even during the existence of the illegal regime. The *Namibia Advisory Opinion* excludes from non-recognition acts the non-recognition of which would act to the detriment of the population. One approach to this formulation is that the obligation prohibits recognition only of acts which strengthen the status of the illegal regime by acknowledging its capacity to act in the public sphere, or which contribute directly to the entrenchment of the illegal regime in the territory. A different approach, advocated in this book, is that the obligation of non-recognition is not limited by the content or purpose of an act, but extends to all acts of the illegal regime. Correspondingly, the exception to non-recognition is not restricted by content or purpose, but can apply to any act, depending on the effect of non-recognition in the specific circumstances, which should therefore be considered on a case-by-case basis. As discussed in Chapter 3, international human rights law has led to a remarkable expansion of this exceptional recognition, to the effect that non-recognition may have become a tool applicable almost exclusively in inter-state relations.

Once the illegal regime has ceased to exist, non-recognition is no longer imperative. One of the issues examined in this book has therefore been the extent to which post-transition regimes have upheld the illegality of the previous regimes and have chosen to maintain the consequences of non-recognition. In southern Africa, the illegality of the regimes was largely set aside, making way for dealing with broader issues of transition to democratic rule. The same issues that underlay the illegality often continued to beleaguer the regime, although they were dealt with as violations of international human rights law. In other cases, illegality of the previous regime held a more central role in shaping the policy of the post-transition regime.

This book has examined diverse transitional processes. Some took place in southern Africa, others in Europe, the Middle East and Oceania; some were consensual, others unilateral; in some the illegality manifested itself only domestically while in others there was a stronger international element. The illegal regimes dated from different periods in time, from 1940 to the late 1970s, the transitional processes themselves spreading from 1980 to the future. Not surprisingly, then, the practices of the post-transition regimes are varied. Yet within this variety, a number of patterns are nonetheless discernible. The following sections address these patterns as they emerge from the individual chapters, as well as the overall picture that they portray of the process of transition.

8.1 Reversion to the *status quo ante* versus continuity

Chapter 4 illustrated that by and large, on the inter-state level, the invalidity of international acts of the unlawful regimes (particularly with regard to treaties) was upheld even after transition. Consequently, the validity of prior treaties was not affected by the existence of the illegal regime, although those treaties were temporarily suspended. Upon the disappearance of the illegal regime they were formally reactivated, even if only to be terminated or replaced immediately due to their unsuitability to modern needs. As for treaties purportedly entered into by the illegal regime on behalf of the disputed territories, a doctrinal analysis indicates that they are invalid *ab initio*, but in practice this has not entirely prevented illegal regimes and their counterparts from acting upon them. Transitional arrangements have been characterized by open-ended formulations, which preserve the post-transition regime's freedom to maintain the relations created under these invalid treaties. Yet despite having reserved their right to succeed to seemingly invalid treaties of the illegal regime, in practice post-transition regimes have not simply succeeded to such treaties. Instead they have sought fresh consent of counterpart states to duplicate the invalid treaties or replace them. Where the post-transition regimes and their counterparts preferred to continue practice that commenced under the illegal regime, this was done by adopting new instruments rather than by validating illegal action. In short, post-transition regimes have upheld the invalidity of treaty relations conducted by the illegal regimes on behalf of their territories.

Chapter 5 demonstrated that under the domestic law of the post-transition regime, acts carried out by the illegal regime, including those which called for non-recognition at the time, have by and large been validated upon transition. The principal reason for this choice is pragmatism. An overhaul of the legal system is a costly and destabilizing process, which is most difficult to justify on political grounds alone. In some contexts, particularly criminal law, such an overhaul is also limited by law. But the continuity in domestic law must be qualified: practice of the post-transition regimes reveals an interesting pattern of engaging, with different levels of enthusiasm and success, in reversion to the *status quo ante* with respect to two areas of law: residence (and nationality) and property rights in land.

Before turning to an examination of these specific areas of law, it is useful to consider the difference between transition with regard to treaty relations and transition with regard to domestic law. In the former, invalidity of the illegal regime's acts was largely upheld. In the latter, it was not. Why were opposite policies adopted? Clearly, political factors were at play with regard to both issues. Nevertheless, the relative uniformity in policy among the post-transition regimes, despite the significant differences in their circumstances, suggests that some underlying principles of law may have also informed the process.

One difference between the domestic legal order and international relations which impacts on the policy of continuity or reversion to the *status quo ante* is the basic norm on which they operate. The legal order against which treaty relations are examined (upon transition) is the same one that applied previously, namely international law. There is no rupture in this order at the stage of transition. The post-transition regime must therefore take cognizance of the fact that its practice reflects on the previous legal situation. Thus opting for continuity from the illegal regime to the post-transition regime may be interpreted as an endorsement of the illegal regime, regardless of any 'no-prejudice' statements that may exist to the contrary. If internal coherence is to be maintained within the international order, affirmation of the previous regime's illegality and of the invalidity of its acts necessitates formal reversion to the *status quo ante*.

The continuity of the legal system on which inter-state relations are conducted implies that rights and legitimate expectations created under that legal system must be respected. The only policy that the post-transition regime can clearly adopt unilaterally without infringing upon these rights and expectations is that of pursuing the legal consequences of non-recognition on which other states have legitimately relied. Any policy other than continuity requires the consent of third parties. Those may be only too happy to give this consent, thereby alleviating many practical difficulties; until then, as a matter of law, the post-transition regime is constrained in its actions.

The situation is different with regard to the domestic law of the post-transition regime, which is constitutionally independent from the domestic law of the preceding regime. Even if it appears to be identical to it, this is only a matter of semblance. The basic norm of the post-transition regime's law is the sovereignty of that regime, rather than any purported authority or effective control of the preceding regime. There is therefore no room for a presumption of internal coherence of a legal order, against which the policy of the post-transition regime has to be measured.

Since, unlike treaty relations, domestic law is not contractual, prima facie the post-transition regime has a great measure of freedom in opting for apparent continuity with or making a clean break from the law of the illegal regime. However, in practice the post-transition regime is not free from legal constraints. The choice with respect to domestic law, too, must take account of the legitimate expectations of individual parties. In some contexts, the post-transition regime is bound by continuity of rights granted in accordance with the law of the illegal regime, for example under the doctrine of acquired rights, which preserves private rights through changes of international personality. In addition, international human rights law requires the post-transition regime to recognize the legal effect of criminal norms of the illegal regimes, in order to avoid retroactive penalization. More generally, international human rights law obligates the post-transition regime to take account of changes that have taken place in the territory, which generate new legal relations that it must respect. This is evident in those areas of law where post-transition regimes characteristically attempt to revert to the *status quo ante*, namely residence and rights in land.

8.2 Exceptions to continuity in domestic law: residence and rights in land

There are two areas of domestic law in which post-transition regimes tend to avoid giving effect to acts of the illegal regime: residence (and nationality) of settlers, and rights in property. In these areas, post-transition regimes have been less than tolerant towards the conduct of the illegal regime, and opted for reversion to the legal *status quo ante*, albeit at varying degrees of insistence and with varying degrees of success. In the southern African states, residence of settlers was a minor issue. In Namibia there was no settler population to speak of, in the TBVC it was of no numerical significance, and in Zimbabwe it was indistinguishable from the White population pre-existing the illegal regime. In contrast, in the three other cases the post-transition regimes took clear formal stances that rejected the notion of residential or national status created under the illegal regime. With respect to land rights, in many instances the post-transition regimes have insisted on reversion to a *status quo ante*. This insistence is most striking in those cases where it stood in the way of effective land reforms which were also undertaken by the post-transition regime, for example in South Africa and the Baltic states. In Timor-Leste the inability to decide on the validity of Indonesian titles resulted in a decade-long stalemate, with the resolution of conflicts being actively explored only after a new wave of displacement threw Timor-Leste into upheaval.

Yet even in the areas of residence and land rights, the post-transition regime is not entirely free to pursue any policy. While the illegality of the previous illegal regime may have precluded it from granting valid status, changes that have been caused by that regime's conduct may give rise to internationally recognized human rights claims that the post-transition regime must respect. Such respect does not constitute continuity of law from the illegal regime, but continuity of practice. For example, grantees of land might not be entitled to proprietary rights, but they might be entitled to continue residing on the land, on the basis of their effective use of a residence under the pretence of ownership for a significant period of time, which substantiates their right to privacy of the home. The acknowledgement of such rights under the law of the post-transition regime constitutes a confirmation not of the legal validity of the acts of the illegal regime, but of the emergence of international human rights entitlements on the basis of relevant practice.

8.3 Reversion to the *status quo ante* and the requisites of statehood

Taking a step back from the detailed discussion of each area of law as provided in the individual chapters, an overall picture emerges from this study. The three areas of law in which post-transition regime did not adopt the policy of the illegal regime as their own correspond directly to the requisites of statehood – population, territory and international relations. This correspondence is not random. Illegal regimes present a challenge in international law because they fulfil the traditional requisites of effectiveness required for the existence of sovereignty – of an independent state, or of a territorial acquisition by an existing state. These requisites disappear when the illegal regime ceases to exist. However, just as legal nullity through non-recognition does not prevent the factual existence of the illegal regime, the latter's formal disappearance does not necessarily prevent the consolidation of its characteristics as a matter of fact. Insofar as the post-transition regime is concerned, removal of the illegal regime entails not only the rejection of that regime's formal existence, which is no longer at issue, but the removal of its substantive characteristics on the political level. Against the background of this challenge, the specific areas of concern of post-transition regimes in rejecting the acts of the illegal regime are all too obvious.

Obviously, rights in land of individuals are not identical to territorial acquisitions by entities claiming international status. However, despite the fact that land rights are a matter of domestic law, they have an international impact, since they are the tangible expression of the claim to territory. The illegal regime may not be able to perpetuate its territorial claim by transferring land to its population under domestic law. But at least where the boundaries of the post-transition regime are negotiable, the aggregation of private claims can carry political weight, particularly if the question of land is regulated in conjunction with the issue of residence of settlers. It is therefore not surprising that post-transition regimes hasten to overturn, as far as they can, any land titles that the illegal regimes may have purported to create. The same is true with respect to residence. Removal of settlers is aimed at protecting the post-transition regime from absorbing the political weight injected into the territory by the illegal regime through its settlers and their influence on the character of the post-transition regime.

By refusing to give effect to the acts of an illegal regime in the areas of treaty relations, rights in land and residence, the post-transition regime guarantees that regardless of any eventual legal stance towards the illegal regime, its effectiveness is excluded. This policy is hardly a conscious attempt to uphold international law. Rather, it aims to achieve a political objective, identical to that which the law aims to achieve through non-recognition: the consolidation of the regime.

The reversion to the *status quo ante* with respect to rights in land, and particularly when combined with reversion to the *status quo ante* with respect to nationality and residence, is based on the perception that conflicts are characteristically between the local, indigenous population on the one hand, and settlers supported by the illegal regime on the other. It is assumed that vindication of the rights of the local population acts to the detriment of settlers. However, the situation is rarely that simple. Controversies that have been framed as conflicts between the illegal regime and its associates on the one hand, and the indigenous population of the post-transition regime on the other, are often actually conflicts among members of the local population. In Timor-Leste, awareness of this was one of the causes of procrastination in resolving the land problem. The bulk of land disputes in Timor-Leste are not between the Timorese and the Indonesians or the Portuguese, but among the Timorese themselves. Whichever way the disputes are resolved, the likelihood of obtaining a common national sense of historical redress to injustice is unlikely. There is no common 'other' against whom grievances are held. In the Baltic states and South Africa, insufficient attention to the internal dimension of the conflict has led the reversion to the *status quo ante* to result in some unintended fallout. Rather than a perceived dispute between the local population and settlers, or between the deprived and the usurpers, reversion to the *status quo ante* has exposed internal conflict within the local population, at times resulting in fragmentation rather than a cohesive stance towards the previous regime based on its illegality.

8.4 The effect of international human rights law on reversion to the *status quo ante*

International human rights law has had a decisive effect on the freedom of action of post-transition regimes, severely curtailing the attempt to return to the *status quo ante*. Not only does it invite an expansive interpretation of the *Namibia* exception, which may later bind the post-transition regime, it also restricts the post-transition regime's ability to reverse the acts of the illegal regime, to the extent that it may have to resign itself, to a large degree, to the situation created by the illegal regime.

Clearly, there is difficulty in pursuing what is essentially a political goal (removal of the legacy of the illegal regime) through measures which directly affect individuals. In the ECtHR, Turkey has repeatedly made the claim that complaints against it should not be admissible since they emanate from a political conflict which should be resolved through political means. The ECtHR has by and large rejected this argument, refusing to allow the human rights regime to be brushed aside by political processes. Although the content and scope of human rights are inevitably shaped by the particular circumstances of the situation, including the political context within which they are considered, as a legal order, human rights are applicable at all times. Conversely, the ECtHR has refused to allow human rights law to be the vehicle for advancing political goals. A third aspect of the independence of human rights law from political considerations is the fact that the process of transition is subject to international human rights considerations. International human rights law entails the fragmentation of a policy of reversion to the *status quo ante* into an accumulation of particularized, and not clearly tenable, interferences with human rights. The political dimensions of the conflict may be present in the evaluation of a specific situation, but they do not alone govern the matter. Instead, the post-transition regime may be constrained by the international human rights entitlements that have accrued through the practice of the illegal regime.

8.5 Conclusion

Both on the inter-state level and on the domestic one, reversion to the *status quo ante* has proven difficult and has rarely led to a reversal of acts already carried out by the illegal regime. Policy and legal considerations have led post-transition regimes to follow pre-existing practice. If non-recognition fails to prevent changes on the ground, it has few *ex post facto* ramifications. If the illegal regime succeeds in withstanding a policy of non-recognition, the long-term risks to it are minimal, and it stands to gain much and lose little. In this respect, emergence from an illegal regime is not very different from emergence from a legal regime with the adoption of a clean-slate policy. The power of non-recognition as a means of enforcing international law is limited. If it fails politically to incentivize an illegal regime to revert to legality, it also does not preserve the freedom of action of the post-transition regime. When all is said and done, non-recognition has proven to be a weak tool of international law enforcement.

Selected bibliography

All Internet sources are correct as of 30 June 2010, unless otherwise noted.

The following list includes the main sources mentioned in this work, as well as principal background material consulted.

SELECTED BOOKS, ARTICLES AND THESES

Akweenda, Sackey, *International Law and the Protection of Namibia's Territorial Integrity: Boundaries and Territorial Claims* (The Hague: Kluwer Law International, 1997)

Andersen, Erik André, 'The Legal Status of Russians in Estonian Privatisation Legislation 1989–1995' (1997) 49 *Europe-Asia Studies* 303

Anonymous, 'Taking Reichs Seriously: German Unification and the Law of State Succession' (1990) 104 *Harvard Law Review* 588

Asmal, Kader, 'The Role and Status of SWAPO in International Law', in Brian Wood (ed.), *Namibia 1884–1984: Readings on Namibia's History and Society* (London: Namibia Support Committee, 1984)

Aust, Anthony, *Modern Treaty Law and Practice* (Cambridge: Cambridge University Press, 2000)

Babo Soares, Dionisio, 'Challenges for the Future', in James J. Fox and Dionisio Babo Soares (eds.), *Out of the Ashes: Destruction and Reconstruction of East Timor* (Adelaide: Crawford House, 2003)

Barrie, George N., 'The "Absorption" of Bophuthatswana March 1994: Extinction of State Personality from a South African Perspective, Irrelevancy from an International Perspective' (1994) *Tydskrif Vir Die Suid-Afrikaans Reg (Journal of South African Law)* 348

Barrington, Lowell W., 'The Making of Citizenship Policy in the Baltic states' (1999) 13 *Georgetown Immigration Law Journal* 159

Bello Hippler, Judith and Bekker, Peter H. F., 'East Timor (Port. v. Austl.)' (1996) 90 *American Journal of International Law* 94

Bello Hippler, Judith, Kokott, Juliane and Rudole, Feate, 'Loizidou v. Turkey' (1996) 90 *American Journal of International Law* 98

Benvenisti, Eyal, *The International Law of Occupation* (Princeton, NJ: Princeton University Press, 1993)

Benvenisti, Eyal, 'Responsibility for the Protection of Human Rights under the Interim Israeli–Palestinian Agreements' (1994) 28 *Israel Law Review* 297

Blacksell, Mark and Born, Karl Martin, 'Private Property Restitution: The Geographical Consequences of Official Government Policies in Central and Eastern Europe' (2002) 168 *Geographical Journal* 178

Blay, S. K. N., 'Self-Determination in Cyprus: The New Dimensions of an Old Conflict' (1981–1983) 10 *Australian Yearbook of International Law* 67

Blix, Hans M., 'Contemporary Aspects of Recognition' (1970-II) 130 *Recueil des cours de l'Académie de droit international de la Haye* 589

Bodenstein, Jobst, 'Elections' (1995) 6 *South African Human Rights Yearbook* 74

Bokor-Szegõ, Hanna, 'Questions of State Identity and State Succession in Eastern and Central Europe', in Mojmir Mrak (ed.), *Succession of States* (The Hague: Martinus Nijhoff, 1999)

Booysen, Hercules, 'Succession to Delictual Liability: A Namibian Precedent' (1991) 24 *Comparative and International Law Journal of South Africa* 205

Botha, Neville, 'To Pay or Not to Pay: Namibian Liability for South African Delicts' (1992–1993) 18 *South African Yearbook of International Law* 156

Brennan, Frank, 'The Timor Sea's Oil and Gas: What's Fair' (North Sydney Catholic Social Justice Series, No. 51, 2004)

Briggs, Herbert W., 'Non-recognition in the Courts: The Ships of the Baltic Republics' (1943) 37 *American Journal of International Law* 585

Brooks, Pierre E. J., 'The Recognition and Enforcement of Foreign Judgments in Transkei, Bophuthatswana and Venda' (1979) 5 *South African Yearbook of International Law* 1

Brownlie, Ian, *International Law and the Use of Force by States* (Oxford: Clarendon Press, 1963)

Brownlie, Ian, *International Law and the Use of Force by States Revisited* (Oxford: Europaeum, 2001)

Brownlie, Ian, 'Recognition in Theory and Practice' (1982) 53 *British Yearbook of International Law* 197

Brubaker, W. Rogers, 'Citizenship Struggles in Soviet Successor States' (1992) 26 *International Migration Review* 269

Bryant, Rebecca and Hatay, Mete, 'Suing for Sovereignty: Property, Territory, and the EU's Cyprus Problem', Global Political Trends Centre Policy Brief (2009)

Budlender, Geoff, 'Urban Land Issues in the 1980s: The View from Weiler's Farm', in Christina Murray and Catherine O'Regan (eds.), *No Place to Rest: Forced Removals and the Law in South Africa* (Oxford: Oxford University Press, 1990)

Budrytė, Dovilė, 'Today's Politics and Yesterday's Embitterments: Ethnic Restructuring and Its Aftermath in the Baltic States', in Rainer Münz and Rainer Ohliger (eds.), *Diasporas and Ethnic Migrants: Germany, Israel and Post-Soviet Successor States in Comparative Perspective* (London: Frank Cass Publishers, 2003)

Cachalia, Firoz, 'A Report on the Convention for a Democratic South Africa' (1992) 8 *South African Journal on Human Rights* 249

Cahn, Hans J., 'The Responsibility of the Successor State for War Debts' (1950) 44 *American Journal of International Law* 477

Carey, Peter and Bentley, G. Carter (eds.), *East Timor at the Crossroads: The Forging of a Nation* (London: Cassell, 1995)

Carpenter, Gretchen, 'Constitutional Implications of the Reincorporation for the Homelands' (July 1990) 16(7) *South African Foundation Review* 4

Cassese, Antonio, *Self-Determination of Peoples: A Legal Reappraisal* (Cambridge: Cambridge University Press, 1995)

Charlesworth, Hilary, 'The New Australian Recognition Policy in Comparative Perspective' (1991) 18 *Melbourne University Law Review* 1

Chaskalson, Matthew, 'Stumbling towards Section 28: Negotiations over the Protection of Property Rights in the Interim Constitution' (1995) 11 *South African Journal on Human Rights* 222

Cheng, Tai-heng, *State Succession and Commercial Obligations* (Ardsley: Transnational, 2006)

Chinkin, Christine, 'Australia and East Timor in International Law', in *International Law and the Question of East Timor* (London: CIIR/IPJET, 1995)

Chitsike, Francis, 'A Critical Analysis of the Land Reform Programme in Zimbabwe', paper presented at the 2nd FIG Regional Conference, Marrakech, Morocco, 2–5 December 2003, www.fig.net/pub/morocco/proceedings/TS4/TS4_4_chitsike.pdf

Cichok, Mark A., 'Independence and Manipulation in the Russian–Baltic States Relationship: 1993–1997' (1999) 30 *Journal of Baltic Studies* 89

Cilliers, Andries, 'Reincorporation of Bophuthatswana and Certain Other States into the Republic of South Africa' (1993–1994) 19 *South African Yearbook of International Law* 93

Clapham, Andrew, 'Human Rights Obligations of Non-state Actors in Conflict Situations' (2006) 88 *International Review of the Red Cross* 491

Clark, Roger S., 'The "Decolonization" of East Timor and the United Nations Norms on Self-Determination and Aggression' (1995), updated and corrected version of article which appeared in (1980) 7 *Yale Journal of World Public Order* (on file with the author)

Clark, Roger S., 'East Timor, Indonesia, and the International Community' (2000) 14 *Temple International & Comparative Law Journal* 75

Clark, Roger S., 'The International League for Human Rights and South West Africa 1947–1957: The Human Rights NGO as Catalyst in the International Legal Process' (1981) 3 *Human Rights Quarterly* 101

Clark, Roger S., 'Obligations of Third States in the Face of Illegality – Ruminations Inspired by the Weeramantry Dissent in the Case Concerning East Timor', in Anthony Anghie and Gary Sturgess (eds.), *Legal Visions of the 21st Century: Essays in Honour of Judge Christopher Weeramantry* (The Hague: Kluwer Law International, 1998)

Clark, Roger S., 'Public International Law and Private Enterprise: Damages for a Killing in East Timor' (1996) 3 *Australian Journal of Human Rights* 21
Clark, Roger S., 'Timor Gap: The Legality of the "Treaty on the Zone of Cooperation in an Area between the Indonesian Province of East Timor and Northern Australia"' in Peter Carey and G. Carter Bentley (eds.), *East Timor at the Crossroads: The Forging of a Nation* (London: Cassell, 1995)
Clark, Roger S., 'UNTAET Regulation No 2000/15 and the Prosecution of Serious Criminal Offences Committed in East Timor during the Indonesian Occupation' (second draft, March 2001, on file with the author)
Cliffe, Lionel, with contributions by Ray Bush, Jenny Lindsay and Brian Mokopakgosi, *The Transition to Independence in Namibia* (Boulder, CO: Lynne Rienner, 1994)
Cohen, David, *Indifference and Accountability* (Honolulu: East–West Center, 2006)
Cooper, Allan D. (ed.), *Allies in Apartheid: Western Capitalism in Occupied Namibia* (Basingstoke: Macmillan, 1988)
Cosslett, Christopher, 'The Economics of "Illegal" Development – International Law and Natural Resource Exploitation in Namibia 1966–1986' (1987) 41 *Journal of International Affairs* 165
Cox, Marcus, 'The Dayton Agreement in Bosnia and Herzegovina: A Study of Implementation Strategies' (1998) 69 *British Yearbook of International Law* 210
Crawford, James, *The Creation of States in International Law*, 2nd edn (Oxford: Clarendon Press, 2006)
Crawford, James, 'The General Assembly, the International Court and Self-Determination', in James Crawford, *International Law as an Open System* (London: Cameron May, 2002)
Crawford, James, 'The Right of Self-Determination in International Law: Its Development and Future' in Philip Alston (ed.), *People's Rights* (Oxford: Oxford University Press, 2001)
Crawford, James, 'State Practice and International Law in Relation to Succession' (1998) 69 *British Yearbook of International Law* 85
Cumes, Guy, 'Murder as a Crime against Humanity in International Law: Choice of Law and Prosecution of Murder in East Timor' (2003) 11 *European Journal of Crime, Criminal Law and Criminal Justice* 40
Cummings, Richard M., 'The Rhodesian Unilateral Declaration of Independence and the Position of the International Community' (1973) 6 *New York University Journal of International Law & Policy* 57
Curtin Knight, Virginia, 'Namibia's Transition to Independence' (1989) 88 *Current History* 225
Czapliński, Wladislaw, 'International Legal Aspects of Polish–Lithuanian Relations' (1991–1992) 19 *Polish Yearbook of International Law* 31
Czapliński, Wladislaw, 'La continuité, l'identité et la succession d'états – évaluation de cas récents' (1993) 25 *Revue belge de droit international* 374
Davidow, Jeffery, *A Peace in Southern Africa: The Lancaster House Conference on Rhodesia, 1979* (published under the auspices of the Center for International Affairs, Harvard University, Epping Bokwer, 1984)

De Kieffer, Donald E. and Hartquist, David A., 'Transkei: A Legitimate Birth' (1978) 13 *New England Law Review* 428

De Smith, S. A., 'Southern Rhodesia Act 1965' (1966) 29 *Modern Law Review* 801

De Villiers, Bertus, 'Land Reform: Issues and Challenges, a Comparative Overview of Experiences in Zimbabwe, Namibia, South Africa and Australia' (Konrad Adenauer Foundation Occasional Papers, Johannesburg, 2003)

Denktaş, Rauf R., 'The Crux of the Cyprus Problem' (1999) 4 *Perceptions* 5

Devine, Dermott J., 'Banda's Case 1989: International-Law Implications' (1990) 107 *South African Law Journal* 434

Devine, Dermott J., 'International Law Tensions Arising from the South African Situation 1976–1986' (1987) *Acta Juridica* 165

Devine, Dermott J., 'Marine Resources and the Namibian Constitution' (1990–1991) 16 *South African Yearbook of International Law* 112

Devine, Dermott J., 'Maritime Conventions and the Reincorporation of the Coastal Homelands into South Africa' (1992–1993) 18 *South African Yearbook of International Law* 127

Devine, Dermott J., 'Recognition, Newly Independent States and General International Law' (1984) 10 *South African Yearbook of International Law* 18

Devine, Dermott J., 'The Relationship between International Law and Municipal Law in Light of the Constitution of the Republic of Namibia' (1994) 26 *Case Western Reserve Journal of International Law* 295

Devine, Dermott J., 'Status of Rhodesia in International Law' (1967) *Acta Juridica* 39

Devine, Dermott J., 'The Status of Rhodesia in International Law' (1973), (1974) and (1975) *Acta Juridica*

Dickinson, Edwin D., 'Recent Recognition Cases' (1925) 19 *American Journal of International Law* 263

Dickinson, Edwin D., 'Recognition Cases 1925–1930' (1931) 25 *American Journal of International Law* 214

Dodd, Clement H., *The Cyprus Imbroglio* (Huntingdon: Eothen, 1998)

Doob, Leonard W., 'Cypriot Patriotism and Nationalism' (1986) 30 *Journal of Conflict Resolution* 383

Dore, Isaak A., 'Recognition of Rhodesia and Traditional International Law: Some Conceptual Problems' (1980) 13 *Vanderbilt Journal of Transnational Law* 37

Dorodnova, Jekaterina, 'The Russian-Speaking Identity under the Latvian Language Policy', in Rainer Münz and Rainer Ohliger (eds.), *Diasporas and Ethnic Migrants: Germany, Israel and Post-Soviet Successor States in Comparative Perspective* (London: Frank Cass Publishers, 2003)

Doxey, Margaret, 'The Making of Zimbabwe: From Illegal to Legal Independence' (1982) 36 *Year Book of World Affairs* 150

Doxey, Margaret, 'Strategies in Multilateral Diplomacy: The Commonwealth, Southern Africa, and the NIEO' (1979–1980) 35 *International Journal* 329

Drew, Catriona, 'The East Timor Story: International Law on Trial' (2001) 12 *European Journal of International Law* 651

Dugard, John, 'Collective Non-recognition: The Failure of South Africa's Bantustan States', in *Boutros Boutros-Ghali Amicorum Discipulorumque Liber: Peace Development, Democracy* (Brussels: Bruylant, 1998) Volume I

Dugard, John, 'The Future of the TBVC "States"' (1992) 8 *South African Journal on Human Rights* iii

Dugard, John, 'Legal Aspects of Investment in Namibia (South West Africa)', in Roger Murray, Jo Morris, John Dugard and Neville Rubin (eds.), *The Role of Foreign Firms in Namibia: Studies on External Investment and Black Workers' Conditions in Namibia* (Uppsala: Africa Publications Trust, 1974) 183

Dugard, John, 'Public International Law' (1993) *Annual Survey of South African Law* 61

Dugard, John, *Recognition and the United Nations* (Cambridge: Grotius, 1987)

Dugard, John, 'Rhodesia: Does South Africa Recognize It as an Independent State?' (1977) 94 *South African Law Journal* 127

Dugard, John (ed.), *The South West Africa/Namibia Dispute: Documents and Scholarly Writings on the Controversy between South Africa and the United Nations* (Berkeley: University of California Press, 1973)

Dunn, James, *East Timor: A People Betrayed* (Milton: Jacaranda, 1983)

du Plessis, Jean, 'Slow Start on a Long Journey: Land Restitution Issues in East Timor, 1999–2001', in Scott Leckie (ed.), *Returning Home: Housing and Property Restitution Rights of Refugees and Displaced Persons* (Ardsley: Transnational, 2003)

du Plessis, Jean and Leckie, Scott, 'Housing, Property and Land Rights in East Timor: Proposals for an Effective Dispute Resolution and Claim Verification Mechanism' (UNCHS (Habitat), 31 May 2000 and 5 August 2000)

Ederington, L. Benjamin, 'Property as a Natural Institution: The Separation of Property from Sovereignty in International Law' (1997–1998) 13 *American University International Law Review* 263

Eekelaar, J. M., 'Rhodesia: The Abdication of Constitutionalism' (1969) 32 *Modern Law Review* 19

Eisemann, Pierre Michel and Koskenniemi, Martti (eds.), *State Succession: Codification Tested against the Facts* (Dordrecht: Martinus Nijhoff, 2000)

Elderton, Catherine, 'Land Issues and Independence' (paper presented at FAO/USP/RICS Foundation South Pacific Land Tenure Conflict Symposium on Transforming Land Conflict, University of the South Pacific, 10–12 April 2002), www.usp.ac.fj/fileadmin/files/faculties/islands/landmgmt/symposium/PAPER52CATH.PDF

Emiliou, Nicolas, 'Cypriot Import Certificates: Some Hot Potatoes' (1995) 20 *European Law Review* 202

Engers, J. F., 'The United States Travel and Identity Document for Namibians' (1971) 65 *American Journal of International Law* 571

Erasmus, Gerhard, 'Namibian Independence and the Release of Political Prisoners' (1988–1989) 14 *South African Yearbook of International Law* 137

Evans, Graham, 'Namibia – South Africa: Relations since Independence' (1992) 302 *Round Table* 293

Evans, Luther H., 'The General Principles Governing the Termination of a Mandate' (1932) 26 *American Journal of International Law* 735

Fawcett, J. E. S., 'Security Council Resolutions on Rhodesia' (1965–1966) 41 *British Yearbook of International Law* 103

Feldman, Merje, 'Justice in Space? The Restitution of Property Rights in Tallinn, Estonia' (1999) 6 *Cultural Geographies* 165

Feldmanis, Inesis, 'The Occupation of Latvia: Aspects of History and International Law' (2004), www.mfa.gov.lv/en/latvia/history/occupation-aspects/

Fischer, Georges, 'La non-reconnaissance du Transkei' (1976) 22 *Annuaire français de droit international* 63

Fitzmaurice, Sir Gerald, 'The General Principles of International Law Considered from the Standpoint of the Rule of Law' (1957-II) 92 *Recueil des cours de l'Academie de droit international de la Haye* 1

Fitzpatrick, Daniel, 'Brief Memorandum of Advice on a Transitional Land Law for Timor Leste' (Singapore, 2008)

Fitzpatrick, Daniel, *Land Claims in East Timor* (Australia: Asia Pacific, 2002)

Fitzpatrick, Daniel, 'Land Issues in a Newly Independent East Timor', research paper No. 21, 2000–2001 (Department of the Parliamentary Library, Australia, 2001)

Fitzpatrick, Daniel, 'Land Policy in Post-conflict Circumstances: Some Lessons from East Timor' (2001) *Journal of Humanitarian Assistance*, www.jha.ac/articles/a074.htm

Foster, Frances H., 'Restitution of Expropriated Property: Post-Soviet Lessons for Cuba' (1996) 34 *Columbia Journal of Transnational Law* 621

Fox, James J. and Babo Soares, Dionisio (eds.), *Out of the Ashes: Destruction and Reconstruction of East Timor* (Adelaide: Crawford House, 2003)

Francis, Laurel B., *State Succession to Rights and Obligations for Namibia* (Lusaka: UNIN, undated)

Freeman, Linda, 'The Contradictions of Independence: Namibia in Transition' (1991) 46 *International Journal (Canadian Institute of International Affairs)* 687

Gamarra, Yolanda, 'Current Questions of State Succession Relating to Multilateral Treaties', in Jan Klabbers, Martti Koskenniemi, Olivier Ribbelink and Andreas Zimmermann (eds.), *State Practice Regarding State Succession and Issues of Recognition: The Pilot Project of the Council of Europe* (The Hague: Kluwer Law International, 1999)

Garner, James W., 'Non-recognition of Illegal Territorial Annexations and Claims to Sovereignty' (1936) 30 *American Journal of International Law* 679

Gerner, Krisian and Hadlund, Stefan, *The Baltic States and the End of the Soviet Empire* (London: Routledge, 1993)

Goldblatt, Israel, *History of South West Africa from the Beginning of the Nineteenth Century* (Cape Town: Juta, 1971)

Goodwin-Gill, Guy and McAdam, Jane, *The Refugee in International Law* (Oxford: Oxford University Press, 2007)

Gowlland-Debbas, Vera, *Collective Responses to Illegal Acts in International Law: United Nations Action in the Question of Southern Rhodesia* (Dordrecht: Martinus Nijhoff, 1990)

Grant, Thomas D., 'East Timor, the UN System, and Enforcing Non-recognition in International Law' (2000) 33 *Vanderbilt Journal of Transnational Law* 273

Grant, Thomas D., 'Hallstein Revisited: Unilateral Enforcement of Regimes of Nonrecognition since the Two Germanies' (2000) 36 *Stanford Journal of International Law* 221

Grant, Thomas D., *The Recognition of States, Law and Practice in Debate and Evolution* (Westport, CT: Praeger, 1999)

Grant, Thomas D., 'United States Practice Relating to the Baltic States, 1940–2000' (2001) 1 *Baltic Yearbook of International Law* 23

Grundy, Kenneth W., 'Namibia's First Year of Independence' (May 1991) 9 *Current History* 213

Gunn, Geoffrey C., *East Timor and the United Nations: The Case for Intervention* (Lawrenceville: Red Sea, 1997)

Gürel, Ayla, 'Population and Property Issues in Divided Cyprus' (2008) (on file with the author)

Gürel, Ayla and Özersay, Kudret, 'The Politics of Property in Cyprus', PRIO Report 3/2006

Gutiérrez, Nicolás J., Jr, 'Righting Old Wrongs: A Survey of Restitution Schemes for Possible Application to a Democratic Cuba' (1995) 4 *University of Miami Yearbook of International Law* 111

Hafner, Gerhard and Kornfeind, Elisabeth, 'The Recent Austrian Practice of State Succession: Does the Clean Slate Rule Still Exist?' (1996) 1 *Austrian Review of International and European Law* 1

Hague Academy of International Law, Center for Studies and Research in International law and International Relations, *State Succession: Codification Tested against the Facts* (Dordrecht: Martinus Nijhoff, 1996)

Hall, Ruth, 'Land Restitution in South Africa: Rights, Development and the Restrained State' (2004) 38 *Canadian Journal of African Studies* 654

Hannikainen, Lauri, 'The Case of East Timor from the Perspective of Jus Cogens', in *International Law and the Question of East Timor* (London: CIIR-IPJET, 1995)

Hannikainen, Lauri, *Peremptory Norms (Jus Cogens) in International Law: Historical Development, Criteria, Present Status* (Helsinki: Finnish Lawyers' Publishing Company, 1988)

Hannum, Hurst, *The Right to Leave and Return in International Law and Practice* (Dordrecht: Martinus Nijhoff, 1987)

Harris, Sidney L., 'The Constitution of Namibia and the "Rights and Freedoms" Guaranteed Communal Land Holders: Resolving the Inconsistency between Article 16, Article 100, and Schedule 5' (1996) 12 *South African Journal on Human Rights* 467

Hatay, Mete, 'Beyond Numbers: An Inquiry into the Political Integration of the Turkish "Settlers" in Northern Cyprus', PRIO Report 4 (Nicosia, 2005)

Hayde, Wayne, 'Ideas and Realties of the Rule of Law and Administration of Justice in Post Conflict East Timor' (2004) 8 *International Peacekeeping: The Yearbook of International Peace Operations* 65

Heinze, Christian, 'Recognition of the Turkish Republic of Northern Cyprus as a State', in Emel Doğramaci, William Haney and Güray König (eds.), *Proceedings of the First International Congress on Cypriot Studies Gazimağusa 20–23 November '96* (Eastern Mediterranean University, 1996)

Henckaerts, Jean-Marie, *Mass Expulsion in Modern International Law and Practice* (The Hague: Martinus Nijhoff, 1995)

Henckaerts, Jean Marie and Doswald-Beck, Louise (eds.), *Customary International Humanitarian Law Volume I: Rules* (Geneva: ICRC, 2005)

Henning, Melber, 'Contested Territory: Land in Southern Africa. The Case of Namibia' (2002) 50 *Namibia Scientific Society (Windhoek) Journal* 77

Henrard, Kristin, 'The Internally Displaced in South Africa: The Strategy of Forced Removals and Apartheid' (1995–1996) *Jura Falconis* 491

Herbst, Jeffrey, 'The Dilemmas of Land Policy in Zimbabwe', in Simon Baynham (ed.), *Zimbabwe in Transition* (Stockholm: Almqvist and Wiksell International, 1992)

Herbst, Jeffrey, *State Politics in Zimbabwe* (Berkeley: University of California Press, 1990)

Herman, Lawrence L., 'The Legal Status of Namibia and of the United Nations Council for Namibia' (1975) 13 *Canadian Yearbook of International Law* 306

Heydt, Donald A., 'Nonrecognition of the Independence of Transkei' (1978) 10 *Case Western Reserve Journal of International Law* 167

Himmer, Susan E., 'The Achievement of Independence in the Baltic States and Its Justifications' (1992) 6 *Emory International Law Review* 253

Hobér, Kaj, *Transforming East European Law* (Uppsala: Iustus Förlag, 1997)

Hoffmeister, Frank, 'Cyprus v. Turkey App. No. 25781/94' (2002) 96 *American Journal of International Law* 445

Hough, William J. H., III, 'The Annexation of the Baltic States and Its Effect on the Development of Law Prohibiting Forcible Seizure of Territory' (1985) 6 *New York Law School Journal of International & Comparative Law* 303

Hughes, James, 'Exit in Deeply Divided Societies: Regimes of Discrimination in Estonia and Latvia and the Potential for Russophone Migration' (2005) 43 *Journal of Common Market Studies* 739

Hugo, Graeme, 'Forced Migration in Indonesia: Historical Perspectives' (2006) 15 *Asian and Pacific Migration Journal* 53

Hugo, Graeme, 'Pengungsi – Indonesia's Internally Displaced Persons' (2002) 11 *Asian and Pacific Migration Journal* 297

Hunter, Justine (ed.), *Who Should Own the Land? Analyses and Views on Land Reform and the Land Question in Namibia and Southern Africa* (Windhoek: Konrad-Adenauer-Stiftung Namibia Institute for Democracy, 2004)

Jagerskiold, Stig, 'The Freedom of Movement', in Louis Henkin (ed.), *The International Bill of Rights: The Covenant on Civil and Political Rights* (New York: Columbia University Press, 1981)

Järve, Priit, 'Estonian Citizenship: Between Ethnic Preferences and Democratic Obligations', in Rainer Bauböck, Bernhard Perchinig and Wiebke Sievers (eds.), *Citizenship Policies in the New Europe*, expanded and updated edn (Amsterdam: Amsterdam University Press, 2010)

Jennings, Robert Y., *The Acquisition of Territory in International Law* (Manchester: Manchester University Press, 1963)

Jennings, Robert Y., 'Nullity and Effectiveness in International Law', in *Cambridge Essays in International Law (Essays in Honour of Lord McNair)* (London: Stevens, 1965)

Jennings, Robert Y. and Watts, Sir Arthur (eds.), *Oppenheim's International Law*, 9th edn (London: Longman, 1996)

Kaeckenbeeck, Georges, 'The Protection of Vested Rights in International Law' (1936) 17 *British Yearbook of International Law* 1

Kaela, Laurent C. W., *The Question of Namibia* (Basingstoke: Macmillan, 1996)

Kask, Peet, 'National Radicalization in Estonia: Legislation on Citizenship and Related Issues' (1994) 22 *Nationalities Papers* 379

Keith, Arthur B., *The Theory of State Succession, with Special Reference to English and Colonial Law* (London: Waterlow and Sons, 1907)

Kelbrick, Roshana, 'Current Developments, Namibia' (1994) 27 *Comparative and International Law Journal of South Africa* 258

Kelsen, Hans, 'Théorie Générale du Droit International Public – Problèmes Choisis' (1932) 42 *Recueil des Cours de l'Academie de Droit International de la Haye* 121

Kiernan, Ben, 'The Demography of Genocide in Southeast Asia: The Death Tolls in Cambodia, 1975–79, and East Timor, 1975–80' (2003) 35 *Critical Asia Studies* 585

King, Robert, 'Certain Maritime Arrangements in the Timor Sea, the Timor Sea Treaty and the Timor Gap, 1972–2007', submission to the Australian Parliament's Joint Standing Committee on Treaties Inquiry into the Treaty on Certain Maritime Arrangements in the Timor Sea (March 2007)

Kingsbury, Damien, 'East Timor to 1999', in Damien Kingsbury (ed.), *Guns and Ballot Boxes: East Timor's Vote for Independence* (Victoria: Monash Asia Institute, 2000)

Kittichaisaree, Kriangsak, *The Law of the Sea and Maritime Boundary Delimitation in South-East Asia* (Oxford: Oxford University Press, 1987)

Klaaren, Jonathan, 'Post-apartheid Citizenship in South Africa', in T. Alexander Aleinikoff and Douglas Klusmeyer (eds.), *From Migrants to Citizens Membership in a Changing World* (Washington, DC: Carnegie Endowment for International Peace, 2000)

Klabbers, Jan, Koskenniemi Martti, Ribbelink, Olivier and Zimmermann, Andreas (eds.), *State Practice Regarding State Succession and Issues of Recognition: The Pilot Project of the Council of Europe* (The Hague: Kluwer Law International, 1999)

Korman, Sharon D., *The Right of Conquest: The Acquisition of Territory by Force in International Law and Practice* (Oxford: Clarendon Press, 1996)

Krause, C., 'The Right to Property', in A. Eide *et al.* (eds.), *Economic, Social and Cultural Rights*, 2nd edn (Dordrecht: Martinus Nijhoff, 2001)
Krieger, Heike (ed.), *East Timor and the International Community: Basic Documents* (Cambridge: Cambridge University Press, 1997)
Krūma, Kristine, 'Checks and Balances in Latvian Nationality Policies: National Agendas and International Frameworks', in Rainer Bauböck, Bernhard Perchinig and Wiebke Sievers (eds.), *Citizenship Policies in the New Europe*, expanded and updated edn (Amsterdam: Amsterdam University Press, 2010)
Kuddo, Arvo, 'Aspects of the Restitution of Property and Land in Estonia', in Ray Abrahams (ed.), *After Socialism: Land Reform and Social Change in Eastern Europe* (Providence: Berghahn, 1996)
Ladas, Stephen P., *The Exchange of Minorities: Bulgaria, Greece and Turkey* (New York: The MacMillan Co., 1932)
Landis, Elizabeth, 'Namibia: A Transatlantic View' (1987) 3 *South African Journal on Human Rights* 347
Landis, Elizabeth, 'Namibia in International Context: The Frustration of Independence', in Brian Wood (ed.), *Namibia 1884–1984: Readings on Namibia's History and Society* (London: Namibia Support Committee, 1984)
Langer, Robert, *Seizure of Territory: The Stimson Doctrine and Related Principles in Legal Theory and Diplomatic Practice* (Princeton, NJ: Princeton University Press, 1947)
Lauterpacht, Elihu, *Jerusalem and the Holy Places* (London: Anglo-Israel Association, 1968)
Lauterpacht, Sir Hersch, *Recognition in International Law* (Cambridge: Cambridge University Press, 1947)
Lawson, Adolphe, *Les accords de Lancaster House en 1979: L'aboutissement de deux décennies de débats sur les conditions de l'indépendance du Zimbabwe* (Uppsala: Uppsala University, 1988)
Leckie, Scott, 'Housing, Land and Property Rights in Post-conflict Societies: Proposals for a New United Nations Institutional and Policy Framework' (UNHCR Legal and Protection Policy Research Series, 2005)
Leckie, Scott, 'The Right to Adequate Housing', in A. Eide *et al.* (eds.), *Economic, Social and Cultural Rights*, 2nd edn (Dordrecht: Martinus Nijhoff, 2001)
Lehto, Maria, 'Succession of States in the Former Soviet Union: Arrangements Concerning the Bilateral Treaties of Finland and the USSR' (1993) 4 *Finnish Yearbook of International Law* 194
Leifer, Michael, 'Indonesia and the Incorporation of East Timor' (September 1976) 32 *World Today* 347
Lerer, David, 'Joint Development Zones – How to Negotiate and Structure a Joint Development Agreement' *Oil and Gas Journal*, 22 September 2003, 38
Lerner, Natan, *The UN Convention on the Elimination of all Forms of Racial Discrimination* (Alphen aan den Rijn: Sijthoff & Noordhoff, 1980)
Levrat, Bertrand, 'Le droit international humanitaire au Timor Oriental: Entre théorie et pratique' (2001) 83 *Revue international de la Croix Rouge* 77
Lieven, Anatol, *The Baltic Revolution: Estonia, Latvia, Lithuania and the Path to Independence* (New Haven: Yale University Press, 1993)

Lillich, Richard B. and Weston, Burns H., *International Claims: Their Settlement by Lump Sum Agreements* (Charlottesville: University Press of Virginia, 1975), Part 2

Linton, Suzannah, 'Rising from the Ashes: The Creation of a Viable Criminal Justice System in East Timor' (2001) 25 *Melbourne University Law Review* 122

Loucaides, Loukis G., 'Expulsion of Settlers from Occupied Territories: The Case of Turkish Settlers in Cyprus', in Loukis G. Loucaides, *Essays on the Developing Law of Human Rights* (Dordrecht: Martinus Nijhoff, 1995) 108

Love, Lucinda, 'International Agreement Obligations after the Soviet Union's Break-up: Current United States Practice and Its Consistency with International Law' (1993–1994) 26 *Vanderbilt Journal of Transnational Law* 373

Lowe, Vaughan, Carleton, Christopher and Ward, Christopher, 'Legal Opinion on East Timor Maritime Boundaries', submitted to Petrotimor (11 April 2002), www.petrotimor.com/lglop.html

Lyons, A. B., 'The Case of Feivel Pikelny' (1955–1956) 32 *British Yearbook of International Law* 288

McDougal, Myres S. and Reisman, W. Michael, 'Rhodesia and the United Nations: The Unlawfulness of International Concern' (1968) 62 *American Journal of International Law* 1

Machover, Daniel, 'International Humanitarian Law and the Indonesian Occupation of East Timor', in *International Law and the Question of East Timor* (London: CIIR-IPJET, 1995)

McNair, Lord Arnold D., 'The General Principles of Law Recognized by Civilized Nations' (1957) 22 *British Yearbook of International Law* 1

McNair, Lord Arnold D., *The Law of Treaties* (Oxford: Clarendon Press, 1961)

Mälksoo, Lauri, *Illegal Annexation and State Continuity: The Case of the Incorporation of the Baltic States by the USSR* (Leiden: Martinus Nijhoff, 2003)

Mälksoo, Lauri, 'Professor Uluots, the Estonian Government in Exile and the Continuity of the Republic of Estonia in International Law' (2000) 69 *Nordic Journal of International Law* 289

Mälksoo, Lauri, 'Soviet Genocide? Communist Mass Deportations in the Baltic States and International Law' (2001) 14 *Leiden Journal of International Law* 757

Martin, David, *The Struggle for Zimbabwe: The Chimurenga War* (London: Faber, 1981)

Martinovic, Louise, 'The Three R's of Land Policy in East Timor: Recognition, Restitution, Reform' (Research Unit Faculty of Law, the Australian National University, 2001)

Mathew, Penelope, 'Lest We Forget: Australia's Policy on East Timorese Asylum Seekers' (1999) 11 *International Journal of Refugee Law* 7

Matsuno, Akihisa, paper on the Balibo Declaration prepared for the Closing Sessions of the 2nd Course on Indonesia and East Timor, Lisbon (March 1995), www.hamline.edu/apakabar/basisdata/1995/04/16/0003.html

Matthews, Robert O., 'Talking without Negotiating: The Case of Rhodesia' (1979–1980) 39 *International Journal* 91

Mattisen, Edgar, *Searching for a Dignified Compromise: The Estonian–Russian Border 1000 Years* (Tallinn: ILO, 1996)

Meissner, Boris, 'The Occupation of the Baltic States from a Present-Day Perspective', in Jundzis Tālavs (ed.), *The Baltic States at Historical Crossroads* (Riga: Academy of Sciences of Latvia, 1998)
Meissner, Boris, 'The Right to Self-Determination after Helsinki and Its Significance for the Baltic Nations' (1981) 13 *Case Western Reserve Journal of International Law* 375
Meitzner Yoder, Laura Suzanne, 'Custom, Codification, Collaboration: Integrating the Legacies of Land and Forest Authorities in Oecusse Enclave, East Timor', PhD thesis, Yale University, 2005
Middlebush, Frederick A., 'International Affairs: The Effect of the Non-recognition of Manchukuo' (1934) 28 *American Political Science Review* 677
Milano, Enrico, *Unlawful Territorial Situations in International Law* (Leiden: Martinus Nijhoff, 2006)
Miller, Mark J., 'Demography and Security (MIT Center for International Studies, December 11–12, 1998)' (1999) 33 *International Migration Review* 193
Mlambo, Eshmael Ephial Mtshumayeli, *Rhodesia: The Struggle for a Birthright* (London: C. Hurst, 1972)
Mndaweni, Cedric B., 'Limping Marriages in the new South Africa?' (1991) 24 *Comparative and International Law Journal of South Africa* 215
Morris, Helen M., 'EU Enlargement and Latvian Citizenship Policy' (2003) *Journal on Ethnopolitics and Minority Issues in Europe* 3
Morrow, Jonathan and White, Rachel, 'The United Nations in Transitional East Timor: International Standards and the Reality of Governance' (2002) 22 *Australian Yearbook of International Law* 1
Mrak, Mojmir (ed.), *Succession of States* (The Hague: Martinus Nijhoff, 1999)
Müllerson, Rein, *International Law, Human Rights and Politics: Developments in Eastern Europe and the CIS* (London: Routledge, 1994)
Mümtaz, Sosyal, 'Inequality of Status: Impediment to a Solution in Cyprus', in Reşat Arim (ed.), *Cyprus and International Law* (Ankara: Bilknet University Foreign Policy Institute, 2002)
Murphy, Craig N., *The United Nations Development Programme: A Better Way?* (Cambridge: Cambridge University Press, 2006)
Necatigil (published as Nedjati), Zaim M., 'Acts of Unrecognized Governments' (1981) 30 *International & Comparative Law Quarterly* 388
Necatigil (published as Nedjatigil), Zaim M., *The Cyprus Conflict – A Lawyer's View*, 2nd edn (A-Z Publications: Lefkoşa, 1982)
Necatigil, Zaim M., *The Cyprus Question and the Turkish Position in International Law*, 2nd edn (Oxford: Oxford University Press, 1993)
Necatigil, Zaim M., 'De Facto Regime in International Law: With Particular Reference to the TRNC' (2001) 6 *Perceptions* 56
Necatigil, Zaim M., 'Judgment of the European Court of Human Rights in the Loizidou Case: A Critical Examination' (1999) 4 *Perceptions* 147
Necatigil, Zaim M., 'The Legal System of the Turkish Republic of Northern Cyprus' (1998) 4 *Journal of Cyprus Studies* 213
Necatigil (published as Nejatigil), Zaim M., *Our Republic in Perspective* (Lefkoşa 1985)

Necatigil, Zaim M., 'The Turkish Republic of Northern Cyprus: Statehood and Recognition' (1996) 2 *Journal of Cyprus Studies* 3

Nkala, Jericho, *The United Nations, International Law and the Rhodesian Independence Crisis* (Oxford: Clarendon Press, 1985)

Norman, Geoffrey E., 'The Transkei: South Africa's Illegitimate Child' (1977) 12 *New England Law Review* 585

Nowak, Manfred, *U.N. Covenant on Civil and Political Rights: CCPR Commentary*, 2nd edn (Kehl: N. P. Engel, 2005)

Nyerere, Julius K., 'Rhodesia in the Context of Southern Africa' (1965–1966) 44 *Foreign Affairs* 373

O'Connell, Daniel P., 'Economic Concessions in the Law of State Succession' (1950) 27 *British Yearbook of International Law* 93

O'Connell, Daniel P., *State Succession in Municipal Law and International Law* (London: Stevens and Sons, 1967) Volume I

O'Linn, Bryan, *Namibia Sacred Trust of Civilization, Ideal and Reality* (Windhoek: Gamsberg MacMillan, 2003)

Okoye, Felix Chuks, *International Law and the New African States* (London: Sweet and Maxwell, 1972)

Olivier, Michèle, 'The Status of International Law in South African Municipal Law: Section 231 of the 1993 Constitution' (1993–1994) 19 *South African Yearbook of International Law* 1

Orakhelashvili, Alexander, *Peremptory Norms in International Law* (Oxford: Oxford University Press, 2006)

Orrego-Vicuña, Francisco, 'Regional Co-operation in Nonliving Resources: Joint Management Zones', in Peter Bautista Payoyo (ed.), *Ocean Governance: Sustainable Development of the Seas* (Tokyo: UNU, 1994)

Oswald, Bruce, 'The INTERFET Detainee Management Unit in East Timor' (2000) 3 *Yearbook of International Humanitarian Law* 347

Özersay, Kudret and Gürel, Ayla, 'Property and Human Rights in Cyprus: The European Court of Human Rights as a Platform of Political Struggle' (2008) 44 *Middle Eastern Studies* 291

Palley, Claire, *The Constitutional History and Law of Southern Rhodesia, 1888–1965, with Special Reference to Imperial Control* (Oxford: Clarendon Press, 1966)

Palley, Claire, *An International Relations Debacle: The UN Secretary-General's Mission of Good Offices in Cyprus 1999–2004* (Oxford: Hart, 2005)

Paraskevas, Costas, 'The Application of the "Pilot Judgment Procedure" to Post-*Loizidou* Cases' (2009) 4 *Annuaire international des droits de l'homme* 573

Pellet, Alain, 'The Opinions of the Badinter Arbitration Committee: A Second Breath for the Self-determination of Peoples' (1992) 3 *European Journal of International Law* 178

Persaud, Motee, 'Namibia and the International Court of Justice' (1975) 68 *Current History* 220

Pettai, Vello Andres, 'The Construction of State Identity and Its Legacies: Legal Restorationism in Estonia' (2007) 3 *Ab Imperio* 1

Pettai, Vello Andres, 'Framing the Past as Future: The Power of Legal Restorationism in Estonia', PhD thesis, Columbia University, 2004 (on file with the author)

Pettai, Vello and Hallik, Klara, 'Understanding Processes of Ethnic Control: Segmentation, Dependency and Co-optation in Post-communist Estonia' (2002) 8 *Nations and Nationalism* 505

Pilgrim, Caleb M., 'Some Legal Aspects of Trade in the Natural Resources of Namibia' (1990) 61 *British Yearbook of International Law* 249

Plasket, Clive, 'The Ciskeian State of Emergency' (1990) 6 *South African Journal on Human Rights* 60

Platzky, Laurine and Walker, Cherryl, *The Surplus People: Forced Removals in South Africa* (Johannesburg: Ravan Press, 1985)

Pogany, Istvan, *Righting Wrongs in Eastern Europe* (Manchester: Manchester University Press, 1997)

Poleshchuk, Vadim, 'Non-citizens in Estonia' (Legal Information Centre for Human Rights, 2004)

Prescott, J. R. V., 'Australia – United Nations Transitional Administration in East Timor (UNTAET)', in Jonathan I. Charney and Robert W. Smith (eds.), *International Maritime Boundaries* (The Hague: Martinus Nijhoff, 2002) Volume IV

Proceedings of the Regional Symposium on International Efforts to Implement Decree No 1 for the Protection of the Natural Resources of Namibia, Geneva, Switzerland (27–31 August 1984)

Pummell, Brandi J., 'The Timor Gap: Who Decides Who Is in Control' (1998) 26 *Denver Journal of International Law and Policy* 655

Quigley, John, 'Baltic States Russians: Entitled Inhabitants or Unlawful Settlers?', in Roger Clark, Ferdinand Feldbrugge and Stanislaw Pomorsky (eds.), *International and National Law in Russia and Eastern Europe: Essays in Honor of Georg Ginsburg* (The Hague: Martinus Nijhoff, 2001)

Raič, David, *Statehood and the Law of Self-Determination* (The Hague: Kluwer Law International, 2002)

Ramutsindela, Maano, 'The Geographical Imprint of Land Restitution with Reference to Limpopo Province, South Africa' (2007) 98 *Tijdschrift voor Economische en Sociale Geografie* 455

Raun, Toivo U., 'Post-Soviet Estonia 1991–1993' (1994) 25 *Journal of Baltic Studies* 73

Richardson, Henry J., 'Constitutive Questions in the Negotiations for Namibian Independence' (1984) 78 *American Journal of International Law* 76

Richmond, Oliver P., *Mediating in Cyprus: The Cypriot Communities and the United Nations* (London: Frank Cass Publishers, 1998)

Rigaux, Francois, 'East Timor and Western Sahara: A Comparative View', in *International Law and the Question of East Timor* (London: CIIR-IPJET, 1995)

Roberts, Adam, 'Prolonged Military Occupation: The Israeli-Occupied Territories since 1967' (1990) 84 *American Journal of International Law* 44

Robinson, Geoffrey, 'People Power: A Comparative History of Forced Displacement in East Timor', in Eva-Lotta E. Hedman (ed.), *Conflict, Violence*

and Displacement in Indonesia (Ithaca, NY: Cornell South East Asia Program, 2008)
Rohland, Klaus and Cliffe, Sarah, 'The East Timor Reconstruction Program: Successes, Problems and Tradeoffs', Conflict Prevention and Reconstruction Unit Working Paper No. 2 (World Bank, 2002)
Ronen, Yaël, 'Illegal Occupation and Its Consequences' (2008) 41 *Israel Law Review* 201
Ronzitti, Natalino, *Rescuing Nationals Abroad through Military Coercion and Intervention on Grounds of Humanity* (Dordrecht: Martinus Nijhoff, 1985)
Rosand, Eric, 'The Right to Compensation in Bosnia: An Unfulfilled Promise and a Challenge to International Law' (2000) 33 *Cornell International Law Journal* 113
Rosand, Eric, 'The Right to Return under International Law Following Mass Dislocation: The Bosnia Precedent?' (1997–1998) 19 *Michigan Journal of International Law* 1091
Roth, Brad R., *Governmental Illegitimacy in International Law* (Oxford: Clarendon Press, 1999)
Sadurska, Romana, 'Threats of Force' (1988) 82 *American Journal of International Law* 239
Salmon, Jean, 'Pays Baltes' (2001) 24 *Review belge de droit international* 262
Satkauskas, Rytis, 'États Baltes: Succession ou identité?', memoire de DÉA Université de Paris I Panthéon-Sorbonne (1999–2000)
Satkauskas, Rytis, 'The Practice of France with Respect to the Baltic States' (2001) 1 *Baltic Yearbook of International Law* 111
Sayre, Francis B., 'Change of Sovereignty and Concessions' (1918) 12 *American Journal of International Law* 705
Sayre, Francis B., 'Change of Sovereignty and Private Ownership of Land' (1918) 12 *American Journal of International Law* 475
Sayre, Francis B., 'Legal Problems Arising from the United Nations Trusteeship System' (1948) 42 *American Journal of International Law* 263
Schaffer, Rosalie, 'Succession to Treaties: South African Practice in the Light of Current Developments in International Law' (1981) 30 *International and Comparative Law Quarterly* 593
Schermers, H. G., 'The Namibia Decree in National Courts' (1977) 26 *International & Comparative Law Quarterly* 81
Schmidt-Jortzig, Edzard, 'The Constitution of Namibia: An Example of a State Emerging under Close Supervision and World Scrutiny' (1991) 34 *German Yearbook of International Law* 568
Schneider, M. B. (ed.), *Namibia: Views and Perspectives since Independence* (Windhoek: Konrad-Adenauer Stiftung eV in co-operation with the Namibia Institute for Democracy, 1992)
Schoiswohl, Michael, *Status and (Human Rights) Obligations of Non-recognized De Facto Regimes in International Law: The Case of 'Somaliland'* (Martinus Nijhoff, 2004)
Schrijver, Nico J., 'The Status of Namibia and of Its Natural Resources in International Law', in *Proceedings of the Regional Symposium on International*

Efforts to Implement Decree No 1 for the Protection of the Natural Resources of Namibia, Geneva, Switzerland (27–31 August 1984)

Schutz, Barry M., 'European Population Patterns, Cultural Persistence, and Political Change in Rhodesia' (1973) 7 *Canadian Journal of African Studies/Revue canadienne des études africaines* 3

Schwebel, Stephen M., 'What Weight to Conquest?' (1970) 64 *American Journal of International Law* 344

Schwelb, Egon, 'Some Aspects of International *Jus Cogens* as Formulated by the International Law Commission' (1967) 61 *American Journal of International Law* 946

Scobbie, Iain G. M. and Drew, Catriona J., 'Self-Determination Undetermined: The Case of East Timor' (1996) 9 *Leiden Journal of International Law* 185

Senn, Alfred E., 'What Happened in Lithuania in 1940?' (2000) 6 *Lithuanian Foreign Policy Review*

Shaw, William H., 'They Stole Our Land: Debating the Expropriation of White Farms in Zimbabwe' (2003) 41 *Journal of Modern African Studies* 75

Sherlock, Stephen, 'Political Economy of the East Timor Conflict' (1996) 36 *Asian Survey* 835

Shihata, Ibrahim F. I. and Onorato, William T., 'Joint Development of International Petroleum Resources in Undefined and Disputed Areas', in Gerald H. Blake, Martin Pratt, Clive Schofield and Janet Allison Brown (eds.), *Boundaries and Energy: Problems and Prospects* (London: Kluwer Law International, 1998)

Slinn, Peter, 'Zimbabwe Achieves Independence' (1980) 6 *Commonwealth Law Bulletin* 1038

Soni, Sushma, 'Regimes for Namibia's Independence: A Comparative Study' (1991) 29 *Columbia Journal of Transnational Law* 563

Sözen, Ahmet and Özersay, Kudret, 'The Annan Plan: State Succession or Continuity' (2007) 43 *Middle Eastern Studies* 125

Spruds, Andris, 'Minority Issues in the Baltic states in the Context of the NATO Enlargement' (2001), NATO Individual Research Fellowship, Final Report 9

Stankevicius, Ceslovas, 'Enhancing Security of Lithuania and Other Baltic States in 1992–94 and Future Guidelines' (1996) Final Report of Individual Democratic Institutions Research Fellowships 1994–6 www.nato.int/acad/fellow/94-96/stankevi/home.htm

Stedman, Stephen J., *Peacemaking in Civil War: International Mediation in Zimbabwe, 1974–1980* (Boulder, CO: Lynne Rienner, 1991)

Stephen, Michael, 'The European Court of Human Rights and Cyprus: The Loizidou Case', in Republic of Turkey, Ministry of Foreign Affairs, *The Loizidou Case – A Dead End* (1999)

Stephenson, Glenn V., 'The Impact of International Economic Sanctions on the Internal Viability of Rhodesia' (1975) 65 *Geographical Review* 377

Stone, Julius, *Aggression and World Order: A Critique of United Nations Theories of Aggression* (London: Stevens and Sons, 1958)

Stranga, Aivars, 'The End Product, a Crisis in Latvian–Russian Relations (March–August 1998)', NATO Research Fellowships Programme 1996–8, www.nato.int/acad/fellow/96–98/stranga.pdf

Strohmeyer, Hansjörg, 'Collapse and Reconstruction of a Judicial System: The United Nations Missions in Kosovo and East Timor' (2001) 95 *American Journal of International Law* 46

Strohmeyer, Hansjörg, 'Policing the Peace: Post-conflict Judicial System Reconstruction in East Timor' (2001) 24 *University of New South Wales Law Journal* 171

Surplus People Project, *Forced Removals in South Africa* (Cape Town: Surplus People Project, 1983) Volume I

Szafarz, Renata, 'The Practice of Poland as the "Other State Party" and as a Depositary – as Regards Succession of Recently Established States in Respect of Treaties' (1995–1996) 22 *Polish Yearbook of International Law* 221

Szasz, Paul C., 'Statement on the Elections Process', in Heribet Weiland and Matthew Braham (eds.), *The Namibian Peace Process: Implications and Lessons for the Future* (Freiburg: Arnold Bergstrasser Institute, 1994)

Szasz, Paul C., 'Succession to Treaties under the Namibian Constitution' (1989–1990) 15 *South African Yearbook of International Law* 65

Talmon, Stefan, 'The Cyprus Question before the European Court of Justice' (2001) 12 *European Journal of International Law* 727

Talmon, Stefan, 'Impediments to Peacekeeping: The Case of Cyprus' (2002) 8 *International Peacekeeping* 31

Talmon, Stefan, 'The Legal Consequences of (Non) Recognition: Cyprus and the Council of Europe', in Malcolm D. Evans (ed.), *Aspects of Statehood and Institutionalism in Contemporary Europe* (Aldershot: Dartmouth, 1997)

Talmon, Stefan, *Recognition in International Law: A Bibliography* (The Hague: Martinus Nijhoff, 2000)

Talmon, Stefan, *Recognition of Governments in International Law: With Particular Reference to Governments in Exile* (Oxford: Clarendon, 1998)

Taube, Caroline, 'Latvia: Political Participation of Linguistic Minorities' (2003) 1 *International Journal of Constitutional Law* 511

Tauber, Laurence, 'Legal Pitfalls on the Road to Namibian Independence' (1979–1980) 12 *New York University Journal of International Law and Policy* 375

Taylor, John G., 'East Timor: Forced Resettlement' (1999) 5 *Forced Migration Review* 31

Temby, Quinton, 'The Blessed Curse' (October 2003) *New Internationalist* 361

Thomson, Wayne C., 'Citizenship and Borders: Legacies of Soviet Empire in Estonia' (1998) 29 *Journal of Baltic Studies* 109

Thos, Baty, 'Division of States: Its Effect on Obligations' (1923) 9 *Transactions of the Grotius Society* 119

Tichy, Helmut, 'Two Recent Cases of State Succession – an Austrian Perspective' (1992) 44 *Austrian Journal of Public and International Law* 117

Tıryakıoğlu, Bilgin, 'Multiple Citizenship and Its Consequences in Turkish Law' (2006) 3 *Ankara Law Review* 1

Tocci, Nathalie and Kovziridze, Tamara, 'Cyprus', in Bruno Coppieters *et al.* (eds.), *Europeanizaiton and Conflict Resolution: Case Studies from the European Periphery* (Gent: Academia Press, 2004)
Tomuschat, Christian, 'International Crimes by States: An Endangered Species?' in Karel Wellens (ed.), *International Law: Theory and Practice: Essays in Honour of Eric Suy* (The Hague: Martinus Nijhoff, 1998)
Tosha, Onkemetse, *National Law and International Human Rights Law* (Aldershot: Ashgate, 2001)
Toth, Akos, 'The Doctrine of Rebus sic Stantibus in International Law' (1974) 19 *Juridical Review* 56
Triggs, Gillian and Bialek, Dean, 'The New Timor Sea Treaty and Interim Arrangements for Joint Development of Petroleum Resources of the Timor Gap' (2002) 3 *Melbourne Journal of International Law* 322
Turack, Daniel C., 'Selected Aspects of International and Municipal Law Concerning Passports' (1970–1971) 12 *William and Mary Law Review* 805
UNIN, *Constitutional Options for Namibia: A Historical Perspective*, based on the work of M. D. Bomany and C. Ushewokunze, Namibia Studies Series No. 2 (ed. N. K. Duggal) (Lusaka: UNIN, 1979)
UNIN, *Economic Development Strategies for Independent Namibia*, based on the work of Harbans S. Aulakh and Wilfred Wasombang, Namibia Studies Series No. 9 (ed. N. K. Duggal) (Lusaka: UNIN, 1985)
UNIN, *Independent Namibia: Succession to Treaty Rights and Obligations, Incorporating Namibian Treaty Calendar*, based on the work of Julio Faundez, Namibia Studies Series No. 13 (ed. N. K. Duggal) (Lusaka: UNIN, 1989)
UNIN, *Namibia: Legal Framework and Development Strategy Options for the Mining Industry*, based on the work of M. D. Bomani, Harbans S. Aulakh, Wilfred W. Asombang and C. Ushewokunze, Namibia Studies Series No. 10 (ed. N. K. Duggal) (Lusaka: UNIN, 1987)
UNIN, *Toward a New Legal System for Independent Namibia*, based on the work of Mengo D. F. Sichilongo, Namibia Studies Series No. 5 (ed. N. K. Duggal) (Lusaka: UNIN, 1981)
Unterhalter, Elaine, *Forced Removals: The Division, Segregation and Control of South Africa* (London: International Defence and Aid Fund for Southern Africa, 1987)
Vagts, Detlev F., 'Rebus Revisited: Changed Circumstances in Treaty Law' (2005) 43 *Columbia Journal of Transnational Law* 459
Valletta, William, 'The Hesitant Privatization of Lithuanian Land' (1994–1995) 18 *Fordham International Law Journal* 198
Van Dijk, Pieter, van Hoof, Fried, van Rijn, Arjen and Zwaak, Leo (eds.), *Theory and Practice of the European Convention on Human Rights*, 4th edn (Antwerp: Intersentia, 2006)
Van Elsuwege, Peter, 'Russian-Speaking Minorities in Estonia and Latvia: Problems of Integration at the Threshold of the European Union' ECMI Working Paper No. 20 (April 2004)

Van Elsuwege, Peter, 'State Continuity and Its Consequences: The Case of the Baltic States' (2003) 16 *Leiden Journal of International Law* 177

Van Meurs, Wim, 'Social Citizenship and Non-immigration: The Immobility of the Russian Diaspora in the Baltics', in Rainer Münz and Rainer Ohliger (eds.), *Diaspora and Ethnic Migrants: Germany, Israel and Post-Soviet Successor States in Comparative Perspective* (London: Frank Cass Publishers, 2003)

Verzijl, Jan H. W., *International Law in Historical Public Perspective* (Leiden: A. W. Sijthoff, 1968) Volume I

Vitas, Robert A., 'The Recognition of Lithuania – The Completion of the Legal Circle' (1993) 24 *Journal of Baltic Studies* 247

Von Carlowitz, Leopold, 'Settling Property Issues in Complex Peace Operations: The CRPC in Bosnia and Herzegovina and the HPD/CC in Kosovo' (2004) 17 *Leiden Journal of International Law* 599

Walker, Cherryl, 'The Limits of Land Reform: Rethinking "the Land Question"' (2005) 31 *Journal of Southern African Studies* 805

Warbrick, Colin, 'The New British Policy on Recognition of Governments' (1981) 30 *International and Comparative Law Quarterly* 568

Watts, Sir Arthur, *International Law and the Antarctic Treaty System* (Cambridge: Grotius, 1992)

Watts, Sir Arthur, *The International Law Commission 1949–1998* (Oxford: Oxford University Press, 1999)

Wegren, Stephen K. (ed.), *Land Reform in the Former Soviet Union and Eastern Europe* (London: Routeledge, 1998)

Werner, Wolfgang, 'A Brief History of Land Dispossession in Namibia' (1993) 19 *Journal of Southern African Studies*, special issue: Namibia: Africa's Youngest Nation, 135

Werner, Wolfgang, 'Land Reform in Namibia: The First Seven Years', NEPRU Working Paper No. 61 (Windhoek: NEPRU, 1997)

Westaway, Ashley, 'Bare Life in the Bantustans (of the Eastern Cape): Re-membering the Centennial South African Nation-State', PhD thesis, University of Fort Hare, 2008

Weston, Burns H., Lillich, Richard B. and Bederman, David J., *International Claims: Their Settlement by Lump Sum Agreements, 1975–1999* (Ardesley: Transnational, 1999)

Whitlam, E. G., 'Australia, Indonesia and Europe's Empires' (1980) 34 *Australian Outlook* 3

Wiechers, Marinus, 'Namibia: The 1982 Constitutional Principles and Their Legal Significance' (1989–1990) 15 *South African Yearbook of International Law* 1

Wiechers, Marinus, 'Reincorporation of the TBVC States – International Law Practice and Constitutional Implications' (1990) 16 *South African Yearbook of International Law* 119

Williams, E. T., 'Japan's Mandate in the Pacific' (1933) 27 *American Journal of International Law* 428

Woker, Tanya and Clarke, Sue, 'Homelands' (1991) 2 *South African Human Rights Yearbook* 104

Woker, Tanya and Clarke, Sue, 'Homelands' (1992) 3 *South African Human Rights Yearbook* 106

Wood, Brian (ed.), *Namibia 1884–1984: Readings on Namibia's History and Society* (London: Namibia Support Committee, 1984)

Wotshela, Luvuyo, 'Territorial Manipulation in Apartheid South Africa: Resettlement, Tribal Politics and the Making of the Northern Ciskei, 1975–1990' (2004) 30 *Journal of Southern African Studies* 317

Wright, Herbert, 'The Legality of the Annexation of Austria by Germany' (1944) 38 *American Journal of International Law* 621

Wright, Quincy, 'The End of a Period of Transition' (1937) 31 *American Journal of International Law* 604

Wright, Quincy, *Mandates under the League of Nations* (Chicago: University of Chicago Press, 1930)

Wright, Quincy, 'Some Legal Aspects of the Far Eastern Situation' (1933) 27 *American Journal of International Law* 509

Wright, Quincy, 'Some Recent Cases on the Status of Mandate Areas' (1926) 20 *American Journal of International Law* 768

Wright, Warren L., 'Final Report on the Review of the Basic Agrarian Law 1960' (AusAID Land Administration Project December 1999), www.landpolicy.org/special_topics/robal1.pdf

Wright, Warren L., 'A Note on Land Rights in East Timor [Government Regulation No. 18 of 1991 on the Conversion of Land Rights in East Timor] and the Purported Suspension of Article 5 by Government Regulation No 34 of 1992' (2004) (No. 1) *East Timor Law Journal*, www.eastimorlawjournal.org

Wright, Warren L., 'An Overview of the Provisions of East Timor's Law No 01 of 2003 on the Juridical Regime on Immovable Properties' (2004) (No. 6) *East Timor Law Journal*, www.eastimorlawjournal.org

Wright, Warren L., 'Some Observations on UNTAET Regulation No 27 of 2000 on the Temporary Prohibition of Transactions in Land in East Timor by Indonesian Citizens Not Habitually Resident in East Timor and by Indonesian Corporations' (2004) (No. 3) *East Timor Law Journal*, www.eastimorlawjournal.org

Wright, Warren L., 'UNTAET Land Policy' (2004) (No. 2) *East Timor Law Journal*, www.eastimorlawjournal.org

Yakemtchouk, Romain, 'Les Républiques Baltes en droit international, échec d'une annexion opérée en violation du droit des gens' (1991) 37 *Annuaire français de droit international* 259

Žalimas, Dainius, 'Legal Issues on the Continuity of the Republic of Lithuania' (2001) 1 *Baltic Yearbook of International Law* 1

Ziemele, Ineta, 'Questions Concerning Genocide' (1999) 7–10 *Latvian Human Rights Quarterly* 327

Ziemele, Ineta, *State Continuity and Nationality: The Baltic States and Russia* (Martinus Nijhoff, 2005)

Zinyama, Lovemore M., 'International Migrations to and from Zimbabwe and the Influence of Political Changes on Population Movements, 1965–1987' (1990) 24 *International Migration Review* 748

Zurjari-Ossipova, Olga, 'Human Rights as the Political–Juridical Issues of the Estonian–Russian Inter-state Relations', 18 NATO Research Fellowships programme 1995–7 (June 1997), www.nato.int/acad/fellow/95–97/zurjari.pdf

SELECTED GOVERNMENTAL PUBLICATIONS

Timor-Leste, Commission for Reception, Truth and Reconciliation in East Timor (CAVR) *Chega!* (31 October 2005) ('CAVR Final Report') www.ictj.org/en/news/features/846.html

UK, 'Documents Relating to the Negotiations between the United Kingdom and Southern Rhodesian Governments November 1963–November 1965' (Cmnd 2807, 1967).

UK, Southern Rhodesia – Report of the Constitutional Conference, Lancaster House, London, September–December 1979 (Lancaster House, 21 December 1979) (Cmnd 7802, 1979)

UK, House of Commons Foreign Affairs Committee, 'Cyprus', Second Report of Session 2004–5 Doc No. 113-I (22 February 2005), www.publications.parliament.uk/pa/cm200405/cmselect/cmfaff/113/113.pdf (UK House of Commons, '2004–2005 Report')

UK, House of Commons, 'How Many Turkish Cypriots Remain in Cyprus', written evidence before the select committee of the House of Commons (22 February 2005), www.publications.parliament.uk/pa/cm200405/cmselect/cmfaff/113/113we33.htm (UK House of Commons, 'Written Evidence')

UK, House of Commons' Foreign Affairs Committee, 'Visit to Turkey and Cyprus', Fifth Report of Session 2006–7, Doc No. HC 473 (9 May 2007), www.publications.parliament.uk/pa/cm200607/cmselect/cmfaff/473/47302.htm (UK House of Commons, '2006–2007 Report')

US, Department of State, 2006 Country Reports on Human Rights Practices, Cyprus

Government of Cyprus Statistical Service Demographic Report 2006 ('Cyprus Demographic Report 2006')

Cyprus, Government of Cyprus PIO, Analysis of the '2006 Population Census' in the Occupied Area of Cyprus and Aide Memoire (undated)

SELECTED PUBLICATIONS OF NON-GOVERNMENTAL ORGANIZATIONS

Amnesty International

'East Timor: Justice past, present and Future' (July 2001), ASA 57/001/2001.

East Timor Violations of Human Rights, Extrajudicial Executions, 'Disappearances', Torture and Political Imprisonment, 1975–1984 (London: Amnesty International, 1985)

'The Right to Return: The Case of the Palestinians, Policy Statement, Amnesty International's Position on Forcible Exile and the Right to Return' (30 March 2001), MDE 15/013/2001

Centre on Housing Rights and Evictions (COHRE)

COHRE Online Newsletter

'Better Late than Never: Housing Rights in East Timor' (Geneva, 2000)
'Housing Rights in Latvia' (Geneva, 2000)
'Land, Housing and Property Rights in Zimbabwe' (Geneva, 2001)

Judicial System Monitoring Programme (JSMP)

(All reports are available on the JSMP website at www.jsmp.minihub.org/reports.htm)
Report on the Court of Appeal Decision in the Case of Armando dos Santos (Dili, August 2003)
Report on the Court of Appeal Decision on the Applicable Subsidiary Law in East Timor (Dili, August 2003)
Dili District Court, Final Report 2003 (Dili, November 2003)
Overview of the Jurisprudence of the Court of Appeal in Its First Year of Operation since East Timor's Independence (Dili, August 2004) (JSMP, 'East Timor Court of Appeals')
Overview of the Justice Sector: March 2005 (Dili, March 2005)
Land Law Report (Dili, 27 September 2005)

Index